MESOAMERICA
AND THE
BOOK OF MORMON

Is This The Place?

Dr. John Lewis Lund

Mesoamerica and the Book of Mormon:
Is this the Place?

Dr. John L. Lund

Published by The Communications Company
Cover Design by Geoff Shupe
Thin Gold Plate used by permission of the
Peabody Museum, Harvard University.

Dr. John L. Lund
via e-mail: drlund@drlund.com

ISBN 978-1-891114-40-3

ACKNOWLEDGEMENTS

As nineteen year old missionaries, my companion and I were lost in the jungles of Mexico for three days. High over our heads was a thick green canopy that made it difficult to tell east from west. Somewhere we had taken a wrong turn. There were no road signs in the jungle except an occasional tree shaped like a large Japanese fan, appropriately called the Fan Palm. There is a legend that this tree's branches point east and west as it follows the path of the sun. True or not, we followed its course due east until we came to a muddy jungle road and civilization. On that journey through the wilderness, we encountered a small plane with human skeletal remains scattered upon the ground. This proved to be a great motivation to keep going. The second thing we happened upon were the ruins of an ancient Maya city. The roots of a tree had grown around a stela with hieroglyphic writing upon it. At the time I had no idea of what we had discovered and I doubt if I could ever find those ruins again. They are somewhere between Campeche and El Mirador in the Yucatan Peninsula of Mexico and Guatemala.

This experience began a life long quest to understand the relationship between the Book of Mormon and the Native Americans. This was 1961. We were taught that the primary American events in the Book of Mormon had taken place around the Hill Cumorah in New York. We also believed that Jaredites, Mulekites and the Lehites were the only ones who settled the Americas. I returned from the mission and attended BYU. There I was exposed to great teachers like Dan Ludlow, Hugh Nibley, Sidney B. Sperry, and Chauncey Riddle. These men inspired a passion for studying the Book of Mormon that has never died. I will be forever indebted to them. After graduation, I taught the Book of Mormon for the next thirty-six years as an Institute teacher for the LDS Church. My own research brought me in contact with Joseph L. Allen and his sons Blake and Todd. I am grateful for Joseph's insights and counsel to be cautious and allow for future finds to disagree with present thinking.

I have led more than fifty land tours and cruises to Mexico and Central America. I am most grateful for those who accompanied me on those journeys. Diane Larsen, the Cruise Lady, is a dear friend who sponsored many of these tours. Jim and Carol Tyndall are the owners of Fun For Less Tours. I am indebted to them for their support, but more importantly for their friendship. As it relates to this book I want to thank Eric and Anita Towner. It was Eric who suggested "Is this the Place?" as a part of the title. Sharon Turner, Marie Lund, Jim Watts, and Eva Olson all helped with the editing. More than dotting the "i's and crossing the t's" their combined insights have made this a better read. Linda Prince from Covenant Communications provided detailed review of the footnotes. The maps were provided by Joseph A. Lund, a professional cartographer, and also my son. Geoff Shupe is a gifted and talented artist whose works speak for themselves. My wife Bonnie is a patient and hardworking companion. Her name as well as mine belongs on the title page. Thanks to all of you.

DEDICATION

This book is lovingly dedicated to our children and grandchildren. May each of you acquire a personal witness of the Book of Mormon by your study and prayer and may each of you teach your children to do the same. My deepest love,

— Granddaddy.

About the Author

By his son, Robert E. Lund, J.D.

For thirty years my father was best known as a popular speaker on the Know Your Religion programs and at BYU Education Weeks. At the Institutes of Religion he taught courses in the Book of Mormon and in marriage and communications. It was his passion for the Book of Mormon that drove him to read it more than a hundred times from cover to cover. His love and testimony of the Book of Mormon has taken him to Mexico, Honduras, Belize, and Guatemala more than twenty times to examine specific issues in the Book of Mormon. His research has included trips to South America and many to Palmyra, New York. My Father has a love of languages. He spent twelve years studying Egyptian hieroglyphics and Old and New World theologies. He is quick to point out that he is not an expert in Egyptian hieroglyphs, Hebrew, or Yucatec Mayan, but he knows enough to ask intelligent questions and is studying to become fluent in both Hebrew and Yucatec Mayan.

Retirement has given him an opportunity to devote significant time and energy to research in the Book of Mormon. He has presented papers and lectures to the Book of Mormon Archaeological Forum and at many Book of Mormon symposia in Mexico City, Guatemala City, Provo, Utah and at Salt Lake City, Utah. This book reflects twelve years of serious scholarship into numerous issues related to the history and geography of the Book of Mormon. My father once commented, "It's ironic that I have an undergraduate degree in both History and Geography, it seems my scholarly life has come full circle."

Dr. John L. Lund at Quirigua, Guatemala

According to him, his doctoral training in "Interaction Analysis" had more to do with statistical "Analysis" than with "Interaction." His post graduate studies were taken at both the University of Washington and at BYU. As a graduate student he resisted having to take various courses in statistics from both universities. In hindsight, it prepared him to be a scholar and to evaluate the research methods and techniques of others. Analysis of the bias of the researcher, the gathering of data, the sampling, as well as the findings and conclusions are critical indicators of the integrity of any research, including his own. Extensive training in scientific methodology has contributed to his ability to evaluate "good science" from "shoddy science."

Dr. Joseph Ginat, a Jewish archaeologist and a vice president of Netanya Academic College in Israel, has introduced Dr. Lund as a "genius" because of my father's ability to retain knowledge, recite scripture, and analyze scholarly data. When he was asked whether or not he has a photographic memory, he replied, "I don't think so, but I do have a photogenic face." His sense of humor has endeared him to many. My own love for the Book of Mormon came directly from my father's teachings. A member of the Quorum of the Twelve Apostles once introduced him as "a great teacher, a brilliant scholar, and gifted with a sense of humor."

— Robert E. Lund, J.D.

TABLE OF CONTENTS

Acknowledgements iii

About the Author v

Introduction xv

Chapter One
The Spirit of Place 1

Spirit of Place 1
Examining the Historical Claims of the Book of Mormon 3
Unanswered Questions 4
What Does a Correlation Prove? 5
What are the "Lands of the Book of Mormon"? 6
Dimensions of the Primary Lands of the Book of Mormon 6
Who is Moroni? 7
Three Geographical Locations Vie for the Lands of the Book of Mormon: Mesoamerica, Great Lakes, South America 8
Why is There confusion? 9
The Major Points of the Great Lakes Advocates 12
Oliver Cowdrey's Cave Experience 13
A Look at Zelph 14
South American Advocates 17

Chapter Two
Things to Consider When Looking at Book of Mormon Geography 19

Examining Book of Mormon Geography
Prophetic and Angelic Considerations 1 9
How Did Joseph Smith Identify Central America as the Lands of the Book of Mormon? 20
Joseph Smith Received Another Book 21
Joseph Identified Specific Sites in Mesoamerica as Book of Mormon Cities and Places 23
1 . Joseph Smith Identified Where Lehi Landed 23
First They Landed,
Next They "Tilled, Planted, and Harvested,"
Then They "Journeyed in the Wilderness," and
Then They Settled in the Land of First Inheritance! 23
2. Joseph Smith Identified the City of Zarahemla 26
3. Joseph Smith Identified the Small Neck of Land 26
4. Joseph Smith Named Palenque and Quiriguá as Book of Mormon Cities 27
5. Other Ruined cities of Central America 31

Joseph Smith as Editor of the Times and Seasons 31
6. Joseph Smith Identified the Land of Bountiful as Being in Central America 32
7. Joseph Smith said that Moroni Walked from Central America to Palmyra, New York 33
A Deeper Look at the Two Cumorahs 36
Moroni Lived Thirty-Six Years After the Last Great War 37
Part One: Moroni A.D. 385 to A.D. 400 37
Part Two: Moroni A.D. 401 to A.D. 421 38
Part Three: Moroni's Post-mortal Mission as an Angelic Messenger 38
From Whence Came the Book of Ether? 40

Chapter Three
A Land of Promise for Many Peoples 43

Preserving a Record of Those in the Promised Land 43
What Happened to the Pre-Columbian People Who Lived in the Promised Land? 44
Looking for a Promised Land 44
Two Lands of Promise 45
The Promised Land is Not Limited to a Single Nation 45
What Does the Land of Promise Mean? 45
The Land of Divine Contract 46
The Mexica (Aztec) Tradition: Looking for their Land of Promise 47
The Snakes of Tizapán 50

Chapter Four
Mapping the Land of the Book of Mormon 53

Mapping the Lands of the Book of Mormon 53
Creating a Template for Book of Mormon Lands 53
Finding Zarahemla 55
How Do We Know Where The Land Of First Inheritance Is Located? . 56
The Ups and Down of Topography 59
The River Sidon 60
New World Changes in Topography at the Death of Christ 61
A Wilderness From East Sea to West Sea 62
Zoramites—Nephite Dissenters in the land of Antionum 62

Chapter Five
Evidences of High Civilization in Mesoamerica: Lost Knowledge and Lost Languages 65

The State of Knowledge About Mesoamerica in A.D. 1830 66
Lost Knowledge of America's High Civilization 68

Hieroglyphic Languages 71
Jaredites 72
Mulekites 72
Nephites 72
The Value of Comparing the Hebrew and Egyptian Languages with the Book of Mormon 73
Egyptian Demotic Anthon Transcript 74
Proto-Hebrew/Early Aramaic of the Time of Lehi 75
Hieratic or Priestly Script 76
Other Untranslated Reformed Hieroglyphic Text 77
Meroitic-Demotic Script 78
Mesoamerica is Home To Four Separate Hieroglyphic Languages 79

Chapter Six
Records in Gold, Records in Stone 83

Language Clues 83
Name Correlations: Laman, Kish, and Lib 85
Laman 85
Kish 86
Lib 86
Literary considerations: Parallelism in Mayan, Hebrew, Egyptian, and the Book of Mormon 87
Understanding Parallelisms 87
An Example of Hebrew Parallelisms 88
An Example of Mayan Poetry and Parallelism 89
An Example of Book of Mormon Poetry and Parallelism 90
Book of Mormon Word Print Studies Word Print Analysis 90
A Record Keeping People 91
Mesoamericans Wrote Upon Thin Gold Plates 92
Gold Records and Stone Boxes in Mesoamerica 93
What Happened to the Other Gold Plates in Mesoamerica? 94
Engraving Upon Stone 96
The Mysterious Olmec 96
From Writing on Stones to Writing on Codices: "Unfold the Scriptures" 100

Chapter Seven
Demographics and a Highly Structured Society 103

Demography: Millions of People? 103
The Great Lakes and Palmyra, New York Demographics 105
What is Known Today About the People Who Lived in Mesoamerica at the Time of The Book of Mormon 106

Mesoamerican City States ... 107
Highly Stratified Society ... 108
Amalgamation and Assimilation of Various Cultures ... 109
Legend of the Light-skinned, Blue-eyed Chanes, People of the Serpent ... 111
Comparison of People of the Serpent and the Book of Mormon ... 113
A Modern Parallel in the Yucatan with the Book of Mormon .. 117
Symbols and Signs of an Advanced Civilization ... 119
Cement and Masonry ... 119
Highways and Roads ... 121

Chapter Eight
Geological Considerations: Gold, Silver, and Copper in Four Different Areas ... 127

Where on the North American Continent Does One Find Gold, Silver, and Copper in at Least Four Separate Areas ... 128
The Mesoamerican Hill Ramah/Cumorah and Gold ... 128
Additional Evidences of Gold, Silver, and Copper in Mesoamerica ... 130
Precious Stones ... 131
Why the New York Cumorah Was Not the Place of the Last Battles of the Jaredites and Nephites ... 132

Chapter Nine
Historical considerations: Mesoamerican Prophets and Unique Mormon Beliefs ... 137

Pre-Columbian Traditions Reported by Bishop Diego de Landa 137
The Mesoamerican Prophet Chilam Balam ... 137
Unique Mormon Beliefs and Mesoamerican Traditions ... 140
Jesus, Our Elder Brother ... 140
The Lacandon Belief in Our Elder Brother ... 144
The Lacandon Tradition: "God's Family Structure is Like Their Own" ... 145
A Name Correlation ... 145
Retaining the Name of an Honored King ... 146
Two Older Brothers Rebel ... 146
The Brother of Jared ... 147
Degrees of Glory in Heaven ... 148
True Men ... 149
Cannibalism ... 150
Blood Sacrifice and the Wearing of Red ... 151
Polygamy ... 152

Apostate Sacrament ... 152
Prophetic Visions of Destruction ... 153
Christopher Columbus ... 153
The Mesoamerican and The Book of Mormon
Belief in "Vision Crystals" ... 153
Idol Worship and the Mesoamericans ... 154
Chacmool ... 154

Chapter Ten
Historical Considerations: A Culture of War ... 157

The Purpose for War ... 157
Traditions Surrounding War ... 60
Mesoamerican and Book of Mormon War Traditions ... 160
War Tactics and Battle Standards ... 161
Captains and Chief Captains ... 163
Ritualized Human Sacrifice ... 163
King Fighting Kings ... 165
The Drinking of Human Blood ... 167
The Taking of Heads ... 167
Slavery ... 168
Marriage Alliances ... 170
Marriage Alliance: Gonzalo de Guerrero ... 171
Marriage Alliance: Amalickiah ... 174
Ammon: The King's Son ... 175
The Taking of Arms, "One Armed Bandits" ... 175
Cities Destroyed in a Single Day ... 178

Chapter Eleven
Historical Records from Mesoamerica: Quetzalcoatl,
The God Who Descended to Earth ... 181

Quetzalcoatl ... 182
Three Distinct Periods of Time For the Descending God ... 184
Good Snake Bad Snake ... 186
Hernán Cortés Arrived on Quetzalcoatl's Birthday ... 188
Looking to the Stars for Signs ... 188
Popol Vuh ... 191
The Popol Vuh and the Book of Ether ... 192
Six Key Elements of the Quiché Story ... 193
The Book of Mormon Story of Acquiring the Book of Ether ... 193
Six Key Elements of the Book of Ether Story ... 194
Title of the Lords of Totonicapán ... 194
Annals of the Cakchiquels ... 196
Obras Históricas ... 196

Chapter Twelve
Historical considerations: New World Calendars and the Climate 199

Unlucky Days 200
The Law of Moses Lunar Calendar 201
The Messiah-Based Book of Mormon Calendar 201
The Influence of the Law of Moses Upon The Book of Mormon 202
The First Month of the Jewish Year 204
Calendars and Climatic Considerations 204
Climatic Conditions and the Book of Mormon 205
Many are Cold and a Few are Frozen 206
Loincloths and Lamanites 207
Illness by the Nature of the Climate 210
Healing Plants and Herbs 211
The Heat of the Day 213

Chapter Thirteen
Faith and Science 215

What Should One Do When the Partial Knowledge Provided by Current Science conflicts With His or Her Spiritual Knowledge? 215
Pre-Columbian Domesticated Barley 216
Science is Knowledge in the State of Flux 217
Science: Tolerating the Unknown 217
Good Science Verses Bad Science 218
There are Scientists and Dogmatists and Some Who are Both 219
The Book of Mormon Under Attack 222
Dealing With the Disingenuous 223

Chapter Fourteen
The One Hundred and Fifty Year Old Battle Between Evolutionists and Diffusionists and The Book of Mormon 225

The "Siberian Land Bridge Only" Scientific Doctrine 226
Pre-Columbian Maritime Sailors in America 227
It Takes Years for the Public Schools to Integrate New Knowledge 230
The Emory University School of Medicine DNA Study 231
The Demise of the "Asian Only" Migrations Theory 232
An Example of Cultural Cross-Pollination or Diffusionism 233
Pre-Columbian Egyptian Influence in America 235
The Book of Mormon as Viable History 235

What Does Accepting the Americas Were Settled by Multiple Maritime Crossings and Not the "Siberian Land Bridge Only" Mean to The Book of Mormon? 235
The Battle continues to Rage Between the Evolutionists and the Diffusionists Regarding Book of Mormon Claims . . 237
Academic Arrogance 238
Scientific Cover-Ups? 240

Chapter Fifteen
The Book of Mormon as History: What About Horses in America? 243

Archaeologists and Anthropologists are Learning the Hard Way 243
Visitors Versus Residents in America 246
The Pre-Columbian Horses of the Yucatan 248
How Could Horses Have Arrived in Mesoamerica? 249
Pre-Columbian Traditions of the Horse Among the Lacandon 250
Is the Loss of Species a Surprise? 254
The Book of Mormon as History 255
What is the Current Level of Knowledge About Book of Mormon Geography? 256

Chapter Sixteen
Why is There a Need for Another Testament of Jesus Christ? 259

The Need for the Book of Mormon 259
The Crisis in Modern Day Christianity 260
A New Generation of Eye Witnesses and Ear Witnesses to the Resurrected Christ 264
The Bible and the Book of Mormon: A Personal Insight 264
Does the Bible Speak of the Book of Mormon? 265
How Does One Obtain A Divine Witness? 267
Recognizing an Answer to My Own Prayer 267
The Simplicity of the Way 268
A Summary Statement 269

List of Credits for Illustrations, Maps, and Photography 271

Endnotes 277

INTRODUCTION

Heavenly Evidence of Earthly Remains

The First Presidency of The Church of Jesus Christ of Latter-day Saints has not taken a position at this time regarding the geography of the Book of Mormon. The absence of a position should not be interpreted as support for, or opposition to, any other statement made by Church members. The lack of a specific position is not to be understood to mean that geography is not important. As the author, I accept full responsibility for the representations made herein. It is, however, the express counsel of modern prophets and apostles that members and scholars gain a spiritual witness of the Book of Mormon by reading it and not by evidences of archaeology, anthropology, or geography alone. For believers in the prophetic mission of Joseph Smith, the Book of Mormon is a history book as well as another testament of Jesus Christ. For some nonbelievers, skeptics, and dogmatists, the Book of Mormon is a fantasy tale from the creative mind of Joseph Smith.

There are those who will look at these evidences who truly have an open mind and a humble heart. To the truth seeker, we declare in the most solemn words: The Book of Mormon is a second witness of God's word to a scattered Israel. Jesus is the Christ and He walked the Americas as the resurrected Messiah. Some of the "other sheep I have, which are not of this fold (John 10:16) that Jesus promised to visit, dwelt in the Americas. There is ample historical and archeological evidence of His visits. Do not be converted by the evidences presented herein. It would be a shallow substitute for a spiritual witness born by the Holy Ghost to your heart. Follow the admonition of the great Apostle Paul, "Prove all things; hold fast that which is good" (1 Thessalonians 5:21). Read the Book of Mormon. Ponder its message and with a sincere heart ask God for a spiritual confirmation to your mind and heart whether or not the Book of Mormon is a true testament of Jesus the Christ.

I believe President Gordon B. Hinckley, who said the following about the Book of Mormon:

> The evidence for its truth, for its validity in a world that is prone to demand evidence, lies not in archaeology or anthropology, though these may be helpful to some. It lies not in word research or historical analysis, though these may be confirmatory. The evidence for its truth and validity lies within the covers of the book itself. The test of its truth lies in reading it.[1]

CHAPTER ONE

THE SPIRIT OF PLACE

Figure 1. Reconstruction View of Palenque, Mexico.

Spirit of Place

The history of the Book of Mormon did not take place in a vacuum. The stage is Mother Earth. History and geography are inseparable. The oceans, the rivers, the mountains and the plains are intertwined with the events that transpired upon them. Knowing the challenges of the physical terrain provides a profound insight into phrases like "We did travel in the wilderness many days." Was the wilderness a tropical jungle, a barren desert, a fertile plain, or a mountainous region? Understanding the topography through which they traveled in the wilderness adds awareness about the trials they faced.

The most significant contribution of geography is to provide a physical setting in which the spiritual message can be appreciated. The higher spiritual purpose of the Book of Mormon is to witness of Jesus Christ as the universal Messiah. The Book of Mormon is the history of real people whose lives were defined by their acceptance or rejection of the Messiah. Geography played a primary role in recognizing the physical struggles the people were willing to make because of their spiritual commitment. Facing difficult terrain exposed the faith of both the believer and the rebellious. This was true for those who wandered in the wilderness of Sinai with Moses and those who came to the New World and journeyed upon the lands of the Book of Mormon. It was not the voyage across the sea or the trek through a difficult wilderness that was important. It was the faith that inspired them. The same is true today. What is important for the student of the scriptures? It is to understand the faith, to sense the courage, and to appreciate the love of God that inspires the journey that gives religious history or geography significant meaning.

Geography helps in understanding history. For some, an examination of geography may peak an interest to visit the lands of the Book of Mormon. Any historical examination of the past can be enhanced by physically standing upon the same sites in the present. For example, those who have been to Jerusalem, Nazareth, Gethsemane, the Sea of Galilee, Golgotha, Bethlehem, Bethany, and the Garden Tomb, all geographical places, have an increased spiritual appreciation for the scriptures. Visits to these sites broaden the understanding of the student of the Bible. One may not always walk exactly where Jesus walked, but in spite of the modern changes, a deeply felt connection to the place is experienced by those who have been to the Holy Land. This is what is meant by the "spirit of place."

A visit to the Sacred Grove in Palmyra, New York; the temple in Kirtland, Ohio; Joseph Smith's grave at Nauvoo, Illinois; or Winter Quarters in Nebraska, all geographical places, is not a visit to a shrine nor is it idol worship for the Latter-day Saint. It is a connection with one's spiritual and historical roots. Among the early Mormon pioneers who came to Utah were the members of the Willie and Martin handcart company. Their story is a historical fact which can be read and intellectually understood. Going to the Platt River in the wintertime and staring at the icy water, feeling the biting wind upon one's face, and sensing the chill of a cold that numbs the toes and chills the bone gives one a deeper appreciation for the struggles they faced. Seeing, smelling, and touching the environment in which the pioneers labored opens the mind to new perspectives. It is taking one's physical feet to where one's spiritual feet have already walked in the history of the Church. This is also the "spirit of place."

It is desirable, but not necessary, to travel to actual locations in order to obtain a greater appreciation of the geography of the Bible, Church history, or the Book of Mormon. When readers of sacred history can move beyond the historical facts, it can touch their souls. For some, a serious study of geography can open a historical window into the past by adding flesh and bone to the pages of holy writ. How this greater appreciation of the Book of Mormon is accomplished, whether by actually visiting the lands of the Book of Mormon or whether it is obtained by a deeper understanding of geography through serious study, or both, may not matter. The "spirit of place" happens when the characters mentioned in the scriptures come alive. It happens when a connection is made between the intellect and the emotions. It is the difference between reading a prayer and feeling the prayer one has offered. Feeling the "spirit of place" is not irrational; to the contrary, it is discovering the truth about the events that transpired at that location. Ultimately, the "spirit of place" is the joining of history and geography with an abiding empathy and a deeply felt appreciation for the events that occurred at that site. Finding the right geographical setting to experience the spirit of place is a major objective of this book.

Examining the Historical Claims of the Book of Mormon

Another purpose in writing this book is to examine some key historical claims of the Book of Mormon. Certain secular claims of the Book of Mormon as history can be examined by the traditional scientific approach. The Book of Mormon asserts that the Americas were settled in part by maritime crossings. There are claims of a high civilization upon the North American continent, of city states, of a people with a written language, of highly skilled artisans who were expert in the crafting of gold, silver and copper. There are absolute statements about the skills of craftsmen who were proficient in the engraving of large stones, of scribes who wrote upon metal plates and of stone boxes. Sepulchers, tombs, altars and trade routes with a merchant class of people were said to have existed. It speaks of a warrior society governed by kings and priests and massive battles with highly structured armies. There were wars of mutual destruction and the abandonment of cities in a single day.

The Book of Mormon talks about social practices of human sacrifices, marriage alliances, polygamy, slavery, and ritualistic cannibalism. It tells of subjugated city states paying tribute to the conquerors. The Book of Mormon claims that the people were a temple building, tower building, cement using, and highway building society. It maintains there were calendars and dating systems in play and a unique structure of weights and measures. There are claims of barley, horses, chickens and a connection to things Egyptian and a hieroglyphic language.

One of the very specific claims of the Book of Mormon has to do with topography and the flow of a major river from the south to the north. Historical claims of Jesus Christ as a resurrected being coming to America and teaching and appearing to many different cities and people are abundant. Prophets and seers were to be found upon the land. Perhaps the most profound historic claim of the Book of Mormon is a demographic one, i.e., that millions of people occupied a relatively small area two thousand five hundred years ago. Where is the evidence on the North American continent of an agricultural base sufficient to sustain a population of millions?

There are many important and significant historical claims made by the Book of Mormon about which Joseph Smith could not have known in his day. Most of these Book of Mormon claims were adamantly denied or overwhelmingly rejected by the scientific community. Nearly every historical claim made in the Book of Mormon was considered absurd when it was published in 1830. One by one these historical claims have been and are being vindicated by modern day scientists. The difference between what Joseph Smith could *not* have known in his day, and the subsequent discoveries in science is a testimony that Joseph Smith did not author the Book of Mormon. He translated it.

What the Book of Mormon does *not* claim is as important as what it does claim in looking at the evidence. Generalizing is a common mistake made by the readers of the Book of Mormon. For example, the Book of Mormon does not claim to be the story of all the peoples of the Americas. It is a partial history of but three of the many societies that dwelt upon this land. The Book of Mormon does not claim that horses were everywhere in North America. Horses were found regionally as they journeyed through the forests and wilderness (1 Nephi 18:25). This is the same general area where the earliest group of immigrants call Jaredites landed around 2200 B.C. with their "flocks and herds, and whatsoever beast or animal or fowl that they should carry with them. (Ether 6:4)" Later, horses were specifically mentioned in their writings (Ether 9:19). The Book of Mormon does not claim that gold, silver, and copper were found everywhere in North America. These minerals were found in the specific areas and limited regions occupied by them. Understanding the exact historical claim made by the Book of Mormon is vital.

Unanswered Questions

Because mankind is not in possession of all historical knowledge and a perfect historical secular record of the inhabitants of this continent, there will always remain some unanswered questions about specific geography in the Book of Mormon. Many previously unanswered questions about the Book of Mormon have been answered, or are in the process of being answered, even now. Some questions will never be answered in this life, in either religion or science. All knowledge awaits a resurrected being, not a mortal one. Absolute knowledge of all things is the prerogative of God. This should not deter researchers from looking at all things and expressing their best opinion based on current information.

In the absence of a perfect knowledge of all things, the prudent scholar and religious believer will allow for future findings that may differ from his or her present understanding. For example, there are some Book of Mormon claims about certain animals for which there are no present evidences. This does not mean there will not be future evidences. Pre-Columbian chickens in the Americas is one example of a recently (2007) discovered animal mentioned in the Book of Mormon, for which there was no previous evidence.[2] The assertion that these animals did not exist in the Americas before the coming of the Spanish has proven to be false.

When writings that were considered scriptures by the LDS Church were being attacked in 1913, President Joseph F. Smith said, "Not only do we testify that Joseph Smith was inspired, [but] ... it is our firm belief that scientific investigation and discovery will confirm our testimony, rather than weaken or repudiate it."[3] There exists, for those interested, an abundance of historical and geographical evidence waiting to be examined. The information already gathered provides a high degree of confidence in various locations as prime candidates for Book of Mormon sites. Further research into specific areas will identify some potential locations as A sites, B sites, and C sites. An A site would represent the best current candidate; a B site means there is significant but not convincing evidence and more information is required; and a C site reflects the location as a possibility among several options. A, B, and C sites are the best-educated opinions of specific areas at this time and not the final word. As one embarks on this geographical adventure, it will be important to look for external evidences that correlate with the internal story of the Book of Mormon.

What Does a Correlation Prove?

It is important to remember that a correlation does not prove anything. Several correlations increase the probability of an association. For example, the correlations between smoking and various forms of cancer are accepted by insurance companies as evidence for some type of connection between the two. However, one cannot prove that smoking causes cancer on the basis of correlated evidences. When there are a significant numbers of correlations, the confidence of the researcher increases that an association exists. The correlations between Mesoamerica[4] and the Book of Mormon are overwhelming. The term *Mesoamerica* defines the geographical region of Southern Mexico and includes Central America. It is used here because in Joseph Smith's day Southern Mexico was considered a part of Central America. There are more evidences and correlations between the historical accuracies of the Book of Mormon and Mesoamerica than there are between smoking and cancer.

For the believer in the Book of Mormon as a real history of a real people, these correlations are expected. For the skeptic, the associations are not conclusive, but raise the possibility and plausibility of a relationship which deserves an open minded evaluation. For the disingenuous no amount of evidence, correlation, or association will suffice. These are they who pretend in the name of science or truth to examine the Book of Mormon. They are held prisoners by their own preconceived notions that the Book of Mormon can not be another testament of Jesus Christ. The solution for the skeptic or the disingenuous remains a spiritual one: humility and prayer.

For those who are already in possession of a spiritual witness of the Book of Mormon as another testament of Jesus Christ, matters of geography bring up questions of "where" and "when" did these events take place? It is not an issue of "if" these events happened. The search begins as a quest for the knowable, not the hoped for. It is much like looking for one's unnamed ancestors in a foreign country. One knows where their progenitors came from and knows they truly existed. The "where did they live" and "how long were they there" are parts of a puzzle that the genealogists are in the process of solving. So it is with the geography of the Book of Mormon. The quest for the location of these historical places of the Jaredites, Mulekites, and Lehites is not without significant clues which come from the pages of the Book of Mormon, from the lips of prophets and angels, and from Mother Earth herself.

What are the "Lands of the Book of Mormon"?

The use of the terms "primary events in the Book of Mormon" will always refer to the history and geography of the Americas. Ninety-nine percent of the stories in the Book of Mormon relative to America take place in five adjoining geographical areas known as the "lands of the Book of Mormon." These sites include

- The Land of First Inheritance of Father Lehi
- The Land of Nephi
- The Land of Zarahemla
- The Land of Bountiful
- The Land of Desolation

Collectively, they are known as the primary lands of the Book of Mormon in America.

Dimensions of the Primary Lands of the Book of Mormon

The Book of Mormon speaks of a land north and a land south, which is divided by a narrow neck of land. Some of the early readers of the Book of Mormon assumed North America was the land north for the Book of Mormon events; that South America was the land south and the Isthmus of Panama was the narrow neck of land separating the two. This position is untenable. Because of the vast distances between North and South America, it would not be possible to move armies and populations over thousands of miles in the limited time outlined in the Book of Mormon for those particular events.

One example will suffice. The distance between the city of Zarahemla, in the Land of Zarahemla, and Helam, in the Land of Nephi, can be reasonably estimated. The people of Alma living in Helam, Land of Nephi, traveled thirteen days to arrive at the city of Zarahemla. They did not leave empty-handed, but left with grain, flocks, little children, and old men and women (Mosiah 24:20-25). How far could that many people travel with flocks and children in thirteen days? The question to the LDS member would be, "How many miles a day could your ward travel?" This has to include the young and the old and some animals along with food stuffs and supplies. Assume one would leave most of the wheat from their food supply behind, especially the wheat grinder. One good Brother commented, "It would take my ward thirteen days to get organized before we could take the first step!" Some have estimated five miles a day. That translates into sixty five miles between the city of Helam, and the city of Zarahemla. A rate of fifteen miles a day equals a distance of one hundred ninety-five miles. Moving twenty miles a day, with young and old, with animals and grain, means that the city of Helam, in the Land of Nephi, and the city of Zarahemla, in the Land of Zarahemla, cannot be more than two hundred and sixty miles apart. Serious scholars question those who require vast distances to make a map of the Book of Mormon fit their favored terrain.

The Book of Mormon makes the rules as to the distances involved and establishes the necessary qualifications for identifying the geographical boundaries of the lands of the Book of Mormon. Any theory not consistent with the internal statements of the Book of Mormon or with the geographical restrictions it imposes remains an unproductive opinion.

Moroni is a key figure in defining the lands of the Book of Mormon. Because he played such a significant role in the coming forth of the Book of Mormon, an introduction to Moroni is in order.

Who is Moroni?

The question is often asked, "Why do you have a statue atop of your temples with a man blowing a horn?" The answer is, "That is the angel Moroni who was sent by God in fulfillment of the promise of John the Revelator:"

> And I saw another angel fly in the midst of heaven, having the everlasting gospel to preach unto them that dwell on the earth, and to every nation, and kindred, and tongue and people (Revelation 14:6).

Moroni was the first of many messengers sent to minister to the young boy prophet, Joseph Smith, and prepare him for his life's mission. The angel Moroni first appeared to the seventeen-year-old in 1823. Joseph was in the middle of a prayer when his room began to fill with light. He related the following experience:

> He called me by name, and said unto me that he was a messenger sent from the presence of God to me, and that his name was Moroni; that God had a work for me to do and that my name should be had for good and evil among all nations ... He said there was a book deposited, written upon gold plates, giving an account of the former inhabitants of this continent ... That the fulness of the everlasting Gospel was contained in it, as delivered by the Savior ...[5]

This was the first of many instructional sessions between Joseph and Moroni over the next ten years.[6] During these visits Joseph discovered in great detail who Moroni was. He was a prophet-historian and the last author in the Book of Mormon. Moroni's father was Mormon, the commander-in chief of the entire Nephite army for more than fifty years. Mormon was more than a great military strategist, he also was a prophet-historian and the one God had chosen to abridge the history of a thousand years. It was the abridgment of the Nephite history that Mormon entrusted into the hands of his son, Moroni (Mormon 6:6). As a mortal, Moroni walked the lands of the Book of Mormon. He was a first person witness to the events leading to the destruction of his people in the Land of Desolation. He was also in charge of ten thousand in the final struggle at the Hill Cumorah where only twenty-four survived.

Moroni spent thirty-six years after the last battle on a journey that would end in Palmyra, New York. There is where the Lord had instructed him to bury the sacred records known as the Book of Mormon. The one undisputed fact among Mormon scholars is that Moroni deposited the Book of Mormon in the Hill Cumorah near Palmyra, New York. The final invitation of the prophet-historian Moroni was poetry to the soul. Here are his very last words following which he buried the records in the stone box near the top of the Hill Cumorah in New York:

> Yea, come unto Christ, and be perfected in him ... and love God with all your might, mind and strength, then is his grace sufficient for you ... And now I bid unto all, farewell. I soon go to rest in the paradise of God, until my spirit and body shall again reunite, and I am brought forth triumphant through the air, to meet you before the pleasing bar of the great Jehovah, the Eternal Judge of both the quick and dead. Amen (Moroni 10:32-34).

Moroni's spirit and body did reunite and he was resurrected like unto the many that came forth after the resurrection of Jesus in Jerusalem as reported by the Gospel writer, Matthew (Matthew 27:52-53). As a resurrected being, Moroni appeared to Joseph Smith. He instructed him in many things related to the coming forth of the Restored Gospel of Jesus Christ of which the Book of Mormon was to play a significant role. Moroni's counsel to Joseph Smith was primarily spiritual. However, within the context of his teaching, specific statements were made relative to the geography of the Book of Mormon. Moroni's declarations help eliminate one of the three candidates that are claiming to be the primary lands of the Book of Mormon.

Three Geographical Locations Vie for the Lands of the Book of Mormon

The three major candidates for the primary events in the Book of Mormon are:

- Mesoamerica (This includes southern Mexico and most of Central America.)
- The Great Lakes and the area surrounding Palmyra, New York
- South America (primarily along the Pacific coast)

Those who advocate for the areas of Southern Mexico and Central America will be known as Mesoamerican advocates. There are some people who advocate for the primary events of the Book of Mormon occurring just south of the Great Lakes near Palmyra, New York. Those who maintain that position will be referred to as the Great Lakes advocates. There are others who believe that South

America was the place where the primary events of the Book of Mormon took place. These will be called the South American advocates.

Regardless of which position one supports, the dimensions of the primary lands of the Book of Mormon are less than six hundred fifty miles from north to south and less than three hundred miles east to west. This is because of the internal restrictions placed on distances traveled in the Book of Mormon. The distances mentioned internally in the Book of Mormon for the primary events require an area somewhat similar in size to the Holy Land.

Dr. John L. Sorenson is the author of what has come to be known as the "Limited Tehuantepec Theory." This means the primary events in the Book of Mormon took place in a relatively small geographical area around the Isthmus of Tehuantepec. In looking at the Book of Mormon geography, Sorenson says,

> The dimensions are small, although hardly tiny. The promised land in which the Nephites' history played out was on the order of five hundred miles long and over two hundred miles wide, according to Mormon's mental map. That is still considerably larger than the stage on which most Old Testament events took place.[7]

I have suggested a six hundred fifty-mile limit from north to south. This is the approximate distance between Mexico City, Mexico on the north and Guatemala City, Guatemala on the south. I also support the position that the primary events of the Book of Mormon took place in a limited area around the Isthmus of Tehuantepec. The single exception was Moroni's journey from Mesoamerica to the Hill Cumorah in New York where he buried the abridged records.

Before proceeding let me set the scope of my own expectations. I will present to you the statements of the Prophet Joseph Smith that are absolutely specific about Mesoamerica as the place of the primary events of the Book of Mormon in North America. By answering the important question, "Where is Zarahemla?" it is my hope that members of the Church will not become confused by alternative claims. Once the Land of Zarahemla is found, so also are the four adjoining lands of Nephi, Bountiful, Desolation, and the Land of First Inheritance. Finding Zarahemla is finding the Jaredites, the Mulekites, and the Nephites.

Why is There Confusion?

Many members of the Church are confused about the disagreements over where the primary events of the Book of Mormon took place. This confusion is the result of well meaning members of the Church advocating three different geographical places. Adding to the confusion are contradictory statements made by some Church leaders. For instance, in 1842 Joseph Smith made definite statements about Central America and Guatemala being the location of the primary events in the Book of Mormon. Later, Joseph Fielding Smith felt strongly

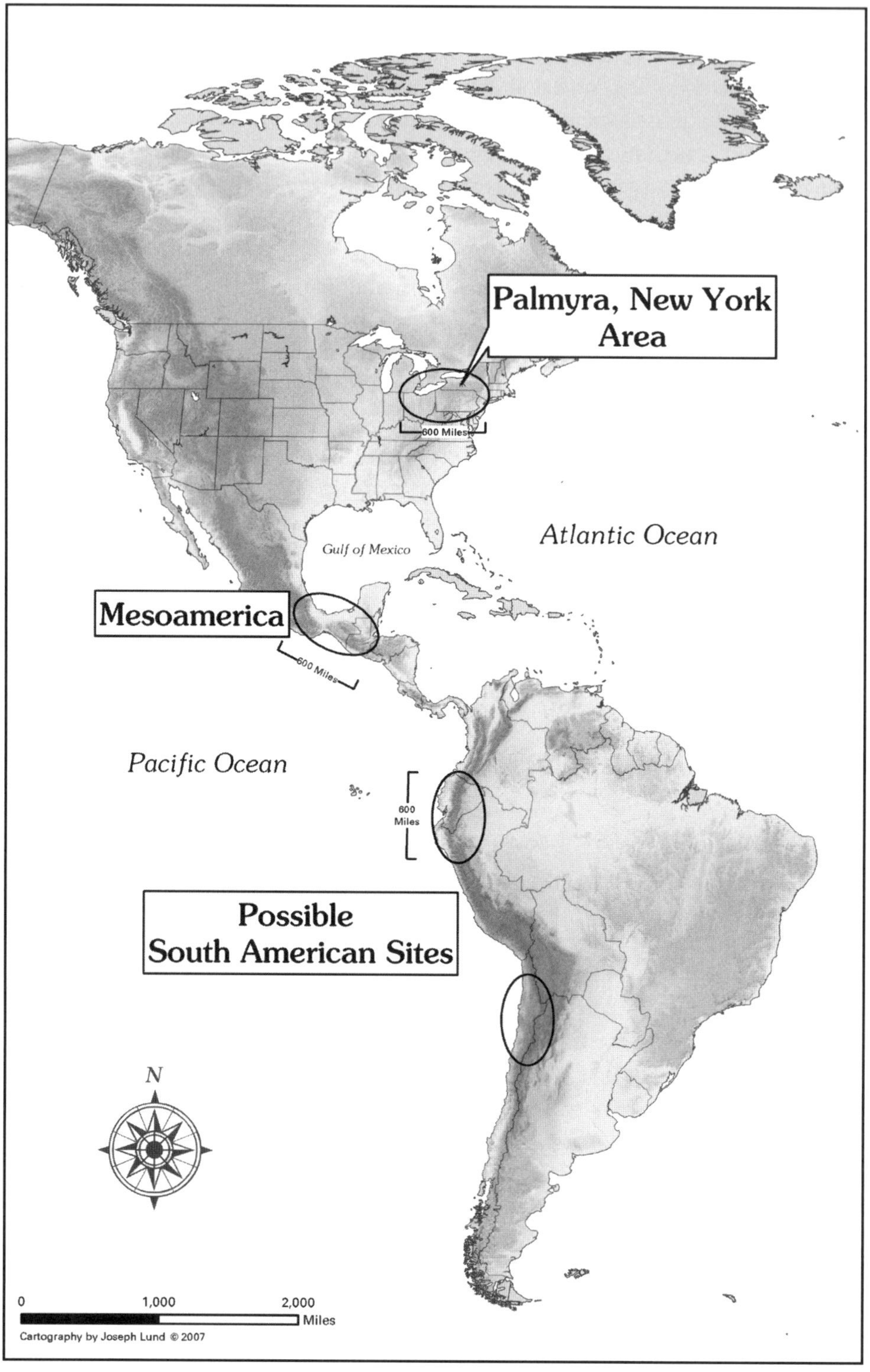

Figure 2. Map: Three Candidate Areas for the Lands of the Book of Mormon

about the primary events of the Book of Mormon occurring near the Hill Cumorah in New York.[8]

There are and will be sincere LDS scholars who disagree with the basic premise that Joseph Smith is an unimpeachable source. Some have taken a point of view that a prophet is only a prophet when he is speaking as a prophet. And unless he says, "Thus saith the Lord," his words, though respected, are nonetheless his opinion. Relegating Joseph's statements to opinion gives them permission to pursue their own theories about the geography of the Book of Mormon. Also, since the Church has no official position on the subject, they are free to speculate. Obviously, I have taken a different stance in regards to the statements of Joseph Smith. Without declaring every word that Joseph wrote or spoke as revelation, there is still merit in sustaining Joseph's opinion over that of someone less acquainted with the coming forth of the Book of Mormon.

Joseph Smith *is* an unimpeachable source for most Latter-day Saints. Independent of being a Prophet, he was a Seer, whose insights alone qualify his opinion to be held in higher esteem and given greater weight than even the most ardent scholar of the Book of Mormon. He was, by vision, a first person witness of the society of the Nephites and Lamanites. Therefore, I have taken the position that the statements made by Joseph Smith and the angel Moroni will have preeminence over the opinions of others. The only exception would be if a modern prophet of the Lord declared, "Thus saith the Lord!" Until that time, the statements of Joseph Smith will be considered a primary source. President Gordon B. Hinckley said the Book of Mormon, "can be explained only as the translator himself explained its origin."[9] The Prophet Joseph's declarations become defining external evidence in the quest for the geography of the Book of Mormon. There is a sincere hope and an expectation that members of the Church will review the statements of the Prophet Joseph Smith and the overwhelming geographical evidence and focus on Mesoamerica confident that they are in the lands of the Book of Mormon.

The real dilemma for both the Great Lakes advocates and those who advocate for South America is reconciling Joseph Smith's statements about Zarahemla being in Guatemala (Central America). All of Joseph Smith's statements are consistent when seen through the eyes of Mesoamerica as the place of the primary events. Those who advocate for the primary events taking place in South America have even a greater objection to overcome. From the lips of an angel named Moroni, Joseph Smith was told that the Book of Mormon was "written upon gold plates, giving an account of the former inhabitants of *this continent*,"[10] meaning the North American continent. Moroni did not say *these* continents.

When retelling his encounter with the angel Moroni, Joseph Smith wrote to the editor of the *Chicago Democrat*, Mr. John Wentworth. From this document written to Mr. Wentworth would be extracted scripture for the Latter-day Saints, called The Articles of Faith and referred to in Church history as "The Wentworth Letter," dated March 1, 1842. In explaining the origin of the Book of Mormon, Joseph retold what the angel Moroni had said to him nineteen years earlier:

> I was also told where were deposited some plates on which were engraven an abridgement of the records of the ancient prophets that had existed on *this continent.* [11]

Joseph distinguished between the North American continent and the Asian continent. Clearly, Joseph understood the term continent as a geographical limitation. In the LDS official publication, *Times and Seasons*, published in Nauvoo Illinois, he declared,

> ... that a great and a mighty people had inhabited *this continent*... and that there was as great and mighty cities on *this continent* as on the *continent of Asia* ... Their ruins speak of their greatness; the Book of Mormon unfolds their history.[12]

There are some great correlations with South America and the Book of Mormon involving seeds, winds, currents, gold, silver, and copper and some remarks ascribed to Church leaders. However, they all fall short when measured against the statements of the angel Moroni and the Prophet Joseph Smith. South America and the islands of the Pacific are part of the eventual spread of the descendants of the Book of Mormon, but not the place of the primary events. It is on the North American continent these first peoples of the Book of Mormon lived, loved, fought wars, raised children, and died. The Book of Mormon is a real history of real people whose descendants created a great civilization on *this continent* which eventually spread to the entire hemisphere.

The Major Points of the Great Lakes Advocates

Advocates for the Great Lakes and the Palmyra area have built their case on the following major points:

1. Moroni buried the records there.
2. It is called Cumorah.
3. Brigham Young quoted the testimony of Oliver Cowdrey who reported that on two separate occasions he and Joseph Smith walked into the Hill Cumorah and found "wagon loads" of ancient records.
4. Mormon's statement about Cumorah being in the "land of many waters, rivers, and fountains" (Mormon 6:4).
5. During Zion's Camp March in 1834
    a. Joseph wrote a letter to Emma and said he was walking on the "plains of the Nephites."
    b. Zelph's grave was found in Illinois and Joseph declared he was a white Lamanite who died in a battle with Lamanites.
6. The United States of America is the Promised Land.

There are other considerations, but most of them are about reinforcing these major points. There are comments throughout this book on why the Great Lake advocates are in error in their understanding and interpretation of the data according to Joseph Smith. Following is a preliminary response to the above issues.

The Great Lakes advocates are sometimes referred to as the "One Cumorah" advocates. This has reference to the belief that two separate events both occured at the same geographical place, i.e., the Hill Cumorah in New York. The buried plates and the wars of destruction are the two events. Great Lakes advocates *assume* that because Moroni buried the gold plates and the interpreters in the stone box in the Hill Cumorah in New York that it must be the same Hill Cumorah upon which the final destruction of both the Jaredites and Nephites took place. It is a natural assumption to make, but as will be seen by the statements of Joseph Smith an incorrect one.

The Mesoamerican advocates are sometimes referred to as the "Two Cumorah" advocates. This means there was one Cumorah where the last battles took place for the Jaredites as well as the Nephites in Mesoamerica and another hill by the same name, Cumorah, near Palmyra, New York where Moroni buried the abridged records. The Jaredites referred to the hill of their final destruction as the Hill Ramah; the Nephites named the same hill, the Hill Cumorah (Ether 15:11, Mormon 6:6). There are testimonies of credible witnesses that tell of Joseph Smith's teaching that Moroni walked to the Hill Cumorah in New York from Central America where the final wars were waged.[13] This was after the last great battle in Mesoamerica. Statements made by Joseph Smith establish there were two Cumorahs. Henceforth, the name Ramah/Cumorah will refer to the place of the final destruction in Mesoamerica of both the Jaredites and the Nephites. In the Book of Mormon, the term Cumorah always means the Hill Ramah/Cumorah. The New York Hill Cumorah, where the plates were buried by Moroni, is mentioned in the Doctrine and Covenants. "Glad tidings from Cumorah! Moroni, an angel from heaven, declaring the fulfillment of the prophets the book to be revealed (D&C128: 20). This has reference to the coming forth of the Book of Mormon from the hill in New York.

Oliver Cowdrey's Cave Experience

Brigham Young, at a special conference in Farmington, Utah for the purpose of organizing a Stake of Zion in 1877, reported on Oliver Cowdrey's experience on two occasions of walking into a cave in the Hill Cumorah with Joseph Smith.[14] Oliver declared that the hill opened up and they saw more gold plates and historical records than probably many wagonloads could hold. The proponents for the Great Lakes and the Palmyra area as the place for the Land of Zarahemla and the Land of Desolation use Oliver's cave experience as evidence to support their view. However, Heber C. Kimball indicated eleven years earlier in 1856 that the experience that Oliver had was a vision.[15] This means that what Oliver saw could have taken place anywhere. That it was a vision affects the entire assumption that the cave in question was in New York.

The scriptures are filled with examples of those who have had visions where their spirits were carried away to view the things of eternity and distant places on the earth. Visions are not bound by time or miles. Moses,[16] Lehi,[17] Nephi,[18] and Abraham[19] are a few of the visionaries. The example of Nephi is of particular interest since he was "caught away in the Spirit of the Lord, yea *into* an exceedingly high mountain" (1 Nephi 11:1, emphasis added). Nephi, like Oliver and Joseph, went "*into*" and not just upon a mountain.

The fact that Oliver had a vision of a cave does not prove what he saw in vision was the hill in New York. It was more likely the Ramah/Cumorah cave in Mesoamerica where Mormon had deposited the Nephite records from which he made the abridgement that he gave to his son Moroni (Mormon 6:6). Joseph Smith's definitive statements about the two Cumorahs, one in Mesoamerica and the other in New York, clear up the misunderstanding.[20] Oliver Cowdrey's vision and the *assumptions* people made about his experience contributed to the confusion.

An example of a geographical correlation for the Great Lakes and Palmyra advocates is the Book of Mormon statement about Cumorah being in the "land of many waters, rivers, and fountains" (Mormon 6:4). The Great Lakes certainly qualify, in general, for this particular requirement. It does not, however, qualify in topography, climatic considerations, geology, demographics, historical records, or Joseph Smith's statements to the contrary. It is not sufficient to have just one or two correlations when there is another area with a myriad of correlations, more qualified, and consistent with Joseph Smith's recorded testimony in the *Times and Seasons.* In addition, there are geographical factors that disqualify the Great Lakes area as the place of the final destruction of both the Jaredites and the Nephites. The other locations in Mesoamerica of many waters, rivers, and fountains do qualify in all the other above-mentioned criteria.

A Look at Zelph

On the Zion's Camp march from Kirtland, Ohio to Jackson County, Missouri, Milton Holmes found human bones in one of the mounds near present-day Griggsville, Illinois on the west bank of the Illinois River on Monday, June 2, 1834. Milton Holmes, Wilford Woodruff, and several of the brethren dug down another foot and discovered the skeleton of a man. Joseph Smith identified the remains as belonging to a man named Zelph.

Dr. Ken W. Godfrey, a Church history scholar, has compiled several separate accounts of this event.[21] Those wishing greater insight into the Zelph incident truly should read his article published in *BYU Studies.* The accounts agree on the following points:

> (1)... members of Zion's Camp, traveling through Illinois, unearthed the skeletal remains of a man, 2 June 1834 near the top of a large burial mound; (2) Joseph Smith learned what he knew about the skeletal remains by way of a vision after the discovery; (3) the man was a white Lamanite named Zelph, a man of God, and a great warrior who served under a widely known leader named Onandagus; (4) Zelph was killed by the arrow found with his remains in a battle with Lamanites.[22]

Dr. Godfrey suggested, "The bulk of Nephite history occurred in Central America while only certain battles or excursions took place in Illinois." [23] There were Nephite populations living both north and south of the Rio Grande.

> Exactly what Joseph Smith believed at different times in his life concerning Book of Mormon geography in general is also indeterminable. Only a few clues remain. For example, while the Church was headquartered in Nauvoo, Joseph read a best-selling book of his day by John Lloyd Stephens, *Incidents of Travel in Central America, Chiapas, and Yucatan*, which John Bernhisel had sent to him from the East. In a letter dated 16 November 1841, the Prophet thanked Bernhisel and wrote of the book that "of all histories that had been written pertaining to the antiquities of this country it is the most correct" and that it "supports the testimony of the Book of Mormon" ... Evidently Joseph Smith's views on this matter were open to further knowledge. Thus in 1834, when Zelph was found, Joseph believed that the portion of America over which they had just traveled was "the plains of the Nephites" and that their bones were "proof" of the Book of Mormon's authenticity. By 1842, he evidently believed that the events in most of Nephite history took place in Central America. [24]

A flawed account of the Zelph story was later corrected by Joseph Smith. However, it was the flawed account that found its way into the *History of the Church.* Joseph Fielding Smith used the flawed account to support the view that the Hill Cumorah of the final Nephite battle in the state of New York was the exact same hill in the Book of Mormon. He may not have been aware of the corrected document or he may have believed the corrected version was in error. In 1950 John A. Widtsoe, former Apostle, scholar, and Harvard Ph.D. graduate added his opinion about Zelph:

> On the journey into northwestern Missouri, led by the Prophet, the skeleton of a large man was uncovered near the Illinois River. Joseph Smith said it was the remains of a white Lamanite named Zelph, a leader among this people. This is not of much value in Book of Mormon geographical studies, since Zelph probably dated from a later time when Nephites and Lamanites had been somewhat dispersed and had wandered over the country.[25]

Zelph was either a Nephite dissenter who joined with the Lamanites or he was a light skinned Lamanite: the product of intermarriage with the Lamanites.

It is an important point to recognize that in A.D. 385, the terms "Nephite, Lamanite, and Gadianton Robbers" were cultural designations and not racial ones. One could be a white or dark Lamanite, a white or dark Nephite, or a white or dark Gadianton Robber. It was the Nephite "culture" that was destroyed. Nephites living in other areas away from their original homeland also survived and were eventually assimilated by surrounding cultures.

Most readers of the Book of Mormon assume that every Nephite was on the Hill Cumorah when the last great battle took place, and that all but twenty-four were killed. *All* is a relative term. Did all the Nephites die on the Hill Cumorah? Yes, all the Nephites that were on the Hill Cumorah, except twenty-four, did die. Was every last Nephite on the earth also a part of the last great battle? No. Were there Nephite dissenters who joined the Lamanites? Yes. Is it also possible there were many Nephite colonies living north of the Rio Grande or in South America away from the main body of the Nephites that also survived? Yes! Moroni commented sixteen years after the great and last battle that any Nephite who escaped and fled south was hunted down and killed by the Lamanites (Mormon 8:2), the rest of the Nephites were hunted down from city to city after the great and last battle. Were these cities north as well as south of the Rio Grande? Yes!

According to the Book of Mormon and Joseph Smith's letter to his wife Emma, there were Nephites living north of the Rio Grande and upon the plains and along the rivers of the United States. The Book of Mormon reports on at least four Nephite group migrations into the land northward involving thousands of people (Alma 63:49). Some migrated by land and others by sea. There were five thousand and four hundred Nephites who migrated to the "land northward" (Alma 63:4). In the same year, 55 B.C., Hagoth, a Nephite, built a large ship and sailed northward. He returned and built other ships in 54 B.C. and sailed northward again. The main body of the Nephites remained in the south including the 230,000 who would die on the Hill Ramah/Cumorah. The last battle was about four hundred and forty years after the great migration of Nephites to the lands northward. Joseph Smith wrote a letter to Emma Smith on June 4, 1834, from the banks of the Mississippi River. He said he had been "wandering the plains of the Nephites."[26] Finding Zelph and other "white Lamanites" and Nephites north of the Rio Grande should be expected in light of thousands who migrated north four hundred forty years before the last great battle on the Hill Ramah/Cumorah. The issue is not the eventual spread of *some* of the Nephites north of the Rio Grande, including the Great Lakes area. In actuality, the mixed seed of the Book of Mormon people did eventually spread to all of North and South America and the isles of the western hemisphere.

By 1842, Joseph Smith was convinced that Mesoamerica was the place of the primary events of the Book of Mormon and that there were two Cumorahs. The Prophet would tell Patriarch William McBride and a Brother Andrew Hamilton that Moroni walked from Central America in the Land of Bountiful to the Hill Cumorah in New York. Moroni made the first part of this trek after the last great battle in Mesoamerica and buried the abridged plates of the Book of Mormon in the stone box on the side of the New York Hill Cumorah.[27] Moroni's statement about being alone occurred sixteen years after the great battle, or about A.D. 401. Could this mean that between A.D. 385 and A.D. 401 that Moroni may have had some of the twenty-four survivors accompany him on the journey north? Yes.

South American Advocates

Frankly, in terms of external evidence the South American advocates have a stronger case than the Great Lakes advocates do. Here is a summary of the major points for South American advocates:

- The winds and the ocean currents favor a landing at Chile.
- Seeds from the Holy Land would not "grow exceedingly," in New York, rather in a climate zone equal to that of the Mediterranean.
- Gold, Silver, and Copper must be present in order to qualify as lands of the Book of Mormon.
- Cultural traditions.
- Unusual animals.

Except for the definitive statements by Moroni and Joseph Smith about the primary events occurring on the North American *continent*, South American advocates would have a stronger case. The lack of a population base in South America of the time of the Book of Mormon is also a major concern. There is currently no evidence of a pre-Columbian written hieroglyphic language that existed in South America. The multiple climate zones, the east and west travel of armies and millions of people impeded by the Andes, the five hundred to six hundred and fifty mile limitation imposed by the Book of Mormon are issues not adequately addressed by the South American advocates. The good news is that all of the blessings promised to the mixed seed of Lehi apply to South America and to the isles of the sea.

CHAPTER TWO

Things to Consider When Looking at Book of Mormon Geography

When Examining Book of Mormon Geography There are Several Areas to Consider

1. Prophetic and angelic considerations
2. High civilization considerations
3. Demographic and Climatic considerations
4. Geological considerations
5. Historical considerations
6. Archaeological considerations

Prophetic and Angelic Considerations

The Prophet Joseph Smith, through his visions and instructions from the angel Moroni, named the North American continent as the right place.[28] There is no question that Joseph Smith also accepted Mesoamerica as a "this is the right place!" location for the Land of Zarahemla, as will be shown. Joseph did not use the term Mesoamerica. Joseph referred to these lands as Central America and Guatemala. Accepting Joseph Smith's geographical insights that Mesoamerica encompasses the lands of the Book of Mormon is profound. It means, among other things, that South America is not the land of Zarahemla, nor is Zarahemla in any area in the United States of America. This does not mean that the wonderful promises extended to South America and the United States of America and Canada are not real or valid. It just means that most of the primary events mentioned in the Book of Mormon transpired in Mesoamerica.

How Did Joseph Smith Identify Central America as the Lands of the Book of Mormon?

Joseph Smith's prophetic mission required him to be a Seer (D&C 107:92; D&C 124:94). As a Seer, Joseph saw in vision the people, their buildings, their engraved monuments, and even their manner of dress and warfare. These visions were received several years before Joseph translated the Book of Mormon. This meant that he could not only translate the words from the engraved plates of the Book of Mormon, but *he could see* the people and their culture from the Tower of Babel to his own day and see into the future. Joseph described the office of a Prophet and Seer:

> They are they who saw the mysteries of godliness; they saw the flood before it came ... they saw the end of wickedness on earth, and the Sabbath of creation crowned with peace; they saw the end of the glorious thousand years, when Satan was loosed for a little season; they saw the day of judgment when all men received according to their works, and they saw the heaven and the earth flee away to make room for the city of God...[29]

As the head of the Dispensation of the Fullness of Times, Joseph was shown what other dispensational heads like Adam,[30] Abel,[31] Enoch, Noah, Abraham, Moses, and the Apostle Peter were shown.

It would be a great mistake to underestimate the preparations which the Lord had given to the Prophet Joseph Smith. Recall Joseph's comment regarding his ability to recognize the place where the plates for the Book of Mormon were buried: "...owing to the distinctness of the vision which I had had concerning it, I knew the place the instant that I arrived there."[32] On another occasion Joseph reported:

> I was also informed concerning the aboriginal inhabitants of the country, and *shown* who they were, and *from whence they came*; a brief sketch of their origin, progress, civilization, laws, governments, of their righteousness and iniquity, and the blessings of God being finally withdrawn from them as a people was made known unto me: I was also told where there was deposited some plates on which were engraven an abridgement of the records of the ancient prophets that had existed on this continent.[33]

Dan Vogel has compiled a number of early Mormon documents and provided a great view into the early life of the Prophet Joseph Smith. Lucy Mack Smith, the Prophet's mother, gave a key insight into the depth and breadth of knowledge Joseph was given by angelic instruction and visions. The information involved the daily life of the peoples of the Book of Mormon and their apostate descendants. Lucy reported that all of this transpired in the year of 1823, or seven years before the publication of the Book of Mormon. Joseph was seventeen years old and had already visited with the angel Moroni several times and had been shown visions of the Book of Mormon peoples.

> In the course of our evening conversations Joseph would give us some of the most amusing recitals which could be imagined. He would describe the ancient inhabitants of *this continent, their dress, their manner of traveling, the animals upon which they rode, the cities that were built by them, the structure of their buildings, with every particular of their mode of warfare, their religious worship as particularly as though he had spent his life with them.* It will be recollected by the reader that all that I mentioned and much more took place within the compass of one short year.[34]

Wandle Mace met Joseph Smith in 1839, and became a friend of the parents of Joseph. Wandle wrote about his interactions with the Smith family:

> In these conversations, Mother Smith related much of their family history. She said their family must have presented a peculiar appearance to a stranger, as they were seated around the room, father, mother, brothers, and sisters, all listening with the greatest interest to Joseph, as he taught them the *pure principles of the gospel as revealed to him by angels, and the glorious visions he beheld*, as he saw the Father and the Son descend to earth. She said: "During the day our sons would endeavor to get through their work as early as possible, and say, 'Mother, have supper early, so we can have a long evening to listen to Joseph.' Sometimes *Joseph would describe the appearance of the Nephites, their mode of dress and warfare, their implements of husbandry*, etc., and many things *he had seen in vision.* Truly ours was a happy family, although persecuted by preachers, who declared there was no more vision, the canon of scripture was full, and no more revelation was needed.[35]

Joseph saw their buildings, their mode of dress, their civilization, their manner of warfare. It is important to note that the young Prophet saw in vision and translated in Holy Writ not only the history of these Mesoamericans, but also many events in North America. This included the coming of Columbus in 1492 (1 Nephi 13:12). Joseph saw in vision the apostate time and the ultimate conquest by the Europeans over the mixed seed of the Lamanites (1 Nephi 13:14-15). Of particular importance was Joseph's vision of the apostate Lamanites and the cultures they built after the demise of the Nephites in A.D. 385 to the coming of the Spanish in A.D. 1519. Why? Most of the ruins that can be seen today in Mesoamerica are from that post Book of Mormon time period. Additionally, many of the current ruins were built upon the structures left by the Nephites and date to the time of the Book of Mormon.

Joseph Smith Received Another Book

In 1841 an American explorer and adventurer by the name of John Lloyd Stephens published a book entitled *Incidents of Travel in Central America, Chiapas and Yucatan.*[36] His traveling companion was an Englishman named Frederick Catherwood, a superb artist and architect and graduate of the Royal Academy in

England whose drawings were published in the Dictionary of Architecture in England. Mr. Catherwood was the graphic chronologist who provided accurate physical drawings of the ruins. This book was sent to Joseph Smith in 1841 by Dr. John M. Bernhisel. Brother Bernhisel was in New York on business for the Church and came across this exciting new best seller. Hundreds of people crowded into lecture halls and exhibition centers to hear John Lloyd Stephens tell of a past civilization buried in the jungles of Mexico and Guatemala. Eager congregations gathered to see the one hundred twenty-four drawings of Frederick Catherwood. So detailed and excellent were the illustrations and renderings of Catherwood's Mayan Hieroglyphs, that modern day scholars can read them with ease.

It had been eleven hard years for Joseph since the Book of Mormon was first published in 1830 in Palmyra, New York. When Stephens and Catherwood's book on Mesoamerica came into his possession, Joseph rejoiced at the external validation of his visions it provided. He instantly recognized the architecture, the Maya temples, the stone monuments, and the ruins because of Catherwood's detailed drawings. They were a part of the history of a fallen society recorded in the Book of Mormon. He identified the location of the Land of Zarahemla, and the small neck of land. The ruins of Palenque and the ruins of Quiriguá and other Mesoamerican ruins were named by Joseph Smith as one time cities of the Book of Mormon.[37]

In 1830, in Joseph Smith's day, Guatemala and Central America also included most of the area in southern Mexico below the Isthmus of Tehuantepec. Joseph identified specific Book of Mormon cities in that area as being in Guatemala or Central America. This included Palenque which is located in present day southern Mexico.

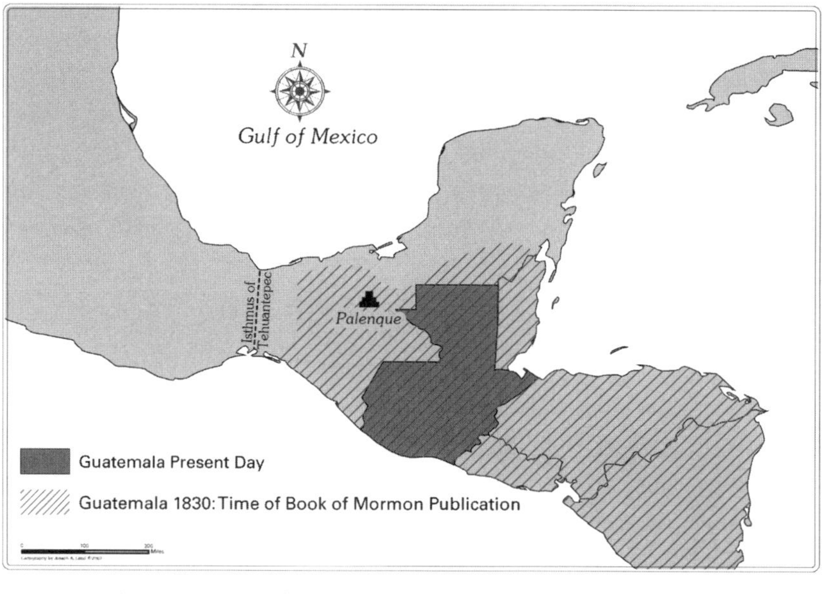

Figure 3. Map of Guatemala in Joseph Smith's Day, 1830

Joseph Identified Specific Sites in Mesoamerica as Book of Mormon Cities and Places

Here is exactly what Joseph Smith said and the specific sites he identified:

- Where Lehi landed
- The Land of Zarahemla
- The small neck of land
- Palenque and Quiriguá as Book of Mormon cities
- Other ruined cities of Central America
- The Land of Bountiful in Central America
- He said Moroni walked from Central America to Palmyra, New York

1. Joseph Smith Identified Where Lehi Landed

Lehi landed, "*...a little south of the Isthmus of Darien.*"[38] Darien is the name the Spanish gave to Panama. Whether this meant that Lehi landed within the current boundaries of the nation of Panama or just "a little south" in northern Columbia is not known. According to Joseph Smith, Lehi landed on the Pacific side.

Joseph Smith identified Lehi's route across the ocean. "Lehi went down by the Red Sea to the *great Southern Ocean*, and crossed over to this land, and landed a little south of the Isthmus of Darien."[39] In the days of Joseph Smith, 1805-1844, it was "customary to speak of the ocean as if divided into three parts, the Atlantic Ocean, the Pacific Ocean, and the Indian Ocean."[40] Today the term "Great Southern Ocean" refers to the entire body of water surrounding the South Pole and Antarctica. However, in Joseph Smith's day the term was applied to the largest of the three oceans, meaning the great Pacific Ocean. Today if you want to enter the "Great Ocean Race," you must go to Australia in the great Southern Ocean to do so. People did not refer to the other oceans as the great Indian Ocean or the great Atlantic Ocean, as wonderful as they might have been. Thomas Suarez reported in his book on *Early Mapping of the Pacific*, that the US Congress on May 14, 1836 authorized the islands south of Hawaii in the "great Southern Ocean" to be charted and mapped.[41] This means that Lehi crossed the Pacific Ocean and landed near the Isthmus of Darien on the western shores of Panama, or a little south of it on the Pacific Coast.

First They Landed, Next They "Tilled, Planted, and Harvested," Then They "Journeyed in the Wilderness," and Then They Settled in the Land of First Inheritance!

There is a difference between where Lehi and those with him landed and where they settled in the Land of their First Inheritance farther north. A careful reading of Nephi's report will reveal that after they landed they pitched their tents, planted seeds and waited for a season. This pattern of traveling and waiting for a season is the same pattern they followed in their journeys along the Red Sea in the Old World. Instead of living on "raw meat" as they did for most of their journeys in the Old World wilderness, in the New World they reaped an abundant harvest. Nephi then indicated they continued their *journey in the wilderness:*

> And it came to pass that after we had sailed for the space of many days we did arrive at the promised land; and we went forth upon the land, and we did pitch our tents; and we did call it the promised land. And it came to pass that we did begin to till the earth, and we began to plant seeds; yea, we did put all our seeds into the earth, which we had brought from the land of Jerusalem. And it came to pass that they did grow exceedingly; wherefore we were blessed in abundance. And it came to pass that we did find upon the land of promise, as we *journeyed in the wilderness*, that there were beasts in the *forests* of every kind, both the cow and the ox, and the ass and the horse, and the goat and the wild goat, and all manner of wild animals, which were for the use of men. And we did find all manner of ore, both of gold, and of silver, and of copper (1 Nephi 18:23-25, emphasis added).

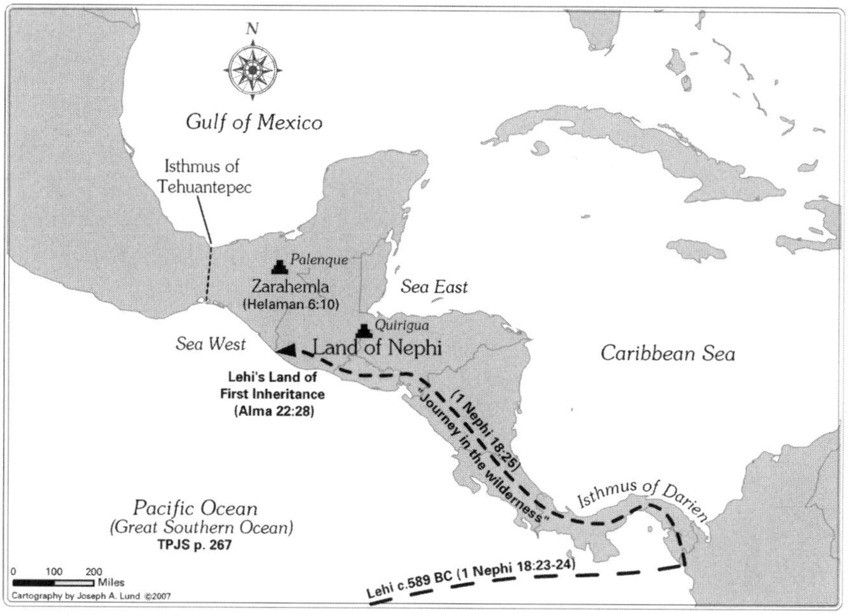

Figure 4. Map of Lehi's Landing and Subsequent Journey in the Wilderness to the Land of First Inheritance.

While on their journey they found all manner of beasts. They traveled through more than one forest as they *journeyed in the wilderness.* They found gold, silver, and copper on their way to the Land of their First Inheritance. The phrase "*journey in the wilderness*" was used a dozen or more times by Nephi in the first two books of Nephi. All uses of these words involved going from one place to another location. It may have been their father's tent, the city of Jerusalem, or the land of promise, but it was always a destination.

This means they did not permanently settle where they landed. From the statement made by the Prophet Joseph Smith as to where Lehi landed combined with the description of Lehi's Land of First Inheritance given in Alma 22:28, we know their *journeying in the wilderness* was from Darien (Panama) northward to a coastal area on the western shores of the Pacific on the border between the Land of Nephi and the Land of Zarahemla. This is a journey of 1100 miles.

I have often wondered why they didn't settle where they first landed near Panama, and why the Lord did not have them sail directly to the Land of First Inheritance? Did they need more trials in a wilderness or was the Lord teaching them how to survive in the New World? We may never know, and it may not matter. We do know that the area surrounding Panama was called the Mosquito Coast by the Spanish sailors, and that years later twenty-two thousand workers would die of yellow fever and other mosquito related illnesses in digging the Panama Canal. Whatever the reasons, the people of Lehi traveled north until they arrived at the Land of their First Inheritance on the Pacific Coast.

From the time Lehi, Ishmael and their families left the banks of the River Laman near the shores of the Red Sea, they had in their possession the Liahona. It was a compass to lead them according to their faith and diligence where the Lord wanted them to be (1 Nephi 16:10, 28). It was more than a north, south, east, and west compass. Nephi makes a point to record that the Liahona was used to acquire various kinds of information. It was the "directions which were given upon the ball" that led him to find beasts for food after he broke his bow in the Old World (1 Nephi 16:30).

There is an indication that once in the Promised Land they continued the use of the Liahona. In the New World, after the death of Lehi, Nephi and the faithful who accompanied him were commanded to leave the Land of First Inheritance. There is reason to believe that the revelation and warning to depart from Laman and Lemuel and "flee into the wilderness," was received on the Liahona. Nephi wrote they took with them the sword of Laban, the plates of brass, and the ball or compass (2 Nephi 5:12). Once again they embarked for many days on a "*journey in the wilderness*" (2 Nephi 5:6-14, emphasis added). It may have led them initially from Panama to the Land of their First Inheritance; but it certainly led them later to the Land of Nephi. The Prophet-Historians of the Book of Mormon safeguarded the records, the sword of Laban, and the Liahona for a thousand years. It may also have led faithful Moroni, after the final battle in Mesoamerica, to the Hill Cumorah in New York.

2. *Joseph Smith Identified the City of Zarahemla*

Joseph Smith said "*Central America, or Guatimala, [sic]* is situated north of the Isthmus of Darien and once embraced several hundred miles of territory from north to south.—*The city of Zarahemla*, burnt at the crucifixion of the Savior, and rebuilt afterwards, *stood upon this land...*" [42]

This is a clear, unmistakable declaration by the Prophet Joseph Smith as to the location of Zarahemla. It was in Mesoamerica and north of Panama. How some people try to rationalize away this statement by Joseph Smith or pretend he didn't say it is beyond my ability to understand. This is not a misprint. It is one of several statements by the Prophet Joseph identifying Mesoamerica as the location where the primary events of the Book of Mormon took place. Establishing the specific area of Mesoamerica narrows the search for other key geographical sites such as the Sidon River and the narrow neck of land spoken of in the Book of Mormon.

3. *Joseph Smith Identified the Small Neck of Land*

In the *Times and Seasons* Joseph identified the *small neck of land* (Isthmus of Tehuantepec in Mexico—not the Isthmus of Panama) "there being a small neck of land between the land northward and the land southward" (Alma 22:32) as being located in "Central America, or Guatimala [*sic*]."[43] Joseph also told Patriarch McBride one had to cross the "Isthmus" or the narrow neck of land to get to Copán.

> [Joseph Smith] Said we should make stations all the way to new, [sic] and Old Mexico until we crossed the Isthmus [of Tehuantepec] and get back to the place where the Covenant was broke by the old Nephites. Spoke of the Great Temple in Central America unfinished...This temple was situated by the River Copán anciently called the River of Nephi.[44]

This means the only viable Isthmus that one traverses going south through "new and Old Mexico" is the Isthmus of Tehuantepec. Palenque, a city of ruins in Southern Mexico dating to 300 B.C., is located just south of the Isthmus of Tehuantepec and was identified as one of the Book of Mormon cities in Central America, meaning that Joseph Smith considered south of the Isthmus of Tehuantepec as being a part of Central America. The term Mesoamerica encompasses all of these locations including Southern Mexico where the Isthmus of Tehuantepec is located. It is of historic note that the Isthmus of Tehuantepec was the third choice for a canal joining the Atlantic and Pacific oceans because it was considered a narrow neck of land.

Joseph identified the "small neck of land" as the same one described by Alma in the Book of Mormon. Joseph urged the readers to turn to the pages of the Book of Mormon published in 1840.[45] These verses include Alma 22:26-35 from the current edition and describe the River Sidon, Zarahemla, and a "small neck of land between the land northward, and the land southward."[46] It is clear that Joseph Smith was confident and convinced that the land of Zarahemla was in Mesoamerica. Because of the six hundred and fifty mile restriction placed on the geography of the Book of Mormon, once we have found Zarahemla, we have found the lands of Nephi, Bountiful, and Desolation. All three lands adjoin or are near the borders of Zarahemla.

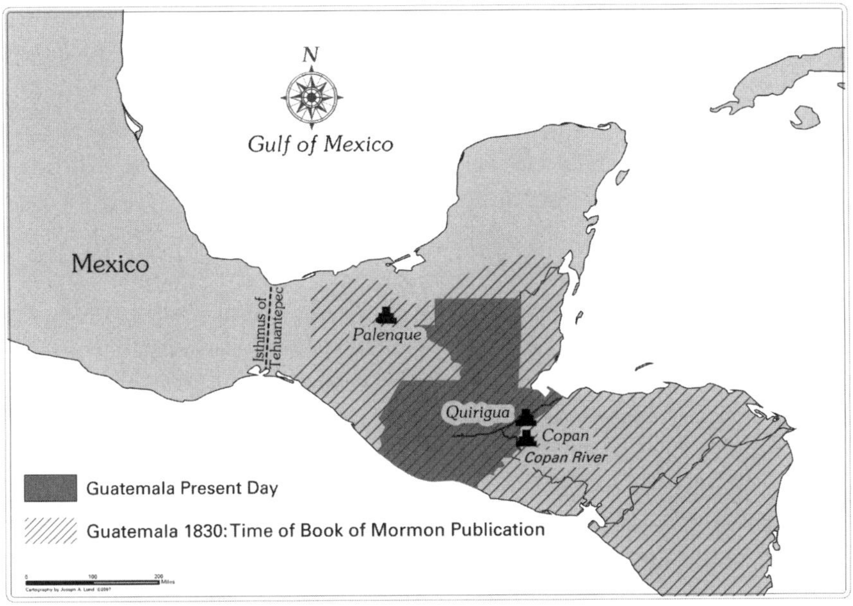

Figure 5. Map of Palenque, Quiriguá, Copán, and the Isthmus of Tehuantepec

4. Joseph Smith Named Palenque and Quiriguá as Book of Mormon Cities

Palenque and Quiriguá were specifically mentioned by Joseph Smith as Book of Mormon cities, with Quiriguá as a candidate for Zarahemla. Quiriguá is another ancient city of magnificent ruins and with stone carvings over thirty feet high. Quiriguá is found in present day Guatemala near the border of Honduras. Palenque is located in southern Mexico.

> Let us turn our subject, however, to the Book of Mormon, where these wonderful ruins of Palenque are among the mighty works of the Nephites:—and the mystery is solved....[47]

> [Joseph would later say] We are not agoing [*sic*] to declare positively that the ruins of Quiriguá are those of Zarahemla, but when the land and the stones, and the books tell the story so plain ... that the ruins of the city in question, are ... *one of those referred to in the Book Mormon.*"[48]

Figure 6. Catherwood's picture of the Palace at Palenque. One of the illustrations seen by Joseph Smith.

One cannot read the writings of Joseph Smith and come away with any other conclusion than Joseph was convinced beyond doubt that Mesoamerica was the land of First Inheritance, the Land of Nephi, the Land of Zarahemla, the narrow neck of land, and the place of the final destruction of Nephites and Jaredites:

> If men, in their researches into the history of this country, in noticing the mounds, fortifications, statues, architecture, implements of war, of husbandry, and ornaments of silver, brass, &c.—were to examine the Book of Mormon, their conjectures would be removed, and their opinions altered; uncertainty and doubt would be changed into certainty and facts; and they would find that those things that they are anxiously prying into were matters of history, unfolded in that book. They would find their conjectures were more than realized—that a great and a mighty people had inhabited this continent—that the arts, sciences, and religion, had prevailed to a very great extent, and that there was as great and mighty cities on this continent as on the continent of Asia. Babylon, Nineveh, nor any of the ruins of the Levant could boast of more perfect sculpture, better architectural designs, and more imperishable ruins, than what are found on this continent. Stephens and Catherwood's researches in Central America abundantly testify of this thing. The stupendous ruins, the elegant sculpture, and the magnificence of the ruins of Guatemala, and other cities, corroborate this statement, and show that a great and mighty people—men of great minds, clear intellect, bright genius, and comprehensive designs inhabited this continent. Their ruins speak of their greatness; the Book of Mormon unfolds their history.—ED.[49]

If there was one obscure statement by Joseph Smith, that statement might be questioned. However, there are numerous clear and unmistakable references published in the official organ of the Church, *The Times and Seasons* newspaper, with Joseph Smith as editor.[50] After quoting two pages from Stephens and Catherwood, Joseph apologizes for not being able to reproduce the pictures, "cuts," in the paper. He announces that the mystery of to whom these ruins in Central America belong is solved. They are the ruins of the mixed seed of the Nephites. He names Palenque as a mighty work of the descendants of the Nephites:

> The foregoing extract has been made to assist the Latter-Day Saints, *in establishing* the Book of Mormon as a revelation from God. If affords great joy to have the world assist us to *so much proof*, that even the most credulous cannot doubt. We are sorry that we could not afford the expense to give the necessary cuts [pictures] referred to in the original [book by Stephens and Catherwood]. Let us turn our subject, however, to the Book of Mormon, *where these wonderful ruins of Palenque are among the mighty works of the Nephites:—and the mystery is solved.*[51]

Palenque has ruins which date back to the Nephite times, i.e., 300 B.C. I have personally stood upon the pre-Classic stones of Palenque, and they are somewhat larger than the stones of the later Classic Maya. The current ruins of Palenque are built upon Nephite ruins which themselves are built upon earlier ruins. This is an important point as it relates to Joseph recognizing the drawings of Catherwood. The Palenque that Catherwood would have illustrated in his artistic rendering was post Book of Mormon time, but not post vision time.

The large structures and ruins that Catherwood captured in his drawings at Palenque date A.D. 700 to A.D. 900. The time period of the Book of Mormon is primarily 600 B.C to A.D. 400. The Jaredite time period was from the Tower of Babel, approximately 2200 B.C. to about 300 B.C. However, Joseph Smith is not claiming that King Benjamin stood atop the current ruins of the Temple of Inscriptions, also known as the Tomb of Pacal, A.D. 700 to 900 and spoke to his people. That would have been impossible. It would be like someone claiming that Benjamin Franklin stood atop the Empire State building in New York and lectured on abolition. The Empire State Building wasn't in existence during the lifetime of Benjamin Franklin. He died in 1790 and the Empire State Building was constructed in 1930. However, Benjamin Franklin was in New York on earlier occasions and did lecture on abolition.[52]

In the fall of 2005, I met with Mexican archaeologist Alfonso Morales at Palenque, Mexico. Both he and his father are highly respected for the work they have done and the archeological digs with which they have been involved. Both he and his father have studied the ruins at Palenque, Mexico, and Quiriguá, Guatemala, over the past twenty years. He said that it was both his and his father's opinion that both of these ruins were built on earlier Olmec sites. The Olmec date to the time of 2200 B.C. to about 300 B.C. This would include Jaredite and Nephite periods of time in the Book of Mormon. Some LDS scholars think the Olmecs may also be the Jaredites or a coexisting society with the Jaredites. Most Mesoamerican archaeologists accept 300 B.C. as a date for Palenque. However, the current dating of Quiriguá is about A.D. 500. When I asked Alfonso Morales why such a recent date for Quiriguá, he said, "They haven't dug deep enough yet; when and if they ever do they will find Olmec ruins."[53]

Palenque is situated in the lowlands where the lands of Zarahemla and Bountiful were located. Mosiah the elder left the highlands of the Land of Nephi about 249 B.C. (Omni 1:12-15). They joined with the people of Mulek and built a great civilization with many cities of which Palenque was one.

Quiriguá was a prime candidate for Zarahemla City, but Joseph would not "declare positively" that such was the case. He was absolutely sure that Mesoamerica or Central America was the *Land* of Zarahemla. The only question was which ruined city qualified for the city of Zarahemla. Joseph published the following excerpt from Stephens and Catherwood in the *Times and Seasons*:

ZARAHEMLA

> Since our 'Extract' was published from Mr. Stephens' 'Incidents of Travel,' &c., we have found another important fact relating to the truth of

> the Book of Mormon. *Central America, or Guatimala, [sic] is situated north of the Isthmus of Darien and once embraced several hundred miles of territory from north to south.—The city of Zarahemla, burnt at the crucifixion of the Savior, and rebuilt afterwards, stood upon this land* as will be seen from the following words in the book of Alma:—'And now it was only the distance of a day and a half's journey for a Nephite, on the line Bountiful, and the land Desolation, from the east to the west sea; and thus the land of Nephi, and the land of Zarahemla was nearly surrounded by water: there *being a small neck of land between the land northward and the land southward.*' [See Book of Mormon 3d edition, page 280-81.]
>
> It is certainly a good thing for the excellency and veracity, of the divine authenticity of the Book of Mormon, that *the ruins of Zarahemla have been found* where the Nephites left them: and that a large stone with engravings upon it, as Mosiah said; and a 'large round stone, with the sides sculptured in hieroglyphics,' as Mr. Stephens has published, is also among the left remembrances of the, (to him,) *lost and unknown.* We are not agoing [sic] to declare positively that the ruins of Quiriguá are those of Zarahemla, but when the land and the stones, and the books tell the story so plain, we are of opinion, that it would require more proof than the Jews could bring to prove the disciples stole the body of Jesus from the tomb, to prove that the ruins of the city in question, *are not one of those referred to in the Book Mormon.*[54]

5. Other Ruined Cities of Central America

Stephens and Catherwood confined their travels to Guatemala, Chiapas in present day southern Mexico, and to the Yucatan. These are the areas Joseph encouraged his readers to explore. These are the lands he identified for future research in discovering other ruined cities of the Book of Mormon. Prophetically, he mentioned the "...preservation of the remains, ruins, *records* and reminiscences of a branch of the house of Israel." Later we will examine some of the Mayan "records" which claimed they were exiles and descendants from the House of Israel.

> It may seem hard for unbelievers in the mighty works of God to give credit to such a miraculous preservation of the remains, ruins, records and reminiscences of a branch of the house of Israel ... It will not be a bad plan to compare Mr. Stephens' ruined cities with those in the Book of Mormon: light cleaves to light, and facts are supported by facts. The truth injures no one, and so we make another EXTRACT From Stephens' "Incidents of Travel in Central America."[55]

Joseph Smith as Editor of the Times and Seasons

In case there is any doubt as to the authorship of Joseph Smith's articles cited in the *Times and Seasons* and Joseph's responsibility for them, it will be instructive to quote him on this very issue. It was March 15, 1842 when he assumed editorship:

> This paper commences my editorial career; *I alone stand responsible for it*, and shall do for all papers having my signature henceforward.[56]

The above quotes identifying Zarahemla and the other locations were from the *Times and Seasons*, September 15, 1842 and October 1, 1842. The statements were made after Joseph Smith assumed editorship. Joseph's signature is at the end of each *Times and Seasons* article as "ED.," meaning editor,[57] and the distinct editorial "we" including the editor as an author.[58] Former Apostle, scholar and Harvard PhD graduate, John A. Widtsoe, referring to the aforementioned editorship of the *Times and Seasons* and Joseph Smith's declaration about Zarahemla being in the land of Guatemala, said:

> The article in the *Times and Seasons* positively stated that Zarahemla, while not necessarily where the Quiriguá ruins now stands, was in "this land." This seems to place many Book of Mormon activities in that region. The interesting fact in this connection is that the Prophet Joseph Smith at this time was editor of the *Times and Seasons*, and had announced his full editorial responsibility for the paper. This seems to give the subjoined article an authority it might not otherwise possess. [*Times and Seasons*, 3:927, stating Zarahemla was in the land of Guatemala].[59]

Between now and the time that additional specific Book of Mormon sites are identified in the future, there is great value in knowing we are looking in an area that will yield productive results. Remember, once we have found the general area of the land of Zarahemla, we have found the Jaredites, the Mulekites, and the Nephites because all of these lands adjoin one another. Equally important is recognizing that most of the events in the Book of Mormon took place in a radius of less than six hundred and fifty miles. Therefore, once we have located the land of Zarahemla, we can limit the search for the River Sidon and the majority of the other Book of Mormon sites to a radius of six hundred and fifty miles.

6. Joseph Smith Identified the Land of Bountiful as Being in Central America

H. Donl Peterson, a past professor of Church History at BYU, published two similar maps of Moroni's travel from Central America to Palmyra, New York with the information on the map coming from two credible contemporaries of Joseph Smith: Patriarch Wm. McBride and Brother Andrew M. Hamilton both from Richfield, Utah. These men credited Joseph Smith with teaching them that the Land of Bountiful mentioned in the Book of Mormon was in Central America. He also taught them that Moroni had traveled from Central America to Palmyra, New York dedicating future temple sites along the way.[60]

Moroni was also given charge of the translating tools called the Urim and Thummim and the breastplate, and by some accounts, the sword of Laban, and the Liahona.[61] However, Joseph Smith does not specifically mention the Liahona. Whether it was a part of the "other things"[62] mentioned by Joseph which were found in the stone box is not known. Moroni had the Liahona in his possession and may have kept it with him to aid him on his journey after he buried the abridged plates in the New York Cumorah. Both the Lord and Moroni's father, Mormon, had commissioned Moroni to care for the gold plates and the sacred things. The abridgment of the gold plates has been estimated to weigh about sixty pounds. Joseph carried the gold plates with one arm as he descended the hill Cumorah. He fought off two men with his other arm.

After the final battle in Mesoamerica, Moroni was inspired to carry the plates northward and to dedicate future temple sites along the way. Moroni had the Liahona in his possession; we do not know whether or not he used it. As a prophet he certainly could have been guided by it to dedicate temple sites all the way from Central America, Mexico, Arizona, Utah, Missouri, Illinois, Ohio, to Palmyra. Moroni not only buried the gold plates at Cumorah, according to McBride's report, he may very well have dedicated the spot where the Palmyra Temple stands today. However, that is speculation based on McBride's claiming that Joseph said Moroni dedicated temple sites "we know not of as yet."[63]

7. Joseph Smith said that Moroni Walked from Central America to Palmyra, New York

The temple sites credited to Moroni were at St. George, Utah and Manti, Utah. Brigham Young met with the leaders of the Church in St. George, Utah to announce the building of a Temple. David Henry Cannon Jr., a member of the St. George Temple Presidency, was in attendance when President Brigham Young said of the St. George Temple site,

> This spot was dedicated by the Nephites. They could not build it [the Temple] but we can and will build it for them.[64]

Those present at the meeting believed Brigham was referring to Moroni as one of those Nephites who dedicated the site at St. George. President Cannon reported that "many rumors" were circulating that Brigham Young had said that "Moroni, the Nephite-General had actually dedicated the site where the Temple now stands."[65]

Brigham Young's statement that "Nephites" dedicated the site for the St. George Temple is consistent with Warren S. Snow's testimony that Brigham Young said that Moroni, a Nephite had dedicated the site for the Manti Temple:

> Early on the morning of April 25, 1877, President Brigham Young asked Brother Warren S. Snow to go with him to the Temple hill … "Here is the spot where the prophet Moroni stood and dedicated this piece of land for a Temple site."[66]

These statements by Brigham Young add considerable credibility to the account given by Patriarch William McBride. Moroni dedicated temple sites at "St. George, Nauvoo, Jackson Co., Kirtland and others we know not of as yet,"[67] according to McBride, Dr. Peterson reported;

> McBride also related that Joseph marked with his cane in the sand the track the saints would take to the Rocky Mountains … described the Valley of Great Salt Lake just as tho [sic] he had lived there … Said we should make stations all the way to new, and Old Mexico Until we crossed the Isthmus [of Tehuantepec] and get back to the place where the Covenant was broke by the old Nephites. Spoke of the Great Temple in Central America unfinished … This temple was situated by the River Copán anciently called the River of Nephi.[68]

Patriarch William McBride and Andrew M. Hamilton drew maps, according to the information they received from Joseph Smith, of Moroni's travels. A Brother Robert Dixon acquired those maps and turned them over to the Church Historical Department. These two very similar maps are currently in the Archives Division of the Historical Department of the Church. H. Donl Peterson published them in a symposium in 1994, after he had rediscovered them.[69] From writings on the maps the following information was given:

- The Book of Mormon Land of Bountiful was in Central America.
- Moroni walked to Palmyra, New York from Central America.
- Moroni traveled through the Great Basin area on his way to New York.

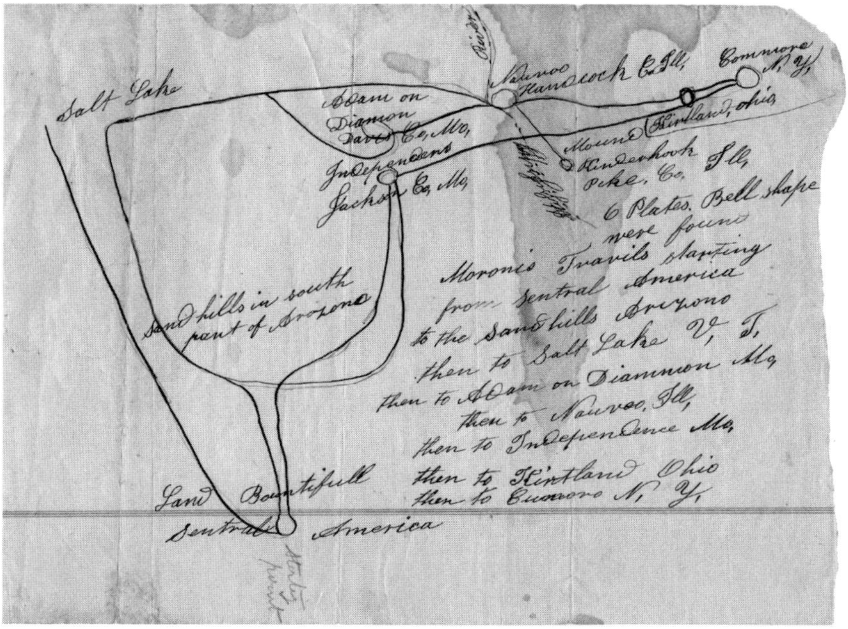

Figure 7. McBride and Hamilton
Map 1 of Moroni's Journey from Central America to Palmyra, New York.

Professor Peterson made these additional remarks concerning the maps:

> On the map "land Bountifull [*sic*]" is listed in "Sentral [*sic*] America." The cartographer wrote "starting point" below the reference to Central America. Above the "land Bountifull" is "Sand hills in the south part of Arizona," and above it to the left is "Salt Lake.... Below this on the right-hand side of the map is written: "Moroni's Travels starting from Sentral America to the Sand hills Arizona then to Salt Lake U[tah], T[erritory], then to Adam on Diammon [*sic*] Mo, then to Nauvoo, Ill, then to Independence Mo, then to Kirtland Ohio then to Cumoro [*sic*] NY."[70]

The reference to Moroni's journey pausing at Adam-ondi-Ahman is consistent with Joseph Smith's comments on May 19, 1838. He said of Adam-ondi-Ahman, "[Lyman White] lives at the foot of Tower Hill (a name I gave the place in consequence of the remains of an old Nephite altar or tower that stood there), where we camped for the Sabbath."[71]

Dr. Peterson goes on to say,

> The second map ... is quite similar to the first.... It is interesting to note that the brethren, [McBride and Hamilton], mentioned on these documents were contemporaries of the Prophet Joseph Smith, and

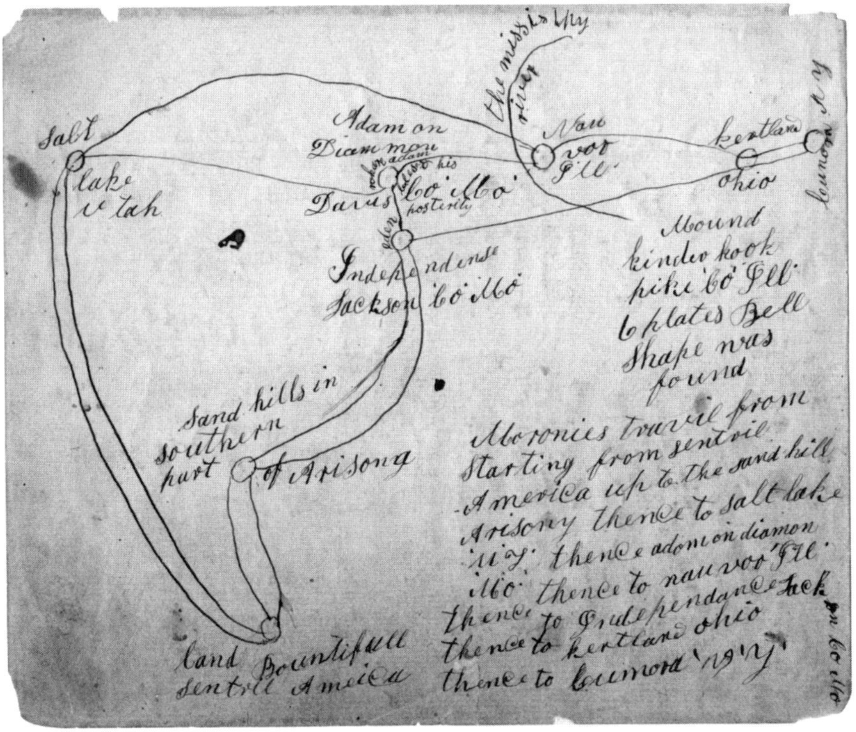

Figure 8. McBride and Hamilton
Map 2 of Moroni's Journey from Central America to Palmyra, New York.

> they credited him with the notion that the travels of Moroni began in the land Bountiful, which was in Central America, and went through the western Great Basin area prior to going east to Cumorah in western New York. Why Moroni took the route he did is still without answers. These men stated that the Prophet Joseph believed Bountiful is in Central America while the Hill Cumorah, the burial place of the plates, is in New York State.[72]

Both McBride and Hamilton were faithful members of the Church. To be a Patriarch in the days of Brigham Young and John Taylor was considered a position of sacred trust like unto that of a General Authority. It was reserved only for the most faithful. Brother Hamilton was an active temple worker at the St. George Temple until he passed away. There are no reasons to question their veracity.

Patriarch McBride was a frequent public speaker because of his association with the Prophet Joseph. Charles Lowell Walker was at the St. George Temple in January of 1881 and heard Patriarch McBride bear his testimony as he quoted the Prophet Joseph on "many issues." In his journal Brother Walker recorded the following by Patriarch McBride:

> ...the Route the old Nephites took traveling to Cumorah from the South and south west; of having to bury their trasures [*sic*] as they journeyed and finally burying the Records and precious things in the Hill Cumorah; of Moroni dedicating the Temple site of what we now call St. George, Nauvoo, Jackson Co., Kirtland, and others we know not of as yet.[73]

According to Patriarch McBride, Moroni was accompanied by other Nephites for a part of that journey to New York. It was sixteen years later, after finishing his father's record, that he announced that he was now alone (A.D. 401). The Lamanites killed his father sometime after the battle at Ramah/Cumorah. Those who took a southern route were hunted down and killed (Mormon 8:1-4). This would be a good reason to travel north.

A Deeper Look at the Two Cumorahs

The McBride and Hamilton maps, and the testimony of Patriarch McBride are consistent with Joseph Smith's statements published in the Times and Seasons. Added to these arguments in favor of two Cumorahs are the many factors that make the New York area an impossible location for the last great battle of either the Jaredites or the Nephites. The objections to the New York Cumorah as the place of the final battles will be addressed in greater detail later. They involve issues of demographics, geology, geography, and climate.

There is no question about a Spirit-guided Moroni who was directed to deposit the plates from which the Book of Mormon was translated in the New York Hill Cumorah. There is also no room to doubt that Joseph Smith believed the final battles of both the Jaredites and Nephites took place in Mesoamerica. This means that the following scriptures apply to the Hill Cumorah in Mesoamerica.

> [Mesoamerican Cumorah] I [*Mormon*] made this record out of the plates of Nephi, and *hid up in the hill Cumorah all the records* which had been entrusted to me by the hand of the Lord, save it were these few plates which I gave unto my son Moroni (Mormon 6:6, emphasis added).

> [Mesoamerican Cumorah] And it came to pass that the [Jaredite] army of Coriantumr did pitch their tents by the *hill Ramah*; and it was that *same hill where my father Mormon did hide up the records unto the Lord*, which were sacred… (Ether 15:11, emphasis added)

Ramah/Cumorah was "Battle Mountain," the place of the final wars in Mesoamerica of the Jaredites around 300 B.C.[74] and of the Nephites around A.D. 385. Except for the abridgment of the records of the Nephites that Mormon gave his son Moroni, Mormon hid all the rest of the plates *in* the hill where the last battle occurred. The Mesoamerican cave is the one Oliver Cowdrey saw in his vision.[75]

Moroni Lived Thirty-Six Years After the Last Great War

Moroni's life after the final battle at the Hill Ramah/Cumorah can be divided into three parts. The first part involved a span of sixteen years from A.D. 385 to A.D. 400. The second part included a period of twenty years from A.D. 401 to A.D. 421. The third part was Moroni's post mortal mission as an angelic messenger.

Part One: Moroni A.D 385 to A.D. 400

1. Moroni survived the great battle at Ramah/Cumorah with twenty-three others (Mormon 6:11-12). A "few" Nephites (not the twenty-four) escaped into the south. A "few" Nephites deserted over to the Lamanites (Mormon 6:15).
2. With some of the survivors, Moroni began a journey north from Central America.[76]
3. Moroni had the abridgment of the "few plates" of the records of the Nephites (Mormon 6:6).
4. Moroni had the Urim and Thummim and Breastplate (Joseph Smith-History 1:52).
5. Moroni had been credited with having the Liahona.[77]
6. Moroni traveled from Bountiful in Mesoamerica to Arizona; Utah; Missouri; Ohio; and to Palmyra, New York, dedicating sites for future temples.

7. Moroni finished chapters eight and nine of his father's record (Mormon 8:1).
8. Moroni commented that those who escaped into the south were hunted down until they were all destroyed (Mormon 8:2).
9. Four hundred years had passed away; he was somewhere on his journey to Palmyra, New York. His father and his companions were killed and he was alone in the north (Mormon 8:3-6).
10. Whomsoever of the Nephites living in and around the Mesoamerica Hill Cumorah were hunted down from city to city and place to place until they were destroyed or assimilated (Mormon 8:7).
11. Moroni would write more, but there was no more room on the existing plates and he had no "gold" ore to make gold plates (Mormon 8:5).
12. Moroni hid up the records in the earth for the first time in A.D. 401 (Mormon 8:4-6).

Part Two: Moroni A.D. 401 to A.D 421

13. Sometime between A.D. 401 and A.D. 421 Moroni wandered "whithersoever" and found gold, abridged the Book of Ether and wrote the Book of Moroni (Moroni 1:1-4).
14. Among the surviving Nephites, any who would not deny the Christ, were put to death. The inference is that those Nephites who did deny the Christ were allowed to live (Moroni 1:2).
15. He was directed to hide the records up *again* in the earth (Ether 4:3). The date was A.D. 421.
16. Moroni wandered or was directed by the Lord to dedicate more temple sites until he dies.

Part Three: Moroni's Post-mortal Mission as an Angelic Messenger

17. Moroni's mission included preparing the New World for the establishment of the Gospel. Orson Hyde referred to Moroni as the "Guardian Prince" of America. In this capacity he inspired both Columbus and George Washington.[78]
18. Later, as an angelic messenger, Moroni appeared to the Prophet Joseph Smith on September 21, 1823.
19. Moroni had at least twenty-three instructional visits with the Prophet Joseph Smith.[79]

An even greater insight, respect, and empathy for Moroni occur as the mind embraces the magnitude of his final journeys in the wilderness from the Mesoamerican Ramah/Cumorah to the New York Cumorah. Moroni had a total of sixteen years to make a journey of about two thousand five hundred miles. Some have questioned the possibility of such a journey. By comparison, Lewis and Clark left St. Louis, Missouri in May of 1804 and traveled over four thousand miles to the mouth of the Columbia River and back in twenty-eight months. Lewis and Clark crossed the great Rocky Mountains twice with a band of about forty-five fellow trekkers. Most of the handcart companies of the Mormon pioneers walked fifteen hundred miles from Nauvoo, Illinois to the Great Salt Lake in less than four months. This also included crossing the Rocky Mountains. Moroni was certainly capable of carrying the abridged records of the Book of Mormon, and other items buried in the stone box, to New York in that period of time. He buried the plates where young Joseph could have access and means to translate them.

There is another important observation offered by Moroni regarding his reasons for not writing more when he buried the plates the first time. He had very little room to write on the plates and there was no gold ore.

> Behold I, Moroni, do finish the record of my father, Mormon. Behold, I have but few things to write, which things I have been commanded by my father ... *if I had room upon the plates, but I have not; and [gold] ore I have none,* for I am alone. My father hath been slain in battle, and all my kinfolk, and I have not friends nor whither to go; and how long the Lord will suffer that I may live I know not. Behold, four hundred years have passed away since the coming of our Lord and Savior (Mormon 8:1-6, emphasis added).

Moroni's message and mission were not over. He traveled for another twenty years. Here is what is known: Moroni traveled to "somewhere" to obtain gold ore to make additional plates. After doing so he engraved an abridgment of the twenty-four gold plates of the Jaredites and wrote his own record. He added approximately forty-four pages to the current edition of the Book of Mormon, which included the Book of Ether and the Book of Moroni.

In The Testimony Of Eight Witnesses, in the introduction of the Book of Mormon, the witnesses bore record that they handled with their hands the individual leaves of the gold plates, *even as many* as Joseph Smith had translated. This included Moroni's contribution of the abridgement of the Book of Ether and his own Book of Moroni, which had "the appearance of gold."[80] This means that the ore Moroni was referring to was gold ore (Mormon 8:5). He buried the records the first time, presumably in the New York Hill Cumorah, in a stone box, and prepared to die.

Some have suggested that Moroni traveled to Canada to find gold ore, while Sperry proposes that Moroni traveled west to the Rocky Mountains where there was a great deal of gold ore and while on this journey may have dedicated future temple sites.[81] It is also a possibility that Moroni returned incognito to the Ramah/Cumorah hill in Mesoamerica. There he acquired the gold and the wherewithal, smelting equipment, bellows, gold presses, etc., to make the plates from the cave where his father Mormon had hidden all the records. Would Mormon have left the equipment to make more gold plates? It's certainly reasonable.

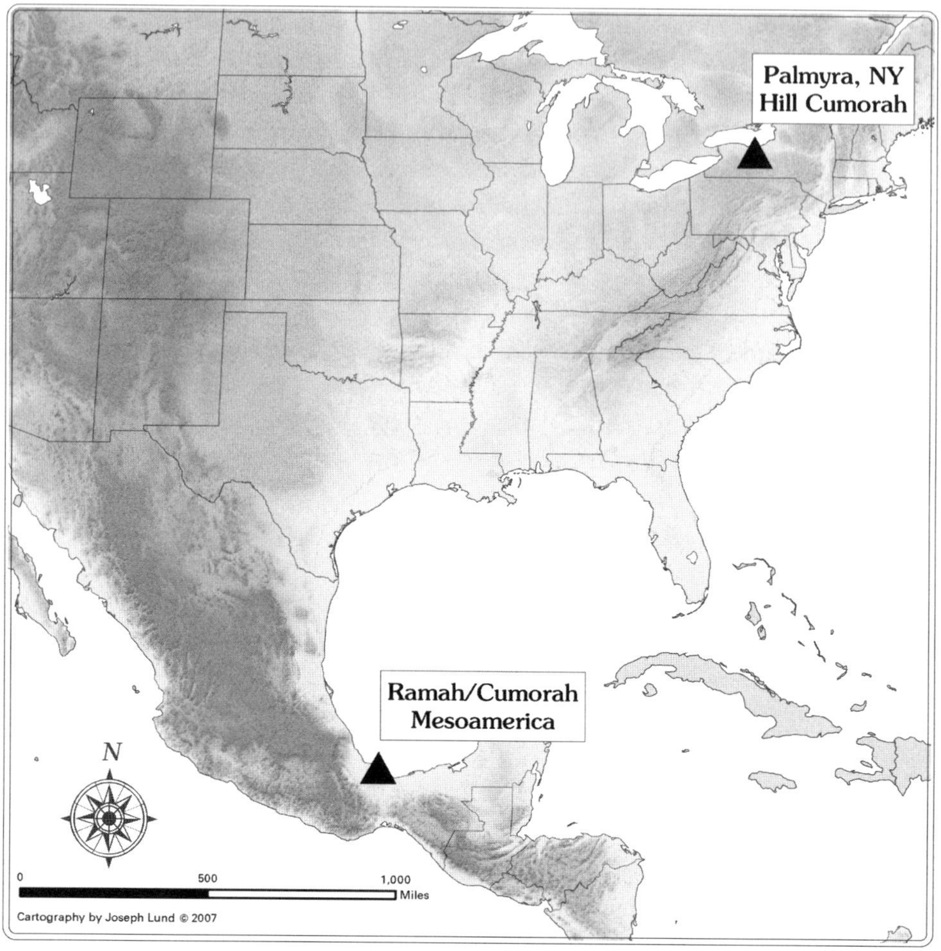

Figure 9. The Distance Between the Two Cumorahs

From Whence Came the Book of Ether?

The Book of Ether was the account of the Jaredites written upon twenty-four gold plates found by the people of Limhi (Ether 1:1-3). Moroni abridged these records (Moroni 1:1). Where was Moroni when he abridged the Book of Ether? He was somewhere in the Land of Desolation in Mesoamerica which Moroni referenced as "this north country" (Moroni 1:1). He did not say *the* north country, rather *this* north country, meaning he was in the Land of Desolation (Alma 22:31). Moroni commented on the Lamanite civil wars going on all about him and of his fear to show himself unto them. It is logical to assume he returned to the cave in the Hill Ramah/Cumorah where all the records had been deposited previously by his father Mormon (Mormon 6:6). This is a reasoned speculation. Otherwise, from whence did Moroni obtain the record of the Jaredites? Did Moroni carry the twenty-four gold plates of the record of the Jaredites with him, as well as his father's abridgement to New York on his first journey? (Ether 1:1-2.) The other option is he returned to the Mesoamerican

Hill Ramah/Cumorah and was then inspired to abridge the Jaredite record there in the cave in Mesoamerica. With only a few gold plates containing the abridgement of the Book of Ether and the Book of Moroni, he returned to the New York Cumorah. He retraced his journey and buried for a second time the Book of Mormon with the additions he had made. He had twenty years to make the second journey. The McBride and Hamilton Map #2 shows Moroni retracing his steps to Mesoamerica. These are only educated guesses. Where Moroni found the additional gold is not as important as the fact that it was not around Palmyra, New York. The abundance of gold, silver, and copper west and north of the Hill Ramah/Cumorah in Mesoamerica is a significant point that cannot be dismissed with impunity (Ether 10:23). The issue of geology, as promised, will be discussed later.

Moroni returned to the buried records and added his gold leaves account of the Jaredites and his own Book of Moroni to the stone box. The Lord commanded him to hide up the records a second time in A.D. 421:

> Therefore I am commanded that I should *hide them up again* in the earth (Ether 4:3, emphasis added).

Moroni engraved his farewell message that included this exhortation:

> Behold, I would exhort you that when ye shall read these things, if it be wisdom in God that ye should read them, that ye would remember how merciful the Lord hath been unto the children of men, from the creation of Adam even down until the time that ye shall receive these things, and ponder it in your hearts. And when ye shall receive these things, I would exhort you that ye would ask God, the Eternal Father, in the name of Christ, if these things are not true; and if ye shall ask with a sincere heart, with real intent, having faith in Christ, he will manifest the truth of it unto you, by the power of the Holy Ghost. And by the power of the Holy Ghost ye may know the truth of all things (Moroni 10:3-5).

CHAPTER THREE

A LAND OF PROMISE FOR MANY PEOPLES

The Lands of Promise encompass all of North and South America and the isles of the sea in the Western Hemisphere. However, Mesoamerica was the place where the primary events of the Book of Mormon occurred. It is a common misunderstanding among many Latter-day Saints that the Americas were *only* occupied by the groups mentioned in the Book of Mormon, that is by Jaredites, Mulekites, and the descendants of Lehi. The Americas have been a promised land for many people other than those mentioned in the Book of Mormon. The archeological evidence is overwhelming that other societies co-existed with the Book of Mormon cultures. The Prophet Lehi acknowledged this when he proclaimed, "Yea, the Lord hath covenanted this land unto me, and to my children forever, *and also all those who should be led out of other countries by the hand of the Lord*" (2 Nephi 1:5, emphasis added).

Preserving a Record of Those in the Promised Land

God commanded his ancient prophet historians to write the Book of Mormon. The title page of the Book of Mormon declares the purposes for which these sacred records have been preserved.

1. To show unto the remnant of the House of Israel what great things the Lord hath done for their fathers
2. That the House of Israel may know the covenants of the Lord
3. That the remnants are not cast off forever
4. Also to the convincing of the Jew and Gentile that Jesus is the Christ, the Eternal God
5. Manifesting Himself [Christ] unto all nations

The covenant people were blessed and prospered upon the Promised Land when they were obedient to the true Messiah. This is a basic message of the Book of Mormon. When they dwindled into unbelief through disobedience, they came to worship false gods. The Lord would lead away a righteous few to proclaim the universal messiahship of Jesus Christ. When the righteous few abandoned their mission God would preserve only their records. Hence the record known as Book of Mormon is all that survived of these once righteous people. Time would pass and whatever truth existed became lost in the traditions of their fathers.

What Happened to the Pre-Columbian People Who Lived in the Promised Land?

Guides in Mexico, Guatemala, Honduras, and throughout Mesoamerica are often asked the question, "What happened to the pre-Columbian people who lived in these ancient ruins?" Most of the guides are the descendants of these people. The answer is they haven't gone anywhere. They are still here. There are more than seven million Maya alone. The Zapotec, the Toltec, the Mexica and the others are a mixed seed living in Mesoamerica today. Their ancestors may have abandoned the ancient ruins and may have lost the truth, but they did not disappear. The Book of Mormon prophets saw in vision the great blending and mingling of these people, called amalgamation and assimilation. They are referred to as the mixed seed (1 Nephi 13:30). They are the Book of Mormon survivors.

In a General Conference address, Elder Ted E. Brewerton quoted the Apostle, Elder Mark E. Peterson: "...the descendants of Laman and Lemuel [sons of Lehi] were sifted over the vast areas of the western hemisphere. They are found from pole to pole."

Elder Brewerton continued:

> *Many* migratory groups came to the Americas, but none were as important as the three mentioned in the Book of Mormon. The blood of these people flows in the veins of the Blackfoot and the Blood Indians of Alberta, Canada; in the Navajo and the Apache of the American Southwest; the Inca of western South America; the Aztec of Mexico; the Maya of Guatemala, and in other Native American groups in the Western Hemisphere and the Pacific islands.[82]

The point that the Americas were a mixed seed was acknowledged by President Spencer W. Kimball in a message from the First Presidency. President Kimball said,

> When Columbus came, these descendants of the Book of Mormon peoples *and those with whom they had mixed numbered in the millions* and covered the islands of the Pacific and the Americas from Point Barrow to Tierra del Fuego.[83]

Looking for a Promised Land

The idea of a "Promised Land" is a concept familiar to Christians, Jews, and Muslims. Christians think in terms of Bethlehem, Nazareth and Jerusalem. Jews focus on Jerusalem as the Holy City. Islamic believers reverence Mecca, Medina, and Jerusalem. For these world religions the Mideast is the Land of Promise. It is a Holy Land.

Two Lands of Promise

The Latter-day Saints believe there are two Lands of Promise. There is, in addition to the Mideast, a Land of Promise in the New World for the descendants of the tribe of Joseph and others led there by the hand of the Lord (2 Nephi 1:5-6). The Resurrected Jesus on four occasions pointed out that where he was standing in the Land of Bountiful on the North American continent was the Land of Promised Inheritance for the descendants of Joseph:

> Ye are my disciples; and ye are a light unto this people, who are a remnant of the house of Joseph. And behold, this is the land of your inheritance; and the Father hath given it unto you (3 Nephi 15:12-13, See also 3 Nephi 16:16, 3 Nephi 20:14, 3 Nephi 21:22-23).

The Promised Land is Not Limited to a Single Nation

The New World Promised Land is all of North and South America and the isles of the sea associated with them in the broadest geographical sense. It would be unproductive to narrow the Promised Land to any political boundary of any nation. The Lord did not reference the political boundaries of the United States nor any other political entity in his remarks. Some have tried to narrowly apply the concept of the Promised Land to the United States. It is true that the United States is a blest land and was the place chosen for the latter-day Gospel to be restored. It is also true that the New Jerusalem will be built upon it. The United States is a significant part of the Land of Promise. "Wherefore, this is the land of promise, and the place for the city of Zion" (D&C 57:1-4). So also are Canada, Mexico, South America, and Mesoamerica part of the Promised Lands. Jesus was speaking from the Land of Bountiful in Mesoamerica when he made reference to "this land," as the Promised Land. It is also true that the Jaredites and the Lehites were told they would be led to a "land of promise, which was choice above all other lands" (Ether 2:7-10). Where did the Lord lead both the Lehites and the Jaredites? It was to Mesoamerica as a part of the Promised Land.

What Does the Land of Promise Mean?

The operative word in the Land of Promise is not "Land." It is "Promise." A promise is a covenant involving two parties. It is a divine contract with responsibilities for each party. If both parties involved in the contract live up to the terms and conditions of the agreement, the promised rewards will follow. If the contract is broken, the promises are null and void and there are penalties. The consequences are serious for either party. If God breaks the agreement he ceases to be God.[84] "God would cease to be God. But God ceaseth not to be God and mercy claimeth the penitent" (Alma 42:22-23).

The Land of Divine Contract

The Land of Divine Contract does not sound as pleasing to the ear as the Land of Promise. What is the Divine Contract? The terms of the contract are simple. God agrees to do everything in His power to help His children become their highest and best selves in time and throughout all eternity. His covenant children promise to love God and to be instruments in His hands to love His other children. The Promised Land is a land under contract with God. The land is given to the covenant people only as long as they continue faithful. Obedience brings blessings[85] (Deuteronomy 28:1-14). Disobedience brings upon His covenant people the curses of war, pestilence, and famine (Alma 10:21-23). These curses are allowed by God as a wakeup call. If the people are willing to repent, they are restored in the contract. If not, they are considered ripe in iniquity and will be removed off the Land of Promise, and the land will be given to another:

> ...he would that they should come forth even unto the land of promise ... which God had preserved for a righteous people. And he had sworn in his wrath unto the brother of Jared that whoso should possess this land of promise, from this time henceforth and forever, should serve him, the true and only God, or they should be swept off when they are ripened in iniquity (Ether 2:7-8).

This is the premise upon which the Jaredites and the Lehites and their families and friends were brought across the waters. Nephi was told that "Inasmuch as ye shall keep my commandments, ye shall prosper, and shall be led to a land of promise; yea, even a land which I have prepared for you..." (1 Nephi 2:20).

The Book of Mormon story includes a group of refugees from the House of Judah called Mulekites. They were also a part of the covenant children who were likewise brought across the sea to a Promised Land. Both the Lehites and the Mulekites were a part of the remnants of the House of Israel. The Prophet Isaiah saw this great escape of a few of the Jews more than a hundred years before it came to pass.

> And the remnant that is escaped of the house of Judah shall yet again take root downward, and bear fruit upward. For out of Jerusalem shall go forth a remnant, and they that escape out of mount Zion: the zeal of the Lord of hosts shall do this[86] (II Kings 19:30-31, See also Isaiah 65:9-10).

The great Jehovah had delivered them from the destructions of Nebuchadnezzar and the subsequent Babylonian captivity. The Mulekites left Jerusalem about 587 B.C. During the unfolding of their history, the Mulekites had themselves encountered in Mesoamerica another more ancient society referred to as the Jaredites. The remnants of these ancient Jaredites claimed to have crossed the oceans in water crafts at the time of the Tower of Babel, or approximately 2200 B.C.

Because the Mulekites were also of the tribes of Israel the Nephites could intermarry with them and continue to abide in the Law of Moses. By marriage and alliance these groups meshed into a common society. Those who were willing to continue the covenant with God and fulfill the intent of the Law of Moses joined with the Nephites. The rebellious followed the Lamanites. The interaction of these two groups of Lamanites and Nephites, their wars and their worship is the essence of the Book of Mormon in Mesoamerica. Is there a complete record of each of these immigrating peoples to Mesoamerica? No! Currently the only records that remain are the remnants of four hieroglyphic languages, the artifacts of several great cultures, and the Book of Mormon. Some of the Mesoamerican traditions, customs, and folklore from the great cultures have survived. In these traditions can be found a common ground with the Book of Mormon.

The Mexica (Aztec) Tradition: Looking for Their Land of Promise

Figure 10. Mexica (Aztec) Altar Stone Formerly called the Aztec Calendar

The story of the Mexicas (Aztecs) is a fascinating one. Current historians and archaeologists prefer the name Mexicas over Aztec. The term Aztec means "man of Aztlan." Mexicas was the name by which the Mexicas referred to themselves. This is the origin of the name for Mexico. The Mexicas appeared in Mexico City (Tenochtitlan) around A.D. 1323. The Mexicas were looking for *their* Land of Promise. They had been taken away from the land of their inheritance and were living as strangers in Aztlan. Many historians believe they came from unidentified settlements somewhere in Northern Mexico and maybe, as some have suggested, the American southwest called Aztlan, hence the name Aztec. In their tradition, Mesoamerica was their original Promised Land. Through centuries of exile they had lost the exact location. What they hadn't lost was their desire to return to their Promised Land. They knew it was somewhere near the Isthmus of Tehuantepec. Their prophets or "Holy Speakers" told the members of their tribe they would find the Promised Land when they found an eagle perched on a cactus growing out of a stone with a serpent in his talons and beak. Some reports of the legend are without the snake and date their exodus towards the south at A.D. 1168.

A significant part of the story is the common belief in being lead to a Land of Promise by prophecy and revelation. This is a tradition shared by the ancient Hebrews as well as the people of the Book of Mormon. Nevertheless, according to the tradition, some Mexican warriors were traveling south from Aztlan, when they came to present day Mexico City. Originally it was an island in the middle of a great lake called Tenochtitlán. On the island these warriors found an eagle

Figure 11. Sign of a "Promised Land" on the Mexican Flag

perched on a cactus growing from a stone with a serpent clutched between its talon and beak. It was the long awaited sign from their god Huitzilopochtli. If these symbols sounds familiar it is because these are the very symbols found today on the Mexican flag.

History records the Mexicas moved in mass from Northern Mexico to an area near Tula, outside of Mexico City. They asked for permission from the local Toltec ruler, Achitometl, to settle on the island as it was for them a Promised Land. The Toltecs worshipped as a primary god, the Feathered Serpent, Quetzalcoatl. The Mexicas worshipped his brother, Hummingbird to the Left, Huitzilopochtli, who was a blood-thirsty War god that required human sacrifice. In a heavenly battle these two god-brothers fought with Huitzilopochtli casting Quetzalcoatl out of heavenly power. This legend was about to be repeated again on earth.

The Toltec King Achitometl had reason to fear the Mexicas because later the Mexicas did indeed conquer the Toltecs and took over the entire empire. Achitometl thought he would devise a clever plan to destroy the Mexicas. He gave them permission to settle in an area considerably south of Tenochtitlan toward the Isthmus of Tehuantepec. This area was known to be infested with snakes by the thousands. The area was called the land of Tizapán.

> Achitometl, governor of Culhuacan, gave them [Mexicas] lands in Tizapán, south of present day Mexico City. This was not a gracious concession but was made in the hope that the plentiful snakes there would kill off all the Aztecs. When some time afterwards Achitometl sent emissaries to see if this had in fact happened, they found instead the Aztecs roasting and eating the snakes.[87]

The irony of this story is amazing. When the Mexicas arrived near Mexico City, they were starving, weak, and about to perish. They had learned to live a nomadic life style and to survive off the game and small animals they captured, including snakes. The problem was they were perceived as invaders. They needed permission to stay upon the land. They could not plant and harvest without being attacked and destroyed. The ground surrounding Tula was the ancient sacred ceremonial center of Tollan, the land of the Toltecs. The Mexicas were denied permission to settle in Tollan. They would have perished or been reduced to insignificant numbers had they not been sent to Tizapán, a land with an abundance of snakes. The Mexicas were thrilled. They were singing praises to their god who had delivered them from destruction.

In two years the Mexicas would become strong enough to overthrow Achitometl and the Toltec nation. A great deal is lost in translation from Aztec to Spanish and from Spanish to English. However, there is a poem written in A.D. 1323 by the Mexicas to celebrate their deliverance from starvation. It was translated from a Nahuatl text into Spanish by Miguel León Portilla and from Spanish to English by Demetrio Sodi:

The Snakes of Tizapán
The Aztecs were overjoyed
When they saw the serpents,
They roasted them all
They roasted them to eat them,
The Aztecs ate them up![88]

This story is amusing. However, there is a great correlation with the Book of Mormon. The land south of Mexico City called Tizapán is located north of the Isthmus of Tehuantepec. This area was identified in the Book of Mormon as a land of poisonous serpents. At times the infestation of snakes was so great that no human beings or animals could pass without being bitten and killed:

> And there came forth poisonous serpents also upon the face of the land, and did poison many people. And it came to pass that their flocks began to flee before the poisonous serpents, towards the land southward, which was called by the Nephites Zarahemla.
>
> And it came to pass that there were many of them which did perish by the way; nevertheless, there were some which fled into the land southward.
>
> And it came to pass that the Lord did cause the serpents that they should pursue them no more, but that they should hedge up the way that the people could not pass, that whoso should attempt to pass might fall by the poisonous serpents (Ether 9:31-33).
>
> ...and in the days of Lib the poisonous serpents were destroyed. Wherefore they did go into the land southward, to hunt for food ...
>
> And they built a great city by the narrow neck of land... (Ether 10:19-20).

The fact that these two historical accounts are about the same specific geographical area is one more correlation between the Book of Mormon and Mesoamerica. It continues to increase confidence in the geography of the Book of Mormon. The Mexicas adopted many of the philosophies of those they defeated. They also integrated many of the traditions of the surrounding cultures. The Mexicas were much like the Romans who adopted much of the Greek culture and religion. The actual Aztec Calendar is only one of the many things adopted by them. Their capital city of Tenochtitlan was as great as any European capital of the time.

Though separated by nearly two millennia, there are some amazing correlations between the Prophet Lehi, his family and friends and their journeys in the wilderness, and their eventual arrival to a Land of Promise. It is the belief of Mormons that the Mexicas are descendants of Lehi and part of the "mixed

Figure 12. Mexico City, Tenochtitlan A.D. 1521

seed" of a former dispensation. It would be natural that the tradition of a "Promised Land" may have passed on into legend. The Mexicas' "journey in the wilderness," their willingness to follow "Holy Speakers" (Prophets) and their belief in a "Land of Promise" relates to the Book of Mormon and especially the commonly shared value of looking for a Land of Promise.

It's possible that the Mexicas were originally a part of the Great Nephite exodus in 55 B.C. who left the Land of Zarahemla and settled in the north:

> ...there was a large company of men, even to the amount of five thousand and four hundred men, with their wives and their children, departed out of the land of Zarahemla into the land which was northward (Alma 63:4).

This group had fallen into apostasy and joined with the Lamanites. They would have abandoned their faith and adopted the idol worship of the Lamanites. However, they may not have abandoned their belief in returning to their Promised Land. Fourteen hundred years later, they did return. This is not unlike the Jews who were scattered to the ends of the earth in A.D. 70 and returned to their Promised Land to become a new nation in 1948, eighteen hundred years after their exile. Whether the Mexicas were descendants of the great Nephite exodus is speculation on my part. The fact they came from the north to Mexico City believing it was their Promised Land is not. It was a religious commitment to their god and to their "Holy Speakers" that motivated an entire nation of people to move across a continent.

CHAPTER FOUR

Mapping the Lands of the Book of Mormon

Mapping the Lands of the Book of Mormon

A map or template shows the relative position of one geographical site to another. Most LDS scholars and writers agree the events in the Book of Mormon regarding the Land of First Inheritance of Lehi, the Land of Nephi, the Land of Zarahemla, the Land of Bountiful, and the Land of Desolation took place in a radius of less than six hundred and fifty miles. Some would say that most of the events occurred less than three hundred miles of one another.

Regardless of the accuracy of a map one creates from the internal clues of the Book of Mormon, applying that map to an actual place is what really matters. Dr. John E. Clark, a recognized archaeological expert in ancient pottery has stated,

> For the New World, dealing with geography is a two-step exercise. An internal geography must first be deduced from clues in the book, and this deduction must then become the standard for identifying a real world setting … The one requirement for making comparisons between archaeology and the Book of Mormon is to be in the right place … Mesoamerica is the right place.[89]

The Book of Mormon identified territorial dominions as "lands." This means there is a Land of Nephi and a City of Nephi, a Land of Zarahemla and a City of Zarahemla, etc. The lands obviously occupy a larger area than a city. Within Mesoamerica the quest for possible sites begins by identifying the general lands. We will refer to these geographical candidates as A sites, B sites, or C sites.

Creating a Template for Book of Mormon Lands

There is a long list of Book of Mormon scholars who have undertaken the task of creating an internal map of the geography of the Book of Mormon based on the clues given within the book. The Book of Mormon does give concrete information about certain lands which can become a fixed point on a template. For example, the Book of Mormon makes it clear that the Jaredites lived north of the Mulekites and the Nephites and Lamanites originally lived south of the Mulekites. By reading in Helaman 6:10 and Alma 22:30 one could draw a map or template. It would look like the one drawn by John L. Sorenson and published in 2000 by F.A.R.M.S. called "Mormon's Map."

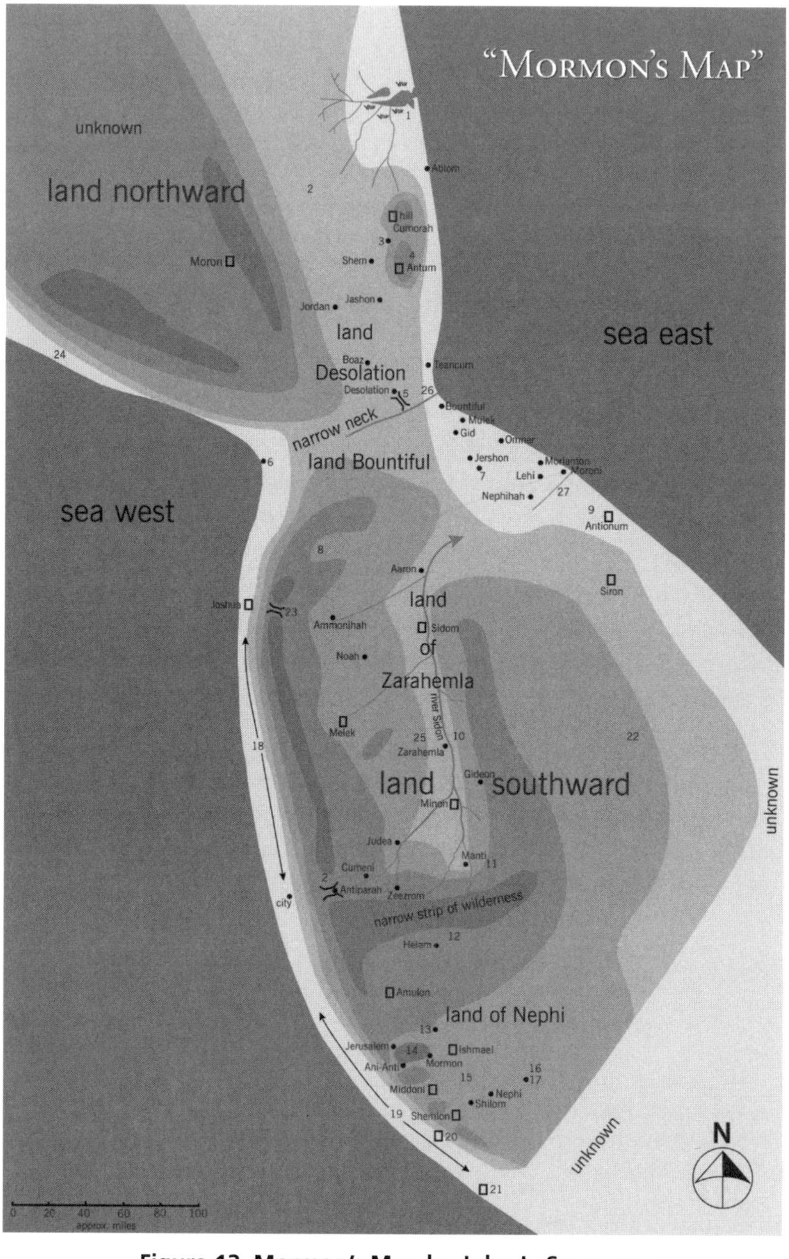

Figure 13. Mormon's Map by John L. Sorenson

Here is how a template is created. There are many verses in the Book of Mormon which give proximities. For example,

> So when he finished his work at Melek he departed thence and traveled three days' journey on the north of the land of Melek; and he came to a city which was called Ammonihah (Alma 8:6).

In that same chapter eight of Alma, verse 3, it locates Melek as being a city to the west of the river Sidon by the borders of the wilderness. Using this information it is accurate to deduce that Zarahemla, which is on the west bank of the River Sidon, is east of Melek. Three days north of the land of Melek is problematic because we do not know the size of the Land of Melek. Ammonihah is three days north of both Melek and the city of Zarahemla. The educated guess comes when one tries to estimate how far a person can travel in three days from the borders of the Land of Melek to Ammonihah. The guesses can range from five miles a day to thirty miles a day depending on the mode of travel, the terrain, etc. So somewhere between fifteen miles and ninety miles north of the Land of Melek, one would expect to find the city of Ammonihah, but not fifteen hundred miles away, nor five miles away.

Finding Zarahemla

Finding Zarahemla is finding a key to all of the lands around it. The Land of Zarahemla becomes a fixed point from which a general map of the area can be drawn.

Joseph Smith identified the lands in which Stephens and Catherwood traveled as the location of the city of Zarahemla. Joseph specifically said Guatemala and Central America, which in his day included most of the area below the Isthmus of Tehuantepec and a significant amount of the Yucatan. Additionally, the Isthmus of Tehuantepec was acknowledged as the "small neck of land." There are numerous Book of Mormon scriptures referring to the up and down topography between the Land of Zarahemla and the Land of Nephi. This establishes Zarahemla as a lower land as does the fact of its location on the west bank of the river Sidon. The physical terrain is a major factor in defining defensible borders. Mountains, rivers, lakes, and oceans all help to define the Land of Zarahemla geographically. Political boundaries ebb and flow according to the ability of the ruling powers to maintain them.

Today the dimensions of the Land of Zarahemla along the small neck of land or Isthmus of Tehuantepec are on the order of one hundred twenty-five miles. Early maps of the flat lands of the Isthmus of Tehuantepec show it to be swampy, much like the Everglades of Florida. This would make travel across the Isthmus more difficult. It would also make the narrow neck of land narrower than it is today.

East of the river Sidon is the Caribbean Sea. Depending on which river one selects as the river Sidon, the distance is again about one hundred twenty-five miles. The southern border as defined by the wilderness of the Sierra de las Minas and the Cuchumantanes could be as much as two hundred twenty-five miles. The northern boundary would include about the same distance. In brief terms the approximate dimensions of the Land of Zarahemla would be a minimum of one hundred twenty-five miles by two hundred twenty-five miles. This would include many of the dependent city states such as Manti to the south and Melek to the west, Antionum to the east, and Ammonihah to the northwest. As a maximum the Land of Zarahemla would encompass the lands of both the Grijalva River and the Usumacinta River basins from the headwaters in Guatemala to the delta at the Gulf of Mexico. The Pacific Ocean on the west to the Caribbean Sea on the east would represent the larger Lands of Zarahemla.

How Do We Know Where The Land Of First Inheritance Is Located?

Alma gave the location of the Land of First Inheritance as west of the Land of Zarahemla. Joseph identified the Land of Zarahemla as being in Central America or Guatemala. The Land of First Inheritance was on the western seashore of the Pacific Ocean:

> ...yea, and also on the *west of the land of Zarahemla*, in the borders *by the seashore*, and on the *west in the land of Nephi*, in the place of their fathers' first inheritance, and thus *bordering along by the seashore* (Alma 22:28, emphasis added).

The internal Book of Mormon description by Alma and Joseph Smith's later declarations would place the Land of Lehi's First Inheritance in the Promised Land somewhere near the ancient site of Izapa which dates to Book of Mormon times. Present day Tapachula, Mexico is only a few miles from the ruins of Izapa. It may be more than a coincidence that the Tree of Life stone, known as Stela 5, was found at Izapa. Many credible LDS scholars believe that the story engraved on this stone represents a form of Lehi's dream in 1 Nephi 8 of the Tree of Life. Some disagree.

Elder John A. Widtsoe preferred the term "fixed point" to elected and stated that the Hill Cumorah where Joseph extracted the plates was a fixed point for Moroni burying the records.[90] Joseph Smith identified the general area where Stephens and Catherwood traveled in Guatemala near Copán and Quiriguá as the Land of Zarahemla. Joseph's statement qualifies Mesoamerica as a fixed point for Zarahemla.

However, in Mesoamerica there are two prime "candidates" for the River Sidon. Notice that the River Sidon runs from south to north. That is because the Book of Mormon always talks about being on the east or west of the Sidon River (Alma 2:15, 34). Because the Land of Nephi is "up" and the Land of Zarahemla is "down," the Sidon River flows from the south to the north.[91] One candidate is the Grijalva River, and the other candidate is the Usumacinta River. Frankly, they are both "A" sites. Both rivers start in the Guatemalan highlands and flow north to the Gulf of Mexico.

Somewhere in Mesoamerica, this template or map is going to fit with some adjustments. Where can one find in Mesoamerica, within a radius of five hundred to six hundred and fifty miles, a place which fits with the information given in the Book of Mormon? The answer is, approximately from Mexico City on the north to Guatemala City on the south.

Following are two maps that I have created using the internal information given in the Book of Mormon plus the insights added by Joseph Smith and then applied to the current Mesoamerican terrain.

1. Lehi landed a little south of the Isthmus of Darien (Panama). They planted their seeds and harvested them. From where they landed in or near Panama they "journey in the wilderness" (1 Nephi 18:25). Eventually, they arrive at the Land of First Inheritance (Alma 22:28). The present day city of Tapachula, Mexico and its environs are great candidates for the Land of First Inheritance. Because of Joseph Smith's statement that Lehi crossed the "Great Southern Ocean," it would have been a Pacific crossing, as previously pointed out, since that phrase was applied only to the Pacific Ocean at that time.
2. The Jaredites probably had a Pacific Ocean crossing as well. In the Jaredite case it took three hundred forty-four days to follow the "wave" driven, "wind" driven waters. Currents are wind driven rivers in the ocean. It takes between 220 to 240 days presently to cross from China or Japan following currents as demonstrated by studies done by oceanographers,

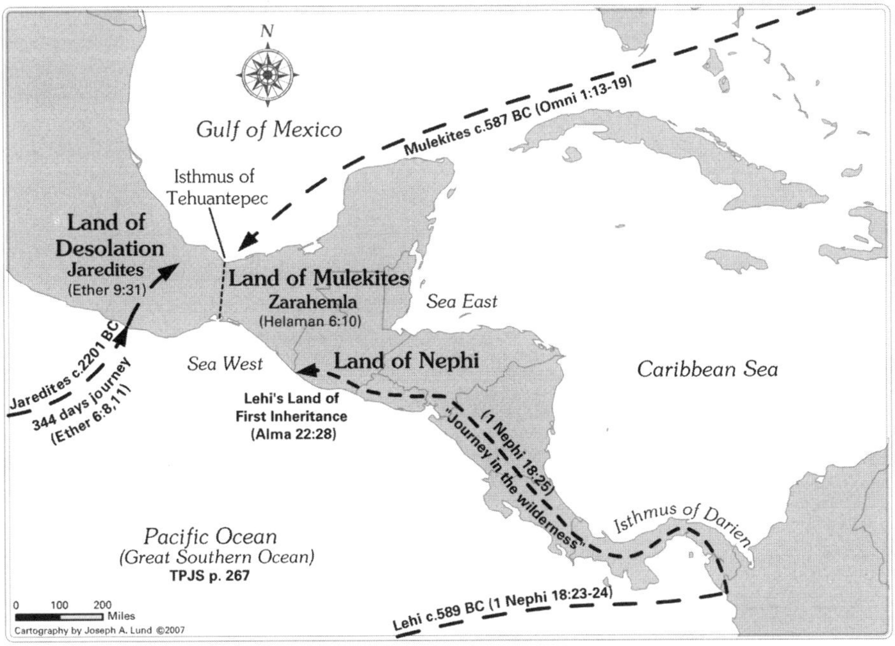

Figure 14. Map of Proposed Landing Sites of the Jaredites, the Mulekites, and the Family of Lehi

Ebbesmeyer and Ingraham from the University of Washington. It takes longer the farther south one goes.[92]

3. The Mulekites are candidates for an Atlantic crossing. Whether or not the Mulekites used Phoenicians is speculative. It was one possible scenario. The Phoenician sailors had a long term relationship with the kings of ancient Israel beginning at 1000 B.C. with King Solomon. Mulek was King Zedekiah's son. Recent discoveries on the Canary Islands indicate a Phoenician presence.[93] After Columbus left the Canary Islands on September 6, 1492, he rediscovered America on October 12, 1492, thirty-six days later. The Book of Mormon gives a more substantial clue. The Mulekites settled where they landed (Alma 22:31-32). They were known to have interacted with the Jaredites in the Land of Desolation (Omni 1:21). Ramah/Cumorah and the "bones of the dead Jaredites" were located on the eastern coast of the Land of Desolation (Ether 14:26, Ether 9:3). Another clue is given by the forty-three members of the expedition of Limhi who headed north from the Land of Nephi in their quest for the Land of Zarahemla. They arrived at the place of destruction of the Jaredites and brought back the twenty-four gold plates and other evidences (Mosiah 8:7-11). The Gulf of Mexico is an "A" candidate for the eastern seashore.

There are the six basic assumptions upon which the maps are based. As new information is discovered the maps will be altered accordingly. Joseph Smith's

Figure 15. Map of Current Cities, Current Ruins, and Geographical Approximations for Book of Mormon Sites

statements, internal information given in the Book of Mormon, and the latest scientific information reveal the following:

1. The Land of Desolation is north of the Land of Mulek/Zarahemla (Ether 9:31).
2. The Land of Mulek/Zarahemla is north of the Land of Lehi/Nephi (Helaman 6:10).
3. The Land of Nephi is in the highlands. The Land of Zarahemla is in the lowlands. Topographically, one always goes "up" to the Land of Nephi and one always goes "down" to the Land of Zarahemla. The one exception occurs after Ammon and his brethren have gone up to the Land of Nephi and are on a "hill" above the city from which they go down into the valley of the Land of Nephi (Mosiah 7:6).
4. The River Sidon flows north from high in the Land of Nephi to the southern lowlands of Zarahemla.[94] The highlands of Guatemala and the lowlands of Chiapas, Mexico are a perfect match. There are two rivers that are considered prime or "A" candidates for the Sidon River: the Grijalva River, and the Usumacinta River. Frankly, I believe we need more research and information before I will be comfortable committing to one or the other. Once a river is selected, the city of Zarahemla will be on the west side of it. I have marked a potential site for the city of Zarahemla, on the west side of the Usumacinta near Yaxchilan until more information is available. The Motagua River and the Rio Dulce are possibilities, and there may be other options.
5. There is a wilderness from the East Sea to the West Sea (Alma 22:27). The Cuchumantanes Mountains and the Sierra de las Minas are located on the border between Mexico and Guatemala. They run from the Atlantic Sea to the Pacific Sea, east and west. This is an "A" candidate for the wilderness which separated the Land of Nephi from the Land of Zarahemla.
6. The Land of Bountiful is located near the small neck of land. It is bordered on the north by the Land of Desolation and on the south by the Land of Zarahemla (Alma 22:29-32).

There are more details about topography, the River Sidon, the New World changes at the time of Christ's death and resurrection, the Southern Wilderness from the East Sea to the West Sea, and some additional insights into the Land of Antionum where Corianton met Isabel that will contribute to a better understanding of the maps.

The Ups and Downs of Topography

Topography is the study of the physical features of the earth's terrain. Elevations are a special focus. It is important to note that whenever Nephi talks about going to Jerusalem from the area of the Red Sea, he consistently uses the term "to go up to Jerusalem." Likewise when he speaks of traveling from Jerusalem to the Red Sea he uses the terms "down."[95] Jerusalem is twenty four hundred feet above sea level while the Red Sea is obviously at sea level. The terms up and down do not describe north, south, east, or west. In common vernacular people say "down south" or "up north." However, in the New World of the Book of Mormon and Mesoamerica one would go up south and down north.

The writers of the Book of Mormon used the same terminology of "up and down" to describe the terrain of the New World. Helaman states that the land of Mulek was north of the Land of Lehi (Helaman 6:10). The land of Mulek and The Land of Zarahemla encompasses the Land of The Mulekites. Whenever one travels north from the land of Nephi to Zarahemla, one must "go down."[96] The converse is also true that to travel south from Zarahemla to the land of Nephi he or she goes "up."[97] In looking for the lands of the Book of Mormon, the topography requires a southern highland for the Land of Lehi/Nephi such as found in Guatemala, and a northern lowland for the Land of Zarahemla, such as located in northern Guatemala and Chiapas, Mexico.

The River Sidon

In the Index of the 1981 edition of the Book of Mormon under the heading of Sidon, River, this definition is given: "—most prominent river in Nephite territory, *runs north* to sea."

As previously mentioned, the topography of the Book of Mormon requires a southern highland and northern lowlands where the Sidon River can flow from south to north. There are numerous references in the Book of Mormon to being on either the east or west of the river Sidon (Alma 2:15, 17, 34).[98] This is a significant topographical feature as it limits an area which can qualify for the lands of the Book of Mormon. Most large rivers in the northern hemisphere flow like the Mississippi, from the north to the south.

The sum of the matter is the necessity of finding upon the North American continent a river of the magnitude and swiftness of the River Sidon into which thousands of bodies can be tossed, which flows from the south to the north and empties into the sea. There are two primary rivers that qualify in Mesoamerica, and each has its champions. The Grijalva River and the Usumacinta River both have their headwaters in the highlands of Guatemala. These are "A" candidates. The Rio Dulce and the Motagua rivers in Guatemala and Honduras near both Copán and Quiriguá are "B" candidates.

The "One Cumorah" advocates for New York seem to focus on the Niagara River or the Genesee River as the only viable options for the Sidon River. Whichever of these candidates is selected as the River Sidon, Zarahemla will be located on the west bank of the river (Alma 6:7). This would place the city of Zarahemla near the present day city of Buffalo, New York or Rochester, New York, for those who hold to the theory that the primary events of the Book of Mormon took place around the Great Lakes and the Palmyra, New York area.

Considering the climate and the lack of gold, silver, and copper in the area, Buffalo and the surrounding environs are not viable candidates for the land of Zarahemla. Also the River Sidon need to be of sufficient size and swiftness to carry thousands of dead warriors into the sea (Alma 44:21-22).

New World Changes in Topography at the Death of Christ

Some ask the question, "Didn't the entire face of the land change at the death of Christ, and, therefore, it would be impossible to recognize significant landmarks, rivers, and mountains such as those mentioned in the Book of Mormon?" The quick answer is: regardless of the geographical changes in the Americas at the death of Christ, they did not prevent both Mormon and Moroni from identifying Zarahemla, the River Sidon, and other key Book of Mormon sites 322 years after the great destruction.[99] The River Sidon still flowed from the south to the north.[100] Zarahemla was rebuilt in the same place.[101] Roads and highways which were broken up and destroyed were rebuilt again leading from one city to another (3 Nephi 8:13).

As extensive as the devastations were in the New World at the time of Christ's death, they were not to the degree some have assumed. Those who postulate that everything was changed so that nothing was the same are overstating the case. The damage was not universally the same. The Book of Mormon reports "And there was a great and terrible destruction in the land southward. But there was even a more great and terrible destruction in the land northward" (3 Nephi 8:11-12). Cities were burned, some were sunk into the sea, and others were covered with earth, and water. Earthquakes, tempests, and whirlwinds raged for three hours. These were followed by a thick vapor of darkness which lasted for three days and ended with the resurrection of Jesus (3 Nephi 8:5-23). The destruction was great but it was not oblivion.

Discovery of buried cities in Mesoamerica from the time of Christ coincides with the accounts in the Book of Mormon. Lake Atitlan in Guatemala is a prime candidate for the Waters of Mormon in the land of Mormon (Mosiah 18:5, 30). This is where Alma fled to hide from the soldiers of unrighteous King Noah. One of the most wicked cities ever to be built stood on the borders of the Land of Mormon. Ironically, it was named Jerusalem. It was destroyed when earth and water came up over the top of it. The cities of Onihah and Mocum, were equally wicked and suffered the same fate. The same type of destruction befell these cities, but they could have been miles apart. A few years ago the water level in Lake Atitlan dropped to an all time low. Some fishermen noticed the remains of what appeared to be a city under water. Divers were sent in and pottery was removed.

> Remains of the ancient Mayan city Chiutinamit have even been discovered near the village of Santiago, Atitlan. Today, underwater archaeology has coughed up ceramics taken out of the water base of the volcanoes. Much of the pottery dates from the late pre-Classic [600 B.C. to A.D. 250].[102]

There are three volcanoes surrounding Lake Atitlan. Displacing the water with rocks and lava would cause the water to "come up in the stead thereof" (3 Nephi 9:7). If these are the Waters of Mormon, Onihah would be the best candidate for "Chiutinamit," because "Hah" in Mayan means "water" or "place of water."

A Wilderness From East Sea to West Sea

North, south, east, and west as well as northward, southward, eastward, and westward were topographical terms understood and used by the people of the Book of Mormon. While still in the wilderness along the shores of the Red Sea, Nephi states they came to a place where they did head "nearly eastward from that time forth" (1 Nephi 17:1). Once in the New World these travelers never lost their awareness of direction. The Book of Mormon is very clear that east is east and west is west. Cartographers can trust them. Imagine a people so good at astronomy they could build a huge temple so perfectly situated, that on the equinox of March twenty-first of each year, the shadow of the sun would crawl down the steps like a snake and connect to a serpent's stone head at the base of the pyramid. Chichén Itza in the Yucatan of Mexico is such a place. The Jaguar Temple is the pyramid. I personally have been there on March twenty-first and witnessed with my own eyes this engineering marvel. Equally amazing are the Temples of the Descending God at Cobá, Tulum, and Dzibilchaltun in Mexico. On March twenty-first and September twenty-first, as the first rays of dawn strike the temples, a small window at the back of each temple creates a sunburst of light which illuminates the inner temple Holy of Holies and sends forth a beam of light directly under the image of God descending to the earth. It is safe to say these people had a good grasp of direction.

The people of the Book of Mormon in the Land of Nephi and the Land of Zarahemla thought of themselves as being "nearly surrounded by water" (Alma 22:32). They described a Sea East and a Sea West. They also identified a "narrow strip of wilderness, which ran from the sea east even to the sea west" (Alma 22:27). This wilderness strip acted as a divider between the Nephites and the Lamanites. Just as the word "sea" can mean any large body of water, so does the word "wilderness" represent any uncultivated region left in its natural state. It could be a desert or a jungle. It could even be the Cuchumantanes Mountain range and the Sierras de Las Minas which cross Mesoamerica from the Atlantic Sea to the Pacific Sea. They remain to this day a natural barrier between the northern lowlands of Mexico and the southern highlands of Guatemala.

> And it came to pass that the king sent a proclamation throughout all the land, amongst all his people ... which was bordering even to the sea, on the east and on the west, and which was divided from the land of Zarahemla by a narrow strip of wilderness, which ran from the sea east even to the sea west ... and thus were the Lamanites and the Nephites divided (Alma 22:27).

Zoramites—Nephite Dissenters in the Land of Antionum

The north, south, east and west description of the Land of Antionum is so precise it is easy to locate:

> Now the Zoramites had gathered themselves together in a land which they called Antionum, which was east of the land of Zarahemla, which lay nearly bordering upon the seashore, which was south of the land of Jershon, which also bordered upon the wilderness south, which wilderness was full of Lamanites (Alma 31:3).

This description would place Antionum at the southeastern most corner of the Yucatan, close to the present day border of Honduras. The Zoramites became idol worshippers and, as many other Nephites had done, they abandoned altogether the spiritual standard of the Law of Moses (Alma 31:1-25). Their apostasy had political as well as religious ramifications. They were located on the southeastern flank of the Nephite territory. An alliance with the Lamanites would open the door for an unencumbered invasion. Topography matters. Later, the feared scenario became a reality: "And it came to pass that the Lamanites came with their thousands; and they came into the land of Antionum, which is the land of the Zoramites… (Alma 43:5)."

Integral to this story is an understanding of *north, south, east, and west* and the basic topography of the land. Captain Moroni, knowing of the Zoramites' treachery, had a massive army near the northern border of the Land of Antionum, which caused the Lamanites and their Nephite defectors to withdraw into the wilderness, which has been proposed as the Sierras de Las Minas. The Lamanites planned to attack the city of Manti, a secondary target located west near the headwaters of the River Sidon. Confident of his enemy's plan, Captain Moroni marched his Nephite army directly to the River Sidon and divided his troops into two bodies. Under the direction of a Chief Captain named Lehi, half of the Nephite army was concealed behind the *south* side of the Hill Riplah on the *east* of the River Sidon. The other half of Moroni's army secreted themselves in a valley on the *west* side of the River Sidon. The trap was set.

True to form the Lamanites and Zoramites passed *north* of the Hill Riplah and began to cross the River Sidon from *east to west.* While the enemy was fording the river, Lehi emerged from the *south* side of the Hill Riplah and surrounded them on the *east* side. The work of death commenced with the advantage to the Nephites. The enemy sped across the River Sidon hoping to regroup and with their superior numbers defeat the Nephites. They came forth out of the River Sidon on the *west* bank only to be met by the rest of the army of Captain Moroni and his fresh troops. The Lamanite army outnumbered the Nephite army more than two to one. Logistics were on the side of the Nephites. The Lamanites were so compacted together that their superior numbers and limited area wherein they could fight worked against them. After being scalped and making a final futile attempt to renew the battle, the Lamanite commander surrendered, delivered up the weapons of war and entered into a covenant of peace. The survivors of the defeated army headed up *south* through the wilderness and into the highlands of Guatemala. The dead numbered into the thousands on both sides but more grievous on the side of the Lamanites and their Nephite-Zoramite allies. The bodies of the dead were not buried; they were cast into the Sidon River. The year was 74 B.C. (Alma Chapters 43-44).

Antionum is the place where Corianton crossed over into the land of Siron among the harlots of a border town and engaged Isabel (Alma 39:3). "Over" implies mountains, hills, or water. It is of curious note that this woman's reputation was known far and wide, and "she did steal away the hearts of many" (Alma 39:4). What is an amazing coincidence is that to this day the largest lake in all of Guatemala is Lake Izabal. It is located exactly where the Land of Siron would have been, if the calculations for the general area are correct. It is said to have received its name from a small village on its southern shores named "Izabal." Corianton, coming from the north, would have crossed "over" Lake Izabal to visit the town. Frankly; it is logical to assume Lake Izabal was named by the Spanish in honor of Queen Isabella. However the Spanish named the lake "Golfo Dulce," a name meaning Sweet Gulf.[103] It is most likely that the name Izabal is a Spanish attempt to pronounce the Mayan words "Itza Balam," meaning "People

CHAPTER FIVE

Evidences of High Civilization in Mesoamerica Lost Knowledge and Lost Languages

Figure 16. Mayan Scribe

The current focus is looking for evidence of a high civilization on the North American continent that corresponds to the time and place of the Book of Mormon. The definition of high civilization includes a written language, city states, political sophistication, architectural achievements, knowledge of science, math, medicine, the stars, a calendar system, etc. These are inportant factors which must exist for an area to qualify as the lands of the Book of Mormon. A highly structured society is one of the critical indicators; a written hieroglyphic language is another. Geologically, gold, silver, and copper are primarily found in each of the lands mentioned in the Book of Mormon. Engraved stones, altars, towers, temples, highways, and cement are all physical evidences recorded in the Book of Mormon. Historical evidences of a society in decline are a part of the Book of Mormon landscape. These include the social institutions of slavery, and the practice of human sacrifice. Finding these evidences are key in locating the correct sites of the Book of Mormon. Even if every item mentioned in the Book of Mormon isn't found, doesn't mean it won't be discovered at a future time. It would be difficult to find even one scientist who believed there were chickens in the Americas before the Spaniards arrived. The 2007 finds of pre-Columbian chickens in the Americas is one example of a recent and previously unknown discovery and will be discussed later.[104]

The State of Knowledge About Mesoamerica in A.D. 1830

Any serious seeker of truth must look at the claims of the Book of Mormon through the eyes of a twenty-four-year-old Joseph Smith in A.D. 1830, when the Book of Mormon was first published to the world. What did the world know about the history, the culture, the language, the archaeology, the anthropology of the Americas? What was the state of knowledge in 1830 available to a young farm hand with a third grade education living on the frontiers of a new and expanding America? These are questions of significant merit. One could safely rule out DNA studies. What was the state of knowledge in A.D. 1830?

A search of the newspapers in the 1820s to the 1830s reveals the common belief that there was no civilized society in the Americas prior to the coming of the Europeans. One should not be surprised by the ethnocentricity of Europeans or the arrogance of such a belief system. It still exists among many. In 1825 the Englishman Thomas Huxley was born and would rewrite history to coincide with Darwinism. Here is a glimpse from the newspapers in 1830. Simon Bolivar died in 1830 after freeing most of northern South America from the Spanish. Other headlines included the fact that two million African slaves were living in the United States. The Monroe Doctrine was being hyped in the press. In medicine the doctors were serious about the bumps on people's heads in a study called "Phrenology." Americans traveled by an improved steamboat built by Robert Fulton and by stagecoaches. The Erie Canal was completed in 1825 and goods and services flowed through it. One of the items brought up the Erie Canal was a new printing press to E.B. Grandin in Palmyra, New York on which the Book of Mormon would be printed. Trains would not traverse the entire nation for four more decades. Newspapers were the primary means of communication and they were often little more than propaganda for the editors. Education was still the domain of the wealthy in 1830. Americans were looked down upon by European travelers who acknowledged them as naturally kind, but ignorant as a whole, with very poor writing, grammar, and speaking skills.

During the early 1800s the belief was commonly held that the original inhabitants of the North American continent were barbarian nomads without any evidence or history of a pre-Columbian civilization. These men had been taught that the earliest Americans were on the low end of the evolutionary scale. The contemporary history book in early America was Dr. William Robertson's, *History of America.* In it he declared unequivocally there were no signs of civilization in the Americas.

> ...a certain principle, that America *was not peopled by any nation of the ancient continent which had made considerable progress in civilization.* The inhabitants of the New World were in a state of society so extremely rude as to be unacquainted with those arts which are the first essays of human ingenuity..., there is not, in all the extent of that vast empire, a single monument or vestige of any building more ancient than the [Spanish] conquest.[105]

The famous dean of U.S. American historians was George Bancroft. In 1841 he argued that prior to the Europeans arriving only tribal barbarians lived in North America. America was "an unproductive waste ... destitute of commerce and political connection ... In the view of civilization the immense domain was a solitude."[106]

There were not supposed to be any signs of high civilizations in America. The great adventurer Stephens, in his *Incidents of Travel in Central America, Chiapas and Yucatan,* sat down on the edge of a wall amidst the splendid ruins of Copán, Honduras. He asked his friend and artist companion, Fredrick Catherwood, a rhetorical question followed by these insightful remarks: "Who were the people that built this city ...? America, say historians, was peopled by savages; but savages never reared these structures, savages never carved these stones."[107]

These two men were trained in post graduate degrees in the finest educational institutions in Europe and America. Yet, these two men, Stephens and Catherwood, were sitting in the midst of the ruins of a society that had developed a high civilization. Stephens and Catherwood were examples of highly educated men who were dumbfounded and perplexed at the cultural sophistication they encountered in Mesoamerica. One trained as a lawyer and the other as an architect. These two men sat and stared for hours pondering the high civilization they had discovered anew. They were contemporaries of Joseph Smith. It was 1839.

Joseph Smith had published the Book of Mormon in 1830, claiming that a high civilization existed on the North American Continent. He was ridiculed, mocked, and scorned. There were no acknowledged evidences of a high civilization on this continent. The general public was ignorant and the scientific community was arrogant. The Book of Mormon was viewed as a fabrication of Joseph Smith because it claimed a high civilization on the North American continent from 2200 B.C. to A.D. 400. The academic community had fully accepted Bancroft's and Robertson's view of pre-Columbian America as devoid of high civilization. Dr. Robertson scoffed at the reports of Cortés and the Spanish priests as gross exaggerations. He believed there were no pre-Columbian high civilizations at any time on the North American continent.

Lost Knowledge of America's High Civilization

Part of the problem of the nineteenth century was the lost knowledge of a high civilization in Mesoamerica as reported by the Spaniards in the sixteenth century. Buried in the royal libraries of Europe and lost in the archives of the Vatican, and written in Spanish, Latin, and Mayan, the minimal knowledge of a high civilization in America remained hidden. Awareness of the existence of letters and codices sent from Cortés to King Charles V was limited. Obtaining royal or papal permission to search their libraries and archives was next to impossible. Travel was difficult. Qualified scholars to research in archaic Spanish were minimal. There were no Mayan language scholars until the late twentieth century. The codices simply remained a novelty. These were some of the reasons the ancient inhabitants of America remained a mystery.

There were greater issues contributing to the void of knowledge about ancient America. Europeans were too consumed with wars of expansionism, consolidating political power, dealing with the Reformation and the Inquisition to appreciate the history of America. Plus, there was another overwhelming issue. The victors of war write the history books. There was a European arrogance of superiority in all things. Everything the Europeans had was better than anything American. Some would say the Europeans still feel that way. Those who were educated during the eighteenth and nineteenth centuries simply ignored any suggestion of a high civilization in America. It was easier to justify their wars of conquest and to view the New World inhabitants as barbarians. Added to that was the notion of divine right. God was on "our side!" Evidences that disagreed with this dearly held view of America were dismissed with impunity. This included the information from the early conquistadors from Spain and Portugal.

The Spanish conquistador, Hernán Cortéz, sent to the Emperor Charles V in the year A.D. 1519, "dos libros delos que tienen los yndios [*sic*]" (two books which are had among the Indians) denoting a high civilization. They were two hand painted pictographic books from the native cultures of Mesoamerica. A year later Cortés sent another letter dated October 30, 1520, to Charles V in which he tried to describe the glory and majesty of the Aztec Capital of Tenochtitlan (Mexico City) which at that time was an island fortress in the midst of a great lake. He described a city of two hundred thousand people complete with temples, towers, and vast market places, political and administrative buildings:

> To give an account, Very Powerful Lord, of the greatness, and the strange and marvelous things of this great city [Tenochtitlan] to Your Royal Excellency, and of all the dominions and splendor of Moctezuma its sovereign; of all the rites and customs which these people practice, and of the order prevailing in the government, not only of this city, but also of others belonging to this lord, much time and many very expert narrators would be required. I shall never be able to say one-

> hundredth part of what might be told respecting them, but, nevertheless, as far as I am able, I shall speak of some of the things I have seen, which although badly described, I know very well will cause much wonder, that they will hardly be believed, because even we, who see them here with our own eyes, are unable to comprehend their reality.[108]

However, all of this knowledge of a high civilization was buried in royal libraries in Europe, and lost in a plethora of political and religious wars. It is also true that the Spanish Conquistadors ignored many of the ruins. They were unaware of most of the ruins which simply stood as mounds in the jungle. Also, as the Mayan scholars, Schele, Sharer, and Coe, had pointed out in various writings, the European conquerors wrote a history casting the defeated Mesoamericans as a barbarous society. It was not until 1839, when John L. Stephens and artist Fredrick Catherwood journeyed to Mexico and Central America and later published their book in 1841, that a new awareness was sparked in the possibilities of a high civilization in the New World.

Egyptian, Persian, Greek, and Roman cultures were the focus of the American universities. Graduates of Harvard, Yale, Dartmouth, or Princeton knew more about Latin and Greek than anything Mayan or even the Native Americans that surrounded their campuses.

Later American historians corrected the mischaracterization of the early inhabitants of America. It has been a gradual and ongoing process. New discoveries have pushed the dating of a high civilization from A.D. 200 back to 600 B.C. – 1200 B.C. It was only in 1941, a hundred years after Bancroft's history, that archaeologist Matthew Sterling convinced a doubting scholarly community that the Olmec, and not the Maya, were the mother culture of the Americas. Current historians now acknowledge the high level of pre-Columbian civilization.

> They had a penal code and an independent judiciary … Their annals were recorded, they were astronomers and had an elaborate calendar. Their engineers were able to design causeways, bridges and aqueducts. Above all, their sculpture was of a very high order … there was a sovereign, a council, an army, a judiciary, a civil service, a treasury and tax collectors…[109]

The Olmec, Zapotec, Mixtec, Mexicas (Aztec) and Maya had written languages and eleven various calendar systems which were more accurate than anything anywhere else in the world. In math and science they had developed the concept of zero (0) centuries before the Europeans. The Mesoamericans possessed solar calendars, lunar calendars, and a calendar based on the five hundred eighty-four day cycle of Venus rising. The two hundred sixty day "Tzolkin," or sacred calendar, and the three hundred sixty (plus five holy days) "Haab" calendar, based on the sun, were used together to form a fifty-two year Calendar Round.

All of this was unknown to a Joseph Smith in upstate New York, and apparently to scholars, until the last fifty years. This is the environment from which Joseph Smith emerged with the publication of the Book of Mormon in 1830. Mockery and scorn awaited those who joined the Mormons. The new converts to Mormonism, who received a spiritual witness of the Book of Mormon, did not lose faith in their spiritual knowledge because of scientific assertions to the contrary. Time and patience would vindicate the Book of Mormon. The early church newspapers were eager to report on any archeological find which might support the claim in the Book of Mormon that a high civilization once existed on the North American continent. While reinforcing the believers, there was also the hope that the skeptics might be convinced by scientific discoveries that the Book of Mormon was a true history of the early inhabitants of this continent and an accurate portrayal of a highly developed society. A year before his martyrdom Joseph Smith stated,

> So when the Book of Mormon first made its appearance among men, it was looked upon by many as a wild speculation ... We were then told that the inhabitants of this continent were, and always had been, a rude barbarous race, uncouth, unlettered, and without civilization. But when they were told of the various relics that have been found indicative of civilization, intelligence and learning; when they were told of the wealth, architecture and splendor of ancient Mexico; when recent developments proved beyond a doubt, that there was [*sic*] ancient ruins in Central America, which, in point of magnificence, beauty, strength and architectural design, would vie with any of the most splendid ruins on the Asiatic continent; when they could trace the fine delineations of the sculptor's chisel, on the beautiful statue, the mysterious hieroglyphic, and the unknown character, they began to believe that a wise, powerful, intelligent and scientific race had inhabited this continent ... [110]

In an editorial column in the *Times and Seasons,* Joseph Smith wrote:

> Every day adds fresh testimony to the already accumulated evidence on the authenticity of the Book of Mormon. At the time that book was translated, there was very little known about ruined cities and dilapidated buildings, [of Mesoamerica]. The general presumption was that no people possessing more intelligence than our present race of Indians had ever inhabited this continent; and the accounts given in the Book of Mormon concerning large cities and civilized people having inhabited this land were generally disbelieved and pronounced a humbug.... it is evident that the Book of Mormon does not give a more extensive account of large and populous cities than those discoveries demonstrate to be even now in existence.—Ed.[111]

The publication of the Stephens' book came eleven years after the publication of the Book of Mormon. If Joseph Smith had been aware of evidences to support the Book of Mormon as a real history of a high civilization in America before Stephens and Catherwood, he would have used that information to silence his critics. President John Taylor spoke about the archeological finds as proof that Joseph Smith was a prophet and the Book of Mormon a true history of these people:

> THE BOOK OF MORMON RECORD—Stephens and Catherwood, after examining the ruins that were found at Guatemala, in Central America, and gazing upon magnificent ruins, mouldering [*sic*] temples, stately edifices, rich sculpture, elegant statuary, and all the traces of a highly cultivated and civilized people, said—"Here are the works of a great and mighty people that have inhabited these ruins; but now they are no more. History is silent on the subject, and no man can unravel this profound mystery. Nations have planted, and reaped, and built, and lived, and died, that are now no more; and no one can tell anything about them or reveal their history." Why, there was a young man in Ontario County, New York, to whom the angel of God appeared and gave an account of the whole. These majestic ruins bespeak the existence of a mighty people. The Book of Mormon unfolds their history. O yes; but his was of too humble an origin, like Jesus of Nazareth. It was not some great professor, who had got an education in a European or an American college, but one who professed to have a revelation from God—and the world doesn't believe in revelation. But nevertheless it is true, and we know it.—[112]

There is one inescapable fact from the testimonies of Stephens and the drawings of Catherwood: the North American Continent and "Mesoamerica" in particular could no longer be dismissed. A high civilization existed at a time and a place consistent with the Book of Mormon narrative. The Book of Mormon as a real history of real people who lived and died as part of the pre-Columbian scene was plausible.

Hieroglyphic Languages

One of the most important characteristics of a high civilization is a written language. Detractors of Joseph Smith believe that the letters and characters he transcribed to what is known as the Anthon Transcript were the imaginary scribbling of an inventive mind. During the translation process Martin Harris imposed on Joseph to copy over a few of the "Caracters [*sic*]" written upon the gold plates in the altered reformed Egyptian. Martin hoped that the world, and in particular his wife Lucy, would know that the Book of Mormon was not a hoax. The characters were copied by Joseph Smith from the Book of Mormon plates and given to Martin Harris in 1828 who in turn took them to Charles Anthon, a Professor of Ancient Language at Columbia University in New York. Martin Harris claimed that Professor Anthon originally agreed that these were ancient writings and then recanted when he found out it was associated with religious claims. These characters have become known as the "Anthon Transcript." Dr. Anthon denied that he ever acknowledged anything to Martin Harris, although he admitted meeting with him. The two separate and opposite accounts amount to which of them you choose to believe.

To qualify as the lands of the Book of Mormon, there had to be evidence of at least three separate peoples migrating to the same geographical area. Two of the three cultures needed to possess a written language. Moreover, it was a requirement of the Book of Mormon that one of the languages be written in hieroglyphics. The Book of Mormon reports that the Jaredites and the Nephites possessed a written language. The Mulekites lost their literacy shortly after their arrival to the New World. Here are a few key Book of Mormon scriptures related to the claims of a written language:

Jaredites

> And as he [Ether] dwelt in the cavity of a rock he made the remainder of this record ... (Ether 13:14). Ye shall write them and shall seal them up, that no one can interpret them; for ye shall write them in a language that they cannot be read [without the Urim and Thummim] (Ether 3:22).... And I take mine account from the twenty and four plates ... (Ether 1:2).

Mulekites

> Mosiah discovered that the people of Zarahemla [Mulekites] came out from Jerusalem at the time that Zedekiah, king of Judah, was carried away captive into Babylon.... they had had many wars ... and their language had become corrupted; and they had brought no records with them ... Omni 1:15-18).

Nephites

> Yea, I make a record in the language of my father, which consists of the learning of the Jews and the language of the Egyptians (1 Nephi 1:2).... Lehi ... having been taught in the language of the Egyptians therefore he could read these engravings, and teach them to his children ... (Mosiah 1:4).

The questions may be asked, why would Lehi know how to write in Egyptian? And why did Lehi choose to write in Reformed Egyptian? In answer to the first question: Jerusalem was tied economically to Egypt. Jerusalem was a tiny city state compared to the larger political empires of Babylon, Syria, and Egypt. The entire reason that Babylon invaded Jerusalem was due to the Jewish King Zedekiah forming an alliance with Egypt against Babylon. In spite of the fact Babylon was the political power, Jerusalem's major commercial trading partner was Egypt. The language of commerce was Demotic Egyptian. Demotic (from the Greek meaning "of the people" or "popular") was a form of hieroglyphic shorthand. It was used from the 7th century B.C. to the 3rd century A.D. It was the commercial "lingua franka" at the time that Lehi and his family left Jerusalem for the New World. Whether Lehi was a caravan trader, as some have speculated, or not, he would have been familiar with the Egyptian language. Later, during the time of Jesus, Rome was the dominant political force but Syria was the chief economical influence, therefore Aramaic was a language spoken by Jesus. Aram was the name by which Syria was known and Aramaic was the economical language of the entire region influenced by Syria. It is much the same today with the English language. Regardless of one's mother tongue, English and the American dollar have made English the language of commerce.

The second question about why Lehi would write in reformed Egyptian was answered by the writers of the Book of Mormon:

> And now, behold, we have written this record according to our knowledge, in the characters which are called among us *the reformed Egyptian*, being handed down and *altered by us*, according to our manner of speech. And if our plates had been sufficiently large we should have written in Hebrew; but the *Hebrew hath been altered by us also*; and if we could have written in Hebrew, behold, ye would have had no imperfection in our record. But the Lord knoweth the things which we have written, and also that none other people knoweth our language; and because that none other people knoweth our language, therefore he hath prepared means for the interpretation thereof (Mormon 9:32-34, emphasis added).

The Value of Comparing the Hebrew and Egyptian Languages with the Book of Mormon

What is the value of comparing the Hebrew, and Egyptian languages with the Book of Mormon? The answer is the authorship of the Book of Mormon. The Book of Mormon claim is that it is an ancient historical record. Additionally, it was written in an "altered" combination of Hebrew and Egyptian.

A visual comparison of the Anthon Transcript with the Hebrew and with the Egyptian Demotic available to Lehi in 600 B.C. will demonstrate the viability of these writings as ancient characters. There are those in academia who would have you believe that you are not sophisticated enough to recognize the similarities or differences between ancient scripts. Translation is not the objective. The issue is the same one placed before Professor Anthon. Are the characters from the Anthon Transcript indicative of an ancient script? You be the judge.

This is what Egyptian Demotic writing of 600 B.C. looks like:

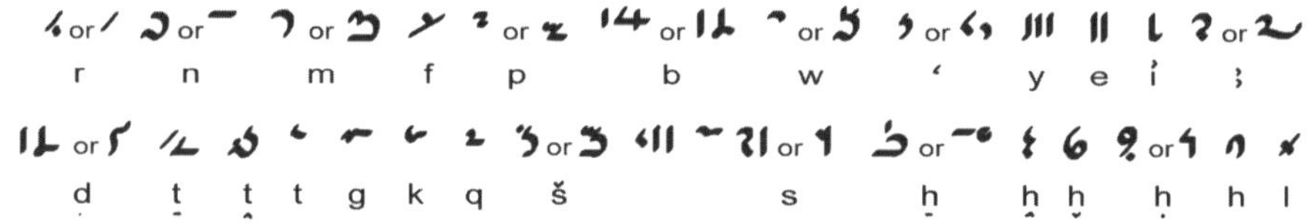

Figure 17. Egyptian Demotic Glyphs

Compare the Demotic characters with those from the Anthon Transcript.

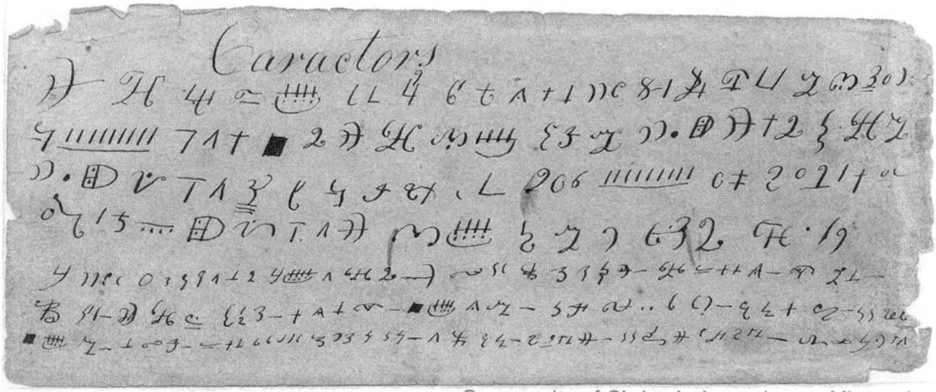

Community of Christ, Independence, Missouri

Figure 18. Characters from the Book of Mormon Known as the Anthon Transcript

It doesn't take a rocket scientist to identify the many common written characters between the Anthon Transcript and Demotic writing. In 1830 the Book of Mormon was published. Very, very little of ancient Egyptian hieroglyphic writings had been translated by that time. Jean Francois Champollion was credited with deciphering ancient Egyptian hieroglyphics from the famous Rosetta stone:

> Champollion did not publish any of his decipherment work, probably secreting it away on purposes [sic] since others had the same goal as he, until in 1822 … In this document he made it known that his efforts had revealed an alphabet of twenty-six letters, including syllabic signs, of which ten were identified completely. However, two others were only partly correct, and fourteen others were later proved to be wrong, or missing…Two years later he followed this with … a more definitive, expanded analysis, and we can only wonder what else he might have accomplished had he not died at such an early age.[113]

Champollion died in 1832. His book entitled *Egyptian Grammar* was published in 1836 or six years after the Book of Mormon had been published and one year after the *Pearl of Great Price*. Both claimed a connection with things

Egyptian. In denouncing Joseph Smith, Dr. James Breasted, a renowned Egyptologist from the University of Chicago, said,

> Little of the [Egyptian] language, comparatively speaking, was understood when he [Champollion] died in 1832.... It would have been impossible for any American scholar to know enough about Egyptian inscriptions to read them before the publication of Champollion's grammar ... It will be seen, then, that if Joseph Smith could read Egyptian writing, his ability to do so had no connection with the decipherment of hieroglyphics by European scholars.[114]

He was right about one thing: Joseph Smith's ability to translate the Book of Mormon from Reformed Egyptian had nothing to do with European or American scholars. Joseph was a Prophet and a Seer. With the aid of special instruments prepared and preserved by God, called the Urim and Thummim, Joseph translated the engraved plates upon which the Book of Mormon was written.[115]

Below is the Proto-Hebrew/Early Aramaic alphabet. This would have been the Hebrew style of writing available to Lehi in 600 B.C.

Proto-Hebrew/ Early Aramaic of the Time of Lehi

Figure 19. Proto-Hebrew/Early Aramaic Writing 600 B.C.

Compare The Proto-Hebrew/Early Aramaic writing with the Anthon Transcript.

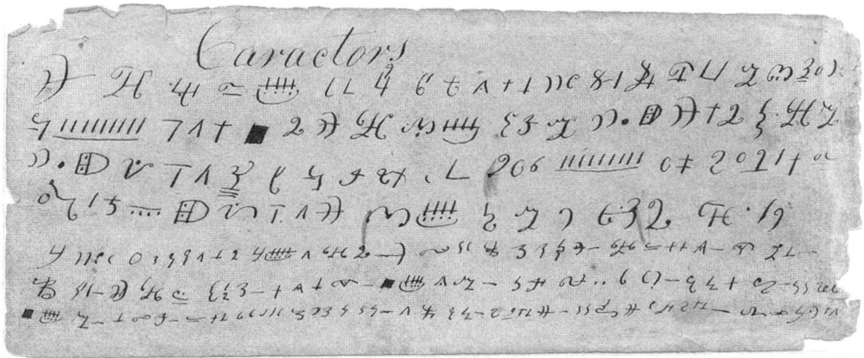

Community of Christ, Independence, Missouri

Figure 20. Characters from the Book of Mormon Known as the Anthon Transcript

The Book of Mormon was written in a combination of Egyptian and Hebrew. This blending of two languages is referred to as "Reformed Egyptian." It is most likely that the writers of the Book of Mormon would have used a combination of the two languages of Proto-Hebrew and Demotic-Egyptian. The writers and prophet-historians of the Book of Mormon made it clear that even these writing were "altered" by them. This means that the Book of Mormon and the Anthon Transcript, which was taken from it, may remain an "isolate," (altered unidentified language) until such a time as a new Rosetta-type stone or its equivalent can be found, or the Lord sees fit to give the keys of translation.

There is another form of Egyptian shorthand writing known as Hieratic that may have been a resource for Lehi and the Book of Mormon writers. Hieratic (from the Greek meaning "sacred") is a cursive script of Egyptian hieroglyphs used from the first dynasty about 2700 B.C. to 400 B.C. Since Lehi left Jerusalem at 600 B.C., hieratic script would still have been in use. It was mostly replaced by the Demotic (common people's) script in most secular writing, but hieratic continued to be used by priests and political leaders for several more centuries. Since the Book of Mormon was considered sacred writing, there is an outside possibility that Hieratic was used by the Book of Mormon writers. It can not be ruled out as a possible resource to Lehi, who was a writer of sacred things (1 Nephi 1:18).

Hieratic or Priestly Script

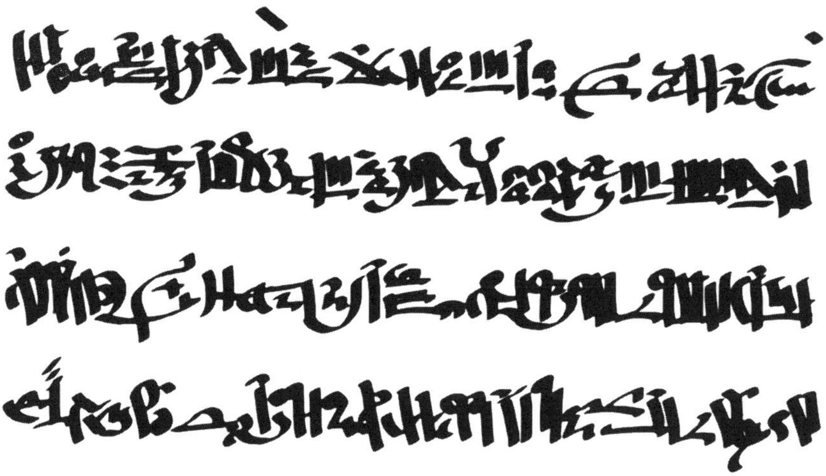

Figure 21. Egyptian Hieratic or Priestly Script

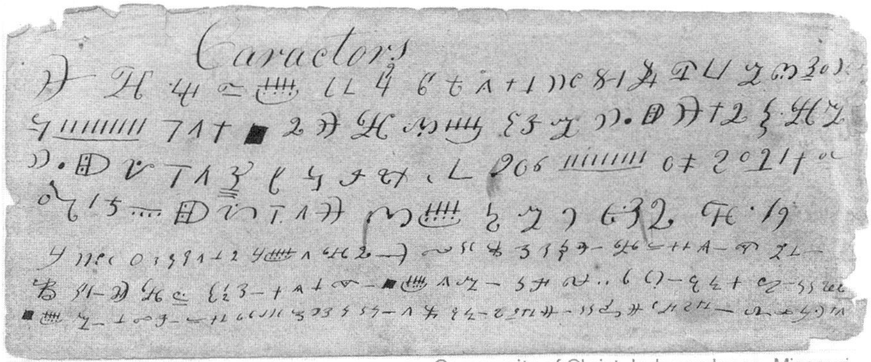

Community of Christ, Independence, Missouri

Figure 22. Characters from the Book of Mormon Known as the Anthon Transcript

The transition from Hieratic to Demotic took place only a few decades before Lehi's exodus from Jerusalem in 600 B.C. Looking at Hieratic, Demotic, Proto-Hebrew writing and the Anthon Transcript and comparing the individual characters, Joseph Smith's credibility is once again reinforced. The existence of hieroglyphic languages at the time and the place where Joseph Smith said they would be requires honest people to keep an open mind to the Book of Mormon as an ancient Mesoamerican script.

Other Untranslated Reformed Hieroglyphic Text

There are other reformed Egyptian hieroglyphic texts of the time of the Book of Mormon which remain undeciphered. The Merotic texts are a prime example. Foreign invaders caused the Egyptian court to flee to Upper Egypt for safety. At the time when Lehi and his family were escaping the Babylonian captivity of Jerusalem around 600 B.C., the Egyptian royal court fled to Meroe near the sixth cataract of the upper Nile River around 590 B.C. It was a place so remote that centuries later the Romans abandoned it as too distant and too unproductive to sustain. Because of its isolated location the Cushitic Pharaohs developed an independent language from Lower Egypt. They adapted the Demotic writing into a "Reformed Egyptian" which has yet to be comprehended even though the individual letters can be deciphered. The Merotic texts were used from the 2nd century B.C. to about the 4th century A.D. This is a prime example of how a contemporary society with Lehi changed the Egyptian language into a Reformed Egyptian that remains misunderstood to this day.

> Merotic was the written language of the ancient civilization of Kush, located for centuries in what is now the Northern Sudan. The word "Meroitic" derives from the name of the city Meroë, which was located on the East bank of the Nile south of where the Atbara River flows off to the east. It is the second oldest written language in Africa after Egyptian hieroglyphs. It is a phonetic language with both a hieroglyph

form using some adopted Egyptian hieroglyphs and a cursive form similar to Egyptian Demotic writing. The language had one innovation uncommon in ancient written languages such as Egyptian hieroglyphics or Greek in that there was a word separator, similar in function to spaces in modern scripts, that looks similar to a colon. Meroitic was employed starting the 2nd century BC and was continuously used until the fall of Meroë in the mid 4th century AD.[116]

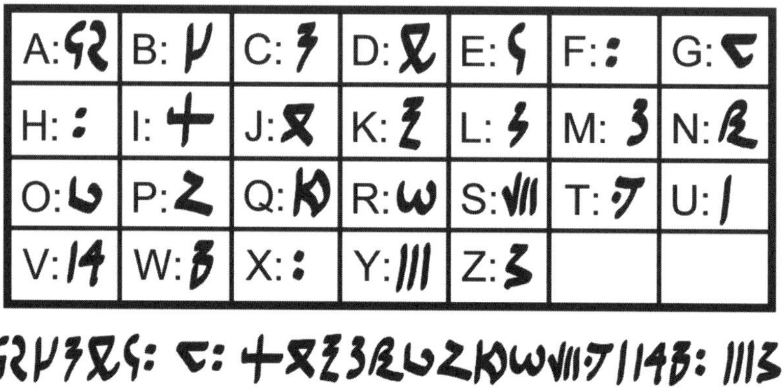

Figure 23. Reformed Egyptian Meroitic-Demotic Script

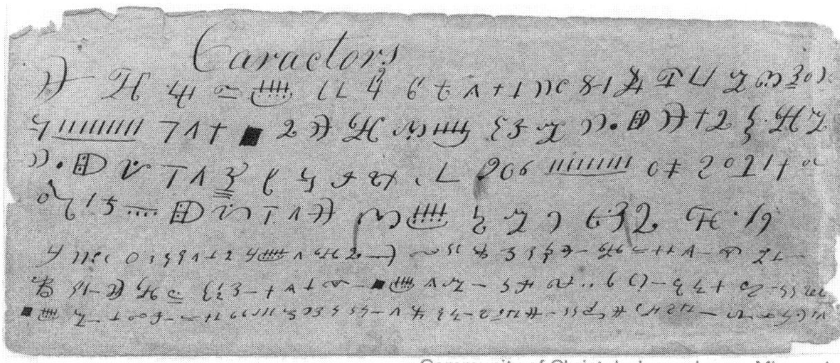

Community of Christ, Independence, Missouri

Figure 24. Anthon Transcript

Compare the "Anthon Transcript" with the Merotic-Demotic texts. For those who would like more examples of Merotic writing, another sample is the stela of Waleye son or daughter of Kadeye, from Sai, now at the British museum and online for the internet user. This is not to suggest that Merotic Reformed Egyptian had any connection whatsoever with the Reformed Egyptian writing in the Book of Mormon. The value of the Reformed Egyptian Merotic in relation to the Book of Mormon is to point out the viability, credibility, and comparative development of various forms of Reformed Egyptian at similar times and places that relate to Book of Mormon history.

Egyptian is phonetic based, which meant that each letter also represented a sound. Egyptian writing lent itself to meshing with other languages. When

Alexander the Great conquered Egypt around 332 B.C., the Greek and Egyptian languages reformed into a blend of both called Coptic. Technically, Coptic is Reformed Egyptian. Instead of Hebrew and Demotic, it was Greek and Demotic. All of this means that the Book of Mormon claim to Reformed Egyptian is not only plausible, but typical of what others had done.

Mesoamerica is Home To Four Separate Hieroglyphic Languages

There is no current evidence of an ancient written language in South America. Hieroglyphic codices in the boundaries of the United States or Canada remain undiscovered. In the Americas, hieroglyphic languages have been found only in Mesoamerica. The bottom line is that in Mesoamerica there are four discovered complicated systems of hieroglyphic and reformed hieroglyphic writing systems. They are divided into three different families, i.e. Zapotec and Mixtec belonging to the Otomanguen family, Aztec (Mexica) to the Uto-Aztecan, and the Maya to the Macro-Mayan. The structure of Zapotec writing was a kind of hieroglyphic writing in vertical columns, and often with numerals. It is in style and format very similar to Egyptian, which most scholars are reluctant to admit. Why? Because it contradicts the "Siberian Land Bridge Only" doctrine. This theory insisted that America was settled *only* from Asia by primitive man who followed the bison and mastodons across the Siberian Land Bridge. To admit a cross-cultural relationship between Egypt and Mesoamerica would be to go against a scientific position deemed sacred. However, Dr. Joyce Marcus, a scholar of the Zapotec, said,

> Zapotec writing was older than the Maya, Mixtec or Aztec systems and may have appeared as early as 600 B.C. in the Valley of Oaxaca. "Although some conventions are shared by the four systems [Maya, Mixtec, Zapotec, and Aztec] ... Zapotec writing system although not fully understood may be partly phonetic and partly ideographic.[117]

Until September 14, 2006 Zapotec was considered the oldest writing system in Mesoamerica. New evidence now reports that the oldest society and the mother culture of America had an acknowledged writing system dating to 1000-800 B.C. New discoveries keep pushing back the date when mankind had the ability to read, write and calculate the revolutions of the stars.

It is a wonderful coincidence that the Olmecs representing one culture have a written language dating now at 1000 B.C.[118] It is equally satisfying to have a second culture known as the Zapotec appear with a writing system around 600 B.C., about the same time as the Mulekites arrived in Mesoamerica. The Zapotec are candidates for being, mixing with, or coexisting with the Mulekites in the southern coastal area of Mexico's gulf to Oaxaca, Mexico. The famous ruins of Monte Alban and Mitla are located in Oaxaca. The Book of Mormon states that eventually the Mulekites lose their own written language skills and amalgamate with the Nephites. After they are discovered by the Nephites they learn the Nephite written language. The Zapotec language underwent some dramatic changes which some scholars believe was the result of cross-cultural pollinating. The mixing of the Nephite and Mulekite cultures would certainly account for those changes. The ancient Zapotec language will be decoded at some future date. We will then be able to gain a greater insight into these people of hieroglyphic language. As a post script, the George Washington of Mexico was Benito Juarez, a full blooded Zapotec, and twice the President of Mexico.

The Book of Mormon claim to be Reformed Egyptian was once thought to be absurd and ridiculous. It now appears plausible, except to most anthropologists who still reject a Mediterranean or African influence in the Americas before Columbus. If there were more of the Anthon Transcript, the Book of Mormon would make another Mesoamerican hieroglyphic text to be translated by modern scholars. But wait! The Book of Mormon has been translated already by the gift and power of God. What a wonderful blessing it would be if the academic community had access to the Urim and Thummim. However, use of the Urim and Thummim requires a belief in God and His specific authority to be a Seer (1 Samuel 9:9, Mosiah 8:13-15).

Suffice it to observe that at least four systems of Hieroglyphic and Reformed Hieroglyphic writing existed in Mesoamerica at the time and place where the Book of Mormon said that two existed, i.e., Jaredite and Nephite. The Mayan language is about seventy-five percent to eighty percent translated as of 2007. The recent discovery of a large Olmec stone with hieroglyphic writing means one more undeciphered hieroglyphic language from Mesoamerica may now be deciphered. Deciphering of the Olmec, Mixtec, and Zapotec are in their infancy, and dedicated scholars are desperately needed to help with the decoding of these hieroglyphic writings.

There are many current examples of how a people lose their written language. There are seven million Maya today who speak a dialect of their mother tongue but have lost the ability for centuries to read and write Mayan. Only recent efforts have codified their language so that modern Mayan dialects can be written and learned in school.

The most logical and rational explanation to the diversification of language is cross-cultural pollination followed by periods of isolation. The most dramatic impact on any language historically is foreign invasion. The present is the key to the past. The best example of cross-cultural pollination today is the impact that the United States of America has had on the world's languages. American movies, music, and television have invaded the world. In addition to the American soldier crossing the oceans, American words have crossed the airwaves and become a part of a global language. American business words, computer phrases and manner of dress have had an effect on the world's languages.

Foreign domination by any conquering army has imposed change upon the languages of the conquered. The Olmecs disappeared as a dominate political culture. However, the Totonac of the Mexican Gulf Coast continue to speak a language isolate that was influenced by the Olmec. There are several Mesoamerican languages that remain isolates.

The question is, "Who influenced the Olmec and Zapotec languages?" These untranslated isolates (altered) languages, such as the hieroglyphic languages of the Olmec and Zapotec may yet demonstrate an Egyptian or even a Chinese influence. Both Egyptian and Chinese began as hieroglyphic languages. There are two possible connections of the Mesoamerican hieroglyphic writing systems to the Book of Mormon. One language could belong to the Olmec, possibly Jaredite connection. The Olmec written language may be more closely tied to ancient Chinese hieroglyphs or Sumerian than to the Egyptian, since the Olmecs/Jaredites came to Mesoamerica around 2200 B.C. from the Tower of Babel (Ether 1:33). They entered that quarter of land where man had not been and crossed over many waters from presumably somewhere along the Asian coast (Ether 2:5-7).[119] The Book of Mormon does not rule out the possibility of the Jaredites coming from Asia across the Pacific. Nor does the Book of Mormon eliminate the possibility of the friends of Jared or the friends of the brother of Jared from being Asian. According to the sixteenth century Mesoamerican historian, Ixtlilxóchitl, his ancestors came from the land of "Tartary." This would include China, Mongolia, Korea and the eastern most parts of the Russian republics. The Jaredites came with the ability to read and write and were commanded to keep a record which the Lord would confound until the time was right (Ether 3:21-24). The other connection the Book of Mormon may have with Mesoamerican languages is with the hieroglyphic writings of the Mixtec and Zapotec. Further research may yet find these latter languages are related to the Egyptian.

This idea will be scoffed at and ridiculed by the same arrogant group of dogmatic scholars who maintained for a hundred years that there were no pre-Columbian maritime crossings and who now finally admit to it. If modern science is ready to admit that America was settled by maritime crossing, is science willing to accept that some of these people just may have brought with them a written language. Indeed, it is possible that one of those transoceanic crossings had people aboard that were influenced in their writings by the Egyptians.

Less than two percent of all known archaeological sites have been uncovered in Mesoamerica. The latest findings at El Mirador and Waka are pushing the boundaries of Maya writing back by hundreds of years. It may be prudent for scholars and religionists to withhold dogmatic assertions on what can and can't be, until a significant and reliable number of sites have been excavated. Less than two percent of known archaeological sites in Mesoamerica have been excavated. Generalizing from a population that is less than two percent is inherently precarious.

There is also the possibility that the four hieroglyphic writings found in Mesoamerica have no connection whatsoever with anything in the Book of Mormon and are the products of other cultures brought to the Americas. What is known is that Mesoamerica is the only place on the North American continent or on the South American continent where there is current evidence of a high civilization with several written hieroglyphic languages.

CHAPTER SIX

RECORDS IN GOLD, RECORDS IN STONE

Figure 25. "Thin Gold Plate" with hieroglyphic writing extracted from the well at Chichen Itzá, Mexico by Harvard Archaeologist, Herbert Thompson, in 1904

Language Clues

There are five basic written languages in the world from which the majority of other languages flow. Scholars believe all five were originally hieroglyphic and pictographic in nature. They are Egyptian, Chinese, Mayan, Sumerian, and Indus. The Mayan scholar, Robert J. Sharer, has given a helpful insight into ancient written languages: "Many writing systems are combinations of different writing systems."[120] For example, combining Hebrew and Egyptian into a reformed Egyptian would be consistent with Dr. Sharer's thinking.

One of the things that most interests linguists are the key words and phrases that carry over from one language to another. These "borrowed" phrases are clues to cross pollination of languages. For example, most English speaking people have used a Mayan word and incorporated it in their regular vocabulary and have not been aware of its origin. The word is "chiclets" as in chewing gum. "Chi" means mouth and "chicle" is a Spanish corruption of "chaaxtik" meaning chew in Yucatec Mayan. Literally the English word Chiclets in Mayan is "mouth chew." That is an amazingly accurate definition of what one does with gum. There was an interaction between the two cultures. More importantly, it demonstrates the influence of one language upon another.

Phrases, names, places, and literary considerations between the Book of Mormon and Mesoamerica are myriad and plentiful. A few only have been chosen to illustrate the similarities.

Figure 26. "And It Came to Pass" Glyph

The phrase "*And it came to pass,*" "*And then it came to pass,*" or a like form of it is found nearly fifteen hundred times in the Book of Mormon. Mark Twain in his witty ways said that if the phrase "And it came to pass" were removed totally from the pages of the Book of Mormon it would be "only a pamphlet."[121] This same phrase is also found over five hundred times in the Bible.

In Mexico are the beautiful ruins of Palenque. Joseph Smith named this site as a former Book of Mormon city. The Mayan glyph pictured above is found on both the Temple of Inscriptions, also known as Pacal's Tomb, and the Temple of the Cross. Mayanists refer to this glyph as the "Ut-chi." It means "it happened," or it can be translated as, "and it came to pass." Neither the Temple of Inscriptions nor the Temple of the Cross existed during the time of the primary events of the Book of Mormon, i.e. 600 B.C. to A.D. 400. However, the use of this phrase was in common practice by tradition in the lands of Mesoamerica. It demonstrates another correlation between Mesoamerica and the Book of Mormon. For a more thorough explanation of this glyph see *Exploring the Lands of the Book of Mormon* by Dr. Joseph L. Allen.[122]

Name Correlations: Laman, Kish, and Lib

Name correlations, especially, in a phonetic language such as Maya, carry over from one society to another. It is this kind of phrase correlation and name correlation one would expect to find when translating from one language to another. Even if the Maya are not a part of the original Book of Mormon people, there would be a language carry over of certain key words, because they occupied the same land mass. Look at how many American cities in the United States, Mexico, and Canada are Native American in origin: Pontiac, Seattle, Tacoma, Seneca, Oaxaca, Manitoba, Saskatchewan, Cancun, Acapulco etc. The examples are myriad. These are name correlations which have been carried over from the previous cultures. They have nothing to do with the English language of the United States, nor the Spanish language of Mexico, nor the French language of the early Canadians. These are phonetic approximations of names that have carried over from the original inhabitants of the land by later foreign invaders.

Some Book of Mormon names such as Laman, Kish and Lib have survived intact. There are dozens more such as the Mayan word *Xul* (x is pronounced 'ish'). Xul is the name of one of the Mayan months. The name of a Jaredite king in the Book of Mormon is *Shule* (Ether 1:30). *Cunén* is the name of a village near the Guatemalan, Mexican border. *Cumeni* is also the name of a Nephite town near the border of the Guatemalan highlands and the lowlands of Mexico (Alma 56:14). Cumeni would have been one of the first cities the Lamanites encountered coming down from the highlands near Manti and the headwaters of the River Sidon. *Kumen* is also the name of a Nephite disciple of Christ. There are variants of the same name which include Kish*kumen, Kumen*onhi (Helaman 1:9, 3 Nephi 19:4). Phonetically, k, ch, c are interchangeable as is x and sh, and m with n.

Laman

The ruins on the New River in Belize are called Lamanai. This is a contraction of "Laman" and "Ayin" or "Ayim." Scholars know that "ayim" means crocodile but are uncertain about the name Laman. They believe it means "submerged." However, the word for "submerged" in the Yucatec Maya is "t'ubik' or "bulik," neither of which has any connection or phonetic approximation with the word Laman in Spanish or English. Laura Howard reported that

> The ancient name of Lamanai was recorded by the Spanish in the 16th century and brought to light again by historian Grant Jones through his work in the archives in Seville, Spain. The name Lamanai is loosely translated as Submerged Crocodile...[123]

Dr. David Pendergast, an expert archaeologist on Lamanai, claims the community of Lamanai developed between 700 to 500 B.C.[124] Laman is the name of one of the most prominent characters in the Book of Mormon which name was subsequently taken by various kings (Mosiah 9:9) and commoners (Alma 55:5). The association of Laman and a river is reminiscent of Father Lehi's plea to his son Laman, "O that thou mightest be like unto this river" (1Nephi 2:9).

Kish

Palenque is a city which dates back to the Jaredite times in the Book of Mormon. The name Kish is found prominently engraved in stone among the predecessors to the great Maya King of Palenque known as Pacal or Lord Shield. Dr. Bruce Warren, a Mesoamerican archaeologist, reported on the name Kish:

> The personal name *Kish* gives us an especially intriguing connection between the Book of Mormon Jaredites and the Olmec culture: In the Old Testament in about one thousand B.C., Saul's father was named *Kish* (1 Samuel 9:1). Interestingly, in the book of Ether, a Jaredite king, King Kish, lived about the same time. The book of Ether's account gives little information about King Kish other than his name. He was the son of a righteous king named Corom and the father of a righteous king named Lib (Ether 1:18-19; 10:17-19). Thus, King Kish was apparently one of the Jaredite monarchs.[125]

My own research into the origin of the name Kish took me directly into a Hamitic (African) source which corresponds to Dr. Bruce Warren's connection to the Jaredites, who may be the Olmecs. Kish is also an Egyptian name meaning "smelter." More than a miner, a kish was a worker of precious metals. He was responsible for extracting minerals from the ore. Those familiar with the Egyptian language and culture, as were the prophet historians of the Book of Mormon, would appreciate Joseph Smith's observation that among the friends of Jared, or the friends of the Brother of Jared, were Hamitic blacks from Egypt.[126]

Lib

There were two different Jaredite kings named Lib in the Book of Mormon. One lived in the ninth century B.C. and the other in the fourth century B.C., approximately. The name Lib was found at Palenque and dated to 800 B.C. Palenque is located just south of the Isthmus of Tehuantepec. The narrow neck of land mentioned in the Book of Mormon is believed to be the Isthmus of Tehuantepec. The ninth century B.C. King Lib built a city near the narrow neck of Land (Ether 10:18-20) There seemed to be few righteous kings whether in or out of the Book of Mormon. However, Lib is identified as one who was "good in the sight of the Lord" (Ether 1:18-19; 10:17-19).

At the ruins of Yaxchilán, Mexico, located just southeast of Palenque, the name Lib emerges again about A.D. 709. It was found on a lentil over the doorway of a palace. Mesoamerican archaeologist, Shelby Saberon said "The name Lib is recorded as the father of Lady Shark."[127] The name of Lib and the date correlation of the ninth century B.C. with the rulers of Palenque and the continued emergence of the name Lib with a specific geographical area near the Isthmus of Tehuantepec is further proof of Mesoamerica as the land of the Book of Mormon.

Those interested in a more exhaustive correlation of Book of Mormon names would be well served by looking at Hugh Nibley's *Lehi in the Desert* or *Since Cumorah*; Hunter and Ferguson's *Ancient America and the Book of Mormon;* Larry Ferguson and Bruce Warren's *The Messiah in Ancient America;* Joseph Allen's *Exploring the Lands of the Book of Mormon;* and specifically J.N. Washburn's *The Contents, Structure and Authorship of the Book of Mormon.* The latter may be hard to find as it is out of print.

Literary Considerations: Parallelism in Mayan, Hebrew, Egyptian, and the Book of Mormon

The purpose of these comparisons is to demonstrate that the Book of Mormon is an ancient text. It was written in a style and manner similar to other ancient text. Most of what is known about the literary styles of ancient languages has been discovered in the last one hundred years. To paraphrase and encompass the spirit of Dr. James Breasted from the University of Chicago; It would have been impossible for any American scholar to know enough about Egyptian literary styles until after 1912 or Mayan literary styles until after 1983. Biblical Hebrew was known, but current literary styles such as the Haskalah did not become well known in America until after 1856.[128] Joseph Smith died in 1844. Current literary information about poetry, style, and syntax was not available in Joseph Smith's day for either Egyptian or Mayan. Six years after the publication of the Book of Mormon Joseph Smith began a study of Hebrew in preparation for doing a new translation of the Bible.[129]

Understanding Parallelisms

The Mayan Bible called the Popol Vuh will be highlighted later under the topic of "Historical Considerations." However, there is a literary consideration that has emerged recently that demands observation. Most translations of the Popol Vuh have been from Mayan to Spanish and then from Spanish to English. This required two translations and with each translation some things were lost.

The reasons are obvious. There have been few English scholars capable of reading, writing and understanding the nuances of the Mayan. The Popol Vuh could not be fully appreciated until Linda Schele and others broke the Mayan code in the early 1980s. There hasn't been sufficient time to train enough scholars to do the work of translation until now.

Professor Allen J. Christenson, a student of Linda Schele, has mastered the Quiches' dialect of the Mayan, one of thirty Mayan dialects, and has undertaken the ten year task of translating the Popol Vuh. In 2003 his work was published. His translation has been heralded by fellow scholars worldwide. I have read the Popol Vuh translations in Spanish and in English. What Professor Christenson has accomplished is a miracle. He has captured the poetry and the parallelism of the language. The significance is profound as it relates to the Book of Mormon.

Some languages use poetry to rhyme ideas the way other languages rhyme words. In English there is a strong bias for the rhyming of words in love songs and poetry.

> Roses are red,
> violets are blue,
> Sugar is sweet,
> and so are you.

In ancient languages one looks for the rhyming of *ideas* instead of words. For example, most of the Psalms and Proverbs are the rhyming of ideas.

> Let us sing unto the Lord:
> let us make a joyful noise (Psalms 95:1).

That which rhymes is the *idea* of "sing" and "joyful noise." In spite of these words being translated from Hebrew to English, the original Hebrew still rhymes ideas as opposed to rhyming words. There are a few languages that use both poetry and parallelism. Ancient Egyptian, Hebrew, and Mayan use these linguistic tools to aid in memory retention and to convey power and magnitude, and so does the Book of Mormon. If the Book of Mormon is a translation of an ancient text, as it claims to be, by Hebrew speaking people who used a Reformed Egyptian writing style, then finding poetry and parallelism would be expected. Imagine the challenge of an unlearned Joseph Smith at age twenty-four being able to convert the entire Book of Mormon into a poetic format.

Though scholars differ in their delineating and categorizing of the types of parallelisms, I have found it helpful to look at four types of parallelisms.

An Example of Hebrew Parallelisms

1. Repeat the same idea as line "one" but in different words.
   Line One: The heavens declare the glory of God;
   Line Two: ...the firmament sheweth his handiwork (Psalms 19:1).

2. Contrast an opposing idea to line "one."
Line One: For the Lord knoweth the way of the righteous:
Line Two: but the way of the ungodly shall perish (Psalms 1:6).

3. Complete the idea of line "one."
Line One: Yea, though I walk through the valley of the shadow of death, I will fear no evil:
Line Two: for thou art with me; thy rod and thy staff they comfort me (Psalms 23:4).

4. Various Chiastic expressions, A B C-C B A; etc.
Line One: Make the *heart* of this people fat, ... [A]
Line Two: and make their *ears* heavy, ... [B]
Line Three: and shut their *eyes;* .... [C]
Line Four: lest [perhaps] they see with their *eyes,* [C]
Line Five: and hear with their *ears,* .... [B]
Line Six: and understand with their *heart* , ... [A] (Isaiah 6:10).

An Example of Egyptian Poetry Parallelism

Notice the parallelism in this 1160 B.C. ancient Egyptian poem translated by J.L Foster:

The Egyptian Harper's Song for Inherkhawy
So *seize the day!* hold holiday! [A]
Be unwearied, unceasing, alive you and your own true love; [B]
Let not the heart be troubled during your sojourn on Earth, [B]
but *seize the day* as it passes! [A][130]

An Example of Mayan Poetry and Parallelism:

Creation of the First Humans
Creation began with a declaration of the first words . [A]
The sky is in suspense ... earth is *submerged in water.* [B]
The creation is to be under the direction of *Its Heart Sky.* [C]
The creation of all things begun. .... [D]
the *creation of Earth.* .... [E]
The creation of mountains. .... [F]
The *division of the waters* into branches. .... [G]
Merely *divided* then existed *waters,* .... [G]
then were revealed *great mountains* .... [F]
Thus its *creation earth* this, ... [E]
Then it was *created by them* .... [D]
Its Heart Sky, [who first conceived the creation] .... [C]
set apart the sky; ...set apart also *earth within water,* [B]
Thus its conception this ... when they pondered. ... [A][131]

An Example of Book of Mormon Poetry and Parallelism

"Wherefore, redemption cometh in and through the Holy Messiah; for he is full of grace and truth. Behold, he offereth himself a

sacrifice for sin, to *answer* . [A]
the *ends of the law,* . . . . . . [B]
unto *all those,* . . . . [C]
who have a broken heart . . [D]
and a contrite spirit; . . . . . [D]
and unto *none else* . . . . [C]
can the *ends of the law* . . . . [B]
be *answered* . . . . [A]
(2 Nephi 2:7, emphasis added.)

For those who want greater depth, the book by Donald Parry entitled, *The Book of Mormon Text Reformatted, according to Parallelistic Patterns* published by FARMS is a worthy work. Parry points out that "three hundred examples of chiasmus exist in the Book of Mormon."[132]

There are many other literary considerations of which poetry and parallelism are but two. Wade Brown and others have done extensive work on "Word Print Analysis." This is a type of *word* fingerprinting of the author. It examines frequency of words used, vocabulary, and idiomatic expressions. It is an exciting study and an intellectually stimulating experience. Word Print Analysis reinforces the reality that Joseph Smith translated the Book of Mormon and not authored it.

Book of Mormon Word Print Studies, Word Print Analysis

Noel Reynolds, the president of The Foundation for Ancient Research and Mormon Studies (FARMS), presented a lecture at a BYU Devotional entitled *The Authorship of the Book of Mormon* on May 27, 1997. He gave the following overview of word print studies:

> In the 1982 authorship volume, Wayne A. Larsen and Alvin C. Rencher, BYU professors of statistics, presented the first comprehensive statistical word print study of the Book of Mormon. Using computerized text and powerful statistical techniques, they were able to establish that the different sections of the Book of Mormon were authored by different people and that none was authored by Joseph Smith, Sidney Rigdon, Oliver Cowdrey, or other 19th-century candidates put forth by Book of Mormon critics. Applied physicist John L. Hilton and five of his fellow scientists in the Bay Area (three of them non-LDS) repeated that study using a wholly different and more conservative form of word printing analysis. Again, different authors were detected, and none corresponded to the nineteenth century candidates. Also, in retirement as an adjunct

> professor of statistics at BYU, Hilton has used his techniques to identify anonymous writings of the seventeenth century philosopher Thomas Hobbes to show which of Francis Bacon's works were authored chiefly by his staff of secretaries. Hilton even used these same techniques to help the FBI identify possible authors of the Unabomber's Manifesto.[133]

The point being that Joseph Smith was a nineteenth century writer with an English bias and orientation. All of Joseph Smith's letters, correspondence, and other writings demonstrated that English propensity. The Book of Mormon, as an ancient script which he translated, was written in a style that is more consistent with Hebrew and Egyptian than English. It would have been impossible in the amount of time Joseph had, and at his tender age of twenty-four, to write the Book of Mormon without formal training in multiple Hebraic styles of writing. Hebrew is a revived language. Most of what we now know about Hebrew writing, parallelisms, repetitions, similes, metaphors, and chiastic expression emerged long after the death of Joseph Smith in 1844. In looking at the evidence from a literary, linguistic, and historic perspective, the Book of Mormon represents a work consistent with its claim to be an ancient writing.

A Record Keeping People

In the beginning of the Book of Mormon is a separate section called "The Testimony of Three Witnesses," and "The Testimony of Eight Witnesses." Eleven men in all were shown the plates from which the Book of Mormon was translated, in addition to Joseph Smith. In the testimony of the eight men, there is a specific reference to the plates of the Book of Mormon having the appearance of "gold."

> Be it known unto all nations, kindreds, tongues, and people, unto whom this work shall come: That Joseph Smith, Jun., the translator of this work, has shown unto us the plates of which hath been spoken, which have the *appearance of gold*; and as many of the leaves as the said Smith has translated we did handle with our hands; and we also saw the engravings thereon, all of which has the appearance of ancient work, and of curious workmanship. And this we bear record with words of soberness, that the said Smith has shown unto us, for *we have seen and hefted*, and know of a surety that the said Smith has got the plates of which we have spoken. And we give our names unto the world, to witness unto the world that which we have seen. And we lie not, God bearing witness of it.[134]

The early detractors of Joseph Smith referred to the Book of Mormon as Joe Smith's Golden Bible. A local newspaper in Palmyra, New York, called the *Palmyra Reflector* printed a six-part series titled "Gold Bible." The articles appeared from January 6, 1831 to March 19, 1831. The term "Gold Bible" was intended to be a derogatory one. The phrase caught on and eventually attracted the attention of scholars. One of the earliest criticisms of the Book of Mormon was to ridicule the idea that anyone would engrave history upon gold plates, or brass plates, or any kind of metal plates. More than a hundred years would pass before the 1933 discoveries of the ancient gold tablets were found in the ruins of the palace of the Persian, King Darius. The gold tablets were written on thin gold sheets and dated to 500 B.C. (All of a sudden it was no longer impossible that Father Lehi could have obtained a record written upon metal plates in Jerusalem that dated to 600 B.C.) In 1952, two bronze or copper scrolls were discovered in a cave near the Dead Sea. The scrolls dated to about A.D. 50. The ancient peoples of the Near East wrote upon metal plates of gold and copper.[135]

Mesoamericans Wrote Upon Thin Gold Plates

At the beginning of this chapter is a picture of one of the thin gold plates found in Mesoamerica. The archaeologist, Edward Herbert Thompson was best known for dredging Chichen Itzá's sacred cenoté in 1904. Among his finds were human sacrifice victims, obsidian knives, vases, jewelry, and seven thin gold plates with pictographic and hieroglyphic writing upon them. They are often referred to in the literature as gold discs. These precious finds were smuggled out of Mexico via diplomatic pouches to the Peabody Museum in Boston, where they currently reside. The translation of this particular gold plate has been rendered as follows, "*All the nations were to be sacrificed before him. Their hearts were to be carved out from beneath their shoulders and armpits.*"[136]

The Book of Mormon claimed the Lamanites abandoned the spiritual symbolic message of the Savior and replaced it with idol worship The irony was their acceptance of literalism over symbolism. The above translation of the gold plate from the cenoté at Chichen Itzá is a sad example of apostasy. It is not a stretch at all to suggest that the Book of Mormon teaching was symbolic. *All the nations were to sacrifice before him a broken heart and a contrite spirit*" (See 2 Nephi 2:7).[137] This doctrine of a broken heart is mentioned nine times in the Book of Mormon. This is a figurative expression inviting humble and teachable souls to come unto Christ. A literal interpretation of a broken heart is to break the heart by carving it out of the chest and offering it unto their idol gods.

There have been several tombs in which thin gold plates have been found in Mesoamerica. In 1932 Alfonso Caso discovered at Oaxaca, Mexico numerous thin gold plates in the famous tomb #7 at Monte Alban.[138] These discoveries of thin gold plates at Chichen Itzá, Mexico and at Oaxaca establish the practice of Mesoamericans using gold as one of the mediums for recording sacred writings. Moroni writing on thin gold plates as a Mesoamerican scribe of sacred texts was well within the norm. More importantly, it identified Moroni as a Mesoamerican scribe.

Moroni buried in Palmyra, New York the abridgment containing the Book of Mormon which was written upon thin gold plates from Mesoamerica. Members of the Church believe this very man, Moroni, came back as an angel.

He instructed the young Joseph Smith for four years with various visits and visions to prepare him to translate the Book of Mormon. Moroni told Joseph that the book was "written upon gold plates, giving an account of the former inhabitants of this continent..."[139]

The "Testimony of the Eight Witnesses," bears repeating. They reported:

> Joseph Smith, Jun., the translator of this work, has shown unto us the plates... *which have the appearance of gold;*...we did handle with our hands; and we also saw the engravings... for we have seen and hefted, and know of a surety that the said Smith has got the plates...[140]

It is clear more people other than Joseph Smith saw the gold plates from which Joseph translated the Book of Mormon. The immediate reaction of many skeptics, then and now, is to dismiss these testimonies as some type of conspiracy theory. Mark Twain called the Book of Mormon "a pretentious affair."[141] Dismissing the Book of Mormon as a conspiracy does not explain how Joseph Smith identified correctly dozens and dozens of historical facts which were not known until decades after his death.

Gold Records and Stone Boxes in Mesoamerica

Of the many claims of the Book of Mormon, the one that seemed the most absurd and outrageous was that the ancient inhabitants of this continent engraved on plates of gold and stored them in stone boxes. Later scholars would acknowledge, "Yes, the Persians did engrave their writing upon gold plates and stored them in stone boxes, but not on the American continent" would be their cry. Without belaboring the point of how many stone boxes have been discovered in Mesoamerica, suffice it to say there are numerous stone boxes on display in the National Museum in Mexico City. A recently discovered stone box, dated from A.D. 485 to A.D. 550 , was on display in a museum in Guatemala until it was stolen in May 2006.[142]

The sarcophagus of Pacal at Palenque is a huge stone box. Several stone boxes were found among the Olmec in Tres Zapotes, Vera Cruz, Mexico[143] near the proposed Hill Ramah/Cumorah. That is of particular interest because Moroni would have constructed a box composed of stone and cement in New York where he deposited the plates and other precious items. Archaeologist Paul Cheesman noted

> Prior to 1823, when Joseph Smith first gazed upon the stone box containing the plates, no record had been found describing any type of stone box from any ancient period. Only in recent years have archaeologists confirmed the idea that this method of storing valuable articles was commonly used in ancient cultures.[144]

Stone boxes such as the one above which dates to the time of Moroni, are typical of Mesoamerican stone boxes used to store ancient records and artifacts.

Figure 27. Mesoamerican Stone Box
Dating to the time of Moroni

What Happened to the Other Gold Plates in Mesoamerica?

The Spanish obsession with gold became a wholesale disregard for culture and human life. They took gold from the teeth of the slain and anywhere they could find it. For a hundred years the smelters and mines burned night and day to satiate the greed of Europe. They melted down every piece of gold they found, unless its value as a treasure exceeded its value as an ingot. If the Spaniards found any gold plates or gold records, they melted them down and sent them to Spain as ingots.

Apparently they did not get all the gold. Some gold plates managed to survive; seven of them. The gold plates lay hidden in the Sacred Well, the cenoté, at Chichen Itzá, Yucatan, Mexico. The fact that gold plates exist as claimed by Joseph Smith validates one more claim of the Book of Mormon, as a historically correct text.

Mesoamericans wrote on bones, on jade, on paper made from the bark of trees, on temples, on tombs. They wrote on thin gold plates and on monuments of stone. Dzibilchaltun is the name given by the Maya to the ruins located in the very northwest corner of the Yucatan. The literal translation of Dzibilchaltun is "The Place of Writing upon Stone." This ancient city was inhabited from 600 B.C. to the time of the Spanish conquest in the late 1500s. Mesoamerica is a repository of thousands of engraved stones from the Atlantic to the Pacific oceans. Near the present day city of Tapachula in Mexico's southwestern corner are the ruins of Izapa. Here is where the famous to Mormons "Tree of Life" stone is found. Because there are so many of these engraved stones at each location, they are numbered. The "Tree of Life" stone is referred to as Stela #5. A stela is an upright engraved stone.

Figure 28. Tree of Life Stela #5 Found at Izapa, Mexico, near Lehi's Land of First Inheritance

What is astounding is to realize that less than two percent of all the known sites in Mesoamerica have been unearthed. What other evidences await discovery in the ninety eight percent that will continue to confirm the Book of Mormon as a true record? Not all societies engraved their histories upon gold plates, copper plates, brass plates, or metal plates of any kind. Many cultures lacked a written language at all. Far more common is to find an illiterate society with idols of gold, silver, wood, or stone. Finding idols with hieroglyphic engravings is a sign of an advanced civilization.

Engraving Upon Stone

Figure 29. Stela F at Quiriguá, Guatemala
Another Catherwood Drawing seen by Joseph Smith

Above is a picture of the famous twenty-three feet high Stela F. It carries the equivalent date of A.D. March 15, 761. It was found at Quiriguá, Guatemala. Notice the man standing by the base of the large engraved stone.[145]

The quote from Omni in the Book of Mormon dates to about 200 B.C. Stela F was still a half of a millennium away from being carved. Stela F was one very large stone monument among many in a tradition of stone carving going back hundreds of years before the Christian era. The evidence of the most ancient carvers of large stones in Mesoamerica belongs to the Olmecs.

The Mysterious Olmec

The Olmec are called the Mother Culture of the Americas. The Olmecs are the authors of the massive stone colossal heads. These heads measure nine feet tall and weigh many tons.

Figure 30. Dr. John L. Lund standing by an Olmec Stone Carved Head

So that people don't become confused, I like to point out that the Olmec head is the big one on the left. This particular Olmec head was found near San Lorenzo, Mexico. More than twenty-two such colossal heads have now been unearthed, which demonstrated the ability of the Olmec to be great stone workers.

The stones the Olmecs carved date to the times claimed by the Book of Mormon. There were large engraved stones with historical hieroglyphic writings on them at the time and the place where the Book of Mormon said they would be. Among the Olmec ruins are found the oldest stone carvings. Harvard graduate and Yale professor, Michael Coe speaks of the Olmecs as the very first Native Americans to

> ...achieve such a high level of social, cultural, and artistic complexity, it would not be stretching a word to call them "civilized." This level was reached three thousand years ago.... In the very hot, very wet, tropical lowlands of the Mexican states of Veracruz and Tabasco, amid a tangle of rivers, swamps, high jungle, and savannas, they built their great temple centers and carved huge stone monuments. It was there that the New World's first civilization arose.[146]

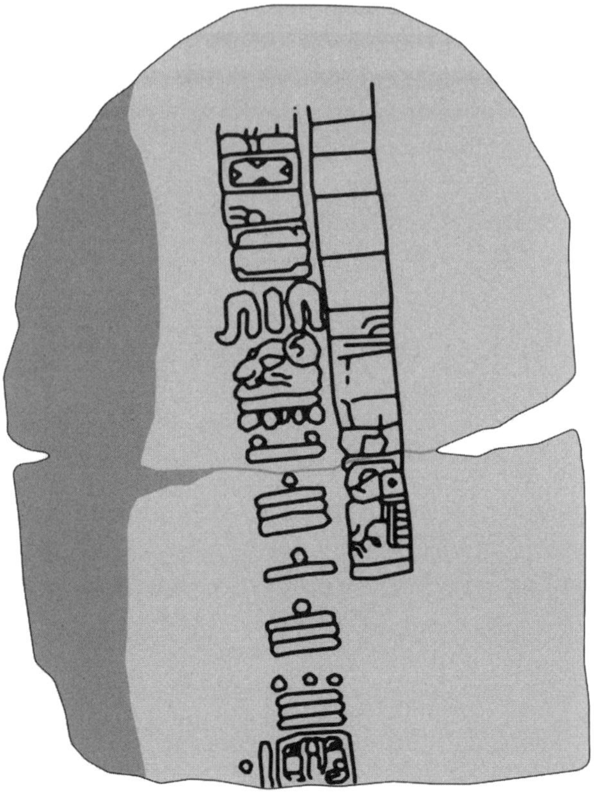

Figure 31. Stela C from Tres Zapotes, Vera Cruz, Mexico, Olmec Hieroglyphic Writing found in Mesoamerica

The Olmecs had hieroglyphic writings on stone dating to the time of the Book of Mormon. Their dominate culture lasted from 2200 B.C to the time of the Spanish conquest. The Olmecs as a people were destroyed and/or assimilated around 300 B.C. However, their influence survived. They were given the credit for inspiring the oldest calendars in the Americas. Stela C is one of the ancient Olmec artifacts using the long count calendar system. The date which appears is 7.16.6.16.18 (September 3, 32 B.C., Julian calendar). The glyphs surrounding the date are some of the few surviving examples of Hieroglyphic Epi-Olmec script.[147] Although the Olmec numbering system has been determined, their hieroglyphic writing has not yet been deciphered. The Olmec, as mentioned, are the best candidates for the Jaredites in the Book of Mormon. There is no question that the Zapotec and Mayan societies were influenced by the Olmec.

Sometime near 200 B.C. the Book of Mormon records that a large stone with engravings on it like unto Stela C above was brought to a Prophet King referred to as Mosiah.

> And it came to pass in the days of Mosiah, there was a large stone brought unto him with engravings on it; and he did interpret the engravings by the gift and power of God (Omni 1:20).

The very beautiful and artistic round zoomorphic stones of the Maya have their tradition in the stone carvings of the Olmec. A large round stone like the one found at Quiriguá, Guatemala, but much older, would have been brought to King Mosiah.

Figure 32. Large Round Stone from Quiriguá, Guatemala
Approximately 8 ft. by 8 ft. by 6 ft. in height

When Joseph Smith read the report of Stephens about "a large round stone with sides sculptured in hieroglyphics..."[148] he said the following:

> It is certainly a good thing for the excellency and veracity, of the divine authenticity of the Book of Mormon, that the ruins of Zarahemla have been found where the Nephites left them: and that a large stone with engravings upon it, as Mosiah said; and a '*large round* stone, with the sides sculptures in hieroglyphics,' as Mr. Stephens published, is also among the left remembrances of the, (to him,) *lost and unknown*.... when the land and the stones, and the books tell the story so plain ... It will not be a bad plan to compare Mr. Stephens' ruined cities with those in the Book of Mormon...[149]

Taken within the context of a Joseph Smith in 1830, the above relationships between the Book of Mormon and the large engraved stones of the Olmecs are remarkable. They can not be dismissed with impunity. Appreciate Joseph Smith's assertion in 1830 of a high civilization in America complete with a hieroglyphic writing system engraved upon large stones. The stones and engraved monuments seen today are ruins built atop ruins of a later time period than the Book of

Mormon. These stones, however, were influenced by the Olmecs who do date to the times of the Book of Mormon.

Imagine the ridicule and mocking one would be subjected to if he or she were to predict that when men landed on the planet Mars they would discover a high civilization complete with a hieroglyphic writing system engraved upon large stones. Projecting into the future a hundred years, assume the reaction of the people on earth when the astronauts verified the claim of hieroglyphic writings on stone on Mars and sent back pictures of an extinct three thousand year old civilization. What conclusions would be drawn about the author's credibility then? This is the position Joseph Smith is in today. Large engraved stones with hieroglyphic writing upon them are facts and not assertions.

The angel Moroni advised the seventeen-year-old Joseph that his name would be spoken of for both good and evil among all nations, kindreds, and tongues around the world.[150] According to official LDS sources as of October 2005, the Book of Mormon has been fully translated into seventy-six languages, and selections of it have been translated into twenty-nine additional languages for a total of one hundred five languages since it was first published in 1830. The printed copies have totaled nearly one hundred twenty million.[151] In spite of concrete evidence, Joseph Smith's name will continue to be spoken of for good and evil. Ultimately, of course, it is not about concrete evidence. It is about "heavenly evidence and earthly remains." Joseph said he was not the author of the Book of Mormon, but he was the translator.

The book by Stephens and the drawings by Catherwood revealed concrete evidence of high civilization in Mesoamerica. The lost worlds of the Maya and the Olmec were brought back to life. With the discovery of the recent Olmecian stone, epigraphers may soon be able to decipher one of the world's oldest hieroglyphic languages.

From Writing on Stones to Writing on Codices: "Unfold the Scriptures"

While anxiously waiting for the translation of the Olmec, scholars have engaged in serious historical analysis of the Maya. Obviously not all Mesoamerican records were engraved on thin gold plates. The most common form of Mayan writing involved "screen folds" or folded manuscripts made from "amate" or the barks of various trees. A screen fold is also referred to as a codex. By far, the most common historical document was the codex. The writings on the codices were "Ideographic" and considered sacred by the Mesoamericans. These manuscripts were family histories and contained the genealogies of many generations. They would be passed on in a patriarchal father to son tradition. These codices were joined together in an accordion like fashion and could be easily added to or lengthened by adjoining more pages.

When unfolded some codices reached lengths of forty-eight feet. When folded together, they were easily stored and carried about as a book. In addition to their marriages and their offspring, these codices recorded their wars and the names of their conquered foes. A typical symbol of a conquered city or village was a mound of dirt with a spear in it. The names and dates of each battle were meticulously copied, as were the names and birthdates of family heroes. A noble family might also possess a codex which was highly religious in nature and would tell of the origin of man, animals, and the cosmology of the universe. It would include man's relationship to the gods as well as prayers and psalms. Some religious codices had content similar to the Popol Vuh and the Bible.

One of the great tragedies in human history is book burning. It happened in Nazi Germany, the barbarian conquest of Rome, and was mentioned in the Book of Mormon. "...and they also brought forth their records which contained the holy scriptures, and cast them into the fire..." (Alma 14:8). The later book burning of the Mexican Inquisition was only an extension of the Spanish Inquisition. For scholars the greatest tragedy was the almost complete eradication of the Mesoamerican codices by a fanatical Franciscan Bishop named Diego de Landa. He personally ordered the destruction of every manuscript he and his priests found among the Maya. Huge bon fires consumed hundreds, if not thousands, of records. On July 12, 1562 de Landa personally supervised the destruction of over five thousand codices and artifacts.[152] Only a handful of these codices are known to have survived and are now identified by the name of the city in which they reside; i.e., The Madrid Codex, The Dresden Codex, The Paris Codex, The Vienna I, II codices. Some are known by the person who found them or cataloged them; i.e. Codex Laud, Codex Bodley, and Codex Selden are all at Oxford. Codex Becker and Codex Sanchez Solis are in London's British museum. Codex Colombino is in Mexico City. Codex Fejervary-Mayer is at Liverpool. Codex Cospi is at Bologne, while Codex Borgia and Codex Vaticanus B are in Rome.

It is believed that one of the two codices sent to Charles V by Cortés in 1519 was the Codex Mixtec, now known as the Codex Nuttall. There may be a few more hidden in museums or still buried in jars, stone boxes, or caves waiting to be discovered.

Codices are to be read from back to front and from right to left, just the way Egyptian or Hebrew would be read. Joseph Smith said the Book of Mormon was read from back to front and from right to left.[153] One can read codices a single page at a time or unfold several pages for a more panoramic view. In Alma 12:1, Alma and Amulek "unfold the scriptures...." This is exactly how one opens a Mayan codex: it is unfolded.

How do these codices relate to the Book of Mormon? It is evidence of a written language. It is evidence of Mesoamericans using a pictographic and ideographic writing style. Like the Book of Mormon these records are considered sacred and they contain a history of the family to whom they belong, their wars, marriage alliances, and their religious beliefs. They were passed down from father to son.

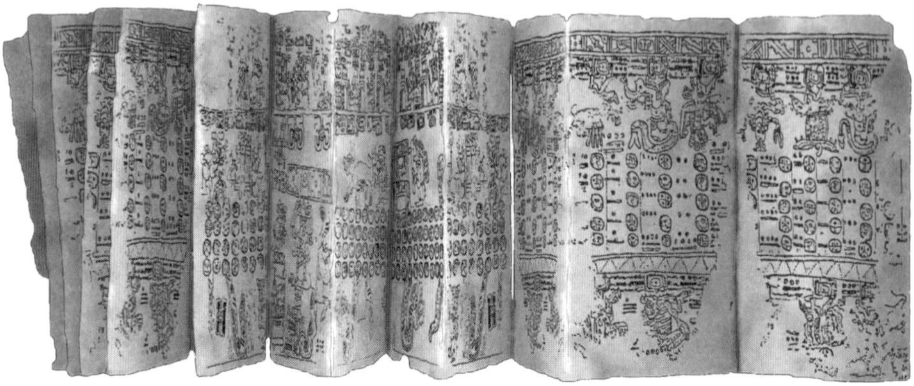

Figure 33. A Mayan Codex

Of the surviving codices and written artifacts none were dated before A.D. 900 until several recent finds. The surviving samples were so small it was difficult to estimate their date of origin. However, all the new evidences coming from El Mirador and other sources keep pushing Maya civilization to an earlier and earlier date. The same is true of the Olmec. The National Science Foundation in a news release dated December 9, 2002 reported:

> The discovery of a fist-sized ceramic cylinder and fragments of engraved plaques has pushed back the earliest evidence of writing in the Americas by at least three 350 years to 650 BC.…Archaeologists uncovered the cylinder and fingernail-sized fragments among debris from an ancient festival at San Andres, an Olmec town on the coastal plain of the Mexican state of Tabasco.[154]

CHAPTER SEVEN

DEMOGRAPHICS AND A HIGHLY STRUCTURED SOCIETY

Figure 34. Reconstruction View of El Mirador

Demography: Millions of People?

Demographics is the study of populations. The Book of Mormon speaks of millions of people living in a relatively small area and of wars of annihilation on a massive scale. In one prolonged war of several years, two million people were destroyed on one side alone (Ether 15:2). What does the academic community who has studied the demographics of Mesoamerica during the time period of the Book of Mormon have to report on the size of the population? Some estimates of the zenith of Mesoamerican populations start at eleven million. Yale professor of archeology, Michael Coe commented on recent discoveries one half of all Maya houses being missed by "archaeological surface surveys."

> What this means is that we may have to double our previous population estimates for the Central Area, which already run into the many millions.[155]

For Joseph Smith in 1830 to suggest that millions of people inhabited North America was one more absurd assertion of the Book of Mormon according to the people at the Smithsonian. In 1928, nearly a hundred years after the publication of the Book of Mormon, "James Mooney, distinguished ethnographer at the Smithsonian, combed through colonial writings and government documents to conclude that in 1491 North America had 1.15 million inhabitants."[156] Once again the Smithsonian scientists were wrong, dead wrong. By 1950, Sherburne F. Cook, a physiologist, and historian Woodrow W. Borah from Berkeley made an exhaustive study of pre-Columbian North America.

> When Columbus landed, Cook and Borah concluded, the central Mexican plateau alone had a population of 25.2 million. By contrast, Spain and Portugal together had fewer than ten million inhabitants. Central Mexico, they said, was the most densely populated place on earth, with more than twice as many people per square mile than China or India ... Another way of saying this is that when Columbus sailed more people lived in the Americas than in Europe.[157]

Dr. John E. Clark, a BYU professor of archeology addressed the issue of demographics in Mesoamerica:

> Could millions of people have lived in the area proposed as Book of Mormon lands? Yes, and they did. Mesoamerica is the only area in the Americas that sustained the high population densities mentioned in the Book of Mormon, and for the times specified.[158]

After Columbus and the Europeans arrived, the populations of North and South America were devastated by European diseases. However, prior to Columbus the decline of populations in Mesoamerica was the result of civil wars and the concomitant woes of famine and pestilence. Coe asserts

> We know from the downfall of past civilizations such as the Romans and Khmer empires that it is fruitless to look for single causes. However, most Maya archaeologists now agree that three factors were paramount in the [pre-Columbian] downfall: 1) endemic internecine warfare, 2) overpopulation and the accompanying environmental collapse, and 3) drought. All three probably played a part, but not necessarily all together in the same time and in the same place. Warfare seems to have become a real problem earlier than the other two.[159]

The Prophets in the Book of Mormon prophesied long before Michael Coe that destruction would come by similar means: "by famine, and by pestilence, and by the sword [war]" (Alma 10:22). The 1830 publication of the Book of Mormon would make Joseph Smith as wise, informed, and accurate as

Mesoamerican scholars of today regarding demographics and, among other things, the reasons for the demise of the Mesoamerican cultures.

Drought is almost always followed by famine as seen in the Book of Mormon. When the rains were withheld and the people were dying by the thousands, the Prophet Nephi prayed:

> O Lord, thou canst bless them according to thy words ... the Lord did turn away his anger from the people, and caused that the rain should fall upon the earth, insomuch that it did bring forth her fruit in the season of her fruit. And it came to pass that it did bring forth her grain in the season of her grain (Helaman 11:16-17).

On the number one issue of war as the major destroyer of civilization on the American continent there is complete agreement between the scholars and the Book of Mormon.

The Great Lakes and Palmyra, New York Demographics

Demographics in a six hundred fifty mile radius of Palmyra, New York during the 600 B.C. to A.D. 401 time frame are void of any populations approaching fifty thousand, much less millions. The five tribes of the Iroquois Nations, according to a 1995 study by Mann and Fields using a combination of documentary sources, solar eclipse data, and Iroquois oral history, claim August 31, 1142 as the ratification of the Iroquois Confederacy.[160] Later in 1722, the Tuscarawas would join the Confederacy and make it the six tribes. The estimated population of the original combined five tribes was less than twenty thousand:

> The Lamoka period, classified in the archaic or hunting, fishing, gathering stage, can be traced back to 3500-1300 B.C.; the Woodland State, which deals with the development of ceramics, agriculture and village life, can be traced to 1000 B.C – A.D. 1600.

> Cultures of the Archaic stage in the Northeast give evidence of mobility, small-band organization, and simple social structuring. Most of the sites are small and show no trace of larger dwellings, fortifications, storage pits, and even graves.

> The Lamoka culture became known though the excavations of the Rochester Museum, begun by Ritchie in 1925, on the Lamoka Lake site in Tyrone ... The original homeland of the Iroquois was in upstate New York between the Adirondack Mountains and Niagara Falls. Through conquest and migration, they gained control of most of the northeastern United States and eastern Canada. The Iroquois did not, however, for the most part, physically occupy this vast area but remained in their upstate New York villages ... Surprisingly, the Iroquois population was not that large. It is believed that in 1600 there were less than 20,000 for all five tribes. By 1650, the spread inland of

> European epidemics and warfare had cut their population in half. The adoption of conquered enemies, such as 7,000 Huron, led to an estimated total of about 25,000 Iroquois in 1660. [161]

There is no historical evidence that the Native North America population in and around the Great Lakes regions, including Palmyra, New York, ever approached even fifty thousand at any historical or pre-historical time period. The land did not sustain an agricultural lifestyle, nor were the people primarily an agrarian society. The Native Americans of this region were primarily dependent upon hunting and fishing. Their lifestyle was nomadic and migratory as they followed the game and moved within the boundaries of their hunting grounds.

Contrast the nature of a city state in Mesoamerica with that of the nomadic Native Americans. It would be similar to the contrast which exists today between the Bedouins of the Mideast and modern day Amman, Jordan or Damascus, Syria. Contrast the Mesoamerican type of highly stratified society with the nomadic culture of the Native North American with which Joseph Smith was most acquainted. The nomadic lifestyle did not involve building city-states. There were no masons and architects. Tents and travel, hunting and fishing, summer camps and winter camps were the characteristics of the Native Americans. Living off the land as hunters and gatherers and moving about in a large territory was the tribal way of life. Their political structure involved chiefs, not kings; medicine men and shamans chanted their prayers, not a priestly hierarchy. There were no epistles sent in hieroglyphic script and no temples and tombs. There were, instead, notches carved on sticks and burial mounds. The northern Native Americans and their lifestyles were appropriate for the nomad. In spite of modern day critics, the Native Americans were the best of environmentalists and lived in harmony with the earth.

As previously established, all of North America was perceived by nineteenth century historians as being a nomadic society. The Book of Mormon's claim of city states existing on the North American continent has been verified by modern archeological evidence; all of which was unknown by the young prophet, Joseph Smith living in upstate New York in 1830. Accompanying the claims of sophisticated city states by the Book of Mormon were the equally preposterous assertions for 1830 that a highly stratified society occupied the land of the Book of Mormon.

What is Known Today About the People Who Lived in Mesoamerica at the Time of The Book of Mormon?

The ancient inhabitants of Mesoamerica were not nomads. The people were city builders. Pre-classic Maya or the Book of Mormon era was also a time of a highly structured, highly diversified, and sophisticated civilization in Mesoamerica. The evidence of this was found in tomb drawings, pottery, temple structures, carved monuments, codices, hieroglyphic texts, and figurines like those shown in the National Museum of Anthropology in Mexico City, Mexico. Kaminaljuyu, Tikal, and El Mirador in Guatemala, Lamanai in Belize, and other Maya sites illustrated a high level of social structure from 500 B.C. According to the Mesoamerican archaeologist Robert Sharer, the Olmecs demonstrated a highly developed social structure. He reports that "around 1200 B.C., the Olmecs had developed a theocratic chiefdom. In this system a complex society is managed by an elite class."[162]

Mesoamerican City States

In Linda Schele's book, *The Code of Kings*, she explained the high degree of societal sophistication the Mesoamerican civilization had achieved. She mentioned sixty city states, their system of kings, priests and nobles, the paying of taxes and tribute, the organization of warrior cults of Jaguars and of Eagles, of merchants who were also spies, of a people who built towers, temples, tombs, and sepulchers. She explained their high civilization and their hieroglyphic writing, their accurate calendars and ability to map the starry universe. In summary, she spoke of all the things represented in the Book of Mormon as being a part of Mesoamerica.[163] The Book of Mormon claims that the entire Land of Nephi and the Land of Zarahemla were covered with city states ruled by kings, priests, and judges (3 Nephi 6:7-8, Alma 50:1).

The Land of Nephi is simply the geographical territory belonging to the City State of Nephi. The size of the territory of a city-state depended on the ability of the local ruler to defend it. Alliances were formed with kingdoms of equal power by marriage or truce agreements. There could be several fortified cities, numerous unfortified cities, various large villages, and a multitude of hamlets all belonging to the city-state of the Land of Nephi or the dominant city state. Smaller city states were often vassals to a larger and more powerful city state than themselves. The kings of the vassal states owed allegiance to the larger city state. Almost always, they had to pay a tribute to the greater king. Gold, silver, copper, jade, obsidian, cocoa beans and even slaves were paid as tribute by conquered city-states. Smaller city-states contributed men and supplies to the larger and more powerful city-state to strengthen their armies in times of war.

From the internal description of an invasion given in the Book of Mormon, the first to be attacked were the shepherds. They fled from the edge of the wilderness where they tended the flocks and herds, across the agricultural fields to within the walls of the city (Mosiah 9:14-5). The king gave the people weapons from an armory and the people were quickly organized into an army with captains of tens, hundreds and a chief captain. The king was expected to lead the army into battle.

Frequently when there were two very large and very powerful city states, the surrounding smaller ones had to choose which one they were going to support. Smaller city-states rebelled when they perceived that larger ones were weak or unable to enforce their dominance. Two of the largest city-states that existed during the Maya pre-classic time of the Book of Mormon in Mesoamerica were Kaminaljuyu in the highlands of Guatemala, where present day Guatemala City is located, and El Mirador, which is situated in the lowlands of the Peten in the Yucatan. El Mirador is an active archeological site which is rendering regular insights into the lives of the classic and pre-classic times of the Maya. Linda Schele said,

> There were many other city states flourishing at this same time, such as Lamanai located on the New River in present day Belize. Eventually, there were as many as sixty city-states among the Maya.[164]

Highly Stratified Society

The Book of Mormon describes a highly stratified society. There were kings (Mosiah 11:1). Sometimes the king was also the high priest; at times the king would consecrate his own priests (Mosiah 11:5). Nobles were "those of high birth" (Alma 51:8). There were lawyers (Alma 10:14), judges (Mosiah 29:11), the laboring class of poor (Alma 32:1-6), farmers (Mosiah 23:25), shepherds (Mosiah 9:14), merchants (3 Nephi 6:11), traders (Mosiah 24:7), slaves (Mosiah 7:15), artisans and craftsmen (2 Nephi 5:15), boat builders (Alma 63:5), stone engravers (Omni 1:20), masons (Alma 48:8), carpenters (Mosiah 11:8), cement workers (Helaman 3:11), road builders (3 Nephi 6:8), fishermen (Ether 2:2), and clothiers (1 Nephi 13:8). There were soldiers (Alma 51:9),

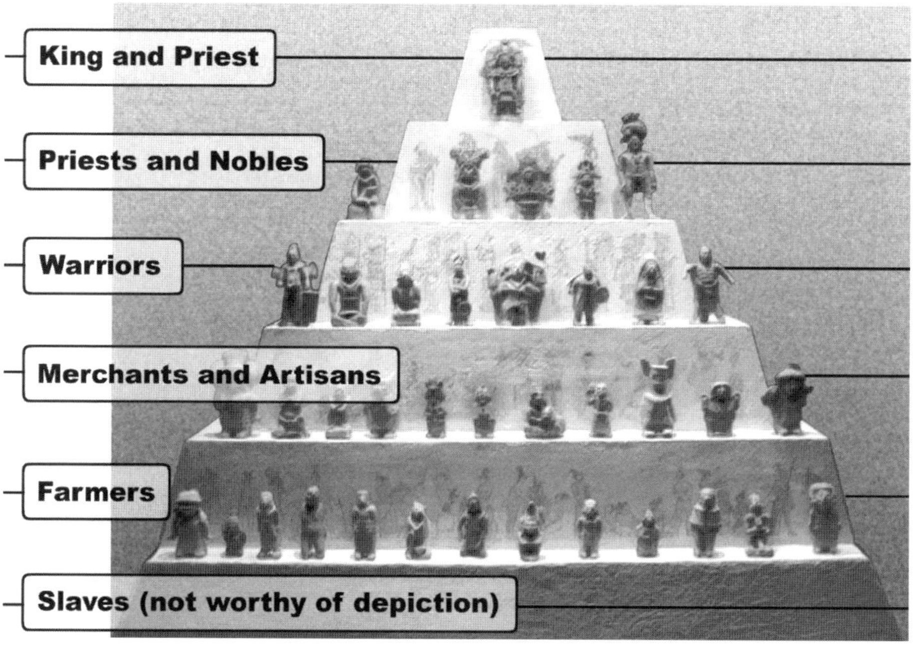

Figure 35. A Highly Stratified Society

a warrior class of captains (Alma 2:16), higher captains (Alma 2:13), and chief captains (Alma 16:5). There were wives which were monogamous (Jacob 2:27), wives which were polygamous (Mosiah 11:2), concubines (Mosiah 11:2), and harlots (Mosiah 11:14). There were miners (Ether 10:23), goldsmiths, coppersmiths, silversmiths (2 Nephi 5:15), jewelers and idol makers (Helaman 6:31), sorcerers, witches, and workers of magic (Mormon 1:19; 2:10), loggers (Helaman 3:5-10), spies (Alma 2:21), architects and temple builders (2 Nephi 5:16), tomb and sepulcher builders (Alma 19:5), and prophets (Alma 37:30). Most everything one would expect to find in a highly diversified society is mentioned in the Book of Mormon.

A caste system was prevalent in Mesoamerica with a highly stratified society. The Book of Mormon identified the time when the society "began to be divided into classes…" (4 Nephi 1:26). It was the year A.D. 201. Mesoamerican scholars mark the classic era of the Maya at A.D. 250. For the next one thousand years civil wars would dominate the landscape. Many empires would rise and fall. Totonacs, Maya, Toltecs, Zapotecs, Mixtecs, and many others tribes began to mix and blend.

Amalgamation and Assimilation of Various Cultures

Many groups who arrived in the Americas blended together over the centuries of time. Coexisting societies commingled. The known historical trends of amalgamation (blending) and assimilation (mixing) of various cultures may be the best key to unlocking the past in Mesoamerica. Mexico is a prime example of a racial and cultural melting pot over the past five hundred years. A Mestizo is a mix of Native American (also referred to as Amerindian) and European. The first documented Mestizos were the children of Gonzalo Guerrero and the Maya Princess Shell from Chetumal in the Yucatan after A.D. 1511. As an ethnic group, Mestizos constitute officially 75% to 90% of Mexico's current population of one hundred six million people. Many define the population by cultural traditions and not by the amount of racially mixed blood they may or may not have in their veins. This in fact is exactly the claim made by the Book of Mormon about the pre-Columbians as well. Lamanites and Nephites were identified by cultural and religious affiliation. Remember Zelph was referred to as a "white Lamanite."

As it pertains to amalgamation and assimilation, the Nephites tried to maintain a separate identity. As keepers of the Law of Moses, they were forbidden to marry outside of Israel (Deuteronomy 7:2). However, many of the Nephites became dissenters and joined with the Lamanites by marriage or war alliance; Amalickiah, the Amlicites, the Zoramites, and the wicked priests of King Noah to name a few. Amalickiah is a case in point:

> Amalickiah [a dissenting Nephite] sought the favor of the queen, [a Lamanite] and took her unto him to wife … yea, he was acknowledged king throughout all the land, among all the people of

> the Lamanites, who were composed of the Lamanites and the Lemuelites and the Ishmaelites, and all the dissenters of the Nephites down to the present time (Alma 47:35).

The Amlicites were another group of dissenting Nephites. They are an interesting study (Alma 3:4). They began to mark themselves with red in their foreheads after the manner of the Lamanites. They rejected the Nephite ways and adopted the customs and traditions of another culture, i.e., assimilation.

The Lamanites themselves had most likely assimilated into the surrounding cultures. They abandoned all vestiges of their Israelite heritage and embraced idol worship and human sacrifice (Mormon 4:14, 21). These practices were known to have existed in Mesoamerica prior to the arrival of the Lehites or the Mulekites. Because of the rapid growth in population among the Lamanites, many have assumed that the Lamanites intermarried with coexisting polygamous cultures and amalgamated with idol worshipping societies in Mesoamerica. They also pursued a war of extermination against the Nephites which was to last for centuries. The Book of Mormon reported that around 550 B.C. the Lamanites were monogamist.[165] Later, and until the time of the Spanish conquest, they were a society of polygamists. There would be no reason for the Lamanites not to intermarry since they rejected the Law of Moses which forbade it:

> When the Lord thy God shall bring thee into the land wither thou goest to possess it ... thou shalt make no covenant with them ... Neither shalt thou make marriages with them; thy daughter thou shalt not give unto his son, nor his daughter shalt thou take unto thy son ... For they will turn away thy son from following me that they may serve other gods... (Deuteronomy 7:1-4).

Fleeing from war, escaping from religious or social persecution, or being brought as a slave to America are historically consistent patterns found in the Book of Mormon and Mesoamerica. The Mulekites fled from the Babylonian war and came to America. Additionally the Lehites came to Mesoamerica to escape religious persecution; the leaders in Jerusalem were going to kill Lehi for his religious teachings (1 Nephi 1:19-20). The Lehites brought a freed slave by the name of Zoram with them (1 Nephi 4:33, 37).

In modern times the Mormons established colonies in Mexico to pursue religious freedom as did the Mennonites, and Molokans (Russian non Orthodox Christians). Nephi, Mosiah, and others in the Book of Mormon fled from one location to another within Mesoamerica seeking religious freedom.

The Nephites kept the Law of Moses and married within Israel. Fortunately the Mulekites were also of the tribes of Israel. However, the combined Nephite and Mulekite populations were less than half the numbers of Lamanites:

> Now there were not so many of the children of Nephi, or so many of those who were descendants of Nephi, as there were of the people

> of Zarahemla [The land where the Mulekites lived], who was a descendant of Mulek ... And there were not so many of the people of Nephi and of the people of Zarahemla as there were of the Lamanites; yea, they were not half so numerous (Mosiah 25:2-3).

By divine intervention, and quite probably by intermarriage with coexisting dark skin cultures, the Lamanites and the Nephites were distinguished by the color of their skin, i.e., a light-skinned society, the Nephites, and a darker skinned society, the Lamanites. The Book of Mormon also relates that the Mulekites, by comparison a light-skinned people, immigrated to Mesoamerica and settled where they landed (Omni 1:16).

Legend of the Light-skinned, Blue-eyed Chanes, People of the Serpent

Edward Herbert Thompson was a highly respected Harvard archaeologist who spent forty years of his life doing field research in the Yucatan. He is the one who found the seven thin gold plates with hieroglyphic writings upon them in the cenoté at Chichen Itzá, Mexico in 1904. In 1932 he published a book titled *People of the Serpent.*[166] Because the comparisons with the Jaredites, Mulekites, and Nephites are so obvious, extensive quotes in his own words are required to remove doubt that he said what he said. Words that are highlighted in *italic* type will be compared with Book of Mormon passages.

> In the legends and folklore of a race, the history of the race is written if we could but read it. It is true that the grain of fact is generally hidden beneath a wealth of imaginative chaff, but it is there nevertheless. During my long career in Yucatan I was fortunately able to prove the truth of certain tales that had passed as legendary for generations and I will touch upon these matters later. But back of tales such as these are many ancient Maya traditions, none the less fascinating because they are as yet incapable of proof, and obviously containing the elements of history. Among these ancient legends none is more alluring to the student, nor more baffling, than that which concerns the landing of the *Chanes.*
>
> In a previous chapter I referred to the fact that the Mayas had their Plymouth Rock as had the Puritans who followed them to the continent of America many centuries later. That is, the legends of the primitive races of Yucatan and of portions of Mexico tell of the *coming in ships* of *a fair-skinned race of men who became the rulers and the leaders of* the dark-skinned aborigines ... But a tradition so widespread and a legend so persistent must have some basis in history, and *it is legitimate for us to hold as probable that at some time in the remote past a group of people representing a civilization of which we have lost all trace made their influence felt upon the races indigenous to Mexico and Yucatan....*

These traditions tell us, and carvings on ancient walls and stone columns sustain them, that unknown ages ago there appeared strange craft at the mouth of what is now known as the Panuco River in the State of Vera Cruz. The sides of these vessels shone like the scales of serpent' skins, and to the simple natives who saw them approaching they appeared to be great serpents coming swiftly toward them.

In these craft were *light-skinned beings* and some of the traditions have it that they were *tall of stature* and blue-eyed. They were *clad in strange garments* and wore about their foreheads emblems like entwined serpents. The wondering natives who met them at the shore saw the manner of their coming with the symbol of the Sacred Serpent, which they worshipped, on their brows, and knew the strangers to be *their gods come down* from their home in the sun to teach and guide them.

Who were these fair-skinned people, tall of stature and strangely clad, *sailing through unknown seas to an unknown land?* The answer to this question has been lost in the passing of the ages and the destruction of the ancient records, and now we know only that they came and that until after the arrival of the Spaniards, *the place where they landed* was known as *Tamoanchan*, which means, in the native language, the place where the People of the Serpent landed. It is near Tuxpan in the Tampico district.

The dark-skinned race took to the light-skinned people to be their guides and teachers and all went well with them. Under the sage counsels and wise teachings of the *Chanes*, the indigenous race was raised from an almost brutish, savage condition to the status of thinking, reasoning people.

In the passing of time—and much time must have passed to have brought all this about—these wise men, *the People of the Serpent, separated*, probably in the furtherance of a concerted plan. *Some went north and some went south, each with a band of dark-skinned followers.* Those who went north were known among the Chichimecas and even more northerly peoples, the savage tribes among whom they worked and taught and whom they left enlightened, as *Tultecas*— "teachers" or "builders."

Those who went south, the tradition tell, forded rivers, lived under the shadows of great forests, and in cave darknesses [*sic*] suffered all things that man may suffer and live. Ever they moved onward, teaching and uplifting into the light the savage peoples among whom they tarried when they met them. They conquered, not by force and strange weapons, but *by binding the primitive peoples to them by force of their power and wisdom.* Among these races, they were known as *Ulmecas*—

the Rubber People. It is known that they used rubber extensively and this is probably the derivation of the name. The leaders of the *Ulmecas* were known as *Chanes*, or, among the Mayas, as *Canob*—Serpents' Wise Men—or *Ah Tzai*—People of the Rattlesnake.

It is impossible from any sources as yet available to reconstruct the details of that pilgrimage of the *Ulmecas*, drawn out over no man knows how long a span of time, but at last they *came to a favored site* by two great wells. There they rested finally and there they built Chichén Itzá—the City of the Sacred Well.

Meanwhile a roving branch of the *Tultecas*, lost brothers of the *Ulmecas*, had turned southward and gone first to the ancient parting-place of the two groups of the *Chanes*. Through the slow-growing centuries they had become near kin in manners, thoughts, and language to the peoples they had neighbored in the north. They drifted along the ancient trail of the *Ulmecas*, down to the capital of the Ulmecas Mayas, Chichen Itzá. This was the so-called Toltec invasion, which occurred but a few centuries before the coming of the Spaniards and when *all the races of the region were merged into one people* under the name of Maya.

Thus, in barest outline, with many breaks and dubious places, runs the history of this ancient race of *Chanes*—People of the Serpent—and the peoples they led from darkness into light, from the landing at *Tamoanchan* down to the Conquest.[167]

Comparison of People of the Serpent and the Book of Mormon

PEOPLE OF THE SERPENT	THE BOOK OF MORMON
"Coming in ships"	Jaredites (Ether 6:4, 11), Mulekites (Omni 1:16), and Lehites (1 Nephi 18:8) *came in ships.*
"Fair-skinned race"	Jaredites: "the daughter of Jared was exceedingly *fair* (Ether 8:9)." Mulekites: came from Jerusalem, a *fair-skinned people* (Omni 1:15). Lehi-Nephites: "white, and *exceedingly fair and beautiful*, like unto my people (1 Nephi 13:15, emphasis added)."

PEOPLE OF THE SERPENT	THE BOOK OF MORMON
"...became *the rulers and the leaders* of the dark-skinned aborigines and all went well with them."	The dark-skinned Lamanites who were called the Anti-Nephi-Lehites were converted by the fair-skinned sons of Mosiah and joined them and *lived among them in peace* (Alma 27:26, emphasis added).
"...probable that at some time in the remote past a group of people representing a civilization of which we have lost all trace made their influence felt upon the races indigenous to Mexico."	Two groups in the Book of Mormon brought with them the ability to read and write. The Lehites brought with them many hieroglyphic writings (1 Nephi 1:2). The Ulmecas or Olmecs are the mother culture of Mesoamerica.
"...carvings on ancient walls and stone columns"	"...there was a large *stone ... with engravings on it*;" with a history of a great battle. This was a Jaredite stone (Omni 1:20).
"...*strange craft* at the mouth ... of the ... River."	The Jaredite barge was completely encased and rode high upon the water. It was tight like unto a dish. It truly was *a strange craft*. The Nephite ship was of "*curious workmanship*" (1 Nephi 18:1, emphasis added).
"...sides of these vessels shone like the scales of serpent's skin." There were several vessels.	Jaredite vessels, *eight of them*, "the sides thereof were tight like unto a dish; and the ends thereof were peaked ... and the length thereof was the length of a tree" (Ether 2:17, emphasis added). "...they were light upon the water, even like the lightness of a fowl" (Ether 2:16). They very well may have had the appearance of the scales of a serpent.

PEOPLE OF THE SERPENT	**THE BOOK OF MORMON**
The light-skinned people "*were tall* of stature."	The breastplates worn by the Jaredites were described as being "large" (Mosiah 8:10). The warriors like Lib were "*of great stature*" (Ether 14:10, emphasis added). "And they were all large and mighty men" (Ether 15:26).
"Strange garments"	The Jaredites wore pectorals called "*breastplates*," (Ether 15:15, emphasis added). These would appear as strange garments.
"...gods come down"	"*The Lord came down* and talked to the brother of Jared (Ether 2:4, emphasis added)."
"...sailing through unknown seas to an unknown land"	Both the Jaredites and the Nephites sailed through unknown seas to an unknown land, "*commending themselves unto the Lord*" (Ether 6:4, emphasis added). "*They knew not whither they should steer* the ship..." (1 Nephi 18:13).
"...the place where they landed" on the Gulf of Mexico's shores.	It is proposed the Mulekites landed on the Gulf of Mexico's shores.
"...the indigenous race was raised ... from an almost brutish, savage condition to the status of thinking, reasoning people."	The brutish dark-skinned Anti-Nephi-Lehites were a savage, blood-thirsty and war-like people who experienced a complete change of heart and buried their weapons of war deep in the earth never to retrieve them again (Alma 24:7-16).

PEOPLE OF THE SERPENT	THE BOOK OF MORMON
"...the people of the Serpent, separated"	Large numbers of *light-skinned Nephite dissenters broke away from the main group and joined the dark-skinned Lamanites,* Amlicites, Zoramites, Amalickiah, and the priests of King Noah to name a few (Alma 2 and 46).
"Some went north and some went south, each with a band of dark-skinned followers."	Mesoamerica was divided by treaty at the narrow neck of land with *some going north and the others going south* just before the end of the Nephites (Mormon 2:29).The greater division occurred when the Lamanites occupied all of the Land of Nephi in the south and the Nephites all of the lowlands in the north (Alma 50:7-8).
"...came to a favored site"	A *Promised Land* is a "favored" site. Both the Jaredites and the Lehites were led to a New World Promised Land (1 Nephi 5:5, Ether 2:9).
"when all the races of the region merged into one people"	In 4th Nephi there was a time for two hundred years when the people had all things in common and there were no "ites" (4 Nephi 1:2-13). They merged into one.

In the foregoing explanation of a light-skinned people and a dark-skinned people by Dr. Edward Herbert Thompson, there is much to appreciate and absorb. Whether these traditions refer to the Jaredites, Mulekites, Nephites, Vikings, or some other seafaring peoples, is not known. The point is that the Book of Mormon's claim of the Americas being settled by multiple maritime crossings is supported by the history and traditions of the Mesoamericans.

There was a time, however, when the darker skinned people become more righteous than the Nephites and re-entered the covenant. The Book of Mormon is clear about how God views all his children:

> Behold, the Lord esteemeth all flesh in one; he that is righteous is favored of God… (1 Nephi 17:35).

> The Lord … inviteth them all to come unto him and partake of his goodness; and he denieth none that come unto him, black and white, bond and free, male and female; and he remembereth the heathen; and all are alike unto God, both Jew and Gentile (2 Nephi 26:33).

A Modern Parallel in the Yucatan with the Book of Mormon

The Book of Mormon tells of a light skinned minority people surrounded by a darker skinned majority culture. There is a striking parallel in the Book of Mormon with a current saga that is going on in Mesoamerica today in the Yucatan Peninsula. Within the borders of Belize, a country of less than one hundred eighty thousand people, there is a community of nearly forty-five thousand Mennonites. They pay no taxes; they build their own roads, hospitals and schools. By agreement with the government of Belize intermarriage is forbidden by law. The Mennonites are white Caucasians. The Mennonites are great furniture makers and they control the dairy industry in Belize to everyone's delight. They speak their own language and keep to themselves. They sell their farm goods to local markets and at an occasional roadside stand. From personal experience, I can vouch for their great tasting watermelon. It is considered an offence to take their photographs. They wear attractive homemade clothes. The Mennonites are a culture within a culture. They choose not to intermarry because they want to preserve their religious beliefs. The rest of Belize is a mix of Africans brought to Mesoamerica as slaves, native Maya, Mestizos (European married to Maya), Chinese and Indians from India. Belize is a country where four-fifths of the racial mix is Black or Brown and one-fifth is White. The Chinese and Indian populations maintain their ethnocentric tendencies but slowly, because of intermarriage, are mainstreaming; not so with the Mennonites. There are "jack" Mennonites, or dissenters, but usually they are swallowed up in the mix and lose their identity and their unique racial characteristics in a generation or two through intermarriage. Racial problems are almost non-existent in Belize today. This lack of racial issues was an observation made by John Lloyd Stephens as early as 1840 when Belize was known as British Honduras.[168]

The Nephites would have been very much like the Mennonites, a culture within a culture. The Lamanites could be compared to the conglomerate general society of Belize. The prime motivation for the Nephites not to intermarry was to preserve their freedom of worship. If the Mennonites were wiped out by plague, famine or war, in a short time the jungle would overtake their once beautiful farms and the Germanic dialect they speak would be lost, except for any written records they might have left. Languages have a way of becoming so specialized and localized that among the Maya about thirty dialects exist. Most can not understand another dialect. If the Mennonites were destroyed, their unique religious worship and their belief systems would be left to the oral traditions perpetuated by their neighbors who would outlive them. Any Mennonites that would survive would be swallowed up in the dominate culture. This was the fate of the Nephites who existed only as a mixed seed in a culture overtaken with pagan idol worship. The Lamanites simply assimilated the surrounding social landscape and became a part of the cosmopolitan community.

This is analogous to the Nephites and the Mulekites coming to Mesoamerica. They came to a place where other cultures had already experienced the rise and fall of their empires, and other immigrant cultures were on the rise. Still, other immigrant societies were in a state of degradation and living in squalor on the glorious ruins of a higher more advanced culture. The Nephites and Mulekites would have interacted with and fought wars with their neighboring societies who saw them as strange and different. Omni reports that the Mulekites had "many wars" (Omni 1:17). He fails to tell which ones were civil wars verses wars with neighboring cultures. Both can be reasonably assumed.

The view that the three immigrant groups of Jaredites, Mulekites, and Lehites came to a pristine America and were the sole cultures to inhabit the land is not true. They were but three of the many groups to come. The principles of assimilation and amalgamation are the keys to understanding the fate of the unique groups that were led by the hand of the Lord to what for them was also a land of promise.

The Prophet Nephi told his posterity they were a remnant of the House of Israel. They were part of the scattered descendants of the Twelve Tribes throughout the earth. It is important to state properly the claim of the Book of Mormon. Some of the descendants of Jacob were dispersed throughout the Old World, while others were led to the New World (I Nephi 22:4). This does not mean that everyone who came to the Americas is from the Twelve Tribes of Israel or is of Jewish descent. Nephi saw in vision the eventual demise of his posterity and the fact his children would lose their identity and only survive as a part of a mixed seed. Commenting on the Prophet Isaiah, Nephi points out that "our seed," i.e. Lehi, Laman, Lemuel, Nephi, et al., will be scattered as well upon "this land" of the Americas (I Nephi 13:39; 22:7). Nephi adds his own testimony that the "marvelous work" the Lord will perform by the gentiles will be to awaken the remnants of Lehi's "mixed seed" scattered throughout North and South America and the Isles of the Sea to the fact they are the remnants of a covenant people (I Nephi 22:9).

The Book of Mormon recorded a promise given by the Lord that scattered Israel in the New World will assist in building the American New Jerusalem (3 Nephi 21:22-29). A milestone was reached in the year 2004, in Mexico alone. In that year LDS Church membership passed the one million member mark in Mexico. There were twelve functioning LDS temples in Mexico in 2004. LDS Church membership in South America and the Isles of the Sea experienced similar growth. Another interesting fact about the demography of LDS Church membership is the expected dominance of Spanish over English. At current rates of growth, there will be more Spanish speaking members of the LDS Church than English speaking members in the not-too-distant future.

SYMBOLS AND SIGNS OF AN ADVANCED CIVILIZATION

Cement and Masonry

The Book of Mormon describes a land where the people were experts in the use of cement, especially in the land northward, where massive populations denuded the terrain of timber (Helaman 3:5). Was it the "slash and burn" tactics used by the early Olmec and Maya farmers that stripped the land of its lumber? The answer is unknown. Swidden is the term for slash and burn type of farming. It involves the cutting down of all the timber and the undergrowth of the jungle in a certain area and letting it dry. Later the area is completely burned filling the sky with clouds of smoke and the ground with ashes. These ashes were rich in potash and enlivened the soil to produce the maize and beans which were the staples of life among the Maya. These "milpas" or farming plots would be abundantly productive for about three years before they were depleted. In addition to the corn and black beans, there were many other items found in the Mesoamerican garden. They cultivated chilies, tomatoes, potatoes, sweet potatoes, squash, onions, and bananas. Near a village could be found groves of oranges, grapefruits, and tangerines. Swidden farming destroyed the environmental habitat of all eco-systems dependent upon the jungle. It also destroyed the trees as a resource for building homes and huts. It required thirty years before the jungle could be restored sufficiently to be "slashed and burned" again. However, many of the trees never came back during that time period. For example, it takes eighty years for a mahogany tree to reach maturity. The forests have survived small populations, but not large ones. Overpopulation contributed to the problem. The only real substantial clue to the lack of timber is found in the Book of Helaman.

> ...many inhabitants ... had before inherited the land ... And there being but little timber upon the face of the land, nevertheless the people who went forth became exceedingly expert in the working of cement; therefore they did build houses of cement in the which they did dwell (Helaman 3:5-10).

In Mesoamerica the making of cement and mortar was a common and easy process because of the abundance of limestone. The entire Yucatan has a limestone substrata located less than two feet below the surface. In most areas the ground is covered only by humus and a shallow soil. Limestone subjected to fire creates a chalky powder which, when mixed with any of a number of local resins, creates a wonderfully strong mortar. There are tens of thousands of these cement and mortar buildings that have been identified, but not yet unearthed, because of the lack of funding. Even the most liberal estimates purport that less than two percent of the known structures have been excavated in Mesoamerica. The October 1989 National Geographic has an insert map showing hundreds and hundreds of unexcavated ruins. Nearly every site involves additional hundreds of cement buildings. David Pendergast reported more than eight hundred such buildings at Lamanai alone. The complex surrounding Tikal numbers in the thousands.

Cement structures have a way of surviving the people who erected them. There is no evidence that significant cement structures of the time of the Book of Mormon existed around the Great Lakes or in South America. The ruins of Machu Picchu are renowned for not using cement and date to A.D. 1460.

> Most of the structures are built of granite blocks cut with bronze or stone tools, and smoothed with sand. The blocks fit together perfectly without mortar, although none of the blocks are the same size and have many faces; some have as many as thirty corners. The joints are so tight that even the thinnest of knife blades can't be forced between the stones.[169]

However in Mesoamerica Michael Coe described the building of a reservoir and canal system of stone and mortar, of stairs and sunken courts, of many carved stones and public buildings. He identified numerous monuments scattered over hundreds of miles by the Olmecs between 1400 B.C. and 900 B.C.[170] The impact of the Olmec society is easily underestimated. The Olmecs had a profound effect on all of the New World cultures with which they associated. Their impact reached into the northern parts of South America and to north of the Rio Grande. Olmec influence was pervasive and transformed the social, economic, and religious landscape for generations to come in America.

> Its rapid spread has been variously likened to that of Christianity under the Roman Empire, or to that of westernization (or "modernization") in today's world. Wherever Olmec influence or the Olmecs themselves went, so did civilized life.[171]

The Mesoamerican "ballgame," involving human sacrifice is traced to the Olmecs. The ballgame was tied to man's relationship with the gods and to all their religious beliefs about the after-life. No group seemed to be more influenced by the Olmecs than the Maya.

Everything in the Maya culture was tied to the Cosmos. The universe was well ordered. The Maya could count on the rising of the sun, moon, and the planet Venus. Their lives reflected the order of a caste system. There were rules to be followed. The gods coexisted with the mortals, and at times they shared the buildings, the temples, and the roads. But the gods were not the only inhabitants of the spirit world. Nothing really died; it only transitioned to another state of existence. Mortals lived with spirit companions. These spirit companions were the dead but not departed spirits of jaguars, eagles, conquered enemies, and beloved ancestors. The architecture and all-pervading art style reflected this relationship with the gods and the spirit companions. Cement, mortar, and stone supported and mirrored the order in the universe. The Maya had a passion for symmetry and both a fear and reverence of offending either the gods or their spirit companions. They too must see the buildings and walk on the roads where the living walked.

Figure 36. Picture of John L. Lund on a Sacbé

Highways and Roads

Certainly, a highly civilized society would have a system of roads and highways. It is an ironic note that prior to the French and Indian War in 1754, Colonial America voted down various proposals for a comprehensive system of roads. Instead they opted for water transportation via rivers and canals. Turnpikes and road building were left to private individuals. Serious commitment to road building by the Europeans, who brought "Civilization" to the Americas, developed in the latter half of the 19th century. Two thousand years earlier it was the Romans and the Maya who were the serious road builders. The Book of Mormon speaks of an elaborate highway system in Mesoamerica:

> And there were *many* highways *cast up*, and *many* roads made which led from city to city and from place to place (3 Nephi 6:8, emphasis added).

Within the cities an organized pattern of roads also existed. A comment made in 23 B.C. in the Book of Mormon indicated how the homes and gardens were placed to conveniently access a "highway which led to the chief market" (Helaman 7:10). The gardens were walled and had a gate which opened up to the highway. In the same verse it stated that a prayer tower was built in the garden of Nephi "also near unto the garden gate by which led the highway."

It is obvious that the gardens served more than a single purpose of raising corn, beans, squash, tomatoes, limes, avocados, chilies, peanuts, cashews, pineapples, yams, potatoes, vanilla, and chocolate. All these items were unique to the New World gardener. The Spanish returned to Europe with more than gold and silver. They brought the foods that would change the diet of the Old World. Imagine Europe without Swiss or Dutch chocolate. Can you think of Italy without the tomato? It was from the gardens of Mesoamerica that all these products came. Also in the garden could be found a few turkeys and a "chicle" tree from which chewing gum was derived. These too would be exported to Europe, but not until a millennium had passed away from the time of the final battles of the Nephites.

The setting for Helaman's comment about gardens and highways was the capital city of Zarahemla. A Prophet named Nephi was praying in a garden atop a platform-type tower. It was both near the garden wall and near the highway which led to the chief market. It would have been a busy street with a heavy traffic flow. Lawyers, artisans, farmers, and a mix of all strata of their society would be traveling to and fro. It was the custom for these people to pray in high places. Mountains or artificial mountains called prayer towers were constructed in the gardens of the city dwellers so that the supplicant might pour "out his soul unto God" (Helaman 7:11).

It is worth noting that the Mesoamerican spent his life outdoors because the climate was conducive to doing so. The temples did not have large rooms, and even the palaces of the nobles were designed with small but elaborately decorated rooms. Archaeologists insist that only the elite and the wealthy lived within the walls of a city. This would mean that this particular prophet was considered elite and here Nephi was "mourning for the wickedness of the people" (Helaman 7:11). Because of its proximity to the highway, people began to stop and wonder what could provoke such a great outpouring. Men ran to report this event and soon "multitudes" of people had gathered in the street to inquire the cause for such grief. He called them to repentance. This was not a pathway in the jungle. It was not a narrow street in Europe; this was a major thoroughfare that led to the chief market place capable of handling a very large crowd.

The purpose in referring to this story is to point out the nature of the highways and roads in the Book of Mormon. High civilizations are marked by a highly developed system of highways and roads. "All roads lead to Rome" is more than a saying. Romans were great road builders. Their roads allowed for the Roman legions to quickly move to a needed site. They also allowed for the free flow of goods and supplies to sustain a concentrated population of a city. By comparison, both the Romans and the Maya were building roads and highways in 23 B.C.

Roman roads were convex. This means they were high in the center. This allowed for the water to quickly run off the road and to be carried away by the gutters built along their sides. Mesoamerican roads however, were built "level" (3 Nephi 8:13). If Joseph Smith created the Book of Mormon at twenty-four years of age from his imagination, why would he have suggested that roads be built level and not convex as was the Roman and European tradition brought to America? In order to qualify as the land of the Book of Mormon, a highway system dating to the time of Christ and before the time of Jesus needs to be found. The Book of Mormon stated that at the time of the Savior's death in the Old World, approximately A.D. 34, that a great many natural disasters occurred in Mesoamerica. Of special concern was the breaking up of the "level" roads.

> And the highways were broken up, and the *level roads* were spoiled, and many smooth places became rough (3 Nephi 8:13, emphasis added).

Such a system of level highways and level roads did exist in Mesoamerica. A highway in Mayan was called a "Sacbé" and it literally meant "white road." Sacbob was the plural.

Figure 37. Maya Sacbé

How did these Mesoamericans build level roads and highways that were "cast up" (3 Nephi 3:8) from the jungle floor and covered distances of sixty-two miles long? The highway between Cobá and Yaxuna in the Yucatan jungle is sixty-two miles long and elevated three to nine feet off the jungle floor. It is thirty plus feet wide and at one time was perfectly "level." Centuries of use rendered many sacbob with a concave and not a convex appearance. These people were amazing engineers. The latest research coming from El Mirador, located in the middle of the Yucatan and a great candidate for the city of Bountiful, shows a spoke-like pattern of highways emanating from the city.

How did the Maya and the Mesoamericans of the Book of Mormon build these highways and roads? Here was how they did it: First, they cleared the jungle floor for about sixty feet. The entire Yucatan Peninsula is composed of limestone which lies only a few inches under the surface of the topsoil. The roots of the trees run across the ground; there is no place for the roots to descend without running into the limestone. After the jungle floor was cleared and a road base of crushed limestone was laid down, mounds of dirt were cast up to the height of three to nine feet and a width of two feet or more to form a rectangular mound approximately thirty feet by thirty feet. A small trench was carved in the top of the mound and made waterproof with a plaster. The trench was filled with water which served as a level. (It still does for anyone that has used a carpenter's level.) A line was drawn at the water's edge and staked out to the level marks with a taunt string made from the maguey plant. The mounds of dirt were removed. Limestone blocks were quarried out of designated areas which would later become plastered and made into artificial lakes and water reserves. The limestone blocks were literally "cast up" (3 Nephi 6:8) to the perfectly level strings resulting in a perfectly level road.

This story was told to me years ago at Dzibilchaltun, Mexico as I stood upon a sacbé leading to the Temple of the Seven Dolls. I spoke Spanish and only a few words in Yucatec Mayan. A very old Mayan, who spoke Mayan and only a few words in Spanish, took me through the process with the aid of a translator who spoke both Spanish and Yucatec Mayan. Later, I learned that this man was a Maya Holy Man who still practiced the burning of incense and the chanting of prayers on Mayan holy days. Some governments have had to build special cement altars on the ground near many of the ruins to provide a place of worship for these people. Otherwise they would sneak into the ruins at night and burn incense on the ruins causing significant damage. The next time you are in Tikal, look for a modern cement disc on the ground in the Grand Plaza between temple #1 and # 2. They are about twenty-four inches in diameter. The old man has since passed away, but everything I have studied confirms the story he told me.

Once again a road was not just a road to the Maya. All things that were temporal were also spiritual. Symbolism and symmetry cannot be separated in Maya and Mesoamerican life. This included wars and roads. There was a fanatical commitment of the Maya to symmetry. One side is just like the other side. To not be symmetrical would be an exception and not the rule. The white road on earth was the symmetrical reflection of the heavenly "Sacbé" or Milky Way along which the souls of man and beast would travel to Xilbalba, the place of the gods. It was a surprise to the 16th century Spanish that the Maya would cry and mourn over a sacbé that had been severed to make way for a Spanish road. It was not just a road; it was an artery to the gods that had been cut. The symbolism had been profaned; the symmetry had been violated. The continuum of heaven and earth, spiritual and temporal, had been interrupted. In order to understand the Maya integration of religious symbolism into every aspect of daily life, one need only to compare the Maya to the ultra orthodox Hasidic Jew, whose every behavior is influenced by their religious beliefs. Life and religion are one and the same. Even something as simple as washing the hands became a spiritual cleansing ritual as well as a temporal behavior.

It is important to reflect on the "mind set" of the people in the Book of Mormon. Laman and Lemuel came to their younger brother Nephi, all from the nation of Judah, with a question about the writings of the Prophet Isaiah. They wanted to know whether the writings of Isaiah were to be interpreted as symbolically "spiritual" in this case or were they were also "temporal." Nephi's response was "both temporal and spiritual" (1 Nephi 22:3). The western European mind influenced by the Plutonic Greek tradition separated the spiritual and the temporal into two realms which were loosely linked together by the whimsical behavior of spectator gods. The concept of a continuum, of everything being tied to a great plan of God, is very much a Hebrew and a Maya thought. Understanding this integration of all things spiritual and temporal helps us to see how the building of a temple, a house, or a road would be a religious experience. It would be accompanied by prayers and by animal or human sacrifice.

If you are able to visit Cobá, Dzibilchaltún, or Chichén Itzá, you can walk on a sacbé. If you have been to Chichén Itzá and if you have walked from the Temple of Kukulcan (El Castillo), to the Sacred Well (also called a cenoté), you have walked upon a sacbé. You have walked upon a once "level" highway which was thirty feet wide "cast up" from the jungle floor.

Joseph Smith as the translator of the Book of Mormon in 1830 could not have known about the elaborate highway systems of Mesoamerica any more than you know about life on another planet. Joseph did not invent the Sacbé or the level roads and was unaware of their existence except for what he translated from the Book of Mormon or saw in vision.

CHAPTER EIGHT

Geological Considerations: Gold, Silver, and Copper in Four Different Areas

The earth bears witness to the treasures she holds as the repository of precious metals. The Book of Mormon reports that the Nephites, Mulekites, and Jaredites lived in lands abounding in gold, silver, and copper. There needs to exist evidence of gold, silver and copper in four separate areas, in order to qualify as the lands of the Book of Mormon. They are the Land of First Inheritance, the Land of Nephi, the Land of Zarahemla, and the Land of Moron, near to the Land of Desolation. All these places were reported to have gold, silver, and copper in abundance. These areas need to be encompassed within a five hundred to six hundred and fifty mile north to south and a three hundred mile east to west zone.

> [Land of First Inheritance]...find all manner of ore, both of *gold*, and of *silver*, and of *copper* (1 Nephi 18:25, emphasis added).

> [Land of Nephi] ... work in all manner of wood, and of iron, and of *copper*, and of brass, and of steel, and of *gold*, and of *silver*, and of precious ores, which were in *great abundance* (2 Nephi 5:15, emphasis added).

> ... many of you have begun to search for *gold*, and for *silver*, and for all manner of precious ores, in the which this land, which is a land of promise unto you and to your seed, doth *abound most plentifully* (Jacob 2:12, emphasis added).

> ... and became exceedingly rich in *gold*, and in *silver*, and in precious things ... and also in iron and *copper*, and brass and steel... (Jarom 1:8, emphasis added).

[Land of Nephi and Land of Zarahemla.] ... they became exceedingly rich, both the Lamanites and the Nephites; and they did have an exceeding plenty of *gold*, and of *silver*, and of all manner of precious metals, both in the *land south* and in the *land north.*

Now the land south was called Lehi, and the land north was called Mulek, which was after the son of Zedekiah; for the Lord did bring Mulek into the land north, and Lehi into the land south.

And behold, there *was all manner of gold in both these lands*, and of *silver,* and of precious ore of every kind (Helaman 6:9-11, emphasis added).

[Land of Moron was near and west of the Jaredite Land of Desolation (Ether 9:3).] Now the land of Moron, where the king dwelt, was near the land which is called Desolation by the Nephites (Ether 7:6).

Having all manner of fruit, and of grain, and of silks, and of fine linen, and of *gold,* and of *silver*, and of precious things (Ether 9:17, emphasis added).

And they did work in all manner of ore, and they did make *gold, and silver,* and iron, and brass, and all manner of metals; and they did dig it out of the earth; wherefore, they did cast up mighty heaps of earth to get ore, of *gold,* and of *silver* ... and of *copper* (Ether 10:23, emphasis added).

Where on the North American continent does one find gold, silver, and copper in at least four separate areas within a six hundred and fifty mile zone?

Four separate mining areas possessing gold, silver and copper are required in order to qualify as the lands of the primary events in the Book of Mormon. Where are those criteria met? The answer is in Mesoamerica, Southwestern United States, the Northern Rockies, and Western Canada. However, there is no single place east of the Mississippi River, including all twenty-six states, where one can find gold, silver, and copper together in one locale in abundance, much less four separate locations. This single fact alone is a nail in the coffin of the Great Lakes advocates.

The Mesoamerican Hill Ramah/Cumorah and Gold

In Mesoamerica there is an abundance of gold within the proposed Land of Desolation; inclusive of the Land of Moron. In general terms the Land of Desolation included the lands north of the small neck of land or north of the Isthmus of Tehuantepec. More specifically, the lands of desolation were the western areas near the Gulf of Mexico. These were the lands where the greatest numbers of Jaredite wars were fought including but were not limited to the Hill Ramah/Cumorah. Two million "mighty men" were reported killed as battle casualties on one side alone. It was the Nephites who referred to the land of the Jaredites as the Land of Desolation (Helaman 3:6). The Jaredites references were to specific cities, hills, valleys, and coastal plains.

At one point, in the Book of Ether, a distinction was made between the land northward and the land southward. A great city, presumably called Lib, was built by the "narrow neck of land" (Ether 10:20). The land southward was used for hunting while the land northward was covered with inhabitants (Ether 10:21). The people living north of the narrow neck of land dug up "mighty heaps of earth" (Ether 10:23) from which they extracted gold, silver, and copper.

The Book of Ether clearly states that Omer, a Jaredite king, was commanded to flea eastward from the Land of Moron to the east coast and eventually to Ablom, a city by the Gulf of Mexico. In doing so, Omer passed by the Hill Shim, where the Book of Mormon plates and records were originally deposited by Ammaron (Mormon1:3). Later Mormon would move the records from the Hill Shim (Mormon 4:23) to the Hill Ramah/Cumorah (Mormon 6:6) where both the Jaredites and the Nephites were destroyed (Ether 15:11):

> And the Lord warned Omer in a dream that he should depart out of the land; wherefore Omer departed out of the land with his family, and traveled many days, and came over and passed by the hill of Shim, and came over by the place where the Nephites were destroyed, and from thence eastward ... to Ablom (Ether 9:3).

Later Omer returned from near Ramah/Cumorah which was next to the Land of Moron, where there was an abundance of gold, silver, and copper (Ether 10:23). This means that west of the Hill Ramah/Cumorah, within a three hundred mile east to west zone, one should find evidence of gold, silver, and copper.

One of the current candidates for the Mesoamerican Ramah/Cumorah are located along the Gulf of Mexico. One in the state of Vera Cruz, Mexico is the Hill Vigia. West of this Mesoamerican proposed Hill Cumorah (Hill Vigia) there are truly a plethora of mines producing an abundance of gold, silver and copper. The Hill Benal in the state of Taumalimpas ner Tampico, Mskico is another candidate. Many of the mines in the heart of Mesoamerica produce both silver and gold from the same mine. In the mountainous area south of Mexico City and west of the candidates for the Hill Ramah/Cumorah are many mining towns of which Taxco, Mexico is the most famous. This particular town is known for its silver. Mexico is still the number one producer of silver in the world today. Nearby are mines of gold and copper. One does not have to travel far from the Hill Vigia to find gold. Directly north of the Hill Vigia in the same State of Veracruz is the Cerro de Oro. A direct translation will suffice: "Hill of Gold." After the Olmecs and before the conquistadores the area was settled by the

Totonacs. A few decades before the Spanish arrived the Totonacs were subjected to the Mexicas. Each conquered nation paid tribute in goods and services for which they were known. The Totonacs were required to pay tribute in gold. Additionally, they were known for their goldsmiths and their fine gold jewelry.[172] The first gold Cortés received after landing on the shores of Veracruz was from the Totonac mines near the Hill Vigia.[173]

There are two points to be made: Mesoamerica qualifies as the only candidate on the North American continent where there are several areas that have gold, silver, copper and other precious gems within a five hundred to six hundred and fifty mile zone.

The Mesoamerican Hill Ramah/Cumorah had gold nearby while the New York Cumorah did not. A point made earlier bears repeating. Moroni said that he would write more but there wasn't enough room on the plates and "ore I have none" (Mormon 8:5). Moroni was required to travel a great distance to obtain the ore necessary to add the Book of Ether and his own Book of Moroni. Had Moroni been in Mesoamerica, there would have been gold nearby. The Hill Ramah/Cumorah where the Jaredite King Omer passed by and where the Nephites and Jaredites were destroyed was near gold. That means the final battles took place in Mesoamerica. Moroni was in New York when he buried the gold plates, a place of no gold. There were two Cumorahs.

Additional Evidences of Gold, Silver, and Copper in Mesoamerica.

An "A" candidate for the frontier area between Zarahemla and the Land of Nephi is Honduras. Tegucigalpa, the capital of Honduras was taken over in 1579 by the Spaniards on the site of a Maya mine that produced both gold and silver. The Mayanist, Robert Sharer, documents gold, silver, and copper as major trade items coming from Mesoamerica.[174]

On the fourth voyage of Columbus in1502, it was reported that he had

> ... a famous encounter with a Maya trading canoe off the north coast of Honduras near Islas de la Bahía [modern day island of Roatan] ... The canoe, described as being as long as a Spanish galley and 2.5 m wide, had a cabin amidships and a crew of some two dozen men, plus its captain and a number of women and children. It carried a cargo of cacao, metal products (copper bells and axes), pottery (including crucibles to melt metal)...[175]

Various gold, silver, and copper products were gathered from many mining sites throughout Mesoamerica. Articles of gold and copper found in the Sacred Cenoté of Chichen Itzá were reported to have come from Mesoamerica. Robert Sharer reported that there were

> ...masks, cups, saucers, gold and copper repoussé plates and gold jewelry. Many copper sacrificial bells of different sizes ... Study of the gold and copper objects ... indicates that they were brought to Chichen

Itzá from points as far distant as Columbia and Panama to the south and from as far north as Oaxaca and the Valley of Mexico.[176]

"...they exchanged manta [patis] of cotton for gold and for certain axes of copper, and gold for emeralds, turquoises and plumes..."[177]

The widespread use of gold, silver, and copper in the Yucatan, as well as obsidian, (volcanic glass) is a testimony of the Maya traders. These products were not native to the Yucatan, but existed in plentiful supply in the southern and western highlands. The issue is not about traders and merchants bringing gold, silver, and copper to an area like the Yucatan that was devoid of them. The issue is from where did these precious metals come? The Mayan scholar, Linda Schele said,

Gold does not represent a problem ... because the import of gold from lower Central America into the Maya (Yucatan) region was found to have been mined near Quiriguá [Guatemala] and many other mines in Mesoamerica.[178]

Linda Schele then quotes Sharer that the gold and copper found in the dredging of the well at Chichen Itzá, "came from Columbia, lower Central America, Guatemala, Chiapas, Oaxaca and the Valley of Mexico." Gold was mined all over Mesoamerica, as were copper and silver. Mexico and Central America are still to this day world class producers of gold, silver and copper. There are many mining companies that specialize in reprocessing the tailings of old mining claims. Unlike some species of animals which may disappear by famine or natural selection, precious metals or traces thereof remain in the earth as silent witnesses.

The other silent witnesses that speak from the ground are the tombs of the dead and the articles they contain. Tomb #7 at Monte Alban, Oaxaca, Mexico is a Zapotec burial chamber. Because it lay undiscovered by the Spanish and by grave robbers, it is a prime example of the artifacts and beliefs of these people. Germane to the search of the tomb was the existence of gold, silver, and copper. Would any of the items be found in tomb #7? More than three hundred objects have been discovered in this tomb. Among the treasures buried with the dead were *rock crystals* and numerous intricate carvings of figurines in *gold, silver, and copper, turquoise, jade, obsidian, alabaster, and dozens of pearls.* Oaxaca is one of several areas where gold, silver and copper are mined in close proximity. It is also a candidate for the Land of the Mulekites and the southern part of the Land of Desolation.

Precious Stones

Along with gold, silver, and copper, the Book of Mormon mentioned "precious stones" (Alma 17:14). As Sharer noticed, the Maya traders trafficked in turquoise, emeralds and obsidian, in addition to the precious metals of gold, silver, and copper.[179] Jade is another precious stone recognized around the globe as intrinsically valuable. Guatemala is the source of the highest quality jade in the world. Precious stones are rated according to their hardness. In China the hardness of the jade rates at 6.5 to 7; the same is true of the jade from New Zealand. The highlands of Guatemala produce a jade of an 8.5 level of hardness. The colors of Guatemalan jade vary from an almost white to the deepest of green. For the Olmecs, Chinese, Egyptian, and Maya, dark green was associated with life after death. Jade death masks of dark green were the most prized, as were figurines made from dark green jade. Most Maya tombs thus far excavated have numerous jade artifacts. A nine pound jade head was found in a tomb at Altun Ha, Belize. It is a national treasure, a precious stone.

Why the New York Cumorah was not the Place of the Last Battles of the Jaredites and Nephites

If the New York Cumorah was in the Land of Desolation where the final battles took place, there would have been an abundance of gold ore nearby to the west as reported in the Book of Ether. There is no evidence of gold anywhere near to Palmyra, New York.

There were people hired specifically to look for the mythical gold and silver mines supposedly to be found in western New York and northern Pennsylvania. They were called "money diggers." Technically they were treasure hunters. Rumors abounded about "Spanish Treasure" and for a short time Joseph Smith worked for Josiah Stoal in looking for a Spanish silver mine in Harmony, Pennsylvania. He was called a "money digger." Joseph was the only one to find a treasure around Harmony. It was not silver or gold but a beautiful young woman named Emma Hale, his future wife.[180]

An exhaustive geological search of all twenty-six states east of the Mississippi found copper in Michigan, Wisconsin and one unproductive copper mine in New Jersey. Gold was found in South Carolina, Georgia, and Maryland, and only trace amounts of gold in the Adirondacks and trace quantities of Silver in the Appalachians. This hardly qualifies as abundance. Furthermore, these areas are separated by distances so great as to exclude the possibility of being in the five hundred to six hundred and fifty mile limitation imposed by the internal restrictions of the Book of Mormon.

There were many attempts to open gold, silver, and copper mines in New Jersey, New York, and New England from the time of the pilgrims. These mines exist as silent sentinels of the dreams of wealth that never materialized. One such place is called "Silvermine" near Norwalk, Connecticut. Its history is recorded at the Silvermine Tavern:

> The Silvermine area got its name from early settlers who came because people thought there was silver here. Unfortunately, there never was the silver that they had hoped. They stayed anyway and made a nice village with a post office, grocery store, and a tavern.[181]

According to the locals the mine was a great producer, but not of silver. It was used to produce alcohol during prohibition. The point is, only trace amounts of silver are found east of the Mississippi. This fact alone would disqualify any area east of the Mississippi as the Land of Desolation. It would also disqualify New York as the site of the Hill Ramah/Cumorah. Remember the Land of Desolation and Moron had gold, silver and copper in them (Ether 10:23).

Some have suggested that the early inhabitants picked up all the gold, silver, and copper that were "placer" deposits and therefore the land was plucked clean of its abundance of gold, silver and copper. Ether 10:23, however, makes it clear that in the Land of Desolation "they did dig it out of the earth." There is no historical or geological evidence of gold, silver, and copper near Palmyra, New York, either placer or dug out of the earth. According to geologists, gold, silver and copper are found in certain rock formations. Some deposits may be washed down rivers and streams and found as placer deposits in small amounts in the Adirondacks; however precious metals came originally from very distinctive rock formations. These collective formations are minimal for gold, silver, and copper within six hundred and fifty miles west, south, or east of Palmyra, New York and certainly did not exist in the abundance spoken of in the Book of Mormon.

There are many reasons why most Book of Mormon scholars believe there were two separate Cumorahs. Here are some serious considerations why the New York Cumorah is not a good site for the last great battles of the Jaredites and the Nephites:

1. How do the one Cumorah advocates reconsile the statments of Joseph Smith to the contrary? The prophet Joseph Smith identified Mesoamerica as the lands of the primary events of the Book of Mormon.
2. Joseph Smith identified Zarahemla as being in Central America. The Land of Desolation adjoins Zarahemla to the north (Ether 9:31). The distance between Mesoamerica and New York is too great to comply with the internal requirements of the Book of Mormon for the last great battles of the Jaradites and Nephites.
3. Since Joseph Smith identified Zarahemla as being in Central America, it would require that two hundred thirty thousand Nephites and twice that many Lamanites (Mormon 6:8) would have traveled two thousand five hundred miles north to die in the last great battle.
4. Mormon, in rallying the Nephites in A.D. 346, challenges them to "fight for their children, and their wives, and their houses, and their homes" (Mormon 2:22-23). This would indicate their houses were nearby in Mesoamerica.
5. There is a lack of abundance of gold, silver, and copper near Palmyra.
6. There is no historical evidence that a population greater than twenty

thousand ever inhabited all of western New York prior to the coming of the Europeans. The Book of Mormon reported nearly fifty thousand warriors died in one year alone in three battles during the fifth year of the reign of judges (Alma 2:15, Alma 3:25). It argues for a warrior population greater than the entire number of all the tribes known to have inhabited the areas of the northeastern United States. The Jaredites reported "two millions," of their people slain in the Land of Desolation (Ether 15:2). The demographics do not support western New York as sustaining a population of millions. The soil and the ability of the site to produce sufficient food staples for millions were not and are not there. Even a migrating population numbering less than two million could not live off the land for "four years."[182]

7. The Nephites signed a treaty with the Lamanites and the Gadianton robbers in A.D. 350. The Nephites settled on the land just north of the "narrow passage" in the Land of Desolation and the Lamanites took possession of all the land south of the "narrow passage" including the Land of Zarahemla. The distance between the narrow pass in Mesoamerica and New York far exceeds the six hundred and fifty mile radius imposed by the Book of Mormon (Mormon 2:28-29, Mormon 3:5).
8. The Hill Cumorah in New York does not have a water supply. The Finger Lakes are too far away. The Nephite army camped "round about the Hill Cumorah" (Mormon 6:4). An army moves on its stomach. The logistics of food and water round about the Hill Cumorah in New York would not sustain an army of 230,000, and twice that number of Lamanites, and not the millions destroyed earlier among the Jaredites. The New York Cumorah does not fit the description of "rivers, and fountains" (Mormon 6:4). The Great Lakes and the Finger Lakes do not compensate for the lack of rivers and fountains close to or on the Hill Cumorah in New York.
9. At least twice as many Lamanites would have come against them as they had in previous battles. That is nearly a million people. The New York Cumorah is 1.7 miles long and .4 miles wide. With 30% trees and vegetation, there would not be room enough to swing a sword or sling a stone without hitting one of your own soldiers in the process. One has to imagine that millions of Jaredites gathered over a four year period at the Hill Ramah/Cumorah. That number represents only one half of the equation in that civil war. The opposing army of Jaredites brought their hordes as well. The New York Hill Cumorah is not a strategically defensible location to handle the demographics of the magnitude spoken of in the Book of Mormon.

10. There are no signs of a high civilization in the New York area during the time period of 2200 B.C. to A.D. 400. There are no remnants of city states, a written hieroglyphic language, or a highly structure political system with kings, priests, and sophisticated artisans anywhere in the northeastern United States.
11. The climate around the Great Lakes and specifically the Niagara-Buffalo-Rochester, New York area is not conducive to nakedness for the entire year. Remember, the Lamanites came to battle many times dressed only in loincloths with their heads shorn. This was their manner of dress from 544 B.C. (Enos 1:20) to 73 B.C. (Alma 43:20). Some of the wars lasted years (Alma 45-62).
12. Abundant cement structures dating to the time of the Book of Mormon do not exist in the Great Lakes area. It is not consistent to suggest they were all destroyed when Mesoamerican cement structures dating to the time of the Book of Mormon are in abundance.
13. Earthquakes are reported on several occasions in the Book of Mormon. These occurred in 100 B.C., 81 B.C., 30 B.C., and in 34 A.D (Mosiah 27:11-18, Alma 27:14, Helaman 5:27-31, 3 Nephi 8:6-19). There may have been more but these were the ones recorded. Earthquakes are the result of movement of the earth's crust. The broken fragments of the crust are called tectonic plates. The movement between the tectonic plates creates seismic activity in the form of volcanoes and earthquakes. The seismic activity of Mesoamerica is well known. There are sixteen active volcanoes in Mesoamerica and *none* east of the Rocky Mountains in the United States. Geological events, such as earthquakes, are consistent with Mesoamerican geography. Current scientific evidence for the past three thousand years has not found in the Great Lakes area the kind of seismic activity reported in the Book of Mormon.
14. Vultures are mentioned twice in the Book of Mormon, i.e., in Alma 2:38 tens of thousands of Amlicites, Nephites and Lamanites were killed within a few days "and were devoured by those beasts and also the vultures of the air." This was in the land of Zarahemla and by the River Sidon. The wilderness which was west and north of where they were killed was called Hermounts:

    > "...and it was that part of the wilderness which was infested by wild and ravenous beasts.... And it came to pass that many died in the wilderness of their wounds, and were devoured by those beasts and also the *vultures of the air* (Alma 2:37-38, emphasis added).

    There are seven New World vultures with three vultures which are native to North America. The Turkey Vulture is found throughout North and South America, and specifically migrating to the northern

> part of the United States and Canada for the summer where they breed and give birth to their young. The majority of the Turkey Vultures are in the New York area between May and August. According to the American Turkey Vulture Association, the birds require a wind current so they can soar with the updrafts. The Turkey Vulture is a glider. Therefore, the areas devoid of thermal updrafts are avoided by the Turkey Vultures.[183] The areas just south of the Great Lakes near Niagara provide no updrafts and only migrating Turkey Vultures are seen. This phenomenon occurs in many areas south of the Great Lakes, including Palmyra, New York. The fact is the Turkey Vultures are only in the area for a few months and they avoid land masses where there are no updrafts. The scarcity of Turkey Vultures in the Great Lakes-Palmyra area argues against the site as the one described by Alma in the Book of Mormon. Contrast this information with the fact that Turkey Vultures live in Mesoamerica year round and they number in the tens of thousands.

These issues of the lack of gold, silver, and copper, lack of any evidence of millions of people, lack of cement structures, and no evidence of a written language, a high civilization, or city states deserve a serious response. The climate around the Great Lakes is a major impediment for this area to qualify for the primary events of the Book of Mormon including the final destruction of the Jaredites and the Nephites. These issues have not been adequately addressed by the Great Lakes advocates.

These are not the only issues but until these areas of concern are met "head on" by the Great Lake advocates, their credibility remains in question. The insurmountable problem for both the South American advocates and the Great Lakes advocates remains Joseph Smith's clear and total commitment to Guatemala and Central America as the place for the primary events in the Book of Mormon including the final conflicts of both the Jaredites and Nephites.

There were two Cumorahs: one in Mesoamerica where the final battles of the Jaredites and Nephites took place, and another Cumorah near Palmpra, New York where Moroni traveled after the last great battle of the Nephites. Moroni had sixteen years to make that journey before he buried the abridgment of the Book of Mormon given to him by his father, Mormon (Mormon 6:6).

CHAPTER NINE

Historical Considerations: Mesoamerican Prophets and Unique Mormon Beliefs

What does pre-Columbian history have to say about the ancient inhabitants of Mesoamerica? What were the customs, religious traditions and social mores practiced by the pre-Columbians? What correlations are recorded in the Book of Mormon? These are the issues that will be explored and compared under the title of historical considerations.

Pre-Columbian Traditions Reported by Bishop Diego de Landa

Prior to the demise of the "'Siberian Land Bridge Only" doctrine in 1998, the historical accounts written by the native inhabitants of Mesoamerica were dismissed as myths and fables. Oral histories reported by contemporary Catholic leaders were rejected as tainted by later scholars. The academics were both arrogant and premature. In A.D.1566 Friar Diego de Landa wrote *An Account of the Things of Yucatan.* In it he discussed the pre-Columbian custom of baptism among the Maya, the local prophet-historians' prophecies of the arrival of a foreign power who would "impose a single god" upon the people, and the teachings of the ancient Maya elders that, "Their ancestors, who populated this land ... came from the east, and that God aided them, opening two paths through the sea."[184]

The Mesoamerican Prophet Chilam Balam

Because there are so many correlations between the Book of Mormon and Mesoamerica, I have chosen to highlight some that are not mentioned by other authors, or to expand on those that seem particularly relevant. For example, the Book of Mormon is a chronicle of prophets. The pre-Columbians also believed in prophets, and one of the most well known was Chilam Balam. Historians are not sure whether there was a single great prophet by that name or whether all Chilams "mouth-speaking prophets, seers and shamans" took the name Balam in his honor. "Balam" is literally, "the jaguar." Figuratively, the jaguar was the symbol of the spirit world and things spiritual. Bishop Diego de Landa spoke of a Chilam from the hills of Maní in the Yucatan. His name was Ah Cambal. It was he who prophesied the Maya "would be dominated by foreign people, and they would impose a single god" upon them.[185]

After the Spanish conquest, the monks and Catholic priests under the direction of Bishop de Landa systematically set about to destroy all of the ancient Mayan texts. Excess in the name of religion was considered a virtue. The Bishop believed the books were Satan inspired and would hinder the process of conversion to the Catholic faith. This was the time of the Spanish Inquisition and the "soldiers of God" were in full array. Huge fires in every village consumed the history and culture of a nation. All records sacred or profane were thrown into the flames. Genealogies for hundreds of years, all of the marriages, the family heroes, and records of wars, psalms, poetry, and prayers were gone. The religious texts which included the teachings of creation and man's purpose on earth and an entire religious belief system had gone up in smoke. It was ethnic cleansing at its worst. The Bishop wrote at the time of his surprise at the tears and sorrow expressed by the people as they watched the flames:

> We found a large number of books of these characters, and as they contained nothing in which there were not to be seen superstition and lies of the devil, we burned them all, which they regretted to an amazing degree and which caused them much affliction.[186]

However, the Spanish Bishop had exceeded his authority and was called back to Spain and severely chastised. Upon his return he set about to recapture what he had destroyed. Many of the bravest Maya had been killed along with their teachers, shamans and the Mayan priests. There were few left who could assist him in recapturing a lost culture. To his credit, Bishop de Landa dedicated his life to translate the Mayan language and to undo the damage he had done.

In truth, Bishop de Landa had done only that which had been done throughout all of Mesoamerica by other priests. The systematic eradication of all the cultural institutions of the Maya was complete. The temples were defaced, the idols destroyed, the records eliminated. All the Maya had left now was their collective memory. Landa's first task was to teach the Maya how to read and write in Spanish and how to use the Spanish language to phonetically write Mayan words and names. The Maya immediately set about to record their traditions, history, and prophecies. Without this effort to teach the Maya how to capture their language using Latin letters, there would be no Popol Vuh, or the various writings of Chilam Balam.

Most scholars believe that the books of the Chilam Balam were written using some hidden ancient Mayan texts that happened to escape the flames. The original manuscripts and primary sources which were pre-Columbian disappeared except for a few which are in the museums of Europe. What are now called the books of Chilam Balam are the compilations made after the Spanish arrived. They were written in the Mayan language using Latin characters.

The writings and prophesies of Chilam Balam were widely circulated. Each village was anxious to record the teachings of their elders. The books of the Chilam Balam were known by the name of the village where it was written. Every village seemed to have a copy to which they would attach the name of the village and some history of the movement of their people. There are sixteen of these books known to exist. The Book of Chilam Balam of Maní, the Book of Chilam Balam of Tizimin and the Book of Chilam Balam of Chumayel have real history in them. The other thirteen contain prayers and poems and celestial records of the movements of the sun, moon, and stars. They speak of the creation, man's relationship to the gods, and of planting and harvesting. They are compilations of centuries of history, myth, and oral traditions.

Part of Chilam Balam's historical value lie in the fact they recorded precise names, places and dates of Mayan history before the Spanish conquest. For example, events with precise dates are recorded such as "Katun 8 Ahau 4," which corresponded to A.D. 415-435. Memory alone would not have provided the numerous specific dates without access to ancient documents. Each community's Chilam Balam was written and maintained by the communities' leading sage, a member of the council of the elders. The books formed a window into the past and demonstrated how totally and completely religious these people were.

Readers who are familiar with the Book of Mormon will notice how the keeping of records was considered a sacred task. Lehi's sons went to Laban, a member of the community of Elders, to acquire the sacred "brass plates" upon which was written the history of the creation of the world, genealogy, and family history (1 Nephi 4:26-27).

The Maya Prophet Chilam Balam predicted the coming from the east of the Bearded White God. The Son of God, Itzamna, would come to reestablish his father's kingdom. One of Chilam Balam's central themes was the coming of a great destruction by war. He prophesied the coming of the foreigners [Spaniards] and foretold of a great punishment that would befall his people. Chilam Balam predicted wars of exterminations.

Some pre-Columbian war traditions that are had in common with the Book of Mormon will also be examined. War itself is a dominant topic in both the Book of Mormon and the prophecies of Chilam Balam. A central theme in the Book of Mormon is war and the prophecy of total destruction of the most wicked. A remnant was prophesied to survive, but they too would be punished by the foreigners who would come across the sea. Nephi saw

> ...other Gentiles; and they went forth out of captivity, upon the many waters. And it came to pass that I beheld many multitudes of

> the Gentiles upon the land of promise; and I beheld the wrath of God, that it was upon the seed of my brethren; and they were scattered before the Gentiles and smitten (1 Nephi 13:13-14).

The prophecy of Chilam Balam was, in historical context, the same as the prophecy of Nephi in the Book of Mormon. Both prophecies dealt with the invasion of the North American continent by foreign nations who would come from the east. The conquest and subsequent destruction of the people was a punishment for abandoning spiritual values. One would be hard pressed to find a more direct correlation.

Unique Mormon Beliefs and Mesoamerican Traditions

There are beliefs, articles of faith, and doctrines that are unique to The Church of Jesus Christ of Latter-day Saints. Mormons are Christians. However, their origin is not founded in traditional Christianity. Most traditional Christian faiths have their beginnings in one of the orthodox catholic faiths, such as Roman Catholic, Greek Orthodox, Russian Orthodox, Armenian, Coptic, et al. By definition, all Protestant faiths are break-offs from a mother church from which they protested.

Latter-day Saints believe that Joseph Smith was a prophet, a Chilam Balam; that he was called of God by direct revelation to restore the original Christianity which had been lost in the traditions of a corrupted Christianity. This knowledge came by direct revelation from God. The Book of Mormon is another testament of Jesus Christ as a resurrected Being. It is a companion witness to the Bible. Among other unique doctrines, the Book of Mormon witnessed of Jesus Christ coming to America as a resurrected Being. Latter-day Saints believe in a Father God, like Hunab Ku. He is Supreme. All mankind lived as a family in heaven before coming to this earth, which had been specifically created for the enhancement of His children. In that family structure in the premortal heaven, Jehovah, also known as Jesus Christ, was the first born of all the spirit children of Heavenly Parents. All human beings on this earth are literal brothers and sisters of Jesus Christ: the Son of the Living God. He came to earth as a part of a Divine Plan of Redemption, and is the Savior. He has many titles. One of the titles by which He is known among Mormons is Our Elder Brother. This specific belief in Jesus Christ as "Our Elder Brother," is unique in the Christian community. Men and women are not simply creations of Heavenly Father; they are His literal spirit children and Jesus is Our Elder Brother.

Jesus, Our Elder Brother

One of the Prophet Chilam Balam's prayers included a reference to "Our Elder Brother," who was also the Son of God, the Lord Itzamna. Some translations in Spanish have Elder Brethren, which is in reference to God's other sons. It is still a correct title and translation from the Mayan to say "Our Elder Brother."

The Father God and God of gods was Hunab Ku, the father of the firstborn Itzamna. In Yucatec Mayan "Hun" = One, "Ab" = Being, and "Ku" = God. Literally it means "The One and Only God."[187] This prayer from Chilam Balam is to Itzamna who will take the prayer to his father, Hunab Ku.

> The raised wooden standard shall come! . . . . [A]
> Our Lord comes, Itza! *Our elder brother comes,* . . . [B]
> oh men of Tantun! Receive your guests, ... [C]
> the bearded men, the men of the east, ... [B]
> the bearers of the sign of God, lord! . . . . [A][188]

There are several phrases of significance in this prayer. It is chiastic. The Book of Mormon is chiastic and the phrase, "Our Elder Brother" is a unique LDS doctrine among Christendom. When traditional Christians speak of the family of God, it is a symbolic expression. It is not literal. Catholics and Protestant creeds define God as an unembodied spirit essence without body, parts, or passions. Mormons are literalists when it comes to man's relationship to God as Our Heavenly Father:

> And now, after the many testimonies which have been born of him, this is the testimony, last of all, which we give of him: That he lives! For *we saw him*, even on the right hand of God; and we heard the voice bearing record that he is the Only begotten of the Father— That by him, and through him, and of him, the worlds are and were created, and *the inhabitants thereof are begotten sons and daughters unto God* (D&C 76:22-24, emphasis added).

Traditional Christians teach that humanity came into existence at the creation of the world. Catholic dogma of "exnihlo" suggests that God created all things from nothingness. They do not support the belief in a premortal existence for man. LDS theology asserts that all mankind are literally the divine spirit offspring of Heavenly Parents. Men and women lived as family members with Heavenly Father before this world was brought into existence (Jeremiah 1:5, Job 38:4-7). Furthermore, Jesus Christ was the first born of all the spirit children. He is Our Elder Brother. This earth was created for a purpose. All mankind are here on earth to obtain a mortal body and a subsequent resurrection of that body to a glorified state. LDS believe that Jesus Christ, who was also known as Jehovah in the premortal existence, was foreordained before the foundations of this world to come to this earth in the middle of time to carry out a two-fold mission (1 Peter 1:18-20). He is the Promised Messiah and Redeemer of the world and came to earth as the Son of God to fulfill the requirements of a great Atonement. This supernal act would provide a way for all mankind to resurrect and to return to live in the Heavenly Family of God. Jesus was both Divine and mortal. The second part of the mission of Jesus was mortal in nature. He was to teach His brothers and sisters how to honor God and how to love their fellow brothers and sisters. The specific commandment of Jesus was to love each other as he had loved (John 13:38). The belief that Jesus, as the Firstborn, had the spiritual stewardship as Our Elder Brother to help his younger brothers and sisters to grow and progress and to become their highest and best selves was a revealed doctrine.

There is a Plan of Salvation for each of God's creations.[189] It involves mortal life, a spirit world existence, a millennial time and a final judgment. In LDS doctrine this earth life is an important learning experience. It is part of a much larger plan of progression. Only after every child of God has received a full and comprehensive opportunity to understand the fullness of the Gospel plan will they be judged by Jesus, Our Elder Brother (John 5:22).

So when the Mayan Prophet Chilam Balam specifically identifies the Son of God as "Our Elder Brother," it is a significant theological correlation between Mormonism, the Book of Mormon and the Mesoamericans that cannot be ignored. There comes a point for honest seekers of the truth when they can no longer dismiss the cumulative correlations as good guesses, random luck, or chance occurrences. In any other scientific investigation these cumulative correlations would qualify as "convincing evidences." Because there are religious ramifications no amount of evidence or correlations will suffice the contrary mindset. But it ought to give the seeker of truth sufficient pause to read the Book of Mormon and ask the Father directly in personal prayer as to the divinity and historicity of the Book of Mormon.

How would the people in Mesoamerica have learned of Jesus as the Only Begotten of the Father on earth, their Elder Brother, and their special relationship to Him? The answer is: through prophets like Chilam Balam and the personal appearances of Jesus in the New World as recorded in the Book of Mormon. The current focus here is on the aspect of the Descending God as "Our Elder Brother." The Cherokees, in particular, referred to the Descending God as "Our Elder Brother." The Native Americans referred to the white men as Elder Brothers because they believed that the white people came in the name of the Elder Brother.[190]

Jesus as "Our Elder Brother" is not a doctrine brought by the Spanish monks and priests. In fact, they would have considered it blasphemy. The Spanish Inquisition became the Mexican Inquisition. There was no tolerance for what the Christian priests labeled false doctrine. Those who would not yield to the cross were killed by the sword. Most of the Mayan writings were destroyed, their temples defaced and their priests were burned at the stake. Many chose conversion over death. The truth was and is that the Maya were never fully converted. They went underground and continued to practice their belief in Elder Brother, while identifying with some elements of the Catholic faith. Today most Maya have a mix of Maya and Catholic beliefs.

It is not difficult to see why many of the Maya in particular would identify with some of the Christian symbols of the Catholic Church. This is especially true because of the prophecy of Chilam Balam.

THE MAYA PROPHET CHILAM BALAM	CATHOLIC AND MAYA SYMBOLS
The "Raised Wooden Standard"	The Crucifix: The Cross of Jesus was similar to the Maya Tree of Life Cross.
"Our Lord Comes, Itzá, Our Elder Brother" "Men of Tantun"	Jesus, The Son of God, a Descending God. The Maya were the "Men of Tantun." Tantun had reference to Cozumel as a spiritual center. Tan means "precious" and Tun means stone. Precious Stone. "Behold, I lay in Sion a chief corner stone, elect, precious; and he that believeth on him shall not be confounded." (1 Peter 2:6)
"Receive Your Guest"	The Catholic Church came in the name of God and represented themselves as God's agents.
"The Bearded Men"	The Spaniards
"Men of the East"	Where the Sun and the Descending God and His representatives were to come from once more.
"Bearers of the Sign of God"	The Mayan Cross, a symbol of eternal life.

It is important to remember that the Maya already worshipped the cross as a symbol of the Tree of Life. The Ceiba tree was the axis mundi of the Maya. Even the poorest and most humble of the early Maya homes were built around a square with an altar or a tree in the middle of the courtyard. Some of the Maya homes of the Quiché that I have personally visited near Quetzaltenango, in the Guatemalan highlands still have the altar or the tree.

Another name by which the Latter-day Saints refer to the Church of Jesus Christ is the "Church of the Firstborn." "For ye are the church of the Firstborn, and he will take you up in a cloud, and appoint every man his portion" (D&C 78:21). This is a phrase that the Apostle Paul also used when writing to the Hebrews (Hebrews 12:23). As the Firstborn of all of Our Heavenly Father's children, Jesus is Our Elder Brother. We are commanded to pray to the Father in the name of Jesus. It would not be inappropriate for a Latter-day Saint to pray as follows:

> Our Father who art in Heaven,
> We thank Thee for Jesus, who died on a wooden cross.
> We pray our Lord Comes, even Our Elder Brother.
> May we as Thy children receive Him as a welcomed Guest.
> May we receive those who come in His Name.
> May we accept the Divine Authorities who function in His Name.
> These things we ask in the Name of Jesus, Our Elder Brother. Amen.

The Lacandon Belief in Our Elder Brother

Among the Maya, there is a dwindling nation of people called the Lacandon. They live in the jungles of Chiapas, Mexico, between the ruins of Palenque and Bonampak. They managed to hide in the wilderness and escape much of the influence of the civilized world. At the same time, they are like a time capsule. They have retained many of the old traditions of the Maya. Their view of the cosmos and their traditions and culture has significant carry-overs from the times of the Book of Mormon. This remnant of the Maya has chosen to reject Christianity and pursue their time-honored Maya religion until just recently. This means they are less tainted by western traditions. Scientists have been eager to study their culture as a window into the past. One hope is to find a bridge between ancient Maya and the traditions and practices of these isolated peoples.

Most Lacandon Maya have very little or no Spanish blood in their veins and have remained isolated from the main stream of Mexican culture. Many speak very little Spanish, and what they do speak they speak poorly. They have no televisions and no radios except for the battery operated kind that stop working because there are no more batteries deep in the jungle. Until recently there was no electricity; only a gas generator that would run out of fuel, and no backup supplies. In 1978 the village Elders decided to buy a radio transmitter to keep in touch with the outside world. They do not use nails in building their huts. Strong twine and a type of board and bat construction or woven sticks and mud are used to keep them safe at night. Otherwise, the Lacandon spends his or her life living off the jungle. The trip to the government operated medical clinic is a bus ride or jeep ride of several hours. Most rely on the village Shaman or on the plants and herbs they have come to depend upon for survival. Money was not needed in their system of barter; however, money has already brought change and has lured many of the young away from the jungle.

The men of the Lacandon wear white dresses, a type of priestly white robe. Some are polygamist and have no leader per se. Instead they function as a counsel of separate families and clans. In lieu of a designated leader, there is one who is respected as a wise man who serves as a spiritual governor and judge in the council of the Elders. There is a northern group and a southern group of Lacandonians whose dialects make it hard for the other to understand. Estimates vary, but there are fewer than three hundred Lacandon still living this life style. They survive in the jungles and worship the Mayan gods. Sadly, like their northern cousins, the Native Americans, they will either be assimilated into the general population or die off. The Lacandon Mountains and the Lacanjá River will remain, as will the mixed blood of their descendants. Soon their Mayan dialects and language will be extinct, and the Lacandon will be a footnote in a history book, an assimilated people. Like the peoples of the Book of Mormon they will be swallowed up by the larger communities that surround them.

The Father God of the Lacandon Maya is the same as Hunab Ku of the Yucatec and Xpiyacoc of the Popol Vuh. The Lacandon called Him "K'akoch." His firstborn son is the God "Sukunkyum." The literal translation of this name is "Older Brother, Our Lord." This is another witness in addition to the writings of the Prophet Chilam Balam of the Son of God being referred to as "Older Brother." Older Brother, Our Lord who ruled the world of spirits and judged the souls of men. Older Brother was also responsible to resurrect the souls of men.[191]

The Lacandon Tradition: "God's Family Structure is Like Their Own."

What is amazing for the Latter-day Saints is the Lacandonians similar belief in a divine family. Heaven will be a continuation of the family unit (D&C 130:2). The Lacandon believe that the same sociality that exists on earth will exist in Heaven. Families are forever and relationships such as father, mother, brother, sister, husband, wife, son and daughter will continue throughout all time and eternity. They believed they were part of the family of God. The following is a quote from Professor McGee who lived among them: "*God's family structure is like their own.*"[192] From the Popol Vuh, the Mayan Bible, the Divine Couple are referred to as "She Who Has Borne [*sic*] Children" and "He Who Has Begotten Sons."[193]

A Name Correlation

From the stand point of the Book of Mormon, the name of the Lacandon is of special interest. "Hack Winik" is the Mayan name the Lacandon use to refer to themselves. It means "Real Man," "True Men," or "Men who are Candid." Lacandon is not a regular Spanish word. Spanish is gender sensitive, and after extensive research it may be a corruption of "Los Candorones." This could be possible given the definition of the word "candor" in Spanish which means candid, candor, or truthful. To magnify a noun in Spanish one adds an "n" or "on" to the end. "Candorón" would mean very candid, major candor, or super truthful. It is the only possible option in Spanish, but it requires the Spaniards to violate the gender rule in Spanish, and it assumes a respect for the people which the Spanish did not demonstrate.

It is plausible that Lacandon is a phonetic approximation given by the Spanish to the original ruler or a geographical designation. James Nations, an early student of the Lacandon, believed the name Lacandon is a phonetic approximation of "Lacam Tun" or "Great Rock" and is named after a stone fortress on Lake Miramar.[194] Equally valid is the phonetic name approximation of "Lachoneus" in the Book of Mormon (3 Nephi 3:1). This is the name of a father and son who both served as judges for their people around A.D. 17. They were wise men of great reputation. They served as spiritual advisors and political governors. Because they were of noble character, the people believed the "words and prophecies of Lachoneus" (3 Nephi 3:16). There was a point in time when the people of Lachoneus were facing annihilation from an army of thieves known as the Gadianton Robbers. By following the wise counsel of Lachoneus and a chief captain appointed by him whose name was Gidgiddoni, the people won a great victory. "And now it was Gidgiddoni, and the judge, Lachoneus, and those who had been appointed leaders, who had established this great peace in the land" (3 Nephi 6:6, A.D. 29).

Retaining the Name of an Honored King

Did the people retain the name of Lachoneus in honor of him? It certainly was a Book of Mormon and a Mesoamerican practice to do so.

> The people having loved Nephi exceedingly he having been a great protector for them, having wielded the sword of Laban in their defense, and having labored in all his days for their welfare–Wherefore, the people were desirous to retain in remembrance his name. And whoso should reign in his stead were called by the people second Nephi, third Nephi, and so forth, according to the reigns of the kings; and thus they were called by the people, let them be of whatever name they would (Jacob 1:10-11).

The Mesoamericans of Palenque called their rulers Pacal, Pacal II, Pacal III, et al., following this same practice of remembering an honored king.

Two Older Brothers Rebel

The traditions and teachings of the Lacandon are as intriguing as their name. One of the most interesting beliefs among the Lacandon has to do with the first family. Those who are familiar with the story of Laman and Lemuel, the first two sons of Lehi and Sariah, and their rebellion against their father will appreciate this story. Keep in mind that Nephi is the younger brother. The Lacandon believe that the first family of gods became embroiled in a feud. The elder brothers, (K'aak' Bäkal äk Yum Chäk Xib and Paal äk Yum Chäk Xib) rebelled against their father and sought to usurp the father's power. The younger brother (T'uup) honored the father's will and was given the birthright over his elder brothers (1 Nephi 2:16, 3:29). T'uup became "Master of the Light" and Lord of the Day. The older brothers were banished to live in the wilderness without the honor given to their younger brother.

The story is even more intriguing as one looks at the names of the older brothers (*K'aak' Bäkal äk Yum Chäk Xib*). "Yum Chäk Xib" means Father of the Red Man. Both brothers carry that title as a part of their names. K'aak' Bäkal äk means literally "Bitter Tongue Maize-Cob." An equally valid rendering would be "Bitter Speaking Man, Father of the Red Man." Laman was an older brother in the family of Lehi. He was known as a complainer and one of the fathers of the "Red Man." He was a "Bitter Speaking Man, Father of the Red Man." (*Paal äk Yum Chäk Xib*) was his younger brother who in the Book of Mormon story followed Laman. His name was Lemuel. "Younger Tongue, Father of the Red Man." It appears that the father cursed the older sons with a colored skin for their rebellion before he exiled them off in the forest.[195] Even a casual reader of the Book of Mormon will recognize the common elements between the two older brothers against their younger brother (2 Nephi 5:21).

The story of the Lacandonian gods is very similar to Greek mythology. It is now accepted by many scholars that Hercules was a real man whose story became embellished with time and was lost in mythology. Similarly, it is consistent to believe that the story of the founding family in Lacandonian tradition is the same story of the Book of Mormon that became embellished with time, and that the characters became deified and exaggerated over centuries of oral tradition.

The Brother of Jared

There is more to explore in the Lacandon tradition of "kin terms." Referring to a member of deity as Older Brother is consistent with how the Lacandon refer to each other. Professor R. Jon McGee explains

> Although the Lacandon use personal names in family situations (context usually makes clear who is being addressed), an elaborate set of kin terms is more commonly used to refer to specific individuals ... For instance, in conversation I might refer to an individual as ... u sukun Kayum, or "older brother of Kayum," to name a specific individual.[196]

It remains a puzzle and wonderment to many as to why the Book of Mormon has as a man's name, the "brother of Jared" (Ether 1:34). It would be normal and natural for the Lacandon to refer to him as 'u sukun Jared," literally, "older brother of Jared." These kinds of language connections in the Book of Mormon with the native populations of Mesoamerica provide a credible link in custom and tradition between the two.

Degrees of Glory in Heaven

Yet another correlation with the Lacandon beliefs with those of the Latter-day Saints relates to Heaven. Traditional Christianity prefers a Heaven and Hell dichotomy with one making it to the one or the other and enjoying eternal damnation or eternal bliss. The LDS believe in the Bible based doctrine of degrees of glory that Jesus taught to his disciples:

> In my Father's house there are many mansions: if it were not so, I would have told you. I go now to prepare a place for you. And if I go and prepare a place for you, I will come again, and receive you unto myself; that where I am, there ye may be also (John 14:2-3).

The Apostle Paul taught that on one occasion, whether in the body or in a vision, he saw someone caught up to the "third heaven" (2 Corinthians 12:2). At another time Paul compared the heavens to degrees of glory:

> There is one glory of the sun, and another glory of the moon, and another glory of the stars: for one star differeth from another star in glory. So also is the resurrection of the dead...
> (1 Corinthians 15:41-42).

It is the belief of Latter-day Saints that every man, woman and child that Heavenly Father has sent to this earth will receive a full opportunity to accept the Gospel of Jesus Christ. As mentioned earlier, either in this life or during a time in the world of the spirits or at some time during the promised Millennium, all the necessary teachings and ordinances required by God will be given to each soul. Accordingly, there will be an accounting, or a judgment made by Jesus Christ as to the individual's ability to love God and love their fellow man. The Lacandon believed in various realms of the gods. Instead of degrees of glory, the Lacandonians referred to layers in the sky. The minor gods live in the remotest layer of the universe. The outer most areas are cold and dark. Think of concentric rings, a kind of Dante's Inferno, but reversed. The farther away one is from the center, the colder it gets. The concept of degrees, or layers of glory, is similar doctrine. Joseph Smith would teach that the closer one is to God, the brighter the light and glory until one reaches the very presence of God which is characterized as "everlasting burnings."[197]

For the Lacandon, the minor gods dwell where there is no Sun or burnings. [U Ka'ani Chembel K'uh] means the Sky of the Minor Gods. [U Ka'ani K'akoch] means K'akoch's Layer of the Sky. K'akoch, the creator of the gods, is the Father and abides in this layer and he is warmed by a sun.

There is a place reserved in the heavens for all humans. It is a special universe. [U Ka'ani K'uh] means the Sky that Belongs to the Celestial God. This is man's universe where he is familiar with the sun, moon and stars. Some will inherit the earth. There will be a mix of gods and humans on the earth's surface. These are referred to as terrestrial gods. [Lu'um K'uh] means the Gods of the Earth, Earth Dwellers.

The Lacandonian believed in a Spirit World, an Underworld (Yalam Lu'um). This is the abode of Sukunkyum and Kisin. After death, the souls of all the people travel through the Underworld. Each soul will be judged by Sukunkyum, Older Brother. If they are found to be unrepentant sinners, they will be punished by the impish God Kisin. He is also a son of God who has gone astray. He is the god of death and earthquakes. He punishes the unworthy who are guilty of being liars, thieves, murderers, and abusers of children. The wicked are punished by alternating between being frozen and burned.[198]

True Men

Whether or not the name Lacandon is a carry over from Lachoneus, there is a more compelling connection. As mentioned, the Lacandonians referred to themselves as Hach Winik or literally "Very Man," "Real Man," or a "True Man," or men who were true. The Lacandonians place a high value on the truth. It was a cultural heritage. Speaking truth and speaking clearly the true Mayan dialect were important. All Maya believe their language was the first language and is the language of the gods. Speaking in another language was gibberish. It placed the person in the category slightly above the monkeys and others who were not clear speaking true men. The Lacandon, the Quiché and the Cakchiquel all believe their dialect is the true language. It's ironic that unless one speaks the exact dialect, they are considered less than a true human. Unclear speakers were men who could not be trusted. Those who could not be trusted to say what they mean and mean what they say with true words were false men. [199]

Why was this great value placed on being able to speak clearly in the true language? The answer lies in being able to communicate clearly with the gods and grant them proper worship. Being a clear communicator became equated with being a truth speaker. The focus became to be true to what you say. True men were men who could be trusted to be where they said they would be, doing what they said they would be doing. It has a familiar Old Testament ring to it: "If a man vow a vow unto the Lord, or swear an oath to bind his soul with a bond; he shall do all that proceedeth out of his mouth" (Numbers 30:2).

In the Book of Mormon there were a group of men who had the reputation of being true men. They were the Stripling Warriors of Helaman. Geographically these young warriors would have crossed and crisscrossed the lands of Palenque many times and may have settled in the very jungle areas now occupied by the Lacandon. Joseph Smith made a point to identify Palenque as one of the cities of the Book of Mormon.[200] There were 2,060 of these stripling warriors. Here is how they were described by Helaman, the commander, who lead them into numerous battles:

> And they were all young men, and they were exceedingly valiant for courage and also for strength and activity; but behold this was not all–*they were men who were true at all times in whatsoever thing they were entrusted.* Yea, they were men of truth and soberness... (Alma 53:20-21, 64 B.C., emphasis added).

These true men and the heritage they left have proven to be an inspiration to many who have read the Book of Mormon. Some of the posterity of these "true and valiant" men could have traveled to South America and to the nearby Caribbean islands even as they fell into a state of apostasy.

Cannibalism

Figure 38. Fattening Pens from Codex Nuttall

When Columbus came to the Caribbean and found some of the first Native Americans on the island of San Juan Puerto Rico, he reported they were cannibals because of their ceremonial eating of human flesh. Carib is a corruption of the Spanish word "Caníb" or the plural "caníbales" or cannibal. However the Caribs referred to themselves as Kallinago which, according to some scholars, meant "valiant man."[201] The latter is much more consistent with other Mesoamerican titles such as the "Hack Winik" or "true man" of the Lacandon. The name correlations of the Kallinago and the Lacandon as men who were "*exceedingly valiant* for courage...–they were *men who were* true at all times," cannot be ignored as insignificant appellations. By themselves they are interesting. Collectively with the other historical ties they demonstrate a viable association.

One of the last of the Book of Mormon prophets was Mormon. In writing to his son, Moroni, he decries the tragic decline of these once spiritual giants:

> O the depravity of my people! They are without order and without mercy ... And they have become strong in their perversion; and they are alike brutal, sparing none, neither old nor young (Moroni 9:18-19).

Here, Mormon was describing his own people, the Nephites. Earlier, he spoke of the Lamanites. He commented on three abominations which included the practices of idol worship, human sacrifice, and cannibalism. The Lamanites also practiced cannibalism as a practical way of feeding prisoners:

> [They] did take many prisoners both women and children, and did offer them up as sacrifices unto their idol gods (Mormon 4:14)....
>
> And the husbands and fathers of those women and children they have slain; and they feed the women upon the flesh of their husbands, and the children upon the flesh of their fathers ... (Moroni 9:8).

All three of these practices of idol worship, human sacrifice, and cannibalism were part of the Mayan and the Mesoamerican tradition. These social and bloody religious ceremonies have their origins with the Olmecs of 2200 B.C .The last recorded human sacrifice for the Lacandon occurred in Chiapas in 1868. If one is going to find the lands of the Book of Mormon, these savage practices need to be extant at the times and the places identified in the Book of Mormon.

When Columbus arrived in the New World, he was shocked at the social customs of the natives, which he perceived as barbaric. Of interest, the Spanish themselves were not beyond slavery, burning humans alive at the stake and informal polygamy in the form of mistresses and consorts. The Lacandon were not the only people to experience these social practices of idol worship, human sacrifice, cannibalism, slavery, and polygamy. They were institutionalized throughout Mesoamerica. Idol worship, human sacrifice and cannibalism were linked as an integral part of religious worship of the Mesoamericans on a massive scale. People were seldom killed just for food. Victims and prisoners were sacrificed on special feast days and reserved for ceremonial occasions. The manner of death was highly ritualized and required a priest to perform it. The priest would dress in special ceremonial garb. Four assistants would hold the arms and legs while the priest cut out with an obsidian knife the beating heart of the victim who was stretched out over an altar. Sometimes those who were to be sacrificed were too skinny to be considered worthy offerings, so they would be placed in stockades and fattened up until they could become a worthy sacrifice.

Blood Sacrifice and the Wearing of Red

It is worth noting a couple of social customs which the Lacandonians do practice today, and which are again mentioned in the Book of Mormon. They believe in blood sacrifice, and in a sacrament, and in holy ceremonies celebrating a future coming of the Son of God. When Jesus (Older Brother) returns He will be wearing red. "And the Lord shall be *red in his apparel*, and his garments like him that treadeth in the wine-vat." (See Isaiah 63:2 and D&C 133:48, emphasis added).

Because the gods of the Lacandon are fond of the color red, a very strong dye is made from the fruit of the "annatto" tree. It is called "k'uxu", and in this dye they will color a number of ritual objects including a special red tunic used only for ceremonies of sacrifice. They have long since forgotten many of their rituals; however, they know that red is important to the gods. It is the color of blood and sacrifice. They also wear a headband called "chak hu'un." It is made from strips of bark which have been died red in k'uxu to remind them of the sacrifice of god, and to honor his return.

Polygamy

Some of the Lacandon are polygamists. Although it is against the laws of Mexico to have more than one wife, these people of the jungle are left alone to pursue a lifestyle they have followed for a thousand years.[202] There are so few women left of marriageable age, the young men of the Lacandon greatly resent the older men taking more than one wife. Instead of increasing their population through polygamy, as one might imagine, it is having the opposite effect. The young men are leaving the jungles and mainstreaming in order to find mates. Very few of the women these young men find in the cities are willing to step back in time and live in the jungle. It is a simple life, but one of hard work and sacrifices. As the Lacandon children are exposed to the material advantages of modern society and to educational opportunities, they are leaving the jungles. There is a desperate awareness in the scientific community that a body of knowledge, language, and culture are on the verge of extinction.

Apostate Sacrament

Sadly, by A.D. 400 the posterity of the Nephites had fallen into total apostasy. Recall that the Nephites and Lamanites were not the only inhabitants of the Americas. Human sacrifice was a part of the Olmec culture, and blood letting was practiced by these people. Assimilation of former or surrounding cultures was a natural occurrence for those who had abandoned the true worship of Jehovah. Instead of offering unto God a broken heart and a contrite spirit (3 Nephi 9:20), they cut the actual hearts out of their enemies and offered them up to their idol gods. To compound their savagery they practiced ritualistic cannibalism. This meant that the eating of human flesh was not out of hunger. It was a part of a ritual or ceremony wherein the symbolism was more important than the food.

Most Christian communities partake of a communion or sacrament in remembrance of the flesh and blood of Christ. Apostate literalism led to the abuse of a once sacred ceremony introduced by revelation to some of the Mesoamericans from the time of the Olmecs (Ether 3:17-19). When Jesus came in the middle of time, he taught his disciples in both the Old and New World to reverence the Sacrament. This was a symbolic partaking of bread to remember his body. He commanded them to partake of wine in remembrance of his blood, which was shed for them as a part of his great Atoning sacrifice (3 Nephi 18:1-30).

Prophetic Visions of Destruction

A Book of Mormon prophet named Nephi foresaw the Mesoamerican apostasy. He spoke of the Lamanites which included the Lacandon, dwindling in unbelief, and of the wars of annihilation (1 Nephi 12:2-23). Like the Mayan prophet Chilam Balam, who saw the men of the east come and destroy his people, so Nephi spoke of those Gentiles who would cross the great sea from the east and afflict the inhabitants of the land:

> And it came to pass that I beheld many multitudes of the Gentiles upon the land of promise; and I beheld that the wrath of God, that it was upon the seed of my brethren; and they were scattered before the Gentiles and smitten (1 Nephi 13:14).

Christopher Columbus

In this same vision Nephi saw a man who was separated from the rest of the Gentiles and crossed the great deep. It is obvious today that these verses were referring to Christopher Columbus:

> And I looked and beheld a man among the Gentiles, who was separated from the seed of my brethren by the many waters; And I beheld that the Spirit of God, that it came down and wrought upon the man; and he went forth upon the many waters, unto the seed of my brethren, who were in the promised land (1 Nephi 13:12, emphasis added).

Not only do Latter-day Saints believe this person was Columbus, who was moved upon by the Holy Spirit, but Christopher Columbus himself believed he was moved upon by the Holy Ghost to carry out this mission of discovery. From the personal journal of Christopher Columbus comes the following entry:

> ...our Lord...unlocked my mind, sent me upon the sea and gave me fire for the deed. Those who heard of my emprise [enterprise], called it foolish, mocked me and laughed. But who can doubt but that the Holy Ghost inspired me?[203]

The Mesoamerican and The Book of Mormon Belief in "Vision Crystals"

The Book of Mormon mentions an instrument of vision called "interpreters."

> And the Lord said: I will prepare unto my servant Gazelem, a stone, which shall shine forth in darkness unto light that I may discover unto my people who serve me ... their secret works...
>
> And now, my son, these interpreters were prepared that the word of God might be fulfilled ... (Alma 37:23-24).

Dr. Allen Christenson, in his introduction to his translation of the Popol Vuh, points out that the contents of the Popol Vuh were based on Pre-Columbian documents:

> The fact that the contents of the original Popol Vuh predated the Spanish conquest gave them an aura of mystery and power. Its authors referred to the ancient book upon which the Popol Vuh was based as an ilb'al, meaning "instrument of sight or vision."[204] ... The word is used today to refer to the clear quartz crystals that Quiché priests use in divinatory ceremonies. It may also be used to refer to magnifying glasses or spectacles, by which things may be seen more clearly.[205]

It was not unusual for Maya leaders, and the priestly class especially, to be buried with their vision "crystals." The famous Tomb 7 at Monte Alban in Oaxaca, Mexico was discovered in 1932 by Alfonso Caso. In addition to gold, silver, jade, turquoise and alabaster were numerous "Rock Crystals."[206] As far south as the tombs of Kaminaljuyu in Guatemala, and as far north as Michoacán in west Mexico, researchers have found these curious "rock crystals" buried with the dead. In the western world, mystics and fortunetellers have long believed in a "Crystal Ball" to help them foresee future events. Sodi reports that among the Tarascans of Mesoamerica, were rock crystals of extraordinary workmanship, as were their works of gold, silver, and copper.[207]

Students of the Bible will find "vision stones" or interpreters referred to as the Urim and Thummim. Urim means "lights" in Hebrew, while Thummim means "perfect truth." The Urim and Thummim were described as special stones worn on the breastplate of the High Priest (Exodus 28:30).[208] The High Priest Eleazar was told the purpose of the Urim and Thummim was to help him counsel the children of Israel (Numbers 27:21). When King Saul inquired of the Lord for counsel and direction, the Lord answered him not, "neither by dreams, nor by Urim, nor by prophets" (I Samuel 28:6). Unger's Bible dictionary defines the Urim and Thummim as the "medium through which the high priest ascertained the will of Jehovah in regard to any important matter affecting the theocracy."[209] The reference in the Book of Mormon to the "Seer Stones" (Ether 3:23-28) are analogous to the "Vision Crystals" of the Mayan priest. It is one more historical connection between Mesoamerica and the Book of Mormon.

IDOL WORSHIP AND THE MESOAMERICANS

Chacmool

That Mesoamericans worshipped idols of wood, stone, gold, silver, and precious stones as claimed by the Book of Mormon is not in dispute. From a nine pound jade head found in a tomb at Altun Ha in Belize, to hundreds of pounds of gold and silver idols melted down by the Spaniards, the issue of idol worship is not in question. Idol worship among the Mesoamericans was

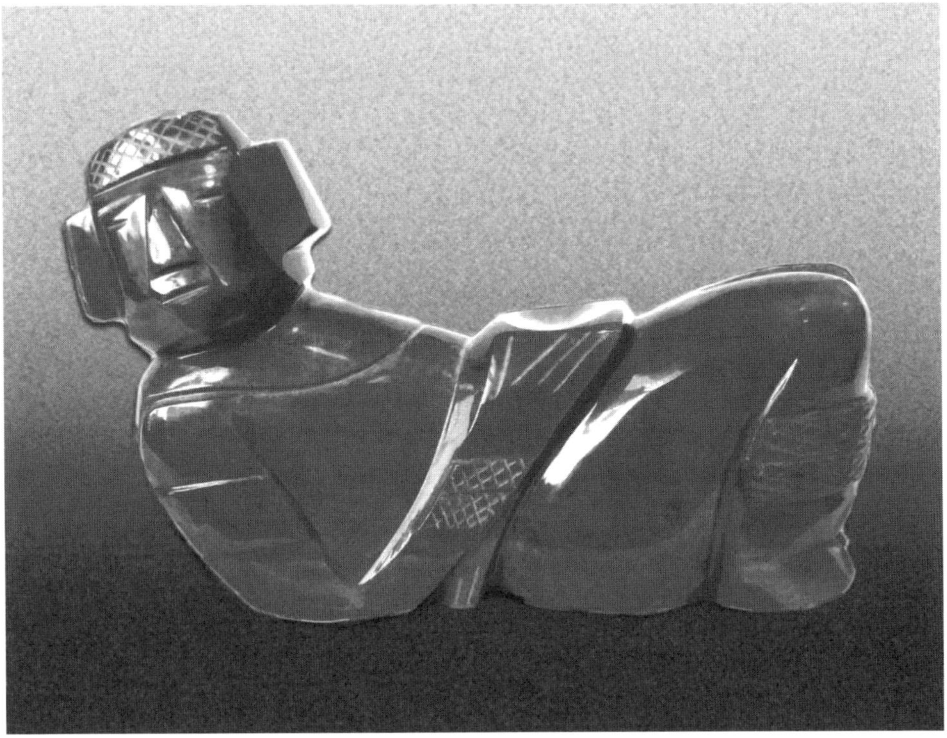

Figure 39. "Chacmool" The Holder of the Hearts of Sacrificed Victims

associated with ritualized human sacrifice. Above is the idol of Chacmool [210] the rain god. He holds over his belly a bowl in which was to be deposited a human heart. Many of the Maya raiding parties were not about power and territory. They had as their objective sacrifice victims. During a raid on an outpost of a rival city state, they only killed those necessary in order to obtain more sacrificial candidates, as Michael Coe explained:

> They fought, not to kill, but to take captives who would later be sacrificed to their gods in elaborate and bloody rituals.[211]

It is also true that slavery was a very important element in their economy. When raids were unsuccessful, the slave population of one's own city was called upon to fill the need for human sacrifice. There were numerous Holy Days and special occasions. There was a constant need for human sacrifice, which guaranteed work for a warrior class and a priestly class in their hierarchy. In their highly integrated society, calendars were a vital part of the formula. The regulation of the heaven, the fertility of the earth, the success of a pending war, the reign of a new king and the death of an old king all called for human sacrifice. The movement of the sun, moon and stars, especially the planet Venus, were all connected to idol worship, human sacrifice, and ritualistic cannibalism.

In Mesoamerica there is overpowering evidence of cross-pollination. The pantheon of gods worshipped by the Olmecs remained consistent with subsequent cultures. The Zapotecs, those of Teotihuacán, the Mixtecs, the Toltecs, the Huastecs, the Mexicas (Aztecs), the Maya, et.al, had different names for the same god. Climate and geography dictated which god would be the local favorite. The god Chacmool was important in those areas subject to draught and dependent upon regular seasonal rain. Tlaloc is the Mexican god of rain. He is the same god as Chacmool among the Maya.

CHAPTER TEN

Historical Considerations: A Culture of War

The Purpose for War

The cultures of war were shared tragedies found in both the Book of Mormon and Mesoamerica. The Book of Mormon prophet and writer Moroni declared,

> The Lamanites are at war one with another; and the whole face of the land is one continual round of murder and bloodshed; and no one knoweth the end of war (Mormon 8:8, A.D. 400).

In the apostate world of the Mesoamerican and in the Book of Mormon war was a part of everyone's life. A culture of war also reinforced the caste system. The warrior class and the priest's class were a permanent part of Mesoamerican society. Some city states, like Dos Pilas, were nothing more than a fortified city filled with warriors. Guy Gugliotta, of National Geographic reported the following:

> Dos Pilas grew no crops and sold nothing. Scholars call it a "predator state" that depended on tribute from the surrounding countryside. War, for Dos Pilas, was not only a ritual to glorify kings and appease gods. War was what Dos Pilas did to survive.[212]

The Book of Mormon refers to a group known as the Gadianton Robbers. They were a secret oath society that had been in existence for four hundred years. At one point they became a political and military power so strong that Mormon in A.D. 350 made a treaty with them (Mormon 2:28). From the Book of Mormon's perspective, they were a mob of thieves and murderers. From the Gadianton's point of view, they were a society of noble warriors; "which society and the works thereof I know to be good; and they are of ancient date (3 Nephi 3:9)." So spoke Giddianhi, the leader of the Gadianton Robbers in A.D. 16. In many ways, they were like the crusaders returning from the Holy Land who occupied Rhodes and later Malta. City states filled with warriors. The Gadiantons were an organization of warmongers who took over cities (3 Nephi 4:1). Their cities were like those of Dos Pilas, filled with predators. There was no merchant class or a highly interdependent society. They could only exist on plunder from war and from tribute "...for there was no way that they [the Gadiantons] could subsist save it were to plunder and rob and murder (3 Nephi 4:5)." The description given of Dos Pilas matches exactly with the Gadianton "Warriors;" a predator state whose very survival was dependent upon war.

The eventual purpose of war among the Mesoamericans was more than territorial. Material gain was appreciated, booty was taken, and power was important. In order to sustain the culture of war, it was important to subject the conquered people to a heavy system of taxation called tribute. The Book of Mormon reports that a tribute of fifty percent was laid upon one city state:

> ...even one half of all they possessed, one half of their gold, and their silver, and all their precious things, and thus they should pay tribute to the king of the Lamanites from year to year (Mosiah 19:15).

It was not just the defeat of an enemy, the paying of tribute, revenge, and the quest for power that motivated the raids and wars. The gods of the Mesoamericans required human blood. It was not about just killing an enemy. It was about pleasing the gods. It was more important to capture an enemy than it was to kill him on the battlefield. Previously pointed out by Dr. Michael Coe was the importance of capturing your enemy for human sacrifice.[213] Dr. Coe's observations were confirmed by Maurice Collis's research in the historical records of Mesoamerica:

> War was the only way to obtain hearts. For that reason the Mexicans were continually making war against the independent states on their borders. In such wars the main object of their generals was to avoid killing the other side. Tactics were directed solely to taking prisoners, and battles were broken off when enough had been secured ... So much was the taking of prisoners considered the greatest service a soldier could render his country, that he was automatically awarded promotion and decorations according to the number he had seized and brought in.[214]

Sacrificing the head or the heart of your enemy upon an altar was considered a true victory. It was an honor to be shared with the gods. Earlier, Mormon lamented that not only had the Lamanites become brutal like unto animals but also his own people, "they thirst after blood and revenge continually..." (Moroni 9:5).

By the 4th fourth century A.D., war had become a way of life and death in the Book of Mormon. Moroni observed,

> And they did take many prisoners both women and children, and they did offer them up as sacrifices unto their idol gods (Mormon 4:14, 21, A.D. 377).

Nearly all of the various cultures of Mesoamerica had adopted a ritualized practice of human sacrifice. This obsession with war and tribal hatred one towards another explains one reason why the outnumbered Spanish were able to conquer the Mexicas (Aztecs). The other tribes in Mesoamerica hated the Mexicas more than they feared the Spanish. Their mantra was, "The enemy of my enemy is my friend." Without the help of these other alliances, the Spanish would not have prevailed as conquerors. The logistics of fighting a war alone from such a great distance from Spain would have ended in frustration. Truly, this coalition of hatred resulted in the demise of the Mexicas and eventually the culture of all the Mesoamericans.

In Guatemala, the same culture of war existed. A new alliance of hatred repeated itself. The Quiche, the Cakchiquels, and the Tzutuhils were all avowed enemies, and had been for centuries. The greatest war confidant of Hernán Cortés was Pedro de Alvarado who was sent by Cortés to subdue these people of the highlands of Guatemala. Alvarado departed on December 6, 1523 with a 120 man cavalry and a 300 man infantry along with four artillery pieces. They first encountered the Quiche and eventually fought a decisive battle at Quetzaltenango. In a letter to Cortés, Alvarado reported

> We commenced to crush them and scatter them in all directions ... Later we returned against them, and our friends [the Nahuatls, Aztecs] and the infantry made the greatest destruction in the world at the river. They surrounded a bare mountain where they had taken refuge, and pursued them to the top, and took [killed] all that had gone up there. That day we killed and imprisoned many people, many of whom were captains and chiefs and people of importance.[215]

Both the Jaredites and the Nephites report a final end of their people on a hill very much like the hill whereon the leaders and captains of the Quiche were slaughtered. The Cakchiquel's capital was Iximche, or present day Guatemala City. Alvarado sent a delegation to the

> ...Cakchiquel capital, asking them to join him in the final defeat of the Quiche. The Cakchiquel were, until the arrival of the Spanish, the paramount new power in the highlands, and the traditional enemy of the Quiche. According to Alvarado, they sent a force of four thousand warriors (although the *Annals of the Cakchiquels* mention only four hundred) and joined the Spanish against the Quiche.... The Cakchiquel appear to have thought that they could use their new alliance to vanquish another of their enemies, the Tzutuhil.[216]

The Cakchiquel were successful with the Spanish in subduing the Tzutuhil at the shores of Lake Atitlan. Later, the Quiche were also defeated. Soon, however, the Cakchiquel faced the wrath of the Spanish brutality. The abundant gold and silver of the highlands of Guatemala were like an addictive drug to the Spanish. In the *Annals of the Cakchiquels,* the bewildered natives wondered about this strange obsession the Spaniards had with metal from the ground:

> There was no fighting and Tunatiuh [Alvarado] rejoiced when he entered Iximche. Thus did the Castilians enter of yore, o my children; but it was a fearful thing when they entered; their faces were strange, and the [Maya] chiefs took them for gods.... Then Tunatiuh began to ask the chiefs for money. He wished that they should give him jars full of precious metals, and even their [gold] drinking cups and [gold] crowns. Not receiving anything, Tunatiuh became angry and said to the chiefs: "Why have you not given me the metal? If you do not bring me the precious metal in all your towns, choose then, for I shall burn you alive and hang you." Thus did he speak to the chiefs.[217]

Traditions Surrounding War

There are a series of traditions surrounding war that are highlighted in both the Book of Mormon and in Mesoamerican history. Some war traditions are unique to both the Book of Mormon and Mesoamerican cultures and some traditions like battle standards are common in many societies. The scholars of Joseph Smith's time did not acknowledge the existence of a highly developed society in North America, nor did they conceive of organized armies numbering in the tens of thousands. The important point is the Book of Mormon claimed that very specific war related traditions and customs were practiced among the Mesoamericans.

Mesoamerican and Book of Mormon War Traditions

1. War Tactics and Battle Standards
2. Captains and Chief Captains
3. Ritualized Human Sacrifice,
4. Kings Fighting Kings
5. The Drinking of Human Blood
6. The Taking of Heads
7. Slavery
8. Marriage Alliances
9. Ammon, the King's Son
10. The Taking of Arms, "One Armed Bandits
11. Cities Destroyed in a Single Day

War Tactics and Battle Standards

The Spanish learned in their first interactions with the New World how sophisticated their military really was. There were three encounters with the Maya of the Yucatan before Cortés landed in Vera Cruz among the Tabascoans. The first was the shipwrecked crew of the ill-fated Valdivía expedition in A.D. 1511. All but two were sacrificed on the altars at Tulum.

In January of 1517 Hernández de Córdoba arrived at Catoche, modern day Cancun, Mexico. The natives seemed friendly and the Spaniards were drawn into an ambush wherein fifteen of them were wounded. The war tactic of *ambush* is quite distinct from European, Roman, Greek, and Persian armies marching in large block-like formations. One of many ambush stories in the Book of Mormon is related to the capture of the city of Manti.

> And when we saw that they were making preparations to come out against us, behold, I caused that Gid, with a small number of men, should secrete himself in the wilderness, and … when they had come and were about to fall upon us with the sword, I caused that my men, and those who were with me, should retreat into the wilderness … the Lamanites did follow after us with great speed … when the army had passed by, Gid and Teomner did rise up from their secret places…(Alma 58:16-20).

Unlike the Book of Mormon story, where the enemy did not overcome the ambush, the Spanish barely survived the ambush. The superior weapons of the Spaniards and Hernández de Córdoba's courage saved them from annihilation. Later at Chanpoton, along the coast of the Yucatan, "A fierce battle followed in which the Spaniards lost fifty men … [later] Córdoba died of his wounds" on his return to Cuba.[218] The last encounter, prior to Cortés, involved the Spanish at Tulum on the eastern shore of the Yucatan in Mexico. In A.D. 1518, under the direction of Captain Juan de Grijalva, the Spaniards approached the shore. In his report to Diego de Velázquez, governor of Cuba, Grijalva reported the following:

> We followed the shore day and night, and the next day toward sunset we perceived a city or town so large [Tulum], that Seville would not have seemed more considerable nor better; one saw there a very large tower; on the shore was a great throng of Indians, who bore *two standards* which they raised and lowered to signal to us to approach them.[219]

Grijalva did not respond to the taunting call to battle at that time; later he would. Battle standards were a regular part of the Mesoamerican culture of war as was the war tactic of *ambush.* From the walls of Bonampak to the prophecies of Chilam Balam, the evidence of the Maya using battle standards and battle towers is abundant. Chilam Balam referred to the large wooden cross of the

Spaniards as, "The Raised Wooden Standard." He also wrote a poem foretelling the doom of his people, in which he spoke of a battle flag:

> On that day, blight is on the face of the earth,
> On that day, a cloud rises,
> On that day, a mountain rises,
> On that day, a strong man seizes the land,
> On that day, things fall to ruin,
> On that day, the tender leaf is destroyed,
> On that day, the dying eyes are closed,
> On that day, three signs are on the tree,
> On that day, three generation hang there,
> On that day, *the battle flag* is raised,
> And they are scattered afar in the forest.
> On that day, *the battle flag* is raised,
> And they are scattered afar in the forests.[220]

There were two military men known as Moroni. One lived around 75 B.C. and his story is told in the Book of Alma. He was referred to as Captain Moroni. He was the chief commander of the Nephite armies. The other Moroni lived around A.D. 385. He was the last of the prophet historians who compiled the Book of Mormon. It was Captain Moroni who required a battle standard on the towers of the cities and towns throughout the Land of Zarahemla to demonstrate loyalty to the cause of freedom:

> ...he caused the title of liberty to be hoisted upon every tower which was in all the land, which was possessed by the Nephites; and thus Moroni planted the standard of liberty among the Nephites (Alma 46:36, 73 B.C.).

It was Captain Moroni who rent his coat, a very Hebrew thing to do (Matthew 26:65, Joel 2:13). Moroni wrote upon it and fastened it upon the end of a pole. And he said

> Surely God shall not suffer that we, who are despised because we take upon us the name of Christ, shall be trodden down and destroyed, until we bring it upon us by our own transgressions. And when Moroni had said these words, he went forth among the people, waving the rent part of his garment in the air, that all might see the writing which he had written upon the rent part... (Alma 46:18-19).

His words inspired courage and united the people behind a battle standard they called "The Title of Liberty."

Captains and Chief Captains

The Book of Mormon talks about a highly structured army. "And there were appointed *captains, and higher captains, and chief captains*, according to their numbers" (Alma 2:13, 87 B.C., emphasis added). Much of the Book of Mormon is dedicated to war and various battle strategies. This is quite consistent with Mesoamerican war traditions. In her book, *The Blood of Kings*, Linda Schele describes the glyph, Stela 11 at Yaxchilán in Chiapas, Mexico. "Shield Jaguar II, a Yaxchilán king of the late eighth century, receives the offering of three captives from a subordinate, identified in the inscription as *a war captain*."[221]

Victories were recorded on engraved stone, on the temple lentils, and in Mayan codices. The defeated were enslaved or sacrificed after being paraded before the victorious kings and gods. In describing Stela 12 at Piedras Negras, Schele says, "A ruler sitting atop a flight of stairs receives *two war captains*, who present him with a pile of captives…"[222]

Ritualized Human Sacrifice

One of the oldest ritualized practices of human sacrifice had to do with a ball game; a very serious ceremony with death on the line. It was much more than a game. It was war on a small scale. As pointed out in the Popol Vuh, a type of Mayan Bible, the game was more of a sacred contest and ritualized ceremony than it was a sporting event or a spectator sport. Because there was a winner and a loser, the concept of a game has been applied to it. There were specific rules of engagement and regulations which had to be followed on the pain of

Figure 40. Ball Player

death. It was ritualistic human sacrifice with one of the combatants being beheaded at the end.

The game was played with a rubber ball weighing between four and nine pounds. Much like soccer, the players were not allowed to use their hands. The teams were even with three to seven players on each team. The object was to pass the rubber ball through a vertical hoop or to strike it with the ball. There is archaeological evidence once again the Olmecs were responsible for the proliferation of the ball game. More than six hundred ball courts have been discovered so far in Mesoamerica. The ball courts can be found as far north as Arizona and as far south as Columbia. Some scholars suggest that the game was played to settle disputes, territorial disagreements, and to gamble. The end of the game involved a death sentence, with the winner or loser being sacrificed. The captain of the winning team was sacrificed because he was the best, a fitting sacrifice for the gods. Some have thought it preposterous that a winner would be sacrificed. Obviously they have never heard of Christianity, which has as its central belief that Jesus Christ gave His life for others precisely because He was the greatest and the most perfect, a winner.

All known ancient Mesoamerican ceremonial centers had a temple and at least one ball court. Chichen Itzá has several ball courts and a large stone mural wall showing a decapitated team captain. The ball court represented the meeting place of man and the gods. By death man was introduced into the world of spirits. The death of man appeased the gods and launched the spirit of the sacrificed on a journey to Xilbalba, the underworld city of the gods. The Milky Way was the heavenly pathway on which the soul would travel.

The Olmecs and the Maya believed in the resurrection of the soul. They believed in a heaven and a hell. Every soul would face a judgment and have to account for their choices in life. Did some of these Mesoamerican people have at one time the Gospel of Jesus Christ? Are these doctrines they believed the apostate remnants of the once true teachings they were given by prophets and divine revelation? The Book of Mormon answers with a resounding, "YES!" to these questions. Did ancient Judaism have the Gospel? Was Father Abraham knowledgeable of the Messiah and did he possess the Gospel? The Apostle Paul taught that the Gospel was indeed taught to Abraham two thousand years before Christ (Galatians 3:8). Did they subsequently fall into various apostasies and spiritually degenerate? Absolutely! Were doctrines perverted, corrupted, and changed? Yes! The idea that man devolves is a hard pill for the Social Darwinist to swallow. Man is supposed to evolve from a lower social creature to a higher one. The truth is there are many societies that stepped backward in time and built their lesser society on the soils of a more advanced, a more civilized, culture than their own.

It is not surprising, therefore, that we should find in the historical records of an apostate people kernels of truth. Evidences of those truths abound in Mesoamerica. Among the greatest evidences of the veracity of the Book of

Mormon in Mesoamerica are the multiple historical correlations with the Book of Mormon.

Kings Fighting Kings

Figure 41. Kings Fight Kings from Codex Nuttall

A curious and somewhat unusual custom among the Jaredites in the Book of Mormon was the practice of kings fighting kings. This practice dates to approximately 1800 B.C. The Book of Ether is a continuous history of face to face battles between kings. The book ends with a battle between two kings who meet face to face. It was King Coriantumr against King Shiz and finally concludes with the taking of the head of the loser, another very Mesoamerican thing to do (Ether 15:30).

The famous Mayanist, Linda Schele, said that it was a universal fact that kings fought kings. "Everywhere, kings faced kings in battle, and so inevitably, many fell in combat and were taken captive."[223] The Book of Mormon reinforces this custom and tradition of kings fighting kings in Mesoamerica. Alma, who was the chief presiding officer of his people, served as both the Chief Judge and as the High Priest (Mosiah 29:42). Because he was the leader of his people, he was required to go to battle and face King Amlici:

Now Alma, being the chief judge and the governor of the people of Nephi, therefore he went up with his people, yea, with his captains, and chief captains, yea, at the head of his armies, against the Amlicites to battle....

> And it came to pass that Alma fought with Amlici with the sword, face to face; and they did contend mightily, one with another.... Alma being a man of God, being exercised with much faith, cried, saying: O

> Lord, have mercy and spare my life, that I may be an instrument in thy hands to save and preserve this people … he slew Amlici with the sword. And he also contended with the king of the Lamanites (Alma 2:16, 29-32).

This fascinating story underscores several important Mesoamerican characteristics. It includes "an alliance of hatred" and "kings fighting kings face to face." Alma had to face two kings on this occasion in order to honor this tradition. There are two possible genealogies for this custom. One is found in the Old Testament among the Hebrews and their surrounding neighbors. Obviously, not all kings felt the need to lead their troops into battle, including King David:

> And it came to pass, after the year was expired, at the time when kings go to battle, that David sent Joab, and his servants with him, and all Israel … But David tarried still at Jerusalem (2 Samuel 11:1-3, circa 1047 B.C.).

A very similar story is told of Amalickiah, a dissenting Nephite, who became a king of the Lamanites:

> Now, if king Amalickiah had come down out of the land of Nephi, at the head of his army, perhaps he would have caused the Lamanites to have attacked … But behold, Amalickiah did not come down himself to battle (Alma 49:10-11).

From a diffusionist point of view, this tradition could easily have been brought across the waters from the old world. The other plausible origin of kings facing kings in battle is the previously mentioned Jaredites. If the Jaredites are indeed the same Mesoamerican society as the Olmecs, then this "Mother Culture" passed on this tradition of kings fighting kings face to face in battle from the time of the tower of Babel.

Hernán Cortés abandoned this tradition at the siege of Mexico City. After fighting for seventy-nine days, the Aztecs held a war counsel. The following story is told by Ignacio Vejar and Professor Mariano Leyva from the Universidad Nahuatl in Cuernavaca, Mexico, in a paper without a date, entitled *The Heroic Defense of Mexiko* [*sic*]*—Tenochtitlan:*

> The Supreme Council of Anahuak decides to propose a duel between the chief of the invaders [Cortés] and the leader of Anahuak … *chief against chief*, with the aim of sparing the civilian population. So, at sunrise on August 13, 1521 … He challenged [Cortés] in front of his troops. Hernán Cortés, the mercenary, refused combat and ordered the Mexican nobles taken prisoner. Dishonor and betrayal was the response. This is the oral tradition, in ueuetlahtolli. This is the true history, and today, we reveal it so that it may never be forgotten (emphasis added).

The Mesoamericans were shocked and dismayed at the refusal of Cortés to honor the tradition of kings fighting kings.

The Drinking of Human Blood

The Book of Mormon referred to a rash promise made by one of the Nephite dissenters. Amalickiah swore he would "drink the blood" of the commander of the Nephite armies whose name was Captain Moroni (Alma 51:9). Drinking the blood of a conquered enemy or sacrifice victim was a very Mesoamerican thing to do. Shortly after Cortés arrived Montezuma sent a peace offering to him: "Cuitlapitoc ... a slave, and [his priests] were instructed to sacrifice him should Cortés want to ... drink his blood."[224] This is an example of a cultural tradition mentioned in the Book of Mormon and found in the social practices of ancient Mesoamerica.

The Taking of Heads

Figure 42. The "Taking of Heads" from The Codex Nuttall

The taking of heads is the first real challenge many people have with Nephi in the Book of Mormon. The time is about 598 B.C. and the place is Jerusalem (1 Nephi 4:8-19). People unacquainted with the Old Testament have said they could not imagine God would command a prophet of God to take a human life. This is a problem of not understanding that God's view of eternity is not the same as man's view (Isaiah 55:8-9). Moses, Joshua, Samuel, Elijah and Nephi are some of the prophets who were commanded to take human life (Deut. 7:2, Joshua 6:21). Samuel upbraided King Saul for not following the Lord's commandment to kill King Agag with these words, "Behold, to obey is better than sacrifice." What follows may seem abhorrent to those who assume that God's primary objective is to preserve human life. Samuel then proceeded with a sword to hew "Agag in pieces before the Lord in Gilgal"

(I Samuel 15:22, 33). This is justifiable homicide; so also is self-defense, warriors who take life in the course of wars of defense, and capital punishment for those guilty of first degree murder (Genesis 9:6, D&C 134:11).

The taking of heads can therefore be righteous or unrighteous. Sadly, the Mesoamericans fell into the latter category. Once a people fall into apostasy, they justify the taking of human life in the name of God even though they have not the authority to do so. This is murder, which is the unlawful and unauthorized taking of human life. The Ten Commandments in Exodus 20:13 reads in English, "Thou shalt not kill." Those who understand Hebrew realize that the original text says "Thou shalt not murder."[225] Murder is different from justifiable homicide or killing in a just cause.

There are those who are satanic and who enter into a secret oath and combination to swear "by their heads" to murder and get gain (Moses 5:29). The early Mesoamerican civilization of the Jaredites swore by their heads "that whoso should vary from the assistance which Akish desired should lose his head" (Ether 8:14). A very beautiful but wicked granddaughter danced and was betrothed on a promise her new husband would bring the head of her grandfather to her father (Ether 8:9-12). This is a preview of a future scene wherein the daughter of Herodias would ask for the head of John the Baptist (Matthew 14:6-12). Ultimately, Jared, the father, lost his own head being decapitated while sitting upon his thrown (Ether 9:5).

On an engraved wall of the largest Ball Court at Chichen Itzá is a warrior player who is carrying the head of his defeated foe in one hand and an obsidian knife in the other. There is a long history and considerable ritual in the taking of heads in Mesoamerica. On Stela 21 from Izapa, Mexico, near the Guatemalan border is a Late Pre-classic stone carving from the time of the Book of Mormon. It is quite simply, "a decapitation scene."[226] It is similar to the decapitation scene from the Codex Nuttall. Evidences found in Maya tombs, have validated the practice of taking heads in Mesoamerica as reported in the Book of Mormon.

> The earliest crypt burial at Los Mangales (c. 400 B.C.) in the Salama Valley was surrounded by a dozen sacrificed individuals, some of whom had been dismembered or beheaded.[227]

The practice of taking the head or the heart of a sacrifice victim as a ritualized part of a religious ceremony was deeply entrenched in Mesoamerican tradition. Captured prisoners were either sacrificed or made to serve as slaves.

Slavery

In the Book of Mormon, slavery was forbidden among the Nephite portion of the descendants of Lehi (Alma 27:9). A Nephite warrior, Moroni, "did joy in the liberty and the freedom of his country, and his brethren from bondage and slavery" (Alma 48:11). A king of the city-state of Zarahemla named King Benjamin declared, "neither have I suffered that … ye should make slaves one

Figure 43. Slavery in Mesoamerica from Codex Nuttall

of another (Mosiah 2:13). Slavery, however, was practiced among those who co-existed with the Nephites. Another king of a city-state, named King Limhi, believed, "it is better that we be slaves to the Nephites than to pay tribute to the king of the Lamanites" (Mosiah 7:15). He was not alone. A disenfranchised group of Lamanites said, "…we will be slaves until we *repair unto them* the … sins which we have committed against them" (Alma 27:8, emphasis added). Apparently, the converted Lamanites felt the same way. However, the Nephites would not allow them to be slaves. Instead, the Nephites gave to them lands and an opportunity to be self sufficient. Among the Mesoamerican Maya if you were a thief and caught, you were obligated to be a slave unto the person from whom you stole until the debt was repaid. The Mayan scholar, Sharer agreed, and answered the question of how one became a slave:

> If a person was caught stealing, he was bound over to the person he had robbed and remained a slave for life or until he was able to make restitution for the stolen articles … At the bottom of the social scale were the *slaves*, the (p'entacob) … Although the high-status captives were usually sacrificed, the lower-status prisoners more likely were made servants and slaves … slaves were created in a variety of ways; by being born to the calling; as punishment for stealing; by being taken prisoner in war; by being orphaned; or through purchase or trade.[228]

The sixteenth century Franciscan Bishop, Diego de Landa, said about the Yucatan that it was "one living rock and has … relied less upon plant husbandry than upon its famed production of honey, salt, and *slaves*."[229]

Marriage Alliances

Figure 44. "Marriage Alliance" from The Codex Nuttall

Finding a tradition of marriage alliances in the Book of Mormon and in Mesoamerica cultural is another claim made by the Book of Mormon which has been validated. It has long been understood that one nation can conquer another nation by war or by marriage alliance. It was also a great way to maintain peace between two political powers. Several Maya scholars assert that Tikal was founded by a marriage alliance between a Maya princess and the son of a ruler from Teotihuacan. The Mesoamericans were politically sophisticated and understood the value of strong political ties.

The traditions of the Mesoamericans did not begin when Cortés landed. Many of the traditions date back three thousand years to the Olmecs. The fact that Cortés was offered multiple marriage alliances was a testimony of the long standing tradition in Mesoamerica.

> Among the presents they [Tabascoan Lords] brought [to Cortés] were twenty women ... After Padre Fray Bartolomé de Olmedo, one of the friars with the fleet, had baptized them, they were given as consorts to the captains, a sort of marriage that was recognized at that time. The women were all daughters of the Tabascoan nobility.[230]

The Totonacs were the next coastal group encountered by Cortés.

> To cement their friendship with the Spaniards, the fat lord [of the Totonacs] brought eight girls, daughters of the aristocracy, and wanted them married to the captains ... The eight girls were brought up and after admonishments were baptized as Christians. Their nuptials with eight selected captains received some kind of minor solemnization.

> Cortés took the fat lord's ugly niece. About this time Doña Marina [one of the twenty Tabascoan women] also became his consort.[231]

Cortés had one wife back in Cuba. She was a Spanish lady named Catalina Xuárez. This form of polygamy to establish political alliances with the native Mesoamericans continued with the Tlaxcalans. Cortés described the town to Emperor Charles V.

> It [Tlaxcala] is so large and admirable that although I will omit much that I might say, the little that I say is almost incredible. It is far larger than Granada and very much stronger. Its population is many more and its provisions better. A huge market, jewellers' [*sic*] shops, as good crockery as anywhere in Spain, barbers and chemist shops and public baths. Order and politeness everywhere in the streets; the people as intelligent as the Moslems. As far as I can judge, the government resembles that of Piza or Venice ... the senior member of the Council of Four ... said [to Cortés] 'I have a beautiful unmarried daughter and I would like to give her to you.'...after [she was] baptized and with her some other girls who had been offered to the captains.[232]

Marriage Alliance: Gonzalo de Guerrero

This is the historical account of a shipwrecked Spaniard named Gonzalo de Guerrero and his marriage to a Maya princess. The year was A.D. 1511. It would be another eight years before the famous Conquistador Hernán Cortés would reach the shores of Vera Cruz, Mexico. The plot sounds more like a movie than a real life event. But it really happened. There are shades of Pocahontas in this story; Pocahontas however, would not be born for another hundred years, and two thousand miles to the north.

Gonzalo was a handsome and dashing young man. He was an adventurer with dreams of sharing the great wealth of the New World promised by Christopher Columbus to Queen Isabella and King Ferdinand of Spain. It had been thirteen years since the discovery of America. The Spanish had set up several colonies with the main one being at Havana, Cuba, to explore and conquer this new continent. Soldiers were paid a salary plus a share in the booty. It was the only way a poor farm boy from the province of Guerrero in Spain could hope to advance his social station in life.

Training in the Spanish army was a grueling experience. The officers came from royalty, wealthy landowners, or by special appointment because of valor on the battlefield. One could also buy a commission from the crown. The officers were ruthless men as were the governors, and their greatest fear was mutiny and rebellion. There was one law in the Spanish army. It was obedience or death. It was reported that Cortés sunk one of his own ships to guarantee that his men would not rebel or retreat from battle. Brutality was a way of life, and mercy meant a quick death.

Priests always accompanied the army. They absolved sin and gave the soldiers the sense that God was on their side. The sword and the cross went hand in hand. If a soldier were dying on the battlefield, the priest would administer the last rites and ensure his passage into Heaven. The soldiers were told that God had chosen their King and Queen and they ruled by divine right with the blessings from the Pope. There were two absolutes. Do not question the King or the Pope. This was the time of the Spanish Inquisition. In was necessary for priests and soldiers not only to kill those who were viewed as unorthodox, but also to do it in a horrific manner. If the natives resisted conversion, they were tortured, maimed and burned alive. All this was done in the name of God. This was the mindset and the conditions of Gonzalo de Guerrero when he left Havana.

Modern day Panama was known as the Isthmus of Darien. It was renowned for its insects and called by the sailors, the Mosquito Coast. It was also a crown colony. An official in the Spanish government named Valdivia was given a charge to inspect the colony at Darien and return and report directly to the Spanish Crown. They embarked in a caravel from Havana intending to visit Darien. In one of the many Caribbean storms, their leaky caravel took on more water than the craft could carry and the ship listed, floundered and began to sink. They were near Jamaica but without means to guide their craft. Eighteen men escaped in a lifeboat designed for twelve. There was no food and no sail. They were prisoners of the sea and the Yucatan current. For fourteen days, they drifted. Seven men starved to death and were sent to a watery grave. The survivors were cast upon the eastern shores of the Yucatan peninsula near the magnificent city of Tulum. The name Tulum means, "Walled City" in Yucatec Mayan. It was also known as "Dawn," because the early rays of the morning sun would first strike the small but glorious Temple of the Descending God and the larger Temple of Hunabku built on the edge of the sixty foot cliff abutting the sea.

The survivors of the Valdivia expedition were too weak and weary to appreciate the splendor of Tulum. Whatever joy they may have felt in being rescued would be short lived. The Maya looked upon the beleaguered group as a gift from the gods, but not as gods. They were too puny to be admired and too scrawny to be gods. These bearded white men would have to be fattened up if they were going to be fit for a sacrifice to the gods. In addition, they wouldn't provide much of a meal when eaten.

Through elaborate communications, the Maya were able to determine that Valdivia was the leader of the ship wrecked sailors. He was immediately taken to the top of the largest pyramid, the Temple of Hunabku. There in front of two rooms on the upper level, one called the Holy Place and the other separated by a veil with an incense altar in front of it, was the Holy of Holies. Outside of these two rooms was a sacrifice altar. Four priests grabbed the arms and legs of Valdivia and stretched him across the altar. The High Priest raised an obsidian knife high above his head and with one swift move severed the heart of Valdivia from his body. In that split second while blood was still in his brain he would have seen his own heart beating in the hands of the High Priest before he died. Four more of Gonzalo's comrades who were the best of the lot met a similar fate. The altar where Valdivia and his four companions were sacrificed is still in tact, and stands directly in front of the upper entrance of "El Castillo Temple" in Tulum, Mexico. Many thousands of tourists have passed by this spot unaware of its bloody, albeit historic value.

Prisoners were placed in fattening pens to increase their size and weight. There was a Catholic priest among the seven who survived that first day. The Priest's name was Geronimo de Aguilar. He said of that occasion in describing their situation:

> I together with six others remained in a coop, in order that for another festival that was approaching, being fatter, we might solemnize their banquet with our flesh.[233]

As the time for their sacrifice approached, the seven survivors were focused on one objective: escape. Aguilar would head north, Gonzalo would flee southward. It was every man for himself. In the dead of night these men fled for their lives. Five of them were recaptured, sacrificed and their hearts were ritually eaten. The priest had traveled north towards Dzibilchaltun, the place of engraving upon the stones. He pled for his life and was granted the status of a slave. He was a novelty; he was white and he had no desire for women. Aguilar was later traded to another Maya chieftain near Uxmal. When Cortés reached the Yucatan in A.D. 1519, the priest was returned to Cortés as a gift. It was then that Cortés was told of another Spanish soldier who had survived the feast of Tulum. It was rumored that this soldier had entered the service of the great Maya Lord Nachan Can at the fortress of Chetumal. It was true.

Gonzalo de Guerrero had fled south to Chetumal. During the time he had been held as a captive in the coop at Tulum, he learned sufficient Mayan to communicate. He was taken prisoner. When he was presented before Lord Nachan Can, he likewise pled for his life and offered his service as a soldier. Lord Nachan Can was a wise and subtle ruler. This white bearded warrior might come in handy to strike fear in the hearts of the enemies of the king. Gonzalo proved to be a fearless warrior. With each victory in battle, Guerrero, a name that means warrior in Spanish, advanced in stature in the eyes of Lord Nachan Can. First, he received a tattoo of honor on his chest and legs. Subsequent victories brought piercing of his ears and nose.

Before proceeding with the story of Gonzalo, a Book of Mormon correlation is appropriate. Ammon, a white Nephite, was taken as a prisoner by a brown skinned Lamanite king named Lamoni, presumably, in the highlands of Guatemala. When asked his intentions by King Lamoni, Ammon replied, "I will be thy servant" (Alma 17:25). There is more that will be compared and explored about Ammon. He proved to be a great warrior for King Lamoni as did Gonzalo Guerrero for Lord Nachan Can.

This handsome Spaniard did not go unnoticed by Lord Nachan Can's beautiful daughter Princess Shell. The attraction was mutual. Lord Nachan Can consented to this Spaniard's request and his daughter's pleading for marriage. The two of them came into the House of Purification. Here in a sauna-like bathhouse the two entered with feathers in their hair, a golden necklace, and earrings shaped into copper bells, which tingled as they walked. They were both naked, and here they would exchange vows of loyalty and drink balché, a mild intoxicant made from honey and the bark of the balché tree. It was believed that drinking balché would make the person both physically and spiritually pure. Water would be poured in from the top of the bathhouse upon the rocks heated by an intense fire. Her mother and a sister of the bride carried out this sacred rite of purification. The Spaniard had no mother to perform this service and so the sister of Princess Shell acted in her stead. Inside the house of purification, there was a large container of fresh water and another of seawater. Each washed the body of the other. No more words were spoken. First, there was a washing of salt water followed by fresh water. There would be sacrifices and a feast. As they exited the place of washing, robes were placed on each of them and they were ushered to the place of the feast. Later, they would consummate the marriage.[234]

There were several amazing footnotes to this story. Aguilar, the Catholic priest, because of his new found language skills, was able to help Cortés as a translator in his conquest of Mexico. Gonzalo de Guerrero became the father of a new race of people referred to as "Mestizos." Their offspring were the first known cross of European with Native Mesoamericans. Gonzalo became a highly respected prince in the Maya fortress city of Chetumal, just north of present day Belize. He also lived up to his name and became a great warrior among the Maya. He convinced the Maya that the Spanish were neither gods nor messengers of Kukulcan. Many believed the Maya were the last to be conquered because of the resistance inspired by this tattooed, white Maya Prince. He was a hero to the Maya and a traitor to the Spanish. Cortés had sent a messenger to Gonzalo asking him to return to Spain. He chose to fight the Spanish and stay with his Maya wife and their mestizo children. Today in the city of Chetumal is a large monument portraying Gonzalo, Princess Shell and their children.

Marriage Alliance: Amalickiah

There are some analogies between the Gonzalo de Guerrero story and that of a man named Amalickiah in the Book of Mormon (Alma 46-51, 73 B.C.). They are different stories separated by hundreds of years. The striking similarities between the two illustrate the Book of Mormon story being historically consistent with Mesoamerican history. The parallels include a white man turning against his own people, marrying a brown-skinned noble woman, becoming a leader of the brown-skinned people, and going to war against his own people as a mighty warrior. In the end both Guerrero and Amalickiah were defeated.

The Nephite sons of King Mosiah in the Book of Mormon petitioned their father to go on a proselyting mission among their avowed enemies, the Lamanites. King Mosiah took their request to the Lord (Mosiah 28). The request was granted, and the four sons embarked on a journey that changed the nature of all future interactions with the Lamanites. What followed was an amazing conversion of thousands of Lamanites.

Ammon: The King's Son

This particular story in the Book of Mormon began with one of the sons of King Mosiah named Ammon. After separating their various ways, Ammon's first stop was the kingdom adjacent to that of his father's: the land of Ishmael. Lamoni was the Lamanite king over this city-state. Because there were many Nephite dissenters who came to live among the Lamanites, it was not unusual for a Lamanite king to imprison and interrogate each Nephite who entered his realm. This was the setting when King Lamoni discovered that his prisoner was the son of a neighboring enemy king. When King Lamoni learned that Prince Ammon wanted to stay in his kingdom and live in peace and was willing to be his servant, the king proposed a marriage alliance between one of his daughters and Ammon (Alma 17:24).

The subsequent refusal of Ammon does not detract from the Mesoamerican tradition of marriage alliances and its historic correlation with the Book of Mormon. Not all nations and religions support marriage alliances. Orthodox Jews, Muslims and Mennonites to name a few are adamantly opposed to marriage outside of their groups. Most religions discourage it. Ammon was on a mission, and because he was commanded not to marry outside of the Nephite community, he refused (2 Nephi 5:21). He chose instead to be a servant. Although the Nephites prohibited slavery, becoming a volunteer servant was approved of as part of the Law of Moses (Exodus 21:5-6).

The Taking of Arms, "One Armed Bandits"

The story of Ammon in the Book of Mormon and Mesoamerican traditions does not end with proposals for a marriage alliance. There is a more profound and unique connection. It has to do with the Mesoamerican tradition of the cutting off of an enemy's arm. Diego Rivera, the famous Mexican muralist, discovered an interesting fact in his research of native Mexican customs and traditions. He found that the taking of a human arm was the sign of a great warrior. On the wall of the National Palace in Mexico City is a painting of a warrior carrying the arm of his vanquished foe. It appears surgically removed. Grotesque as it may appear to some, it was a trophy of this warrior's prowess in battle. It wasn't about food; it goes beyond cannibalism.

Figure 45. "The Taking of an Arm as a Trophy"

The Popol Vuh spoke of a battle where the prideful Seven Macaw fought with Hunahpu, one of the Hero Twins. In the struggle Seven Macaw took the arm of Hunahpu as a trophy. He carried it to his home and hung the severed arm above the mantle of fire. It was not consumed as food. It was kept as evidence of being a mighty warlord. Even after the flesh had fallen from the arm, the bones were kept and some were engraved upon as trophies and buried with the warrior. Seven Macaw said "It will dangle over the fire until they come to take it back again. Truly they are demons," said Seven Macaw as he hung the arm of Hunahpu.[235]

In Mesoamerica the hearts were offered to the gods. The skulls of the beheaded were polished and stored. But the arm of a defeated enemy belonged to the conquering warrior. Because human flesh rots in time, wooden arms were made to commemorate the warriors' prowess. These wooden arms were kept in special rooms in the palaces of the warrior nobles. They were more than trophies; the wooden arms transferred the power of the vanquished to the victor.

The following story involving wooden arms demonstrates the ruthless conquest of Mexico by the Spanish. Montezuma had yielded to Cortés; many of the other Mexican nobles and warriors had not. The murder of some Spanish soldiers by a high ranking Ahau (Lord) named Quauhpopoca and three of his captains led to a brutal reprisal. By the order of Cortés these four men were to be burned alive at the stake.

> The sentence was carried out in the square in front of Montezuma's palace. The fuel used was a quantity of wooden arms collected from the palaces. By this black and violent deed Cortés let the public see that he had assumed executive function.[236]

The only way to advance in the Mesoamerican caste system was through the military. Warriors and slaves were the only flexible positions in the caste. Nobles were almost always sacrificed when captured, or reserved for special sacred days and then sacrificed. Other prisoners were sacrificed or reduced to slavery. One could move down in the caste system but not up. The only exception would be the warrior. As it was with Gonzalo Guerrero so also was it with Ammon. The battlefield was the pathway to social advancement. Taking the arm of an enemy was proof positive of a warrior's greatness.

As the servant of Lamoni, Ammon was assigned to be a shepherd. A large band of thieves periodically raided the flocks of the king, when the shepherds took them to be watered. The thieves were frequently successful. The result being that an irate King Lamoni would have one or two of the shepherds killed as a consequence for allowing the animals to be stolen. This was the pattern before Ammon became one of the king's shepherds. Ammon and his fellow shepherds would take the flocks to be watered at Sebus.[237] As the shepherds approached the waters of Sebus, a band of thieves proceeded to scatter the flocks. Immediately, Ammon's fellow shepherds began to fear for their lives. Their major concern was not the thieves; rather it was the wrath of King Lamoni. Ammon rallied the shepherds. He instructed them to gather the scattered flocks while he contended with the thieves.

> But Ammon stood forth and began to cast stones at them with his sling; yea, with mighty power he did sling stones amongst them; and thus he slew a certain number of them insomuch that they began to be astonished at his power; nevertheless they were angry because of the slain of their brethren, and they were determined that he should fall; therefore, seeing that they could not hit him with their stones, they came forth with their clubs to slay him.
>
> But behold, *every man that lifted his club to smite Ammon, he smote off their arms with his sword;* for he did withstand their blows by smiting their arms with the edge of his sword, insomuch that they began to be astonished, and began to flee before him; yea, and *they were not few in number*; and he caused them to flee by the strength of his arm. Now

> six of them had fallen by the sling, but he slew none save it were their leader with his sword; *and he smote off as many of their arms as were lifted against him, and they were not a few* (Alma 17:36-37, emphasis added).

This is the kind of event of which legends are made. The story of Seven Macaw and Hunahpu in the Popol Vuh may be the origin of the latter practice of warriors taking a human arm as a testament of their prowess in combat. It is also possible that Ammon's great victory over the thieves may have spawned this Mesoamerican custom.

The year was 90 B.C. As a testament to his heroism, his fellow shepherds picked up the arms of the thieves that lay scattered upon the ground and carried them unto the king. If the Mesoamerican traditions were already in place about the taking of an enemy's arm as a sign of a warrior's prowess, it would explain the king's reactions. If the tradition were not in place, this may well have been its origin.

For more than an hour the king stared at Ammon without saying a word. The king was convinced that "the Great Spirit" had come among his people to preserve their lives. The first question asked Ammon by King Lamoni was "Art thou that Great Spirit, who knows all things?" (Alma 18:18). Ammon proceeded to convert the king and his servants. The issue is the correlation of a uniquely Mesoamerican tradition and the Book of Mormon. The 3rd grade equivalent knowledge of Joseph Smith would hardly have allowed such an invention.

Cities Destroyed in a Single Day

The priests and rulers of the Book of Mormon city state Ammonihah were confident in their walled city. The Prophet Alma came to call the people of Ammonihah to repentance. They rejected his message with this rebuke: "We will not believe thy words if thou shouldst prophesy that this great city should be destroyed in one day" (Alma 8:5). Later, the city of Ammonihah was destroyed in a single day and the bodies of their priests, rulers, and inhabitants were heaped upon the earth and covered with a shallow covering of earth (Alma 16:9-11).

The Mesoamerican city state of Cancuén was known for its greatness as

> a strategic trading post ... a stunning ceremonial center. Its heart was a 270,000-square-foot, three-story royal palace with vaulted ceilings and 11 courtyards, made of solid limestone and elegantly placed on a riverside promontory.... Within five years the spreading chaos had reached the gates of the city. In *one terrible day* its glory winked out, another light extinguished...[238]

> [Cancuén] reaped the whirlwind ... the attackers quickly overran the outskirts of the city ...The speed of the attack is obvious even today.... The invaders took 31 hostages.... All were led to the ceremonial courtyard of the palace and systematically executed....

> They laid the corpses in the palace cistern.... Kan Maax and his queen were not spared. They were buried a hundred yards away in two feet of construction fill.[239]

This is not to suggest the two accounts are the same story. The similarities are a testimony of the traditions of a shared culture, separated by time but not by miles. The destruction of a city in a single day and the covering of the dead bodies with shallow rubble are reflective of a common practice of warfare. The historical records confirm a powerful relationship between the Book of Mormon and Mesoamerica.

CHAPTER ELEVEN

HISTORICAL RECORDS FROM MESOAMERICA: QUETZALCOATL THE GOD WHO DESCENDED TO EARTH

Figure 46. Quetzalcoatl Teaching Twelve Men

Many in the scholarly community see the native records of Mesoamerica as tainted by the Christian priests and therefore of little value. What scholars cannot explain are the many unique Book of Mormon doctrines, which could not have been taught by the Catholic priests, which show up in abundance among Mesoamerican historical documents. These unique doctrines found in the native texts establish an authentic relationship between Mesoamerica and the Book of Mormon.

Figure 47. A representation of The Descending God

At Tulum, Mexico, and at Cobá, Mexico there are ancient Maya temples dedicated to the "Descending God." The image is like a child being born with his head down. At the vernal equinox around March 21st, there is a blast of light that illuminates the inner Holy of Holies and shines forth directly under the Descending God announcing his coming to the earth. There are representations of The Descending God engrave in stone and in figurines throughout Mesoamerica.

The relevance of the Book of Mormon to the historical documents in Mesoamerican are the references to doctrines that are unique to LDS theology, and not to Traditional Christianity. The Spanish monks and friars would have indoctrinated the natives of Mesoamerica with Catholic dogma, not LDS doctrine. For example, the belief that Jesus Christ visited the Americas after His resurrection was not an article of faith sustained by the Pope. There were other unique LDS doctrines from the Book of Mormon captured in the writings of the *Popol Vuh, The Title of the Lords of Totonicapán,* and the *Annals of the Cakchiquels.* All of these historical documents of the Maya add credibility to the Book of Mormon. One of the most important historical records written by a descendant of the Mexicas was *Obras Históricas.* Its message will be reviewed in this chapter as well as the legend of *Quetzalcoatl.*

Quetzalcoatl

The "White Bearded Descending God" was the first and most important God worshipped by the Toltecs and most other tribes except the Mexicas. The Mexicas were committed to the brother of Quetzalcoatl known as Tezcatlipoca or Smoking Mirror. Tezcatlipoca's other title was Huitzilopochtli or Hummingbird of the Left, a blood thirsty war god. As a practical matter, the rain god was very popular, but not the most feared. In A.D. 1325 the Mexicas conquered the Toltecs and replaced Quetzalcoatl with Tezcatlipoca. When Cortés arrived in Mexico City in A.D. 1524, Montezuma was afraid that Quetzalcoatl had returned to assume his rightful throne. Montezuma's greeting to Cortés, as recorded by the Franciscan Friar Sahagún, revealed it all.

> O Lord, our Lord, what fatigue, have you journeyed to reach us, [you] have arrived in this land, your land, your own city of Mexico, to sit on your mat, [territory] your stool, [throne] which I have been guarding for you this while. Your vassals, the old kings, my ancestors, are gone, after they too had kept ready your mat. Would that one of them could rise from the dead and, astonished, see what my eyes truly see … For the kings, my ancestors, told that you would appear, that you would return to sit on your mat, your stool. Now it has come true; you have returned.[240]

In describing Quetzalcoatl, Collis pointed out the following:

> Quetzalcoatl (The Feathered Serpent). This was the god referred to above as the great teacher who had declared against human sacrifice. It was believed that in a remote past he had descended from heaven and taking mortal form had, as a priest-king, preached against the great tribal god….He embarked on a magic raft on the coast near Tabasco and departed to an unknown region in the East. But before going he had uttered a prophecy: 'I will return in a One Reed year and re-establish my rule. It will be in a time of great tribulation for the people.'[241]

Historically, there were two major beings identified as Quetzalcoatl. One was a man who lived about A.D. 1100, although there have been other men who claimed the title of Quetzalcoatl at various times. The other major claimant to the title was the god of Mesoamerica who had a history all the way back to the Olmecs. The two of them and their identities have been mixed up and are easily confused. Scholars continue to argue the origins of Quetzalcoatl. Archaeologists Michael Coe and Jacques Soutelle claimed that evidence at La Venta, Mexico and at Las Limas, Mexico in the heart of Olmec country demonstrated that the worship of Quetzalcoatl as the Feathered Serpent began with the Olmec as early as 2200 B.C. Miguel Covarrubias, Alfonso Caso, and Ignacio Bernal are equally respected archaeologists and historians. They have another viewpoint that Quetzalcoatl was more recent. Truth for the archaeologist is lost in myths and legends among the native Mesoamericans. None questioned the overwhelming evidence that the Mesoamericans believed in a white descending god who came among them and promised to return. He is Quetzalcoatl, the Feathered Serpent.

L. Taylor Hansen published more than fifty-five legends from both North and South America and from the isles of the sea of the white God who descended to the earth.[242] Hansen was not LDS and her compilation was not comprehensive, but indicative of the strength of the legend in the western hemisphere.

One of the many similar unreported stories of the "White Descending God" occurred on the island of Puerto Rico. The natives of Adjunta, a town in the tropical highland of Puerto Rico, believed the Spaniards to be immortal representatives of the White Descending God. The natives improvised a simple test. They drowned several Spanish soldiers who were bathing in a pool. They waited three days to see if they were going to resurrect. When the soldiers did not resurrect, the natives massacred the remaining Spaniards in Adjunta.[243]

It is obvious that the legends of the White Descending God appearing to many throughout the western hemisphere were abundant. The Book of Mormon declared that "soon after the ascension of Christ into heaven he did truly manifest himself unto them" (3 Nephi 10:18). The appearances to his *other sheep* as the resurrected Jesus Christ and his universal mission as the Messiah are seminal messages of the Book of Mormon.

Three Distinct Periods of Time When the Descending God of the Book of Mormon Interacts with Man on Earth

Quetzalcoatl, Qucumatz, and Kukulcan all mean "Feathered Serpent." In human form Quetzalcoatl is represented as the light-skinned dark-bearded descending God. If Quetzalcoatl was known 2000 years before Jesus Christ, how could Quetzalcoatl be Jesus Christ? If the Mesoamerican traditions about Quetzalcoatl are based in the actual appearances of Jesus Christ in the New World, then there are three distinct periods of time when Jesus Christ as the Descending God or Quetzalcoatl interacts with man as recorded in the Book of Mormon:

1. As the Premortal God (The Great Spirit)
2. As the Mortal and Divine Messiah on earth (The Earthly Ministry of Jesus)
3. As a Resurrected Being (Jesus, the Risen Lord)

In Mormon doctrine, the Olmecs and/or the Jaredites would have dealt with Jesus (Quetzalcoatl) as the "Great Spirit," or Jesus in his premortal state. This is the Descending God who interacted with all the inhabitants of the earth prior to his birth as the mortal Jesus. For the time before Jesus came to earth, the name Jehovah was often used. Because He was a Spirit Being at that time, He was referred to as the Great Spirit. It was as Jehovah, the Great Spirit that He spoke to Moses face to face. "And the Lord spake unto Moses face to face, as a man speaketh unto his friend" (Exodus 33:11).

Jesus or Jehovah is the God of the Old Testament. In LDS theology Jehovah was a Spirit Being at the time he talked with Adam, Noah, Abraham, Moses, and the Brother of Jared. It was in his premortal existence that he spoke as the great "I AM." Man's communication with the Descending God involved dreams, visions, and prophetic utterances to prophets and others in both the New World and the Old World centuries before his actual appearance on earth as the promised mortal Messiah. The Bible accounts of spiritual manifestations from Adam to Moses and from Joshua to Joseph and Mary attest to the Book of Mormon assertion that "Jesus is the Christ, the Eternal God, manifesting himself unto all nations" (Book of Mormon, Title Page).

The Book of Mormon records multiple visits of the "Descending God" as a Spirit Being to a Jaredite, possibly an Olmec, by the name of the Brother of Jared at the time of the Tower of Babel or approximately 2200 B.C.

> And it came to pass at the end of four years that the Lord came again unto the brother of Jared, and stood in a cloud and talked with him. And for the space of three hours did the Lord talk with the brother of Jared (Ether 2:14).

On another occasion, this very Descending God as a Great Spirit identified himself as the One who would be known in a future time as Jesus Christ:

> Behold, I am he who was prepared from the foundations of the world to redeem my people. Behold, I am Jesus Christ ... In me shall all mankind have life, and that eternally, even they who shall believe on my name; and they shall become my sons and daughters....
>
> Seest thou that ye are created after mine own image? Yea, even all men were created in the beginning after mine own image.
>
> Behold, this body, which ye now behold, is the body of my spirit; and man have I created after the body of my spirit; and even as I appear unto thee to be in the spirit will I appear unto my people in the flesh (Ether 3:14-16).

In 148 B.C. the Prophet Abinadi said that "God himself should come down among the children of men" (Mosiah 17:8)." Earlier, about 544 B.C., the Prophet Enos was told "And many years pass away before he shall manifest himself in the flesh" (Enos 1:8).

The second interaction of God with man occurred as the Mortal Messiah, the New Testament Jesus Christ. As the Babe of Bethlehem, He was given the name of Jesus. He lived on earth in the Holy Lands surrounding Jerusalem and began his ministry at the age of thirty. It was during His mortal ministry that He taught us how to love and treat one another. He was and is man's Great Exemplar. The life of the Mortal Messiah was well attested in the New Testament by the Gospel writers, i.e., Matthew, Mark, Luke, and John. On earth, Jesus was a perfect example of a willing and obedient son. Through discipleship to Jesus He becomes the Father of our spirituality and we become His adopted "sons and daughters" (Mosiah 5:7). His mortal ministry culminated on the cross with his death. Jesus commended his living spirit into the hands of his Heavenly

Father and his body was laid in the tomb. As a spirit, Jesus spent three days in the Spirit World. This was followed by his glorious resurrection.

His third interaction with man was as the Resurrected Jesus Christ. It will be seen that the revelations of a Descending God and Jesus are not confined to the time of Christ's mortal ministry. Jesus died on the cross and rose again in three days as the Resurrected Redeemer with a glorified tangible body of flesh and bones (Luke 24:36-39). He did not return to his former state of being a spirit after his resurrection (James 2:26, Romans 6:9). He returned to heaven and stood on the right hand of His Father as a resurrected being (Acts 7:55-56). It was the resurrected Jesus that Paul encountered on the road to Damascus. As the resurrected Jesus he appeared to Peter, the twelve Apostles, and more than five hundred brethren in the Jerusalem area (I Corinthians 15:4-6). Later he showed himself to more than two thousand five hundred people in Mesoamerica and elsewhere (3 Nephi 17:25).

Dr. Joseph Allen, whose doctoral dissertation was on Quetzalcoatl, and many other LDS scholars believe that the man Topilzin, who was known as Quetzalcoatl around A.D. 1100, and the Mesoamerican God Quetzalcoatl of 2200 B.C. have their origin in Book of Mormon teachings about the Jehovah-Christ. Whether there were later men who took the name Quetzalcoatl isn't as important as the surviving Mesoamerican belief in a god who came to the earth and visited Mesoamerica. It is apparent that scholars and seekers of truth will continue to sift through the myths and legends of Quetzalcoatl to see if they can understand the Descending God. Meanwhile, the very fact that the Mesoamericans worshiped such a being is an important point to document as a unique LDS belief among the society of Christians.

Good Snake Bad Snake

Quetzalcoatl means "Feathered Serpent" in the Nahuatl language of the Mexicas. Kukulcan and Qucumatz are the same name in Mayan dialects. Jesus was symbolized in the Bible by different prophets as a lion, as a lamb, as an eagle, and as a serpent. Many Christians have a problem with Jesus being identified as a serpent. The snake as a symbol conjures images of Satan. The fallen serpent was Lucifer, the Devil who tempted Adam and Eve in the Garden of Eden (Genesis 3:1-6, Isaiah 14:12, Revelation 12:9). Also there is an aversion to snakes by most humans. The belief in a good serpent and an evil serpent is however, a Bible doctrine. Christ was portrayed as the good brazen serpent lifted upon a pole by Moses to heal the sick (Numbers 21:6-9, also John 3:14).

The Mesoamerican belief in two serpents, a good serpent with feathers and an evil serpent without feathers, was a distinction easily understood. The serpent with feathers had the power to fly between heaven and earth and to do good as characterized by Quetzalcoatl, Qucumatz, and Kukulcan. The serpent that lost his feathers, which fell from grace and forfeited his divine power, was evil. The serpent therefore, was a symbol of good or evil among the Mesoamericans depending on whether or not he had feathers. Because of the snake's ability to shed its skin and generate a new one, the serpent was recognized as the symbol of resurrection and regeneration of life. Power hungry priest claimed that the gods could only be worshipped by the shedding of human blood. "Quetzalcoatl had declared human sacrifice unnecessary."[244] With the passage of time this was ignored and the feathered serpent was worshipped by human sacrifice.

The greatest temples in Mesoamerica were dedicated to Quetzalcoatl. Cholula was the city of Quetzalcoatl. It was sixty miles east of Mexico City. Located on the eastern side of the volcanoes of Popocatepetl and Ixtaccihuatl, Cholula's temple to the great Quetzalcoatl stood two hundred fifty feet high. Its base was larger than any in Egypt. Once a year the merchants and priests of Cholula enacted the death and resurrection of Quetzalcoatl.

> Forty days before the festival the merchants bought a slave, the most beautiful youth they could find, and dressed him as Quetzalcoatl with a butterfly jewel, feather mantle and a diadem on his head. Flowers were brought him and exquisite food. He went through the city, dancing and singing. For forty days he was the god and the people crowded to adore him. Nine days before the forty were ended, two old priests came bowing to him and said: "There is an end to dancing and singing. Nine days hence you must die." And if he were sad and danced without joy, they gave him a drink of chocolate and human blood, in which some drug-perhaps peyotl-was mixed, that rendered him insensible to sorrow, as if he were under an enchantment ... The forty days ended, they took him at midnight and on the top platform before the image of Quetzalcoatl stretched him on the sacrificial stone, opened his breast and pulled out his heart. The heart was offered on a dish to the image which they spattered with his blood. The magic ritual had turned the victim's flesh into divine flesh, and that night it was eaten by the merchants, a sacred repast that gave them communion with Quetzalcoatl. At dawn they danced and sang the mystery: by killing Quetzalcoatl by proxy, they had given him new life. It was, as it were, a resurrection; he had died and risen from the dead.[245]

The parallels between the sacrament and the life of Jesus are obvious in this story. Unfortunately, these people fell into apostasy and forsook all the symbolic doctrines of the Gospel taught to them by Jesus. The essence of a kind and loving Messiah were lost. The literalism of idol worship once again replaced the symbolism in the Gospel. Some remnants of the Gospel survived in corrupted rituals, traditions and myths. The original believers in Jesus Christ had reverted to the beliefs of the pagan societies that once surrounded them. In their fallen state, the love of God was replaced by a fear of offending the gods. What remained were the brutal literalism of human sacrifice and the transformation of Quetzalcoatl into a bloodthirsty god. This was in spite of Quetzalcoatl's teachings against human sacrifice. The stage was set. The people were looking fearfully for the return of Quetzalcoatl. The Mesoamericans were ripe and ready for a counterfeit imposture of the White Bearded God. Cortés was circumstantially mistaken for the returning Quetzalcoatl.

Hernán Cortés Arrived in Mesoamerica on Quetzalcoatl's Birthday

Hernán Cortés arrived on the shores of the Gulf of Mexico on the very day the Mesoamericans were celebrating the birthday of the Descending God Quetzalcoatl. Cortés was perceived as the incarnate Feathered Serpent. The day was "One Reed, Nine Wind" according to Mayanist Randolph J. Widmer, Ph.D., Professor of Anthropology, at the University of Houston:

> Quetzalcoatl, the feathered serpent god is one of the oldest and most important deities of ancient Mesoamerica.... The Maya called him Kukulcan.
>
> A god of many aspects, Quetzalcoatl was the creator god.... It was prophesied that Quetzalcoatl would return and reclaim his earthly kingdom. This was still believed by Montezuma II, who thought Hernán Cortés was a deity because he landed in Mexico on the day One Reed [April 21st] in our calendar year 1519, the day of Quetzalcoatl's birth.[246]

Cortés actually landed on a small spit or isle called San Juan de Ulúa, which was only separated from the mainland by a shark infested channel less than a hundred yards from the mainland. Ironically, the celebration was very akin to a modern Christmas which celebrates a Christmas Eve and a Christmas Day. Both April 21st eve and April 22nd day would honor the coming of Quetzalcoatl. The Jews also celebrate their holy days on the eve and the next day. Cortés arrived to the isle on the 21st and came ashore to the mainland on the 22nd of April, 1519.

In the Calendar Round there were only certain hundred plus year cycles that the Feathered Serpent could return. It would be on the day of his birth, One Reed, Nine Wind. He did not come on that date in A.D. 1363, nor did he come in A.D. 1467. His next possible appearance was One Reed, Nine Wind, Ce Acatl, or the day April 21, 1519. Hernán Cortés arrived that very day. Had it not been a case of mistaken identity and subsequent hesitancy on the part of Montezuma, the standing army of 80,000 warriors could have destroyed the Spanish with ease. The sheer numbers would have more than compensated for the superior weapons of the Spaniards. Had Cortés shown up on another day, his fate might have been similar to that of Commander Hernández de Córdoba. He returned to Cuba and died from wounds received when his men were overwhelmed by the superior numbers of the Mesoamericans.

Looking to the Stars for Signs

Looking to the heavens for signs and wonders was another common link between the Mesoamericans and the people of the Book of Mormon. A Lamanite prophet named Samuel came among the Nephites and climbed upon the walls of the city of Zarahemla and began to prophesy unto the people of the coming birth of the Son of God. This was a time when the Lamanites were more righteous than the Nephites. His message was rejected, and they tried to kill him by casting stones and shooting arrows as he spoke to them from the walls of the city. Speaking to the people from the walls of the city was also a Mesoamerican tradition. Montezuma was hit by a volley of stones from the slings of a mob, from which he later died, while speaking to his people from the high city walls of Tenochtitlan.[247]

In the Book of Mormon Samuel gave the following warning:

> Five more years cometh, and behold, then cometh the Son of God. [Birth] ... this will I give unto you for a sign at the time of his coming ... there shall be great lights in heaven, insomuch that in the night before he cometh there shall be no darkness, insomuch that it shall appear unto man as if it was day ... there shall a new star arise, such an one as ye never have beheld; and this also shall be a sign unto you. And behold this is not all, there shall be many signs and wonders in heaven. And it shall come to pass that ye shall all be amazed, and wonder, insomuch that ye shall fall to the earth (Helaman 14:2-7).

It was six hundred years from the time that Lehi left Jerusalem that the Promised Messiah was born (3 Nephi 1:19). There were heavenly signs of his birth; a new star shone in the sky (3 Nephi 1:21). There was a day, a night, and a day with no darkness:

> And it came to pass that there was no darkness in all that night, but it was as light as though it was mid-day. And it came to pass that the sun did rise in the morning again, according to its proper order... (3 Nephi 1:19).

The events transpired as prophesied and the signs impacted all of Mesoamerica. However, rather than turning to Christ, many of the idol worshipping heathens only increased their beliefs in Satanic cults with secret oaths and covenants to overthrow the government and destroy the believers. Swearing by the gods who ruled the heavens, these secret societies began to gain power in the land. Whatever proclivity they may have had before these signs and wonders were now reinforced tenfold.

By the time of Montezuma, the rulers would make no decisions without consulting the stars. The Mesoamericans were obsessed with astronomical signs. Especially important to the Mesoamericans was the 584 day calendar for Venus. Quetzalcoatl's star was Venus.

So were there sky watchers among the faithful believers in the Book of Mormon, but in a different way. Both shared an interest in heavenly signs. After the birth of the Messiah which was made known by heavenly signs, the Nephite Calendar changed:

> Now the Nephites began to reckon their time from this period when the sign was given, or from the coming of Christ; therefore, nine years had past away (3 Nephi 2:8).

The Law of Moses calendar would have celebrated the Passover as they still do in late March or early April. Usually it is the first Sabbath day after the new moon after the vernal equinox. The Book of Mormon prophets were advised as to the very day of the birth and resurrection of the Messiah (3 Nephi 1:13, 3 Nephi 8:5). Both the birth and resurrection of Christ were celebrated in April which was the first month of the year.

Thirty-four years later at the death of Jesus there were signs in the heavens above and earthly signs of destructions. Natural disasters abounded and the greatest light of them all, the sun, was darkened for three days. The significance of these events would awaken the watchers of heaven in subsequent generations.

> And it came to pass in the thirty and fourth year, in the first month, on the fourth day of the month, there arose a great storm, such an one as never had been known in all the land....
>
> And there was not any light seen, neither fire, nor glimmer, neither the sun, nor the moon, nor the stars, for so great were the mists of darkness which were upon the face of the land (3 Nephi 8:5, 22).

After the three days of total darkness, imagine the impression that it made upon one and all that survived the great destruction of tens of thousands of lives. There are those who remember Pearl Harbor and December 7, 1941, a day that will live in infamy. Others remember where they were on November 22, 1963, when John F. Kennedy was assassinated. More recently, the date of September 11, 2001, will have a lasting impression upon all those who saw on live television the second jumbo jet crash into the tower. It is emblazoned upon their minds forever. Those who witnessed the destruction of 3000 lives in the Twin Towers of the New York Trade Center call it "911" or "nine eleven."

The birth of Jesus Christ is still a world wide celebration for millions of people even after more than 2000 years. It would not be difficult to believe that the survivors of the New World destructions at the time of the death of the Savior would have it forever engraven upon their souls. The only event to surpass the destruction was hearing His voice after the three days of darkness. Before He appeared to some of them, He spoke to all of them from Heaven, and all the inhabitants of "this land" in Mesoamerica heard His voice (3 Nephi 9:1). To engrave upon their souls the message, He allowed significant time for them to ponder in silence. They contemplated his words for the "space of many hours" (3 Nephi 10:1-2). Giving the inhabitants of Mesoamerica time to reflect upon these words was important. They remained in darkness for the space of many more hours when the voice of the resurrected Jesus Christ spoke to them a second time. The survivors in Mesoamerica were all "ear witnesses" to the voice of the Lord. Later, many would become "eye witnesses." When Jesus came to Mesoamerica, He came from the sky, and He appeared in brightness above the glory of the sun. One of His many appearances was to those of the city of Bountiful.

> Behold, I am Jesus Christ the Son of God. I created the heavens and the earth, and all things that in them are.... all the people of the land did hear these sayings... (3 Nephi 9:15; 10:1).

This was an overwhelming experience. It was then followed by multiple visits of the risen Lord. He taught. He loved and healed their sick. He wept with them. He prayed with them and for them. He blessed their little children one by one. So powerful were these experiences, they were indelibly impressed upon the minds and hearts of all the people for the next two hundred years. There was a great period of subsequent peace with only minor interruptions of pride. The peace was not just the absence of war, but the spiritual peace which comes with the companionship of the Holy Ghost.

As with Pearl Harbor, or J.F.K., and sadly with Nine Eleven, in a few generations the fervor will fade. There was a great apostasy within four generations of the coming of Christ both on the American continent and in the Roman world. The Holy Spirit left them because of their willful choice to disregard the teachings of the Messiah to love one another. Consistent with most apostates, they would continue to celebrate the event of the "Descending God" coming to earth. They would perpetuate the memory of Christ's coming and surround the event with pagan rites and rituals which served the purposes of power hungry kings and priests. Within eight generations the Nephites would be completely destroyed, except for a history engraven on thin gold plates called the Book of Mormon. Their seed would only survive as a mixed seed. What also would survive was the strong tradition of the white bearded God. He promised to return and to descend anew to the earth.

How does such a sacred event become surrounded by pagan rituals? One has only to look at Santa Claus, the Christmas trees, the Easter bunnies or the Easter eggs to understand. I personally enjoy these traditions, as long as the distractions do not become the primary focus. The problem with the Mesoamericans was that the pagan rituals became more important than the original event. Many of these great events survived in the myths and legends of the people Some oral traditions were written down on Mesoamerican documents.

Popol Vuh

The *Popol Vuh* is a record of the Quiché Maya. It was rewritten by indigenous historians in A.D. 1550. It had to be rewritten because the originals were burned in the fires by the Catholic priests. As soon as the Quiché Maya learned how to write in the Spanish alphabet, they gathered all of the ancients and rewrote their story of the creation. It is called the Mayan Bible. It tells of the creation of the earth, man, and all things. In beautiful chiastic poetry, the Popol Vuh relates the appearance of the first dawn, the requirements of the gods for sacrifice and tribute, and the mystical origins of the clans and places of the Quiché. The book relates the story of the Quetzal Serpent also known as Qucumatz. He is God of Heaven with his feathers, and God of the Earth and the Water as represented by the serpent. He is all-powerful and can move freely between the earth and sky. Quetzal Serpent is the son of the father, "Heart of Sky." Together they created the earth and humanity.

Traditional Christianity has a single God with multiple dimensions, the three-in-one doctrine. The belief in two separate beings such as Joseph Smith saw in the First Vision, a Father and a Son as two distinct identities involved in organizing the earth and all things thereon, was restored light and knowledge. This once known truth had become lost in the early councils of Christianity. Elements of the truth mixed with legend and folklore survived in Mesoamerica. From the Popol Vuh one reads:

> They thought and they pondered. They reached an accord, bringing together their words and their thoughts. Then they gave birth, heartening one another. Beneath the light, they gave birth to humanity ... together [Heart of Sky and Qucumatz] they conceived light and life.[248]

From LDS scriptures one reads:

> And the Gods took counsel among themselves and ... watched those things which they had ordered until they obeyed ... with the lesser light they set the stars ... So the Gods went down to organize man ... male and female to form they them (Abraham 4:26; 3:18,16).

The Popol Vuh and the Book of Ether

The origin of the Popol Vuh and how the Quiché Maya acquired it relates to an account in the Book of Mormon of how the twenty-four gold plates which contained the record of the Jaredites were obtained. Dr. Dennis Tedlock is a highly respected Professor of Anthropology at State University of New York at Buffalo. He has also produced a translation of the Popol Vuh and focused on its origin. One of the names by which the Popol Vuh was known is "The Light That Came from *Beside* the Sea."

> ...the phrase becomes one of a number of clues that converge to indicate that the east coast of Yucatán was the region where Quiché ancestors acquired the hieroglyphic Popol Vuh, or some part of it, on a pilgrimage.... Because they obtained the book (or some section of it) on a pilgrimage that took them down from the highlands to the Atlantic shore, they called it "The Light That Came from Beside the Sea." Because the book told of events that happened before the first

> true dawn, and of a time when their ancestors hid themselves and the stones that contained the spirit familiars of their gods in forests, they also called it "Our Place in the Shadows." And because it told of the rise of the morning star and the sun and moon, and foretold the rise and radiant splendor of the Quiché lords, they called it "The Dawn of Life."[249]

The content of the Popol Vuh relates the story of the creation. There are several key words and phrases that refer to Biblical stories. "The first true dawn" relates to the creation of the earth. "When their ancestors hid themselves" may refer to Adam and Eve hiding from the Lord in the Garden of Eden (Genesis 3:10). "The stones that contained the spirit familiars of their gods" is a poetic reference to vision stones that revealed the future through spirit companions. The Quiché believed in vision crystals or stones that revealed future events. The Bible refers to similar stones (or crystals) as the Urim and Thummim (Exodus 28:30). "The rise of the morning star and the sun and moon" also reference the creation.

Six KeyEelements of the Quiché Story:

1. The Quiché obtained the book
2. While on a pilgrimage
3. Down from the highlands
4. On the Atlantic shore
5. The book contained the story of the creation of all things
6. It was a hieroglyphic book

The Book of Mormon Story of Acquiring the Twenty-four Gold Plates of The Book of Ether

> And the king said unto him: Being grieved for the afflictions of my people, I caused that forty and three of my people should take a journey into the wilderness, that thereby they might find the land of Zarahemla, that we might appeal unto our brethren to deliver us out of bondage.
>
> And they were lost in the wilderness for the space of many days, yet they were diligent, and found not the land of Zarahemla but returned to this land having traveled in a land among many waters,...
>
> And for a testimony that the things that they had said are true they have brought twenty-four plates which are filled with engravings, and they are of pure gold ... (Mosiah 8:7-9).
>
> ...And now I, Moroni, proceed to give an account of those ancient inhabitants who were destroyed by the hand of the Lord upon the face of this north country.

> And I take mine account from the twenty and four plates which were found by the people of Limhi, which is called the Book of Ether.
>
> And as I suppose that the first part of this record, which speaks concerning the creation of the world, and also of Adam, and an account from that time even to the great tower, and whatsoever things transpired among the children of men until that time, is had among the Jews ... but they are had upon the plates; and whoso findeth them, the same will have power that he may get the full account ... (Ether 1:1-4).
>
> ...I am commanded that I should hid them up again in the earth. Behold I have written upon these plates the very things the brother of Jared saw...wherefore I have sealed up the interpreters [Urim and Thummim], according to the commandment of the Lord (Ether 4:3, 5)

Six Key Elements of the Book of Ether Story

1. The Nephites obtain the book (twenty-four gold plates)
2. Forty-three men went on a pilgrimage
3. They came down from the highlands
4. On the Atlantic shore
5. The book contained the story of the creation
6. The plates were engraved upon [hieroglyphics]

The king mentioned in The Book of Mormon story is Limhi. They were living in the highlands (Mosiah 8:2) and went in search of their brethren in the lowlands of Zarahemla (Omni 1:13). It was a "pilgrimage." If one went directly north into the "land of many waters" he would encounter the Atlantic Ocean. Both the Usumacinta River and the Grijalva River flow north and meet just before they empty into the Gulf of Mexico (Atlantic Ocean). Moroni abridged the twenty-four gold plates and found on them the story of the creation of the world, of Adam, and all things down to the great tower (Genesis 1-10).

Is this conclusive evidence? No. But it is one more story like unto the Mexicas looking for a promised land, the Snakes of Tizapán (Ether 9:31), the People of the Serpent, the belief in the Descending God, and the tradition in Oaxaca that a group of highlanders came down and taught the people to read and write for which the highlanders were made their rulers. These are unique LDS doctrines and beliefs that are not espoused in Christendom.

Title of the Lords of Totonicapán

Title of the Lords of Totonicapán is another wonderful Quiché Mayan rewritten text. Indigenous historians recorded it in 1554. It follows in precise order the book of Genesis and claims that the Bible story of the scattering of the Lost

Tribes of Israel is their story. The parallels between the Bible and their own history were so plain to them, that it was impossible for the two to be anything different than the same story told in two places. When the monks and the friars arrived in the New World, they also accepted the story from the natives that their ancestors came across the sea. It was the scientific community and the "Siberian Land Bridge Only" dogma, believing that primitive man could not have crossed the seas in watercrafts, which discounted the testimony of the indigenous historians. Now that the scientific community has accepted that pre-Columbians traversed the oceans, the information given by native historians needs to be reevaluated. This includes the possibility that some of the Mayan descendants were indeed immigrants from the tribes of Israel.

In all of Christianity, it is the LDS doctrine in 1830 which is specific in identifying two of the three immigrant maritime groups discussed in the Book of Mormon as coming from the Tribes of Israel. Here one reads from *The Title of the Lords of Totonicapán*:

> These, then were the three nations of Quichés, and they came from where the sun rises [east] descendants of Israel, of the same language and the same customs ... [our ancestors] were the sons of Abraham and Jacob...[250]

> Now on the twenty-eighth of September of 1554 we sign this attestation in which we have written that which by tradition our ancestors told us, who came from the other part of the sea, from Civán-Tulán, bordering on Babylonia.[251]

When the Quiché say they have the same language as the Hebrew, there is merit in a closer look at this claim. For example, "woman" in Hebrew is pronounced "eesha." The Quiché word for "woman" is ix_k. The x is pronounced with a "ish" sound and "k" as "ch" or "eeshach." Other Mayan dialects are similar; Chortí is ixik. Obviously, over time all languages change and evolve as testified by nearly thirty Mayan dialects. Some key words and phrases are bound to survive, such as "woman." Recall the Book of Mormon does not claim to represent all the migrations to the New World or that Hebrew was the universal tongue. However in the spirit of diffusionism there may have been significant cross cultural pollination and influence.

Title of the Lords of Totonicapán has been rejected by the Darwinists and the Evolutionists as impossible because they believed there was no pre-Columbian contact with the Old World. Why? Would it be surprising at this point to know it was because of the "Siberian Land Bridge Only" doctrine? The Monks and Friars accepted the story of the natives that their ancestors "came across the sea."[252] It wasn't until the late 19th century and post Stephens and Catherwood that the "Siberian Land Bridge Only" theory became dogma for the scientific community. My prediction is the evolutionists will find other reasons to reject the Mayan historical documents; now that pre-Columbian maritime crossings are accepted as one of the ways that the New World was settled. It is no longer "impossible" that the ancestors of the Quiche were not indeed the descendents of Abraham as they claimed. That which was discarded as impossible and labeled as tainted, the Book of Mormon proclaimed both viable and real. God would remember his covenant that he made with Abraham to bless all nations of the earth and gather them again in the latter-days (1 Nephi 22:9-12). A disservice and a great injustice have been done to the Quiché in being discounted so whimsically by the scientific community. This includes the Quiché's witness of Qucumatz as the Descending God who came among them and promised to return.

Annals of the Cakchiquels

Annals of the Cakchiquels is an indigenous document of the highland Cakchiquel Maya collected between A.D. 1550 and A.D. 1560, and written in A.D. 1605. This is another document that had to be rewritten because the originals were destroyed by the Spaniards. In many ways, it is similar to the Popol Vuh but more historical in nature. It is certainly a second witness of what the original Maya believed. The Cakchiquels were arch enemies of the Quiché; however they shared common religious beliefs. The *Annals* reinforces the belief in a Father God, "Tepeuh," and his son, "Topilzin-Quetzalcoatl" Feathered Serpent. The writers tell of wars of conquest and annihilation, of their kings who were made prisoners and forced to live in captivity. It speaks of the eternal ties of the family and records an accurate genealogy. Its relevance to the Book of Mormon is the belief in Quetzalcoatl who would come to the earth. Also the reference to "captive kings or kings held in captivity." Usually the Maya sacrificed kings who were captured. This is an anomaly. However, in the Book of Mormon several captured kings were held in captivity for forty-two years, and some their entire lives. Holding kings captive for years was a Book of Mormon practice as well as Mesoamerican:

> And his brother did rise up in rebellion against him [Kim], by which he did bring him into captivity; and he did remain in captivity all his days...
>
> ...And when Hearthom had reigned twenty and four years, behold the kingdom was taken away from him. And he served many years in captivity, yea even all the remainder of his days (Ether 10:14, 30).

Obras Históricas

Fernando de Alva Ixtlilxóchitl was born in A.D. 1568 in Mexico of Mexica royalty. His great-grandfather was the King of Texcoco, and his mother Beatriz was the daughter of the last Aztec King Cuitlahuac. Ixtlilxóchitl was the most illustrious of the native Mexican historians. He wrote various books, but his two-volume work called *Obras Históricas*[253] is the most quoted. There are several significant points of correlation between the Book of Mormon and *Obras Históricas.* The acknowledgement of the Mexica's belief in the Descending God Quetzalcoatl, the Tower of Babel, the Flood, and that their ancestors arrived in North America by crossing the great waters from Asia are a few of the most obvious.

The original brass plates, from which the prophet-historian Mormon abridged the Book of Mormon, included the accounts of the creation, the Tower of Babel and the first five books of Moses in the Old Testament (I Nephi 5:11). The Book of Mormon claims that the Jaredites came to Mesoamerica from the Tower of Babel. The prophet historian Moroni said of them: "But a part of the account I give, from the tower down until they were destroyed" (Ether 1:5). Now, from the writings of Ixtlilxóchitl, one can read the same or a parallel historical account:

> The Tultecas had good knowledge of the creation of the world (before the Spaniards arrived) ... They said the world was created in the year Ce Técpatl, and from this time until the great flood they called Atonatiuh, which means the age of the sun and water, because he destroyed the world by flood ... the high tower was built to save themselves from the destruction of the second world. Languages were changed, no one understood the other and they were dispersed to the many parts of the world, the Tultecas, seven men, each with his wife who understood the same language, came to this country, *after having traversed lands and seas, living in caves and enduring hardships until their arrival to this land, which they found to be fertile and desirable to live in.*[254]

The Book of Mormon records the journey of the Jaredites across *lands and seas* from *the great tower* and during their crossing of the great waters in eight barges with covered tops. Because the covered barges had no light in them they appeared to be like floating caves (Ether 2:16-22). Others also found America a fruitful land.

> And we did call it the Promised Land. And it came to pass that we did begin to till the earth, and we began to plant seeds; yea, we did put all our seeds into the earth, which we had brought from the land of Jerusalem. And it came to pass that they did grow exceedingly; wherefore, we were blessed in abundance (1 Nephi 18:23-24).

Both the sincere and the curious might ask, "What else did the Book of Mormon predict?" The answer is a resounding "The return of Jesus Christ to America as a resurrected being!" "His "Second Coming." It is not about archaeology. It is about the Book of Mormon as a second witness to Jesus as the Son of God and the son of Mary, and the Savior of mankind.

It would be gratifying if the Olmecs turn out to be the Jaredites. It would be confirming if the Mulekites are the Zapotecs, or some of their mixed seed, or if the original Quetzalcoatl turns out to be based in the actual visits of Christ to the Americas. However, what matters is the witness of the Book of Mormon. There is a God. Jesus is His Divine Son. Man will resurrect and there is life after death. This was the message the early Mesoamericans received.

CHAPTER TWELVE

HISTORICAL CONSIDERATIONS: NEW WORLD CALENDARS AND THE CLIMATE

Figure 48. Tzolkin Calendar

The Mesoamericans were obsessed with calendars. Why? The need for order in the universe required it. Man's very existence depended upon maintaining that order. The gods were a whimsical lot. They were easily upset. Unlike the Christian God who was all-knowing, the Mesoamerican gods were not all-knowing, and they were imperfect. As demonstrated by the "Hero Twins," Hunahpu and Xbalanque, in the *Popol Vuh*, the gods could even be tricked.[255] However imperfect the gods may have been, they nevertheless had life and death control over mankind. They could deny rain in due season. They could give you an unlucky child. They could cause volcanoes to erupt and hurricanes to destroy entire villages. Historian Maurice Collis reported that

> The day and the hour, for instance, when each god should receive his blood offerings, had been worked out in immense detail. The right time was determined by astronomy. The priests of Central America had not gone to the labour of calculating a calendar, as perfect or more perfect than any in Europe, simply for the convenience of knowing the dates. They had done so because they conceived it to be a matter of life and death to approach the gods at the most auspicious moments.[256]

There are at least eleven different Mesoamerican Calendars involving the sun, moon, Venus and combinations of them in Olmec, Toltec, Aztec, Zapotec, and Maya dating systems.

The cultures that occupied Mesoamerica based their sacred calendars on pleasing the gods, of which Quetzalcoatl was but one. The Mesoamericans knew there was a time to plant, a time to harvest, a time for Quetzalcoatl to come, and a time to go to war. Waiting to attack your enemy until a certain day, and according to the stars, was very Mesoamerican. The risings and settings of the 584 day Venus calendar were consulted before going to war. The day of your birth and your fortunes in life were tied together. The concept of being born on "unlucky days" (1st, 3rd, or 5th) is also an Egyptian belief, as reported by Wallace Budge, Curator of the British Museum.[257]

Unlucky Days

If you were born during the Mayan five unlucky days of August 6th to August 10th, you were born during the unlucky days of chaos and sorrow. Trouble was bound to be your lot, and it would affect those around you. The five unlucky days were called Wayeb. There is evidence of some parents giving away their children for adoption because of the stigma of having that child born on an unlucky day. Probably the most famous of these would be the consort of Cortés. Her Spanish name was Doña Marina. Maurice Collis in his book, *Cortés and Montezuma,* said of her

> She is described as good looking, intelligent and not at all shy. Her value to Cortés was great at this moment, for she spoke both Mexican [Aztec Nahuatl] and Maya ... she became indispensable to Cortés in all his delicate negotiations. Moreover, she grew very fond of him, and later on, bore him a son, Don Martin ... In Mexico a person's name had an astrological significance; it indicated what would befall him. Marina's name, One Grass of Penance, was a name which a female born on a particular date would be given ... That it was believed that Marina would be mixed up with troubles of this sort was probably the reason why her mother got rid of her. From the Mexican point of view she was an unlucky person, somebody dangerous to have to do with.[258]

One can see just how important calendars were to the Mesoamericans from this story of Doña Marina. Since the Book of Mormon calendar was not Mesoamerican, and was Law of Moses oriented, what was the significance of Mesoamerican calendars? The basic point is the Mesoamericans of the time of the Book of Mormon had exact and precise calendar systems. This was indicative of a highly sophisticated and advanced civilization. This is accepted today as a matter of fact. It wasn't even acknowledged as a possibility when the Book of Mormon was published in 1830. Secondly, there is no evidence of this kind of high civilization anywhere north of the Rio Grande in North America or in South America dating to the time of the Book of Mormon. Some have argued the Europe of 1492 still did not function with a calendar system as accurate and astrologically correct as those of Mesoamerica.

The Law of Moses Lunar Calendar

Lunar months are twenty-nine and thirty days long. The current solar months are thirty and thirty-one days long with the exception of February. The shorter lunar year requires an annual adjustment on the Jewish calendar so that the Passover is celebrated in the spring. This adjustment on the Jewish calendar results in the Passover fluctuating between March 20th and April 21st. on a solar calendar.

Lehi left Jerusalem before the Babylonian captivity and would have referred to the names of the months as the first month, second month, etc. Lehi would have used a lunar calendar based on the Law of Moses with the first month being celebrated at the Passover (Exodus 12:2). The names of the months of the present calendar used by the Jewish community were originally the Babylonian names for the Babylonian lunar calendar. During the time they were in captivity in Babylon the Jews altered the names and order slightly of the Babylonian named months. Nisan, Iyar, Sivan, Tammuz, Av, Elul, Tishrei, Heshvan, Kislev, Tevet, Shevat and Adar I and II are the Jewish-Babylonian influenced names. By the time of Joseph Smith, the month names of the Jewish calendar had been used by the Jewish community for two thousand years. It would have been natural for Joseph Smith, if he had written instead of translated the Book of Mormon, to use the names for the Jewish months. Joseph did not use month names because they did not exist when Lehi left Jerusalem. The months mentioned in the Book of Mormon include the first, second, sixth, seventh, tenth and eleventh months, just as the Jewish people had referenced their months from the time of the Exodus to the Babylonian captivity (Numbers 10:11). The new moon marks the beginning of each new month.

The Messiah-Based Book of Mormon Calendar

The calendar systems of the Book of Mormon will be discussed in greater detail later. What is important in this context is the understanding that the Nephite calendar was Messiah-Quetzalcoatl based. The Mesoamerican Long

Count calendar was based on the time from the creation of man. The Book of Mormon record keepers were focused on the birth of the Messiah Quetzalcoatl. They were also devout adherents to the Law of Moses.[259] This meant they used a sacred calendar which was lunar (Omni 1:21, Exodus 12:2). The sacred calendar was based on God coming to the earth and his birth. The Book of Mormon Prophet Abinadi said, "God himself should come down among the children of men, and take upon him the form of man" (Mosiah 13:34). For more than six hundred years, the Nephite subculture of Mesoamerica persisted in keeping the Law of Moses being surrounded in a pagan society that worshipped idols and offered human sacrifice.

One cannot read the Book of Mormon and not be aware of the focused attention that is placed upon the birth of the Messiah.

> Yea, even six hundred years from the time that my father left Jerusalem, a prophet would the Lord God raise up among the Jews—even a Messiah, or, in other words, a Savior of the world (1 Nephi 10:4).

No other single event in the Book of Mormon affected the calendar system more than that prophecy of the birth of the Savior. The prophet-writers of the Book of Mormon kept track of time by the number of years until the birth of the Promised Messiah. His birth would occur exactly six hundred years from the time Lehi left Jerusalem; therefore, their departure date signified more than just leaving Jerusalem, Nephi said, "And thirty years had passed away from the time we left Jerusalem" (2 Nephi 5:28). Omni recorded "Three hundred and twenty years had passed away…" (Omni 1:5).

There were different ways of keeping track of time. There was a secular calendar recording the reign of kings and judges, and a sacred calendar relating to the Messiah Quetzalcoatl. It was "in the thirty and third year of his reign [King Mosiah]…making in the whole five hundred and nine years from the time Lehi left Jerusalem" (Mosiah 29:46). Keeping two calendars, one religious and one secular, was very much a Hebrew thing and blatantly a Mesoamerican thing to do.

The Influence of the Law of Moses Upon The Book of Mormon

It is important to remember the Law of Moses calendar system influenced the Book of Mormon. The Nephite calendar in the Book of Mormon was not of Mayan or of Olmec derivation. The Nephites would have been aware of the various other calendars and may have used them for planting and harvesting. The main characters in the Book of Mormon were devout followers of the Law of Moses. They would have used a twelve month pre-Babylonian Jewish calendar, as did the Jews that were scattered in many parts of the earth. Whatever adjustments that were made in the calendar system used by the Book of Mormon people, one thing was certain; the changes respected the Laws of Moses and focused on the coming of the Messiah.

> And notwithstanding we believe in Christ, we keep the law of Moses, and look forward with steadfastness unto Christ, until the law shall be fulfilled (2 Nephi 25:24).

To understand how totally and completely devout Lehi was, a brief look at his behavior revealed his devotion to the Law of Moses. The first thing that Lehi did after he fled from Jerusalem with his family near the shores of the Red Sea was to build an altar and make a "thanksgiving offering" unto the Lord (1 Nephi 2:7). This is consistent with a devout keeper of the Law of Moses (Leviticus 7:11-13). Later, his sons returned with the Plates of Brass, which Nephi had obtained from Laban. When faithful Father Lehi received these sacred writings, once again he "did rejoice exceedingly, and did offer sacrifice and burnt offerings unto the Lord; and they gave thanks unto the God of Israel" (1 Nephi 5:9).

In spite of all the apostasies, desertions, and the dissenters in the Book of Mormon, the prophet leaders and righteous kings exhorted the people to keep the Law of Moses until it should be fulfilled in the atoning mission of the Messiah. After Jesus Christ, who was identified as the Messiah by revelation in the Book of Mormon, was born (2 Nephi 10:3), many thought they were released from the Law of Moses. However, the Messiah had not yet shared his teachings, or set up his church. Important aspects of the Atonement had not been completed, and Christ had not yet suffered in the Garden of Gethsemane, died on the cross, or resurrected.

> And there were no contentions; save it were a few that began to preach, endeavoring to prove by the scriptures that it was no more expedient to observe the law of Moses. Now in this thing they did err, not having understood the scriptures.
>
> But it came to pass that they soon became converted, and were convinced of the error which they were in, for it was made known unto them that the law was not yet fulfilled, and that it must be fulfilled in every wit ... (3 Nephi 1:24-25).

For more than six hundred years, the Nephite subculture in Mesoamerica persisted in keeping the Law of Moses although they were surrounded in a pagan society that worshipped idols and offered human sacrifice. As mentioned, there were as many as eleven different calendar systems used in Mesoamerica by the various inhabitants who coexisted one with the other. The focus here is the Nephite Calendar derived from the Law of Moses. This means that the first month of the Nephite calendar would begin on the New Moon nearest to the vernal equinox, around the first day of April.

> Now nine years had passed away from the time when the sign was given, which was spoken of by the prophets that Christ should come into the world.

> Now the Nephites began to reckon their time [years] from this period when the sign was given, or from the coming of Christ... (3 Nephi 2:7-8).

They were confident in the date because of the many heavenly signs that had been given. The specific sign of the birth of Christ was marked in the New World by a day and a night and another day of "no darkness" (3 Nephi 1:13-15). What better sign for Him who was to become the "Light of the World?" The Nephites were equally confident about the death date of the Savior because of the signs given. The death of Christ was marked by temporal disasters and an all pervading "darkness," which lasted for three days:

> And it came to pass in the thirty and fourth year, in the first month, on the fourth day of the month [approximately April 4th]... for the space of three days that there was no light seen... (3 Nephi 8:5, 23).

The First Month of the Jewish Year

The foregoing explanation has been given in order to demonstrate that late March or early April on a solar calendar was the first month of a twelve month lunar calendar. The Nephites, as devout followers of the Law of Moses, followed the Lord's commandment to Moses to have the month that the exodus occurred from Egypt mark the New Year:

> This month [Passover] shall be unto you the beginning of months: it shall be the first month of the year to you (Exodus 12: 2).

The Book of Mormon believers in the Messiah celebrated what the Bible called Abib, or Nissan, around April 1st which was the first month of the New Year. This information is valuable when studying Book of Mormon dates. For example, Amalickiah was killed on the last day, of the year and he was discovered dead on the first day of the first month of the 26th year of the reign of the judges (Alma 52:1). This means he died about the 1st of April 66 B.C.

Knowing the correct months which correspond to the dates in the Book of Mormon, gives direct information about temperature, clothing, battle dress for war and a number of other issues related to climate.

Calendars and Climatic Considerations

In addition to the lack of population, civilization and overall demographics, the climate in and around western New York does not qualify the region as the lands of the last great battles of the Jaredites and the Nephites. Both the demographics and the climate of Mesoamerica are consistent with the claims of the Book of Mormon and reinforce there were two Cumorahs.

Climatic Conditions and the Book of Mormon

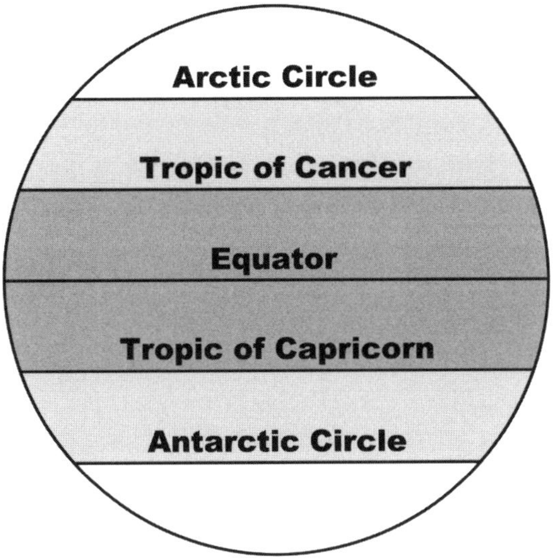

Figure 49. Tropic of Cancer

Mesoamerica, which is south of the Tropic of Cancer, is hot and humid all year long except in the higher elevations. In the highlands of Guatemala or Mexico City, you can experience more moderate weather. A mild climate in the midst of a hot and humid one becomes a refuge. This may explain why Mexico City is listed as one of the largest cities on earth with twenty-plus million inhabitants in the greater suburban area.

However, in the lowlands the average daily temperature range is in the 81 to 88 degrees in the Yucatan year round. There is a wet season, which begins in May-June and ends in October-November and a dry season, which runs from December to May with some obvious local fluctuations. When people ask about the weather in Mesoamerica, they are informed it is either "hot and wet or hotter and wetter."

People who have to deal with snow as a part of their environment are abundantly aware of how snow impacts their lifestyle. Only once in the entire Book of Mormon is the word "snow" used. Nephi, at the time his family was still in the Old World, used the word snow to describe the tree which his father had seen in a vision: "and the whiteness thereof did exceed the whiteness of the driven snow" (1 Nephi 11:8). There was, and still is, snow on Mount Hermon, a mountain of 9,400 feet high in the northernmost part of the Holy Land. Nephi understood what snow was. There was no mention of snow in the area where the primary events of the Book of Mormon took place in the New World. The pilgrims of Plymouth, Massachusetts in 1620 often referenced the cold and the snow. If the major events of the Book of Mormon all happened around the New York Hill Cumorah, one would expect to hear about snow.

In Mesoamerica, one would not expect to hear about snow in their writings, and snow is not a topic about which they write. To the contrary, one would expect to find expressions like, "heat of the day," and "fevers." Indeed, those very expressions are in the Book of Mormon.

Many are Cold and a Few are Frozen

Equally revealing about the climate were the comments involving Alma and Amulek. The setting for the story took place in the city of Ammonihah. The Book of Mormon says that Ammonihah was located three days journey north of Melek, which was west of Zarahemla (Alma 8:3-6). Zarahemla is located on the west of the river Sidon. This river has a west bank and an east bank. As the Book of Mormon Index points out, the River Sidon runs from the south and goes "north to [the] sea."[260]

Some, who believe that the primary events of the Book of Mormon took place within six hundred and fifty miles of Palmyra, have postulated that the Niagara River is a viable candidate for this essential landmark. Others have considered the Genesee River in Rochester, New York as a candidate. Both rivers flow north. If the Genesee or Niagara River were the River Sidon, then somewhere to the west of Niagara or Rochester one would expect to find the best candidate for Zarahemla. Some advocates for the Great Lakes have suggested Buffalo, New York and its environs as a likely spot. Approximately one day's journey west from Zarahemla and three days journey north of the Land of Melek places one in Ammonihah (Alma 8:6). At fifteen or thirty miles a day, a three-day journey north could place a person traveling alone between forty-five to ninety miles north and west of Zarahemla. If Buffalo, New York is located near Zarahemla, then forty-five to ninety miles northwest would place one in Canada at or near Hamilton, Ontario. This place would be and is colder than Buffalo.

Back to the story of Alma and Amulek, who as prophets, were taken and cast into prison at Ammonihah. A causal reading will reveal that these two men suffered great physical and emotional abuse at the hands of their captors. Among other things, they were forced to watch the burning of women and children in human fires, as well as the burning of "the Holy Scriptures." They were bound with cords, and on five separate occasions they were physically beaten, spit on, and bitten; "many came forth also, and smote them" (Alma 14:8-25).

> And many such things did they say unto them, gnashing their teeth upon them, and spitting upon them, and saying: How shall we look when we are damned?
>
> And many such things, yea all manner of such things did they say unto them; and thus they did mock them *for many days*. And they did withhold food from them that they might hunger, and water that they might thirst; and they also did take from them their clothes that they were naked; and thus they were bound with strong cords, and confined in prison.

> And it came to pass *after they had thus suffered for many days*, (and it was on the twelfth day, in the tenth month, in the tenth year of the reign of the judges over the people of Nephi) ... (Alma 14:21-23, emphasis added).

"Many days" is a phrase of uncertain duration. Alma returned to Ammonihah after his first rejection there. Amulek set the date as the "forth day of this seventh month" (Alma 10:6). The 7th month and the 4th day on a lunar calendar of twenty-nine or thirty days per month would be around September 27th. The day they were delivered from prison was "on the twelfth day in the tenth month" (Alma 14:23). This would have been approximately ninety-six days later. This date corresponds to around the first week of January. The minimum amount of time they would have spent in that condition would have been five days (Alma 14:18, 20, 23-28). They would not have been able to go without food and water for much longer without the Lord divinely intervening. The Lord did deliver them after many days. There is no indication that the Lord divinely intervened to spare them from the deprivations and physical sufferings they endured prior to their deliverance. Suffice it to say, many days of physical abuse, battery, and deprivation in a state of complete nakedness with their hands being bound would leave them in a physically weakened condition. They would be fortunate to survive in any climate, and certainly would have perished in a cold one. The areas of Rochester, New York and Buffalo, New York are known for their harsh winters, freezing cold and raging winter storms. The same is true of Hamilton, Canada.

Among the Nephites in the Book of Mormon, and according to the Nephite calendar, they were delivered sometime between December 25th and the 1st of January. It seems unreasonable to assume that one can be stripped naked and left for many days and not die of exposure in Hamilton, Ontario, Canada in late December or early January. The average "high" temperature for January 1st to January 12th in Hamilton is 31° degrees Fahrenheit.[261] The average nighttime temperatures drop to 19° degrees Fahrenheit. The conditions that lead to death by hypothermia are cold temperatures, improper clothing, wetness, fatigue and exhaustion, dehydration, and poor food intake.

In the Mesoamerican lowlands, the average lowest temperature in late December and early January is in the mid-sixties.[262] Wherever three days journey northwest of Zarahemla may be, it has to be a climate conducive to nakedness during the coldest months of the year. Mesoamerica is situated wholly south in the Tropic of Cancer and has a climate conducive to nakedness.

Loincloths and Lamanites

Germaine to the issue of climate is the Lamanite dress, or the lack thereof. For the same reasons that Alma and Amulek could not have survived death by hypothermia in a cold climate, so also the Lamanites would have perished had they come to battle dressed only in a loincloth. Enos, who is estimated to

Figure 50. Loincloths in Mesoamerica

have lived between 544 B.C. and 421 B.C. described the Lamanites as "wandering about in the wilderness with a short girdle about their loins and their heads shaven" (Enos 1:25). Around 178 B.C., Zeniff, a Nephite King, portrayed the manner of dress among the Lamanites in the highlands of the Land of Nephi as follows: "And they had their heads shaved and they were naked; and they were girded with a leathern girdle about their loins" (Mosiah 10:8). In 87 B.C. Alma compared the dissenting Nephite-Amlicites to the Lamanites and observed of the Amlicites: "They had not shorn their heads like unto the Lamanites. Now the heads of the Lamanites were shorn; and they were naked, save it were skin which was girded about their loins" (Alma 3:4-5). In the 18th year of the reign of the judges, or about 74 B.C. a description of the approaching army of Zarahemnah is given. The army was composed of Amalekites and Zoramites (Nephite dissenters) and a massive army of Lamanites: "...they were naked, save it were a skin which was girded about their loins, yea all were naked save it were the Zoramites and the Amalekites" (Alma 43:20).

The actual description of the battle revealed the great loss of life among the Lamanites because they wore no protective cover: "And the work of death commenced on both sides, but it was more dreadful on the part of the Lamanites, for their nakedness was exposed" (Alma: 43:37). Moroni, a Nephite general, who destroyed the combined armies arrayed against him, made this comment: "Behold, their naked skins and their bare heads were exposed to the sharp swords of the Nephites" (Alma 44:18). Nearly a hundred years later, after the birth of Jesus Christ, about A.D. 19, Giddianhi, the leader of a band of robbers composed of Nephite dissenters and Lamanites, came to war against the city-states in the land of Zarahemla to the borders of the Land Bountiful. In preparation for the battle, all of the Nephites gathered together in a single massive encampment with a seven-year supply of food and weapons (3 Nephi 4:4):

> And it came to pass that they did come up to battle; and was in the sixth month; and behold, great and terrible was the day that they did come up to battle; and they were girded about after the manner of robbers; and they had lamb-skin about their loins, and they were dyed in blood, and their heads were shorn, and they had headplates upon them ... (3 Nephi 4:7).

The point is that for nearly six hundred years the Lamanites came to battle dressed only in loincloths with their heads shaven. At least they had learned to wear protective headgear by A.D.19 (3 Nephi 4:7).

The internal evidence in the Book of Mormon confirms that the Lamanites came to battle year round. Some of the wars lasted for six years and they were not seasonal, but one continuous struggle (Alma 51-62). As previously quoted, the naked and shorn Lamanites came to war in the sixth month (September) (3 Nephi 4:7) and in the commencement of the year (April), and at the year's end (March) (3 Nephi 4:1; 3 Nephi 2:17; Alma 56:20). Teancum's killing of Amalickiah was on the last day of the last month (March), and on the first day of the new moon near April 1st, they found Amalickiah dead in his own tent (Alma 51:33-37). Supplies are brought to the Stripling Warriors of Helaman in the second month (May) (Alma 56:27). And these same groups of young soldiers were fighting in the seventh month (October): "In the morning of the third day of the seventh month..." (Alma 56:42). On another occasion, Alma records a battle in the eleventh month (February 10th): "In the eleventh month of the nineteenth year on the tenth day of the month, the armies of the Lamanites were seen approaching the land of Ammonihah" (Alma 49:1). For the interested, there are many more confirming scriptures that duplicate the aforementioned months.

The sum of the matter is that the Lamanites came to battle and war dressed in only a loincloth, and their heads were shaven. This tradition was perpetuated for centuries. They came to battle in February, March, April, May, September, and October as specifically mentioned in the Book of Mormon, and some wars lasted for years. It is doubtful these battles took place in a climate not conducive to nakedness and loincloths. February in New York with loincloths is a stretch for the most avid adherent to the Canadian border believers. Year-round loincloths in Mesoamerica are a well-established fact. When the explorer John Lloyd Stephens first arrived in Mesoamerica he made some preliminary observations: "The Indians were naked, except a small piece of cotton cloth around the loins, and crossing in front between the legs."[263] It was November, 1839.

Illness by the Nature of the Climate

Climate is mentioned in the Book of Mormon as a contributor to the cause of disease: "...the cause of diseases, to which men were subject by the nature of the climate" (Alma 46:40).

The phrase "by the nature of the climate" is a relevant one. Tropical climate areas are inherently more disease prone because the warmer climate is a friendly host to disease causing agents. This means that some climates are more prone to disease by nature of the climate. Warmer and wetter climates such as Mesoamerica are inclined to disease. The observation that a change in weather can lead to the appearance of epidemic disease has been appreciated since the dawn of medical science. The Center for Disease Control in Atlanta Georgia published a report, "Linkages between Climate and Infectious Diseases":

> The characteristic geographic distributions and seasonal variations of many infectious diseases are prima facie evidence, linked with weather and climate. Studies have shown that factors such as temperature, precipitation, and humidity affect the lifecycle of many disease pathogens and vectors [direct and indirect carriers of disease] and thus can potentially affect the timing and intensity of disease outbreaks.[264]

The whole debate on global warming has raised serious questions about the spread of tropical diseases to an epidemic level. The fear is that tropical climates will move father north. If this occurs, it will subject an entire population to disease carrying pathogens. The West Nile Virus and Bird Flu are only the tip of the iceberg. The point is climates south of the tropic of Cancer are, by their very nature, more disease friendly.

Fevers are certainly not the prerogative of Mesoamerica. Fevers are, however, much more abundant in tropical climate zones around the globe because of the heavy seasonal rain. Among other things, mosquitoes spawn on water. There are few places on earth that killed more Europeans than the yellow fever and the malaria of Central America and the similar tropical climate zones around the world. As deadly as small pox was to the Native American populations brought to them by the Europeans, so was the yellow fever of Mesoamerica, and similar climate zones, a killer of Europeans. The early Spanish explorers named the eastern shores of Costa Rica and Darien (Panama), Mosquito Coast. It retains that name to this date.

BOYD'S LDS BOOKS

03/07/08 17:10 E 0 29949

1@ 9.95 MP97417		$	9.95
	BLACKS AND THE M		
1@ 17.95 GP8088X		$	17.95
	GLIMPSES BEYOND		
1@ 20.00 GP14403		$	20.00
	MESOAMERICA AND		
SUBTOTAL		$	47.90
SALES TAX @ 6.500%		$	3.11
TOTAL		$	51.01
TENDER VISA		$	51.01

**FAMILY OWNED AND OPERATED **

OUR 31ST YEAR

VISIT US ONLINE www.boydsldsbooks.com

If it were not for Dr. William Gorgas, later a US Surgeon General, many more thousands would have died in Mesoamerica. It is estimated conservatively that 25,000 workers and family members died from malaria and yellow fever in the digging of the Panama Canal.[265] The same French engineer who built the Suez Canal began construction on the Panama Canal in 1878. His name was Ferdinand de Lesseps. Tropical disease and fevers halted construction on the canal, and eventually brought in the Americans. Dr. Gorgas supervised the elimination of the stagnant pools that served as breeding grounds for the pesky mosquitoes. The insects thrived in murky pools and ponds so common in Mesoamerica. An anonymous canal worker complained, "Mosquitoes get so thick you get a mouthful with every breath."

Healing Plants and Herbs

In Belize and the surrounding rain forest of Mesoamerica, there are over 3,000 healing plants and herbs that a team of doctors and natives have identified.[266] The amount of information is overwhelming. Coca, Guaiacum, Ipecac and Curare were a few I recognized from the list. There is a derivative from the "Curare" plant that is used in most operations involving internal medicine. One very interesting quote claimed "without it (Curare) open heart surgery would be impossible."[267]

> Guaiacum, *Guaiacum officinale*: Relied upon in pre-Columbian South and Central America, guaiacum was used for rheumatoid arthritis, respiratory problems, gout and skin disorders. It is used as an anti-inflammatory, local anesthetic and herpes treatment.
>
> Ipecac, *Psychotria ipecacuanha*: Currently used as an emetic, and anti-amoebic, its traditional uses include as a treatment for gastrointestinal diseases, diarrhea, intermittent fevers, bronchitis, bronchopneumonia, asthma and mumps.
>
> Cayenne, *Capsicum frutescens*: The first documented use of cayenne was at least five hundred years ago by the Aztecs. Historically, it has been used to treat dyspepsia, colic and chronic laryngitis. Currently, it's used to relieve pain from diabetic neuralgia, osteoarthritis, rheumatoid arthritis. Research is underway for its potential use on cluster headaches.
>
> Curare, *Pareira, Chondrodendron tomentosum*, is a vine that grows in the tropical and subtropical rainforests of South and Central America. Amazonian tribes make curare, a deadly arrow poison, from the bark. Western medicine makes d-tubocurarine which enhances general anesthesia. Without it, open-heart surgery would be impossible.

> Quinine, *Cinchona officinalis*: Cinchona, or Peruvian bark as it was called, produces a chemical called quinine that reduces fevers and combats the parasites that cause malaria. Quinine was the first line of defense against malaria until the development of synthetic drugs in the 1940s.[268]

The Native Mesoamericans had built up a tolerance for local fevers and diseases and learned to use herbal remedies to lessen their impact. Mostly, they made tea from the bark of various trees, leaves, and roots. The Book of Mormon makes a point to mention both the seasonal fevers and their herbal remedies. The seasonal rains bring the seasonal fevers caused by the spawning of mosquitoes and other vectors.

> And there were some who died with fevers, which at some season of the year were very frequent in the land—but not so much so with fevers, because of the excellent qualities of the many plants and roots which God had prepared to remove the cause of diseases… (Alma 46:40).

My own experience in Mesoamerica for more than four decades has brought me into contact with native shamans and Maya healers. There are several ways to use the mango fruit and the Mango tree bark to ward off mosquitoes. Typical of the many plants and roots God has prepared to remove pain and disease is a spiny vine. In the jungle, this vine is known by the natives as the "Give and Take" vine. It is obvious and easy to spot as it has two to three inch needles protruding all up and down the vine. When pricked, the poison in the needles gives excruciating pain, which lasts for several hours. The inside of the bark looks like pink cotton candy. When the pink "cotton" is applied to a cut, it will stop the bleeding and ease the pain. A tea made from the bark and needles takes away the pain and is used as a pain remedy. Because it both gives pain and takes pain away, it is appropriately called the "Give and Take" vine. It certainly qualifies for one of the plants, which God had prepared to help with pain and illness.

It is an ironic footnote that the two adventurers who brought Joseph Smith confirming evidence of the Book of Mormon would fall victims to the fevers of Mesoamerica. Even their fevers were an evidence of the veracity of the Book of Mormon. This reference to climate and disease is consistent with Stephens and Catherwood's experience who were both sick with tropical fevers at various times during their Mesoamerican journey. On one occasion Stephens was required to move on and leave Catherwood, "broken down with fever," and later reunited.[269] Reporting on his own experience with fever, Stephens refers to it as "my old enemy."

> At three o'clock I felt uncertain in regard to my chill, but, determined not to give way, dressed myself, and went to dine with Mr. Steiples. Before sitting down, the blueness of my lips, and a tendency to use superfluous syllables, betrayed me; and my old enemy

> shook me all the way back to the convent, and into bed. Fever followed ... For four days in succession I had a recurrence of chill and fever."[270]

Among the sad footnotes of history is the fact that a decade later John Lloyd Stephens returned to Central America and died from his exposure to the Mesoamerican climate and environment. Frederick Catherwood offered these comments upon the death of his friend and fellow explorer:

> Subsequently Mr. Stephens returned to the Isthmus, and by long and incautious exposure in that deadly climate in forwarding the interest of the Railway Company, brought on a disease which terminated fatally in the autumn of 1852.[271]

The Heat of the Day

On the Nephite calendar on the first day of the first month when Teancum killed Amalickiah, they were all tired from "the heat of the day" (Alma 51:33, 37; Alma 52:1). In the eastern Mesoamerica coastal area, the average high temperature on April 1st is 88 degrees. The Book of Mormon reports that Amalickiah camped in tents, "on the beach by the seashore" (Alma 51:32). In the northern climates around Rochester, New York, the average "mean" temperature for April 1st is 42° with the evening minimum "mean" temperature at freezing. The heat of the day is a phrase that best applies to Mesoamerica for late March and early April. Even five hundred miles south at Virginia Beach, Virginia, the average April 1st temperature is 64° for a high and 45° for a low at night. These places in North America at this time of year do not qualify for "heat of the day." Mesoamerica does. And no, the weather patterns have not changed dramatically in the past two thousand years so that the Great Lakes climate was consistently balmy on an April 1st. If there were a variance for two thousand years ago, it would swing to the side of a colder climate north of the Rio Grande according to the global warming people.

As the evidence mounts it becomes clear that Mesoamerica is the only North American climate that is consistent with the internal saga of the Book of Mormon.

CHAPTER THIRTEEN

FAITH AND SCIENCE

Think of what the person who does not have a spiritual witness of the Book of Mormon is being asked to accept; i.e., prophets, revelations, visions, angels, and a resurrected Jesus visiting the Americas. Of course those who truly believe in the Bible are asked to believe in prophets, revelations, visions, angels, and in a resurrected Jesus. If one accepts the Bible and the Book of Mormon on the basis of a spiritual confirmation born of the Holy Spirit, there isn't a problem believing in a Shepherd who visits all his sheep" (John 10:16).

Faith is called one of the gifts of the Holy Ghost (1 Corinthians 12:1, 9). The witness most often comes by the invitation we call prayer (Matthew 7:7-11; D&C 19:28, 38). Faith is not a perfect or complete knowledge, but true faith is a partial knowledge that comes as a spiritual gift from the Holy Ghost. After having read, pondered, and sincerely prayed unto God about the validity of the Book of Mormon, one is better prepared to begin a historical quest for the historical sites of the Book of Mormon. A person is also better prepared to embrace another field of "partial knowledge" called science.

What Should One Do When the Partial Knowledge Provided by Current Science Conflicts With His or Her Spiritual Knowledge?

When teaching a graduate class at the LDS Institute adjacent to the University of Washington, one of the students working on his Ph.D. in horticulture told me privately that he could no longer believe in the Book of Mormon. He said that he had learned in his research that there was no pre-Columbian domesticated barley in the Americas. The Spanish had imported barley. However, the Book of Mormon speaks of barley as a medium of exchange (Alma 11:7, 15; Mosiah 7:22). This student approached me in the early 1970s. What should he do with the partial knowledge provided by current science that conflicted with his spiritual knowledge? My counsel to him and all my students was this: *Don't lose faith in what you know because of what you don't know!* In other words, apparent conflicts need to be placed on hold knowing that truth will not conflict with truth. Either in time, through more research, or when all things are made known by God will he then understand. The tragedy is this young man lost his faith and his commitment to feed that faith and eventually dwindled into inactivity.[272]

This very bright and young doctoral student in horticulture at the University of Washington was a returned missionary. He had received the witness of the Holy Ghost and had faith. However, he allowed doubt to rob him of his faith. Rather than allowing his spiritual knowledge to coexist with the scientific knowledge of 1970, he chose to abandon his religious faith and commit totally to his faith in science. Each person must still gain their own independent testimony through prayer and a witness of the Holy Ghost that the Book of Mormon is a true witness of the resurrected Messiah. Scientific inquiry and faith need not be at war one with the other. In the case of the Book of Mormon, the Bible, Joseph Smith's first vision, or the very existence of God, faith and science can coexist, if people are humble enough to admit they are only in possession of partial knowledge.

Faith must be nourished by study and prayer and acts of loving service (Alma 32:30-43). These behaviors bring with them the reinforcing power of the Holy Ghost that keeps the faith alive. That which brought faith is the same that sustains faith. In a moment of candor, the horticultural student admitted he had stopped any serious study of the Gospel, and his prayers were few and far between. He lost faith in what he once knew, because of what he thought he knew about pre-Columbian domesticated barley, and then he stopped nourishing his faith. The key is not to lose faith in what you know spiritually, because the "current" partial or limited knowledge of science may challenge it.

Pre-Columbian Domesticated Barley

When scholars examine the Book of Mormon, whether they profess a pro, con, or no bias at all, they look for evidences of internal consistency comparing external realities. For example, for decades scholars believed there was no pre-Columbian domesticated barley in the Americas. Therefore, some rejected the Book of Mormon as real history, as did the horticultural student. The belief was the Spaniards brought barley to the New World. However, the Book of Mormon people used barley as a medium of exchange. "A senum of silver was equal to a senine of gold, and either for a *measure of barley*" (Alma 11:7, emphasis added). In *Science Magazine* in December 1983, it was reported that pre-Columbian domesticated barley had been discovered in the Americas.[273] This is an example of looking for evidence to collaborate the internal story of the Book of Mormon. Did world scholars declare the Book of Mormon a true history after the discovery of pre-Columbian domesticated barley in the Americas? No! Those who believed in the Book of Mormon saw this evidence as a confirmation of its truthfulness. Others dismissed it as a coincidence.

I have asked myself many times, where is that young man who lost his faith and left the Church back in the 1970s over an apparent conflict between what he had been taught in science and what the Book of Mormon said? His story is a profound example of why it is important not to lose faith in what one knows by the Spirit just because it may conflict with contemporary science. It is also a testimony of the importance of nurturing faith by continued study of the gospel, ongoing prayer, and of involving oneself in loving service.

This leads me to reiterate a fundamental guideline in my own life. *I will not lose faith in what I know because of what I don't know.* My spiritual knowledge is a gift from God. The real or apparent conflicts between what I know spiritually and what current scientific information may contradict will be set on the back burner of my mind with the quiet assurance that at some future date all truth will be harmonized.

Science is Knowledge in the State of Flux

One significant find can change an entire paradigm. Finding prehistoric Caucasians in North America, as recently occurred, contributed to the downfall of the Americas being settled by the "Asians Only" doctrine. If life is found on another solar system, there will be new theories to replace the old ones. Dearly held scientific beliefs will be supplemented. Science is knowledge in the state of flux.

I attended an informal meeting of retired university professors who had joined me on a cruise ship. They represented soil scientists, genetic engineers, an anthropologist, several medical doctors in highly specialized fields, and an applied math professor. The setting was informal and causal. These were professionals from highly respected universities. Two were former deans, and all were published. It was a time to reflect. The topic was "How has your field of knowledge changed over the past thirty-five to forty years? Each shared comments about things they were taught forty years ago which today have been proven entirely false. One very insightful comment from the soil scientist was that he believed the purpose of science was to prove something wasn't true, not necessarily to find truth. Maybe the most sobering comment was made from the retired dean of a medical school. He said, "I brought in my old textbooks from fifty years ago and quoted from them to the new medical students. It was both humorous and instructive. It was my way to tell them not to become too smug about what they are now learning, because in forty to fifty years new insights will make what they are now learning equally laughable."

Science: Tolerating the Unknown

Most of science involves tolerating the unknown. It is the process of slowly building a case to support a particular hypothesis. Is it not the approach of a true scientist to move from the known to the unknown? Discovery is the work of the dedicated scholar. The search for evidence and truth to strengthen a specific position is consistent with the scientific effort. It does not require that one be in possession of all knowledge before one's confidence can remain high in a particular hypothesis. The history of science is the history of challenging basic assumptions.

It was not many decades ago that doctors assumed that "bleeding" their patients to remove impure blood was good science. The afore-mentioned *science* of bloodletting was universally accepted and practiced in the medical community, and had been for hundreds of years. It is now acknowledged that George Washington died from being bled to death while treating him for a lethally sore throat; but it was deemed good science at the time.[274] The finest and best trained doctors were assigned to save the Father of our country, George Washington. So common was the practice of bloodletting that a family friend named Rawlins with a practice in veterinary medicine was called to draw a pint of blood from the General. Everyone believed this would fix the problem. It didn't. George Washington was suffering from a staff infection in his throat. Four hours later, Dr. Craik extracted more blood. Washington drew weaker and weaker. Blood was once more taken. Two more doctors arrived: Dr. Gustave Brown and Dr. Elisha Dick. It was explained to them that blood had been taken three times that day. After serious consultation, the doctors decided to use drastic bloodletting extraction and siphoned off a significant amount of Washington's blood. George Washington knew the end was near and made some final adjustments to his last will and testament. He died shortly thereafter. Current science had killed him. The date was December 14, 1799. The moral to the story is this: Just because there is current universal agreement in the scientific community doesn't mean it is true or right.

Lining the Roman aqueducts with lead was considered great engineering until it was found centuries later that practice was lethal. Lead based paint and the chips from this paint ingested by infants in New York tenant buildings still cause brain damage today. The list of "good science" that has changed is endless in most fields of study. The truth is, there will always be unanswered questions and new theories to replace old ones. Some like me find this exciting and invigorating. The quest for knowledge remains a passion for man and has since the day Adam and Eve partook of the Tree of Knowledge in the Garden of Eden.

Good Science Verses Bad Science

The danger for most scientists is to become so invested in a conclusion that it prevents them from being open to new or contrary information. The difference between "Good Science" and "Bad Science" is just that simple. Once a scientist sells his soul for a particular hypothesis and refuses to be open to contrary information, he is no longer committed to the truth and becomes a dogmatist. These bad scientists then appeal to their authority status, Ph.D.s, or collective agreements from other bad scientists whose opinions agree, to impose their conclusions as facts. The theory of evolution is a prime example of dogmatism and scientific "bullying."

The challenge for science is deducing from a few facts accurate conclusions. Conclusions are not facts. If one were to find a "black diamond" in South Africa, the diamond would be a fact. Other than tell say it was found in South Africa, everything said about that diamond would be conclusions based upon assumptions, and not facts. Conclusions may coincide with the truth; however, they may not. New information may radically change conclusions. One may deduce that because it takes so much heat, pressure and time to make a diamond, that particular black diamond is 3.3 billion years old and came from South Africa. That would be the best educated opinion at the time. However, new information revealed this particular "black diamond" was made commercially in a machine in Israel and used for drilling. The truth was that this "black diamond" fell out of a truck on its way to a drilling rig. The assumptions initially made were reasonable based on the partial knowledge. Yet, both assumptions and conclusions were wrong in light of the new information.

Conclusions are subject to change as new information is discovered that may alter the basic assumptions. Truth exists independent of scientific conclusion or religious belief. There is an irony about both science and religion. Once committed to a conclusion, the person is exercising a type of "faith" in that conclusion. Science is as much faith based as is religion, although most scientists would not admit to it. The fundamental danger for both religious belief and scientific reasoned belief is one can believe or reason anything into existence, and that doesn't make it true. The fact there is an ancient artifact does not justify the assumed subsequent conclusions, which may or may not be in harmony with the truth. Both religionists and scientists are equally guilty of dogmatism.

There are Scientists and Dogmatists and Some Who are Both

Professor Hugh Nibley once pointed out to a group of graduate students, that the most exact science on the planet was meteorology. Science has more than a hundred years of actual data on the past weather conditions on most parts of the earth. They possess sophisticated weather satellites circulating the globe and giving real time reports on the status of the atmosphere. With all of the past data and with abundant current information, the weather person is prepared to form a hypothesis and make a prediction on the weekend weather. Frequently one laughs at how wrong the weather person was. To protect their credibility wise meteorologists often include a probability of error factor. So now there is a 30% chance of rain on the weekend, or a 10% chance of snow tomorrow. Why? Everyone can test their hypothesis.

Here is the question asked by Dr. Nibley. "If the most sophisticated of all the sciences are willing to give us probabilities of error, why is it that most anthropologists are so dogmatic and do not give us a probably of error of their hypotheses?" This is especially relevant when one's hypotheses cannot be tested. Any hypothesis, which cannot be tested, must remain in the domain of opinion.

Unfortunately for anthropology and most of archaeology their hypotheses can not be tested. It has been said that where there are two anthropologists one will find three firm opinions.

Why is it that the most dogmatic seem to be those who are the least scientific? Of all the sciences, the fields of anthropology, archeology, religion and history are the least scientific and can scarcely be called a science because they cannot field test or laboratory test their hypotheses.

Dogmatism is certainly not confined to religionists. Dogmatism on the part of anyone seems to be as much a function of insecurity as it is a deterrent for the quest for truth. There are some scientists whose dogmatic assertions and close mindedness surpass even the most religiously fanatic. Here is a sample from the Davistown Museum, Liberty, Maine, of how a significant number of current (2007) anthropologists, archaeologists, and historians feel about pre-Columbian visitors to America, and how all evidence is still not given an intelligent and unbiased examination:

> Most all professional archaeologists and historians consider the topic of Pre-Columbian visitors to be a preposterous and, in fact, a ridiculous subject of study of far less serious consideration than alchemy, Ouija boards, flying saucers and moon cheese.[275]

Go to their "web site" and check it out. It will be interesting to see how long it will take them to modify and cloister their arrogance. One of the greatest and saddest examples of scientific dogmatism relates directly to the translation of the Mayan text in Mesoamerica. One of the most respected Harvard professors of Anthropology was J. Eric Thompson. His major contribution was the interpretation of Mayan dates. However, this man single-handedly held back the decipherment of the Mayan language by 30 years. He insisted that Mayan language was not syllabic or phonetic, which it is and was proven so by a Russian named Yuri Valentinovich Knorosov. It is hard to keep a straight face and not laugh Thompson to scorn in light of present knowledge. Thompson was wrong. Being wrong was not his greatest sin; being an arrogant dogmatist was. Thompson used his dominant position at Harvard to crush Knorosov and ridicule any and all who attempted to support the Russian or the idea that Mayan was a phonetic language. Those who knew Thompson best reported on his rage against the Russian Knorosov and tantrums against anyone who held an alternative view. Tatiana Proskouriakoff, a colleague at Harvard and great Mayanist in her own right, was fearful to bring to light any evidence contrary to Thompson's dogmatic assertions. She also opposed the phonetic-syllabic approach. She was wrong. In addition, Tatiana Proskouriakoff adamantly maintained that the Maya were non-religious. She was not just wrong, she was 180 degrees wrong. The Maya were obsessed with religion, and it impacted on every phase of their lives. In the early 1960s, I recall being told by professors and by the guides at the ruins of the Maya in Mesoamerica how peaceful, peace loving, and non-warlike these ancient Maya really were. Unlike some of the warrior societies such as the Mexicas, who practiced human sacrifice on a monumental scale, the Maya were genteel, peasant farmers, and craftsmen. This was another erroneous position held by J. Eric Thompson. He knew that the Maya had weapons of war. He assumed they fought to defend themselves if they had to, but preferred a docile, tractable, and harmonic life of non conflict. How did these scholars miss the mark by so far? Should it call into question anything they might have said, believed or asserted? Status quo intelligentsias are sometimes the greatest dogmatists of all. As Michael D. Lemonick reported, "Among the first myths about this [Maya] population to be debunked is that they were a peaceful race."[276]

Figure 51. Sacrifice Altar Q at Copán, Honduras

I remember looking at Altar Q at Copán, Honduras and asking what its purpose was and being told there was no evidence of human sacrifice among the Maya. Not until Linda Schele, et. al., in the 1980s broke the Mayan code were scientists able to understand the extent to which the Maya were not the peaceful, dossal, peasant farmers earlier scientists claimed them to be. How did modern day scientists miss that one? The Maya lived and breathed as a warrior society. War was ritualized to such an extent among them that, as Linda Schele reports, kings fought kings and victims of human sacrifice were offered up to coincide with the rising of Venus. Eagle warriors, jaguar warriors, war games played on a ball court were all a part of the Maya war-like nature. Harvard scholar, Michael Coe admits in his fourth edition of *The Maya*, these scientific miscalculations and mischaracterizations of the Classic Maya in the following words:

> On the basis of older and now out-dated notions about what the Classic Maya were supposed to be like, it used to be thought that the Classic throughout Mesoamerica was a time of peace and tranquility, without the obsession with warfare and human sacrifice considered typical of the Post-Classic.[277]

Maybe the most recent and ongoing example of scientific dogmatism is the prohibition of teaching "Directed Intelligence" as an alternative to the "Big Bang" theory of creation. Of the two hundred plus major universities in America, where are the deans of the colleges of any of the sciences hiring anyone who would dare suggest an alternative to Darwinism? The point is one is not dealing with professors who hold truth as the highest value, but with human beings who cling to their dearly held bias. Some scientists are threatened by an unfettered search for truth as are some religionists.

The Book of Mormon Under Attack

Those who attack the Book of Mormon on whatever grounds follow a pattern of strategic retreat. First, there is a "*declaration of impossibility.*" The Book of Mormon can't be true history because...America wasn't settled by maritime crossings; it was settled by migrations across the Siberian Land Bridge. The Book of Mormon can't be true history because...nobody knew how to translate Egyptian in 1830. The Book of Mormon can't be true history because...everyone knows that the Spaniards brought domesticated barley to the Americas. The Book of Mormon can't be true history because...there was no evidence of a high civilization in America at the time claimed by the Book of Mormon. The Book of Mormon can't be true history because...ancient peoples didn't write upon metal plates.

At the time the *declarations of impossibility* were made, the defenders of the faith had no concrete proof in archeology to contradict the scientific pontifications. As time marched on, evidence of maritime crossings were admitted by the scientific community in 1998. Hugh Nibley's works on Joseph Smith as a translator of Egyptian emerged in the 1960s. In December 1983, *Science Magazine* announced the discovery of pre-Columbian domesticated barley in America. In 1839, Stephens and Catherwood rediscovered that indeed a high civilization did exist upon the North American continent. The 1933 and 1952 discoveries of gold and copper plates demonstrated that it was possible for the ancients to engrave upon metal plates many hundred years before Christ in the Mideast. In 2007 pre-Columbian chickens were discovered in the Americas.

The next point of strategic retreat on the part of the Book of Mormon detractors is to say, "*It may be possible, but it is not probable.*" OK, but just because ... America was settled by maritime crossings doesn't mean the Book of Mormon happened. OK, but just because ... Joseph Smith may have guessed right on a few Egyptian characters doesn't mean anything. OK, but just because ... pre-Columbian domesticated barley has been found in America doesn't mean it was used as a medium of exchange. OK, but just because ... Stephens and Catherwood discovered evidence of a high civilization in Mesoamerica doesn't mean it has anything to do with the Book of Mormon. OK, but just because ... there is evidence of the ancients writing upon metal plates doesn't mean the peoples in the New World used metal plates. OK so we were wrong about pre-Columbian chickens in the Americas. And on it goes.

The next to last stance taken by the strategic retreaters is to say, "*You can't prove it.*" That, of course, is a standard to which they will not hold themselves, or their own theories. Most of the current scientific theories are based upon probabilities, not upon possession of all knowledge. Some smugly require a standard of perfection. They feed upon doubt and try to find points of apparent contradiction to justify their entrenched positions. Absolute proof that the Book of Mormon is a true history can be obtained by humble prayer and Divine witness. Most defenders of the Book of Mormon are trying to point out the possibility and probability of its claims as a true history. This is why it is a waste of time and energy to try and convince the disingenuous.

The final position taken by the detractors is to "*dismiss the Book of Mormon as a religious issue*" to which they do not want to embroil themselves, or *to jump to another issue without admitting the previous point.* This kind of posturing and strategic retreat is important to recognize so that the sincere students of the Book of Mormon don't waste their time and energies needlessly.

Dealing With the Disingenuous

The motives of the disingenuous are not centered in the quest for truth, although this is a mask they commonly wear. Knowing their primary motive is to prove the Book of Mormon false, they will ignore all evidence that supports the Book of Mormon as real history. Like Paul on the road to Damascus, they are obsessed with persecuting the "heretical" Christians. The Lord's counsel is not to revile against the revilers (D&C 19:30). Under most circumstances the most prudent response is to answer the question, avoid conflict or the spirit of contention, and bear testimony. Sometimes an honest "I don't know" is the best and most appropriate reply. The Apostle Peter admonished

> Be ready always to give an answer with meekness and fear to every man that asketh you a reason of the hope that is in you: Having a good conscience; that whereas they speak evil of you, as of evil-doers, they may be ashamed that falsely accuse your good conduct in Christ (Joseph Smith Translation, 1 Peter 3:15-16).

In spite of the fact the disingenuous have never bothered to truly read the Book of Mormon except to find fault with it, they will jump from issue to issue and ask, "Where are the horses in the Americas talked about six hundred years before Christ?" (1 Nephi 18:25.) Can you predict their response when they find out there is evidence of pre-Columbian horses in America; not prehistoric ten thousand years-ago horses, but 1800 B.C. to A.D. 1200 horses? Before examining the evidence for pre-Columbian horses, it will be instructive to see the Book of Mormon's place in the battle between evolution and diffusionism in the next chapter.

CHAPTER FOURTEEN

The One Hundred and Fifty Year Old Battle Between Evolutionists and Diffusionists and The Book of Mormon

There is a one hundred and fifty year old battle between diffusionists and evolutionists, and the Book of Mormon is in the middle of it. Diffusionism is the belief that information and influence is spread from one culture to another. Another term with similar meaning is cultural cross-pollination. Diffusionism exists independent of Mormonism as a scientific field of study. Many diffusionists are uncomfortable with any religious claims. Like it or not, when it comes to ancient American cultures, Mormons are diffusionists. For example, the statement that the Americas were settled by multiple immigrant groups who crossed the great waters is a diffusionist position. That position alone put the Book of Mormon into the diffusionist camp. The Book of Mormon asserts that two of the groups that were brought across the waters came from Jerusalem and another from the tower of Babel. Mormons believe that the Book of Mormon was written in Reformed Egyptian, and Lehite immigrants brought with them a culture that influenced those in the New World. It is recorded in the Book of Mormon that the resurrected Christ visited the Americas and left a lasting impact upon them in the customs and beliefs about the "Descending God." Mormons believe that the Native Americans are the mixed seeds of the surviving Lamanites. All of these beliefs define Mormons as cultural diffusionists.

At the core of evolutionary thought is the idea that things evolve from a simple to a more complex nature by adapting to their environment. The theory of evolution assumed there was no God, or directed intelligence, and that all things came into existence as the result of chance. Evolution was invented as an alternative explanation to divine creation as told in the Bible. It is the Darwinistic belief that all humans share the mental ability to invent and create similar innovations without any interaction with outside cultures. When a caveman in

Africa and a caveman in South America both invent an axe, this is called in evolutionary terms "Independent Invention." The Darwinists rejected any notion that America was settled by maritime immigrants. Primitive man was too ignorant and lacked the knowledge and skills to construct ocean going crafts according to Darwinians. The evolutionists argued instead that America was settled *only* from Asia across the Siberian Land Bridge.

The "Siberian Land Bridge Only" Scientific Doctrine

The theory that became a scientific doctrine was that the ancient Americas were settled *only* by the Siberian Land Bridge. No one was allowed to challenge this position without being excommunicated from the scientific community. A recent publication of the Smithsonian reviewed these earlier beliefs.

> The traditional theory held that the first Americans crossed the land bridge from Siberia to Alaska around 11,500 years ago and followed an "ice-free corridor" between two large Canadian ice sheets ... to reach unglaciated lands to the south. These first inhabitants, whose archaeological sites are scattered across North and South America, were called the Clovis people, named after the town in New Mexico where their fluted spear points used for hunting mammoth were first found in 1932.[278]

In February of 1998 at the annual meeting held in Philadelphia of A.A.A.S., the American Association for the Advancement of Science, the anthropological community was forced to accept that America was settled by multiple maritime crossings. Charles Mann, a correspondent for *Science* magazine, the official publication of the A.A.A.S., made the following comments:

> When I went to high school, in the 1970s, I was taught that Indians came to the Americas across the Bering Strait about thirteen thousand years ago, that they lived for the most part in small, isolated groups ... At the time, the ice pack extended two thousand miles south of the Bering Strait and was almost devoid of life ... And it happened just before the emergence of what was then the earliest known culture in the Americas, the Clovis culture, so named for the town in New Mexico ... [Haynes] made the theory seem so ironclad that it fairly flew into the textbooks. I learned it when I attended high school. So did my son, thirty years later. In 1997 the theory abruptly came unglued ... an archeological dig in southern Chile had turned up compelling evidence of human habitation ... thirty thousand years old. Or perhaps the first Indians traveled by boat, and didn't need the land bridge ... "We're in a state of turmoil," the consulting archaeologist Stuart Fiedel told me. "Everything we knew is now supposed to be wrong."[279]

Zimmerman, in a report on the "Kennewick Man," in Washington State, reported that the discovery of the "Kennewick Man and other recent finds [in

Chile] are currently causing scientists to reevaluate their theories about how the Americas were first populated."[280]

Sixty years before the first diffusionist, the Book of Mormon was at the forefront of those who proclaimed the Americas were settled by maritime crossings. At long last, the cultural diffusionists might have their day in the court of serious scientific evaluation. The Cultural Diffusionists were right on the issue of pre-Columbian crossings to the Americas. These are the people, like Thor Heyerdahl, who believed that the abundance of cultural similarities between Europe and America were the result of cross-cultural pollination.

Prior to the great admission in 1998 by the scientific community that America was settled by multiple maritime crossings, all artifacts, horse finds, inscriptions, and Book of Mormon claims were labeled as fakes, forgeries and immediately rejected. They ran contrary to the "Siberian Land Bridge Only" doctrine and the current theories about man's evolutionary development.

Pre-Columbian Maritime Sailors in America

No single event in the last hundred years may yet prove to be as significant for scholars as the demise of the "Siberian Land Bridge Only" theory. It was not until his 6th edition of *The Maya* in 1999 that Michael Coe admitted that the Americas may have been settled by maritime crossings of the Atlantic and Pacific Oceans. He confessed "the first Americans may well have taken a maritime route."[281] After February, 1998 the A.A.A.S. threw open the door for America to be inhabited by maritime crossings by prehistoric man thousands of years ago. However, they still advocated that some came across the Siberian Land Bridge. It is now open for serious scholars to look at the consequences of the Americas being settled by multiple migrations across the oceans without being overtly rejected. Only among the diehards, who have made their science into a religion, does the "Siberian Land Bridge Only" theory continue to thrive.

Acknowledging that primitive man was able to build seaworthy transoceanic crafts thousands of years ago is a significant admission.[282] It also means that the scholarly community has decided that primitive man was not that primitive; he was much more intelligent and evolved than they imagined. Professor Coe observed:

> Yet long before this [Siberian Land Bridge], boats must have been available to the peoples of Eurasia, for recent evidence shows that Australia, which was never connected to Asia by a land bridge, was settled as far back as 50,000 years ago.[283]

Thor Heyerdahl is dancing in his grave with joy. It was Thor Heyerdahl who proved that both Atlantic and Pacific crossings were possible in primitive water crafts. In 1947 he made the famous Kon-Tiki craft and traveled 4300 miles across the Pacific Ocean from South America to the Polynesian islands in one hundred and one days. It was not a quirk. Olav, the grandson of Thor Heyerdahl, duplicated his grandfather's feat in April of 2006. Olav's balsa wood raft named *Tangaroa* crossed the Pacific in seventy days.[284]

There are other reasons why Thor Heyerdahl believed that primitive man had great seafaring skills. The Maori in New Zealand had sweet potatoes before they had contact with the Europeans. Kumara is its name. Genetic engineers say that the origin of the Kumara is Central America, and other varieties of the sweet potatoes, come from Peru. Columbus, on his forth voyage, is credited with introducing the sweet potato to Europe. The Portuguese carried it to Japan, China, and to the world. How did the sweet potato arrive in New Zealand before Columbus discovered America? New Zealand was settled in A.D. 1300 by the Maori.

> Kumara: is a sweet potato of tropical origin, a member of the plant family Convolvulaceae, which was the major cultivated food crop of the pre-European Maori. This is grown successfully here only on sheltered north-facing gardens in the north of the North Island. Some of the varieties grown today are believed to have been introduced by 19th century whalers and sealers, but Maori tradition claims the origin of the NZ kumara as Hawaiki, the legendary homeland, and that it was brought to this country [New Zealand] by the migrating canoes ... The Kumara homeland ... is most certainly a Central American plant originally.[285]

Matthew Cowley, a Mormon Apostle, reported that he received a most curious response to a question he asked an old Maori man in 1914:

> "Where did you come from?"
>
> [The man responded] "We came from the place where the sweet potato grows wild, where it is not planted, does not have to be cultivated." There is only one place in the entire world where the sweet potato grows wild...[286]

The sweet potato grows wild in Mesoamerica and also Peru. Thor Heyerdahl knew about the sweet potato and the Maori-Mesoamerican-Peruvian connection, and it was a major inspiration for him to embark on Kon-Tiki:

> It [kumara] was used by the anthropologist Thor Heyerdahl, to support his claim that Polynesians moved into the Pacific from America, rather than from the East.[287]

Heyerdahl based his theory that the Islands were settled by ancient Americans on the fact that the kumara, which was a staple cultivated food crop of the pre-European New Zealand Maori, originated from the Americas.

To demonstrate how close minded the scientific community was to any alternative to the "Siberian Land Bridge Only" doctrine one has just to review their rebuttals to Thor Heyerdahl. The "scientific explanation" for how the sweet potato traveled 4300 miles across the salty Pacific Ocean is that it floated across. It simply uprooted itself, rolled to the Pacific shore from the mountains of Peru or Mesoamerica and survived at least 101 days soaked in salt water (which alone would destroy its ability to germinate), rolled up the sandy beaches of New Zealand, and planted its tubers in kindred soil. Or ancient Americans dumped a load of sweet potatoes on the Pacific shore and the sweet potato rafted itself 4300 miles, drenched in salt-sprayed water, remained unaffected by the salt water, and were picked up along the shore by the Maori who knew exactly where to plant them. Even today the sweet potato is only grown along the north coasts of their islands in New Zealand.

It would be comical except for the arrogance behind it, which continues. The "Floating Sweet Potato Theory" is also called the Accidental Drift Theory. This is an absurd speculation. Where is the convincing evidence of the "Floating Sweet Potato Theory?" The British Broadcasting Company (BBC) devoted an entire satirical article to the "Mystery of the Sweet Potato" including the Accidental Drift Theory on June 11, 2004.[288] There is no convincing evidence that the sweet potato floated 4300 miles across the ocean. However, there are scientists whose whimsical and unsubstantiated statements are accepted as convincing evidence because it supports a preconceived bias that New Zealand was settled from Asia and not from the Americas. The truth is no amount of evidence can convince the recalcitrant or closed minded scientist.

The same people who accept the "Floating Sweet Potato Theory," which is without the least substantiation, reject the many significant and convincing evidences that Book of Mormon history corresponds to Mesoamerican history. There are archaeologists and anthropologists who would stake their professional credibility there were no chickens in the Americas before the Spanish brought them from Europe.[289] They would lose whatever credibility they have left. One of the most prestigious scientific journals in the world is the PNAS or *Proceedings of the National Academy of Sciences.* In the June 19, 2007 Journal the title of the article says it all: "Radiocarbon and DNA evidence for a pre-Columbian introduction of Polynesian chickens to Chile."[290] The highlights of the study are as follows:

1. Chickens could not have gotten to South America on their own—they had to be taken by humans.
2. Radiocarbon dating places them at A.D. 1304 to 1424.
3. The breed of chicken found comes from Polynesia, rather than any chickens found in Europe.

This is a journey of 4300 miles across open seas. It is the reverse journey of Thor Heyerdahl. The story in the Book of Mormon of Hagoth is a case in point. He built several large ships which he launched in the "west" sea or Pacific Ocean near the "narrow neck" of land, or the Isthmus of Tehuantepec (Alma 63:5). The date is 55-54 B.C. He returns from his ocean voyage and recruits more people to go with him. There are two points: first, the Hagoth story is viable. He could cross the Pacific Ocean and settle on any number of Pacific Islands. The islands were, after all, inhabited by many groups of immigrants from diverse countries and distinct ethnic backgrounds. The Fiji islanders are the most obvious example. The Second point: there were pre-Columbian chickens in the Americas (3 Nephi 10:4-6). It is reasonable to believe that Hagoth and those who sailed with him could have been the forefathers of some, not all, of the Pacific islanders. They could easily have taken the sweet potato with them.

Thor Heyerdahl died in 2002 and never received from the scientific community their blessing or approbation. He was a diffusionist. He was mocked, ridiculed, and "persona non grata" because his evidence contradicted the "Siberian Land Bridge Only" doctrine, and the belief of evolutionary anthropologists that primitive man was not bright enough to build a watercraft sufficient to make such a long voyage. With Ra-I and again with Ra-II, Thor Heyerdahl crossed the Atlantic Ocean in fifty-seven days. Compare that with Columbus whose first voyage was thirty-six days and the fourth voyage twenty-two days.

It Takes Years for the Public Schools to Integrate New Knowledge

In the past two years I have made several more trips to Mesoamerica and to South America. On the walls of the Natural History museums in all these countries are large maps which show how the Americas were settled by the Asians coming to America across the Siberian Land Bridge. Because I am fluent in Spanish, I followed a class of Guatemalan 5th graders through the museum and listened carefully as the children were instructed on the "Siberian Land Bridge Only" doctrine. It will take years before these people will be taught from the scientific community that the traditions of their Native American forefathers were correct when they claimed they arrived in the Americas in ships and that the "Siberian Land Bridge Only" doctrine was an error.

Ironically, the ancestors of these very students told the Spanish conquistadors and priests that their fathers had arrived in the New World from across the seas in watercrafts.[291] It will take another generation before current scientific information trickles down to these wonderful people. The rivers of evidence will soon break the dam of resistance. It has already begun. The *Christian Science Monitor* reported in November 18, 2004:

> A Clovis-first [Asian only] approach fails to explain significantly older sites in Central and South America. And while genetic similarities between modern native Americans and Asiatic people have been documented, the high level of genetic diversity seen in native Americans "is difficult to explain in a Clovis time frame. It points to a deeper time."[292]

The Emory University School of Medicine DNA Study

Nine highly respected genetic scholars from America, Italy, and Germany collaborated on an extensive DNA study of Native American tribes. For those interested, the Smithsonian has accepted this study as valid research.[293] The study was conducted by the Center for Molecular Medicine, Emory University School of Medicine in Atlanta, Georgia; Department of Genetics and Molecular Biology, University of Rome in Italy; and Statistical Department, University of Hamburg in Germany. The results were published by the University of Chicago October 6, 1998.[294] This was eight months after the A.A.A.S. meeting in Philadelphia where they had announced that the "Siberian Land Bridge Only" doctrine could no longer be sustained, and that the Americas were settled by multiple maritime crossings.

> On the basis of comprehensive RFLP analysis, it has been inferred that ~97% of Native American mtDNAs belong to one of four major founding mtDNA lineages, designated haplogroups "A"-"D." It has been proposed that a fifth mtDNA haplogroup (haplogroup X) represents a minor founding lineage in Native Americans ... supporting the conclusion that the peoples harboring haplogroup X were among the original founders of Native American populations. *To date, haplogroup X has not been ... identified in Asia, raising the possibility that some Native American founders were of Caucasian ancestry.*[295]

The translation of the above is this: About three percent of Native Americans have Caucasian ancestry and came from the Mediterranean or European areas. The obvious question is how did they arrive in America? Recent DNA discoveries in South America's Chile suggest that Paleo-Mongolois from Japan arrived by sea. The Emory University DNA study and later genetic research into the American Ojibwa Peoples have found genes in common with Italian, Finnish, and Israeli peoples that are not found in the Asian population. Professor Brown was interviewed after their findings were made public:

> Haplogroup X was different. It was spotted by Torroni in a small number of European populations. So the Emory group set out to explore the marker's source. They analyzed blood samples from Native American, European, and Asian populations and reviewed published studies. "We fully expected to find it in Asia, like the other four Native American markers," says Brown. To their surprise, however, Haplogroup X was only confirmed in the genes of a smattering of living people in Europe and Asia Minor [mid-East], including Italian, Finns, *and certain Israelis.*[296]

Professor Brown said the three percent came from Europe and Israel. Were there Jews? Is that what he meant by Israelis? mtDNA from the tribes of Israel? Two of the three immigrant groups talked about in the Book of Mormon were from the tribes of Israel. The Brown study has a time reference of 9,500 years ago. From the Bible's point of view the tribes of Israel came from Abraham, and Abraham came through the lineage of Shem, who was Noah's son. Semite is the term used to describe the descendants of Shem. Were there Semites in America thousands of years ago? If Semites found their way to America around 7,500 B.C., could they also have found their way later around 600 B.C.? There was no Asian origin in three percent of the Native Americans. The most logical argument is that various groups of Finns, Italians, and "Israelis" crossed the great deep, and intermarried after their arrivals in America. This is precisely the claim of the Book of Mormon.

Among the pure-blooded Apache there is evidence of type "B" blood. The Native Americans were all to have had type "O" blood. Germans and "Jews" have type "B" blood.[297] These are the findings, among others, that are forcing a rethinking on the part of some evolutionists and retrenchment on the part of others. A second comprehensive DNA study confirmed diversity of origin for the settling of the Americas. After the examination of 22,808 individuals from sixty groups of Native Americans, including Eskimos, North Americans, Mesoamericans, and South American, it was obvious that a homogeneous group crossing the Siberian Land Bridge did not settle the Americas. Indeed, as this DNA study bluntly stated, "The notion of a homogeneous Amerind genetic pool does not conform with these and other results."[298] The translation of this scientific jargon is this: The Americas were settled by diverse groups other than Asians.

For those seriously interested in the complete Brown, et al., DNA report, it is available online at the footnoted citation. Pre-1998 Darwinists called any DNA evidence contrary to their "Asian Only" theory as tainted, unreliable, and rejected it.

The Demise of the "Asian Only" Migration Theory

To review: the "Asian Only" theory was the belief that only Asians settled the pre-Columbian Americas by crossing the Siberian Land Bridge. Various Asian "hunters and gatherers" migrated across the Siberian Land Bridge following the bison and mastodon herds, and then moved south. According to this theory civilization flowed from the north to the south. Many a die-hard adamantly maintained, and some still do, an Asian only attitude in spite of evidence to the contrary. Sound familiar? Archaeologist Thor Heyerdahl and others have identified some of the oldest tribal artifacts as coming from the South American Continent. These findings presented the "Asian Only" advocates and archaeologists with a big problem. The facts didn't fit the theory. The oldest artifacts should have been found in the northernmost part of North America. They were not. However, if the Americas were settled by various Pacific and Atlantic maritime crossings, as advocated by the Book of Mormon, the artifacts and findings are consistent.

In the 1890s the diffusionist philosophy was used to explain the similarities between Mesoamerica and Egypt. Cultural diffusionists were willing to accept that geographical groups of people separated by thousands of miles could develop independent of each other, inventions, cultural mores against adultery, and some theological beliefs. However, when artifacts, cultural mores, or theological beliefs were identical in form, and practice to those of another society of people, the cultural diffusionists insisted it was time for serious scientific consideration of cross-cultural pollination.

How does all this relate to the Book of Mormon? Cross-cultural pollination is independent of Mormonism, but coincides with the Book of Mormon. As another testament for Jesus Christ, the Book of Mormon is an affront to everything evolution represents. The Book of Mormon supports God as the Divine Creator of all things in heaven and earth. It supports the Bible, and diffusionism as a correct principle. The Book of Mormon will continue to be rejected by evolutionists, except for "theistic evolutionists" who believe that God used evolution as His means of creation. President Hinckley was quoted in the *Deseret Morning News* on March 1, 2006, regarding the Church's position on theistic evolution. He said, "What the church requires is only belief that Adam was the first man of what we would call the human race."[299]

An Example of Cultural Cross-Pollination or Diffusionism

The Egyptians believed that the four sons of Horus represented the four cardinal points of the earth: north, south, east, and west.[300] These four brothers held up the four corners of the earth.[301] The following is from the 1895 *Book of the Dead*:

> Originally they represented the Four Horus gods, who held up the four pillars which supported the sky, or their father Horus. Each was supposed to be lord of one of the quarters of the world, and finally became the god of one of the cardinal points. Hep represented the north, Taumutef the east, Amset the south and Qebhsenuf the west.[302]

Likewise, in the Maya theology, the four brothers of Bacab are identified with the cardinal points of the earth. These four brothers also held up the sky.[303] In 1566 Diego de Landa reported on the Maya creation theology:

> These were, they say, four brothers placed by God when he created the world, at its four corners to sustain the heavens lest they fall. They also say that these *Bacabs* escaped when the world was destroyed by the deluge. To each of these they gave other names, and they mark the four points of the world where God placed them holding up the sky ... [Ix, the north; Muluk, the east; Kan, the south; Cauac, the west].[304]

One translation of Chilam Balam has a different designation for the brothers on a calendar. Muluk is North, Cauac is South, Kan is East, and Ix is West. To avoid confusion, de Landa's explanation will suffice to point out the comparison between Egyptian theology and Maya theology.[305]

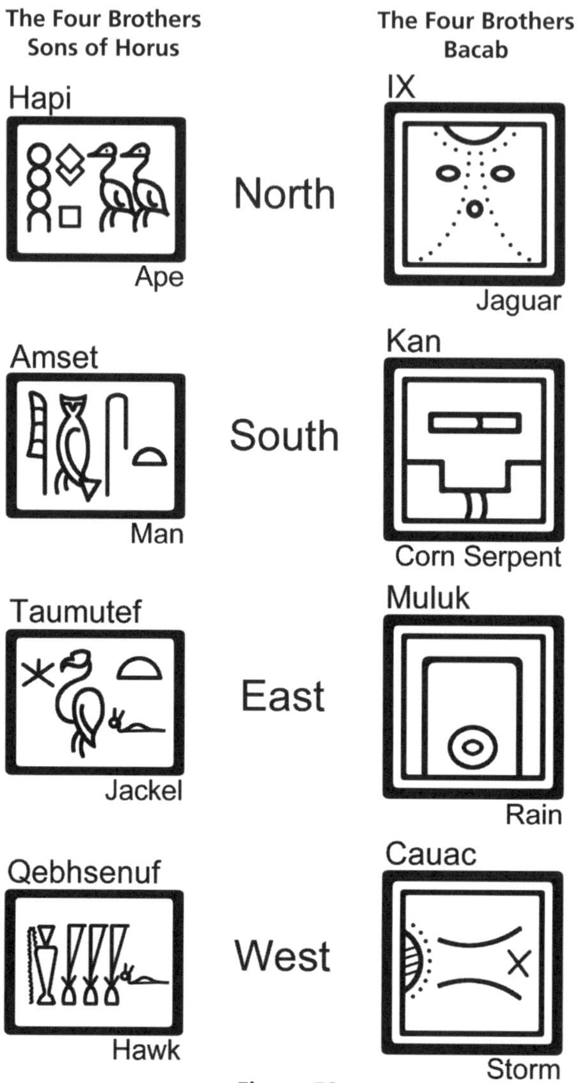

Figure 52.
Old World Egyptian Theology New World Maya Theology

This is an example of one culture influencing another. It would be unwise and premature to dismiss this exact theological parallel as a coincidence or "Independent Invention." This is especially so when one considers that it is now acknowledged that America was settled by many maritime crossings over thousands of years. It is also significant to note that Wallace Budge, compiler of the Egyptian *Book of the Dead* in A.D. 1895, and Diego de Landa, Bishop of the Yucatan, in A.D. 1566, reported their findings about the Sons of Horus and the Brothers Bacab independent of each other. It is possible therefore that people of the Book of Mormon, could have brought to the Americas knowledge of things Egyptian. It is also probable that other people from the Mediterranean and North African communities could have influenced the Mesoamericans.

Pre-Columbian Egyptian Influence in America

The pyramids, the large carved monoliths, and hieroglyphic writings reminded John Lloyd Stephens instantly of his "wandering among the ruins of Egypt."[306] Stephens is credited with rediscovering the ruins of Mesoamerica and of awakening the world to the high civilization that once existed in southern Mexico and Central America. The highly respected Mayanist, Robert Sharer, of the University of Pennsylvania, admits that many of the early explorers of Mesoamerica advanced the theory that Mesoamerica was settled by immigrants from the old world. "Egypt was perhaps the most commonly attributed source."[307] A Professor of Anthropology, and Curator of the American Section of the University Museum of Archaeology and Anthropology at the University of Pennsylvania, Dr. Sharer was steeped in his belief that America was settled only across the Siberian Land Bridge as portrayed on the museum walls. Any alternative view was labeled a "shabby purpose."[308] Dr. Sharer would be well served to read linguist J. Marcus, "Zapotec Writing," *Scientific American.*[309] Dr. Marcus believes that Zapotec hieroglyphic writing shares a similar style to that of the Egyptian. This does not mean that Marcus herself believed they were Egyptian, only that there was a commonality between them.

The Book of Mormon as Viable History

Current information and findings argue for the Americas being settled by many different peoples at various levels of civilization. It may well be that most of the early immigrants to the Americas did come from Asia and crossed the Pacific Ocean. Joseph Smith said that Lehi crossed "the great southern [Pacific] ocean."[310] The Jaredites also are candidates for a Pacific crossing and may very well have come from Asia around 2200 B.C. The Book of Mormon claims to be the history of only three groups of the hundreds of maritime immigrants to the Americas. People from various historic cultures crossed the great oceans over the centuries of time and lived out their human dramas in localized areas with little or no contact with their far flung neighbors. As populations increased there were wars, power struggles, marriage alliances, and a mixing of the various groups that survived.

What Does Accepting That the Americas Were Settled by Multiple Maritime Crossings and Not the "Siberian Land Bridge Only" Mean to The Book of Mormon?

Accepting that the Americas were settled by multiple maritime crossings over thousands of years of time has multiple ramifications:

1. The Maya, Mexica, Toltec, Zapotec and other Mesoamerican, North American, and South American histories, both oral and written, about their ancestors coming to the Americas from across the great waters, is viable.

2. The Book of Mormon claim that three migrating groups, the Jaredites (2200 B.C.), the Lehites (600 B.C.), and the Mulekites (587 B.C.) is also a viable and plausible historic option.
3. The Vikings may have had a more profound pattern of settlement than previously accepted. For the Book of Mormon, it establishes pre-Columbian transoceanic travel and shows that Atlantic as well as Pacific crossings were possible.
4. Each of the above groups of seafaring immigrants and the many other unknown cultures arrived with various levels of civilization. One should expect to find pockets of high and less advanced civilizations in North and South America.
5. Each "Pocket Culture" or regional settlement would expand according to the political and military influence it could exert. Less cultured societies, barbarians, who were more militarily aggressive, could eradicate or assimilate those who had attained a higher civilization without adopting the advancements of the higher civilization. The Spaniards did not adopt the more accurate Mesoamerican calendars, in spite of the calendars superiority.
6. Where there was interaction between expanding groups, one should find war, marriage alliances, trade and cultural blending and a mixing of seed through amalgamation and assimilation over time.
7. Immigrant cultures to America would bring animals with them, as did the Vikings. Some animals would survive and others not. The ability of the animals to adapt and expand beyond their geographical pocket would vary.
8. Geographically isolated communities could rise and fall over hundreds of years and be wiped out by plague, famine, civil wars, or natural disasters and leave little or no measurable historic footprint.
9. Specifically for the Book of Mormon it means:
   a. The animals mentioned in the Book of Mormon do not have to cover all of North and South America in order to support Book of Mormon history.
   b. Maritime crossings were viable.
   c. Amalgamation and assimilation of Jaredite, Mulekite and Nephite societies into the corpus Americana should be expected.
   d. It is not necessary to find a sign that says "Nephi lived here." Instead one should be able to find footprints in the history, the culture, and the traditions of the surviving cultures that correspond to the Book of Mormon.

The battle in science between Diffusionists and Darwinists has been going on for a century. Many of the current attacks against the exclusivity of the "Siberian Land Bridge Only" and "Asian Only" theories are being made by fellow Darwinists. The theory that civilization flowed from the north down to South

America, as a logical extension of the Siberian Land Bridge theory, is not a sustainable position. Glaring problems for the "Asian Only" theory continue to mount.

Here is another problem for the "Siberian Land Bridge Only" advocates: the demise of their theory weakens the position of the social evolutionist. According to Darwinists man evolves from a lower creature to a higher and more intelligent one. Survival of the fittest, adaptation and mutation applied to man's social progress was the expected pattern of human development. There is more evidence of de-evolution of societies than of evolution. The uneducated sit on the ruins of a higher society from Egypt to Mesoamerica even today.

It has taken a hundred years for the Darwinists to entrench their theories in the school systems. Significant numbers of the entrenched Darwinists are willing to misrepresent, manipulate, summarily reject, and hide evidence that runs contrary to the evolutionary theory. Evolution as a theory can not be proven. It must remain in the area of opinion or "best educated guess." As it relates to "Clovis" and the "Siberian Land Bridge Only" doctrine, now the general public is told that a new pharaoh, "Kennewick Man," who knew not "Clovis" has arrived in the land, and new dogmatic assertions are being made to replace the old ones. The graveyard of anthropological theories is filled to overflowing.

The Battle Continues to Rage Between the Evolutionists and the Diffusionists Regarding Book of Mormon Claims

Many in the scientific community believe, contrary to convincing evidence, that the Spaniards introduced horses, cattle, chickens, as well as barley, to the Americas. It is one thing to state that the Spanish brought with them to the New World Spanish horses, Spanish cattle, Spanish chickens and Spanish barley, and the use of these Spanish imports impacted in a major way upon the native populations. That is a reasonable and proper assertion. It also supports the diffusionists' theory of one culture influencing another. If the issue is that European contact after Columbus had a greater impact on both South America and North America than Vikings or any other previous transoceanic crossings, then the answer is yes, they probably did. However, to say there were *no* pre-Columbian horses, cattle, chickens or barley in the Americas prior to Columbus is dogmatic, wrong and arrogant. It supposes all knowledge on the part of the advocates of such a statement and does not allow for future findings which might contradict the theory.

Society has just witnessed the egg-on-your face dogmatic overstatements on the part of scientists in regards to the "Siberian Land Bridge-Asian-Only" fiasco. Equally foolish was an earlier overstatement made by the Smithsonian. The Smithsonian in their "Statement Regarding the Book of Mormon," prepared by the Office of Anthropology, National Museum of Natural History, reported in the summer of 1996:

> American Indians had no wheat, barley, oats, millet, rice, cattle, pigs, chickens, horses, donkeys, camels before 1492 (Camels and horses were in the Americas along with the bison, mammoth, and mastodon, but all these animals became extinct around 10,000 B.C.)...[311]

Academic Arrogance

Notice there is no room for future horse finds, cattle finds, chicken finds, or any wisely stated "wiggle room" that a prudent scholar would allow himself or herself. For example, saying there was not a horse in America after 10,000 B.C. and before the Europeans came in A.D. 1492, is too dogmatic. It is not good science. To have said that there is no current evidence of which we are aware that there were pre-Columbian horses, chickens, and cattle is prudent. The fact is there are numerous evidences of pre-Columbian horses, chickens and cattle that were ignored or summarily dismissed. The Smithsonian has a long standing tradition of eating crow; of being wrong and having to restate a more modest position as they have recently done in relationship to the Siberian Land Bridge.

For those who may not be aware, there has been a long standing feud between the Smithsonian's anthropologists and the Book of Mormon believers dealing with dozens of issues. Why? Because of dogmatic statements like the one above, which are recanted or modified later by the Smithsonian. Betty J. Meggers, of the Smithsonian has made similar dogmatic statements regarding populations in South America, which have been proven wrong.[312] It is a violation of true science and it is irresponsible. The general populous ought to be able to trust the scholars who are sustained in their livelihoods by public and private funds. Look again at the attitude of current diehard evolutionists:

> Most all professional archaeologists and historians consider the topic of Pre-Columbian visitors to be a preposterous and, in fact, a ridiculous subject of study of far less serious consideration than alchemy, Ouija boards, flying saucers and moon cheese.[313]

Beware of those who claim to be scientists. They may only be bigots masquerading as scientists. It would be foolish to place greater faith in the partial evidence of even well meaning scientists than in spiritual knowledge obtained by prayer and a witness of the Holy Ghost. The above statement is reflective of the majority of today's scientists in this field. Truly, all in current science received their graduate degrees from institutions that indoctrinated them with evolutionist theories. Professor Edward J. Vajda, a linguist and Ph.D. graduate of the University of Washington, wrote an article for his current students (2007) titled "The Siberian Origins of Native Americans."

> Virtually all scholars agree that the aboriginal populations living in North, Central and South America at the time of Columbus' voyages originated from small groups of prehistoric immigrants from North

> Asia. *No sober anthropologist* would defend the notion that Pre-Columbian Native Americans sailed across the Atlantic from Europe or Africa or that Native Americans have lived in the Western Hemisphere from time immemorial.[314]

This would be laughable except for the arrogant mentalities which still persist in the large and spacious buildings we call institutions of higher education. These people are so closed minded they refuse to acknowledge Atlantic crossings of the Vikings or attempt to minimize it. Professor Vajda's attitude is typical of those who have sold their soul to a theory, and nothing can budge them from their dearly held faith; not even the truth and concrete evidence. It must be terribly painful for Professor Vajda and others to read the latest revised statements of the Smithsonian about the death of the "Asian Only" theory:

> There is now convincing evidence of human habitation sites that date earlier than the Clovis culture ... A coastal migration route is now [2007] gaining more acceptance, rather than the older view of small bands moving on foot across the middle of the land bridge between Siberia and Alaska and into the continents ... Archaeological evidence in Australia, Melanesia, and Japan indicate boats were in use as far back as 25,000 to 40,000 years ago. Sea routes would have provided abundant food resources and easier and faster movement than land routes ... In addition ... skeletal remains show a range of physical attributes suggesting separate migrations of different populations of modern humans from Asia ... Spirit Cave Man from Nevada and ... Kennewick Man found in Washington in 1996 [are two examples] ... Physical anthropologist see a greater similarity in these crania to certain Old World populations such as Polynesians, *Europeans,* and the Ainu of Japan.... *At this time, scientists are not ruling out the possibility of a migration from Europe* ... Recently, however, a fifth mtDNA linage named "X" has turned up in living American Indians and in prehistoric remains for which there does not appear to be an Asian origin.[315]

According to Vajda, the people at the Smithsonian must not be "sober." The "Asian Only" theory is going to die a slow and agonizing death. Prior to 1998 only the heretical anthropologist would seriously risk his or her career and future grant money by going against the holy doctrine of "all of the Americas were settled by multiple Asian migrations across the Siberian Land Bridge prior to the coming of the Spaniards in A.D. 1492!" Most anthropologists gave the doctrine the spiritual weight of a "Papal Bull." And some still do. Mocking, scorning, and ridicule were and are the lot of any who dared challenge it. This included the Book of Mormon which proclaimed in 1830 that the Americas were settled by various maritime crossings. Frankly, as a group, anthropologists lack credibility. It is difficult to trust the "science" of most anthropologists. Guess what? They haven't gone away. They are just as self-righteous and condescending as always.

Dennis Stanford, then the Curator of the Smithsonian, admitted after the 1998 American Association for the Advancement of Science held in Philadelphia that the possibility of serious scholarship to reexamine some former artifacts, which were summarily rejected, is now possible.[316]

Scientific Cover-Ups?

There is incontrovertible evidence that pre-Columbian horse finds were summarily rejected or labeled as a hoax without serious scholarship. One example was an anthropologist from the Milwaukee Public Museum, Dr. Robert Ritzenthaler.[317] Recall the sentiment expressed by the Maine Museum, "the topic of Pre-Columbian visitors to be ... preposterous."[318]

Morley, Thompson, and Proskouriakoff are names revered among Mesoamerican scholars. It is akin to blasphemy to point out their ludicrous blunders. In balance these Mesoamerican scholars did add to the body of knowledge, and indeed their contributions may have outweighed some of their arrogance. Are they are all dishonest? No! There are many competent scientists who are willing to accept "truth" as their highest value. They have the courage to stand against the elite and admit error. They appear to be in the minority. It is to the credit of the Smithsonian they were willing to admit error.

Soon many scientists will see the wisdom and the new opportunities for studying the impact of pre-Columbian crossings on the settlement of the Americas. The "Siberian Land Bridge Only" doctrine will be a concept buried and not praised. Like Marc Antony at the funeral of Julius Caesar, "I come to bury Caesar, not to praise him."[319] Most scholars will bury their former beliefs. They were not really wrong. They simply made miscalculations. Many former advocates of the Americas being settled by the "Asian Only-Siberian Land Bridge Only" theory will put as much distance between themselves and their former published opinions to the contrary as they can. There will be a few who will go down with the ship. Those who do are most likely also members of a lead-water drinking, blood-letting, flat earth society. The fact that it took a hundred years to abandon the "Siberian Land Bridge Only" doctrine bodes well for cautious and qualified assertions in science.

I will be forever grateful to my own doctoral committee who forced me to pursue a doctoral minor in statistics. The key to valid conclusions relies heavily on proper sampling. The first concept we were taught was "Gin-Gout." This was an anagram which meant "Garbage-**in** equals Garbage-**out**." If the sample is bad, equally bad is the conclusion based upon the poorly acquired sample. When statements are made in science based upon research, I am anxious to see all phases of the sampling process, control groups, and the biases of the researcher. The LA Times reported on a DNA study claiming that all Native Americans came from Asia. They eliminated from their samples vital information that led them to false conclusions. The biases of the "Siberian Land

Bridge Only" advocates prevented any evidence to the contrary to be seriously evaluated. How many more of these theories based upon bad sampling are we to accept? This is not my only concern about scientific theories.

The Thompson story about preventing the deciphering of Mayan is not an isolated example. Until Michael Coe's sixth edition of *The Maya* in 1999, acknowledging his belief that the Americas were settled by many maritime crossings, the "Siberian Land Bridge Only" doctrine was the only permitted theory to be advanced in college classrooms. Those who dared to propose a contrary view would find it a block to academic advancement. Those who have spent their lives in academia, such as I have, know an unwritten policy exists for excluding from hire or advancement those who hold alternative but opposing views from the college Deans. This unwritten policy of hiring those who agree with the Deans has created an unhealthy educational environment that stifles the quest for truth. The inbreeding that has resulted from a limited gene pool of diverse thinkers on the college campus opposes the very purpose of science, which is the search for true knowledge.

I once asked a graduate student who was ready to receive his doctorate in microbiology if he would be willing to read the Book of Mormon and pray about it. He said it was too subjective. I responded by telling him that I didn't believe in micro-organisms because I couldn't see them. All of his assurances would not convince me. He invited me to come to the laboratory and see for myself. "All you have to do is to look through this very powerful microscope and you will know for yourself." I told him I would feel silly and would have to decline his invitation. He was very bright, and understood that I was inviting him to look through a spiritual microscope. He softened his heart and took the challenge. Suffice it to say, it has changed the course of his life. He is a brilliant researcher today who seeks for truth in the laboratory using all his resources including his intuition and the gift of the Holy Ghost. The hypothesis that the Book of Mormon is another true witness of Christ can be tested. Read it and ask of God.

God also loves the scientist, and there are and always have been great scientists who believe in God. Some have been members of the LDS Church, and others of various faiths, and some of no organized religion at all. Apparent differences and incongruence between spiritual knowledge and secular knowledge should be left for further study and research, with some questions that will remain unanswered until the Great Beyond.

CHAPTER FIFTEEN

THE BOOK OF MORMON AS HISTORY: WHAT ABOUT HORSES IN AMERICA?

Figure 53. Man Missing a Head Standing at the Side of a pre-Columbian Horse at Chichen Itzá, Mexico

Archaeologists and Anthropologists are Learning the Hard Way.

Based on the broad sweeping statements and generalizations that are made by the Smithsonian and most archaeologists, historians, and anthropologists about the Americas, there is a problem of perception. The Americas are perceived as a whole and not as regional geographical areas. The 1996 Smithsonian statement regarding the Book of Mormon is typical. "American Indians had no wheat, barley, oats, millet, rice, cattle, pigs, chickens, horses, donkeys, camels before 1492,"[320] is one example. Professor McGee's declaration is truly reflective of nearly all pre-1998 archaeologists, historians and anthropologists, "The first cattle, horses, chickens, and pigs were all brought to the New World by the Spanish."[321] In a field of study where their credibility is already suspect because they can not field test their hypotheses, one would hope for more prudent statements.

Passionate assertion is a poor substitute for good science. This is another problem that afflicts many in all the sciences, and, in particular, archaeologists, historians, and anthropologists. It is the Gnostic mentality. Because they have specialized knowledge in their area of expertise, they are arrogant. What they fail to recognize is they are not the only ones who have been trained in the scientific process. How they gather information, and their preconceived biases, affects their findings and conclusions. All scientists are subject to scrutiny by those equally educated in the methods of scientific investigation. In this case it was the preconceived bias that the Spaniards brought "The first cattle, horses, chickens, and pigs ... to the New World..." that has resulted in flawed conclusions and hasty judgments against the Book of Mormon. This same bias still persists with many in the scientific community.

Instead of evaluating as an option the written histories and oral traditions of the Mesoamericans which claimed their ancestors had traveled across the great waters to Mesoamerica, they were summarily rejected in favor of the preconceived bias of the Siberian Land Bridge. The evidence for multiple Viking settlements and the artifacts associated with them were, and are still, considered by most archaeologists and anthropologists "a ridiculous subject of study of far less serious consideration than alchemy, Ouija boards, flying saucers and moon cheese."[322]

The Book of Mormon claims need to be evaluated on a regional or micro-regional basis. Most of the statements made in the Book of Mormon are time and place sensitive. There are regional statements which are true for that area. After the Lehites arrived in Mesoamerica and were journeying in the wilderness, Nephi commented on the gold, silver, copper, and on the animals in that region (1 Nephi 18:25). His statement must be taken to mean that particular habitat, and not all of North and South America. If pre-Columbian chickens are found in South America, that does not mean they were to be found in Mesoamerica. Finding chickens in South America increases the probability of finding chickens in Mesoamerica, given the diffusionist reality, but would be an overstatement. With less than two percent of the known Mesoamerican ruins excavated, one would want to error on the side of caution. Book of Mormon scholars need to be equally cautious about archaeological claims.

The current focus has been on the viability of the Book of Mormon as history. The basic assumptions of the majority of archaeologists and anthropologists have been wrong regarding many vital issues affecting the viability of the Book of Mormon as history. One of the most important is how the Americas were settled. Their obsession with the "Siberian Land Bridge Only" doctrine precluded serious examination of pre-Columbian transoceanic travel to the Americas. The anthropological disdain for diffusionism from Europe, Africa, or the Mid-east to the Americas from 2200 B.C. to A.D. 1500 has prevented an open and honest look of legitimate artifacts. The arrogant dismissal of the extent of Viking influence in North America and their continued refusals to acknowledge hard evidence, i.e., pre-Columbian peppers from Mexico found in Medieval Lund Sweden by a Paleo-botanist, butternut wood found at L'Anse aux Meadows demonstrating Viking penetration as far south as the Great Lakes, the Viking coin of Olaf Kyrie dated A.D. 1065 to A.D. 1080 found in Maine and called the Maine Penny. The assumption that the Spanish were the first to introduce horses, cattle, chickens, etc. to the Americas, and the rejection of any evidence to the contrary, does not bode well for their scientific credibility.

The fact is the Spanish introduced new breeds of European horses to the Americas, just as Canadian wolves were introduced into Yellowstone National Park to replace the smaller and extinct American wolf. Evidences of pre-Columbian horses are just now being allowed to come forth. There are horse bones, not prehistoric, but pre-Columbian, at the caves in the Yucatan at Uxmal, that date to the time of the Book of Mormon. There is a stone engraving of a horse at Chichen Itzá on the Temple of Tableros, which I have personally seen. At Tulum in Mexico's Yucatan there is an embossed equine on the northern wall of El Castillo. This would indicate awareness of horses two hundred years before the Spanish arrived.

People who sailed the oceans brought animals with them. Think of the Vikings. Also, who is to say the chickens traveled from the islands to South America? They may also have traveled from South America to the islands carried by humans.

There are today 80,000 horses in Iceland. How did they get there? They were originally brought in ships by the Vikings around A.D. 800. "When peaceful Vikings settled Iceland more than a thousand years ago they brought their horses with them in open Viking long boats, braving the cruel North Atlantic."[323] These are the same Vikings who came to North America in ships and established several communities along the St. Lawrence Seaway as well as L'Anse aux Meadows in Newfoundland.[324] It is absurd to believe that a group of settlers would have not taken cattle, horses, sheep, and chickens with them.

> The Vikings caught fish, hunted game animals, picked berries, and had brought meat, cattle, and poultry from Iceland. The cattle not only provided food, but some also produced milk (and eventually dairy products). The chickens not only provided meat but also eggs and their chicks maintained the poultry system.
>
> In A.D. 1008, Thorfinn Karlsefni brought sixty people (including five women) to Vinland. He continued the practice of bringing cattle

> and sheep from Europe, and traded furs, skins etc. with the aboriginal people.[325]

Also there is concrete evidence of pre-Columbian cayenne pepper found in Lund, Sweden from the Middle Ages long before Columbus set sail. It was discovered by an evolutionist, the renowned Paleo-Botanist Hakon Hjelmqvist.[326] The Vikings obviously had contact with the people as far south as the Gulf of Mexico. Capsicum annuum, from which cayenne pepper, bell peppers, jalapenos, and paprika come, "originated in Mexico and Central America."[327] Later, cayenne peppers along with many other Mesoamerican foods were introduced to the rest of the world by Spanish and Portuguese sailors.

Visitors Versus Residents in America

It is the position of the Book of Mormon that many groups were led to the Americas by maritime crossings over hundreds of years. Some travelers became visitors while other adventurers became residents. The Vikings were proclaimed visitors; however, some scholars believe many remained for generations until they were killed or assimilated. They set up camp at Vinland on Newfoundland's shores around A.D. 1000, and recent archaeological evidence indicates that they may have experimented with other settlements near the Great Lakes.[328] Oklahoma, where the twelve-foot-high "Heavener" Runestone was found needs to be reevaluated as a potential Viking site. Some researches believe "The Heavener Runestone on Poteau Mountain in eastern Oklahoma is most likely a boundary marker."[329] Remember, there is a bias in the scientific community against all pre-Columbian finds supporting maritime crossings of Vikings. Also near the Bay of Campeche in Mexico there is a carved stone under investigation as a potential "Viking Stone." Viking contact with Mexico and Central America was a reality based on the Paleo-Botanist Hakon Hjelmqvist, who reported cayenne pepper in medieval Lund, Sweden.[330] Because some of the Vikings returned to their homelands, they are not given credit as permanent residents of America, but rather as visitors. Time and further research may yet prove that the Vikings in America, like the Olmec, were a vanishing culture and not just visitors. The Vikings who stayed may have been assimilated into the native populations. The three groups mentioned in the Book of Mormon stayed and became residents of America and eventually by wars of conquest, intermarriage, and miscegenation became a part of the corpus Americana.

How many groups came to the Americas over these hundreds of years is not known. What is known is that many diverse and distinct racial characteristics abound. Certainly there were dozens if not hundreds over the past three thousand years. Ronald H. Fritze authored a book in 1993 entitled, *Legend and Lore of the Americas before 1492: An Encyclopedia of Visitors, Explorers, and Immigrants.* In it he pursues the expeditions of the Chinese, the Arab, the African, and the Europeans and concludes that most, but not all, were seafaring tales. Some may have perished unto themselves and have left traces of their existence such as the Olmec. Ivan Van Sertima in his book, *African Presence in Early America,* makes a rational case for the Olmecs being all or partly of African origin. The colossal heads found along the gulf coast of Mexico look African. It is of interest to note that Joseph Smith mentioned to his scribe, William Clayton, and to his compatriot, Parley P. Pratt, that there were blacks of African descent among the friends of Jared who came to the Americas in 2200 B.C. Pratt recorded that the bones of a man discovered in Kinderhook, Illinois, were from a "descendant of Ham through the loins of Pharaoh, king of Egypt..."[331] Ham was Noah's son. He married a righteous black woman named Egyptus (see Abraham 1:21-26, I Peter 3:18:20).

The two authors, Fritze and Sertima are not LDS. John L. Sorenson is. His book is called *Pre-Columbian Contact with the Americas across the Oceans.* These are all worthwhile reads for those who desire more information. But because of the "Siberian Land Bridge Only" theory and its avid adherents in the past and some in the present, the obvious fact of pre-Columbian maritime crossings were dismissed for a far less probable explanation: they all walked to America. Now that serious scholars such as Michael Coe accept pre-Columbian and prehistoric maritime crossings, Sertima's claims and others can receive a legitimate scientific examination.

Might the Vikings have perhaps brought horses with them to America, or did they leave all the horses in Iceland in A.D. 870? In spite of the time difference between the Vikings and the Book of Mormon, the point is the "scientific" assertion that there were no pre-Columbian horses is incorrect.

Evidence of pre-Columbian horse bones have been ignored for years and summarily rejected because they were not supposed to be in the Americas. Henry Mercer, an early American paleontologist, encountered horse bones in the caves of the Puuc in the Yucatan. He found horse bones in three of the caves (Actun Sayab, Actun Lara, and Chektalen). He identified ten layers of strata. Near the top stratum he found two horses. If we give him the benefit of the doubt, he assumed they had to be Spanish since they were not Pleistocene. Being pre-Columbian was not an option.[332] Why? Because it was universally accepted there were no horses in America prior to the Spanish bringing them. Now that science is open to America being settled by multiple maritime crossing from the Atlantic Ocean and the Pacific Ocean, the probability that even a few of these mariners brought horses, cows, and chickens with them must be a viable option.

Here is one example of summarily rejecting horse finds. In 1936, W.C. McKern excavated a mound at Spencer Lake in Wisconsin (47BT2), and vouched for by McKern in the *Wisconsin Archaeologist.* Here is his simple testimony:

> There remains no reasonable question as to the legitimacy of the horse skull that we found as a burial association placed in the mound by its builders.[333]

> Carbon 14 dating on all the surrounding charcoal, charred wood, and bone has been dated to A.D. 750-900 (+or- 65 years).[334]

A questionable "anonymous confession" was given by a Mr. P., who supposedly told the anthropologist from the Milwaukee Public Museum, Dr. Robert Ritzenthaler, that as a lad he had buried a horse head as a prank in a mound at Spencer Lake. Further investigation revealed there were two mounds. The Ritzenthaler and Mr. P's mound was on the west side of the lake, while the McKern mound (47BT2) was on the north side of the lake. Additionally, Mr. P's horse's skull had a missing mandible, while the McKern horse skull had the mandible in place. Rather than publish the findings, Dr. Ritzenthaler, who was also the editor, "took it upon himself to expunge all mention of the skull from the official report."[335] What was Ritzenthaler's motive? Why didn't he feel a moral commitment to science and to truth to publish what he had found? He is the only one who has the answer. The fact he would have been mocked, scorned and laughed out of the anthropological community might have contributed to his decision to "cover up" contrary information. What is equally disgraceful is that current archaeologists are still trying to declare the issue a hoax.[336]

The Pre-Columbian Horses of the Yucatan

There is an engraving of a pre-Columbian horse at Chichen Itzá. It is located near the observatory at El Templo del Tableros. There are other examples of Yucatec horses. In the 1950s excavations at the pre-Columbian site of Mayapan were reported. Horse bones were discovered in four different locations. Because two of the finds were close to the surface, they were "summarily dismissed" as being Spanish. The others could not be. They were found in two meters of unconsolidated earth almost six feet deep. Two partially mineralized horse teeth were found at the same stratum with Maya pottery. This means there was an association of horses with humans. This contradicted the science of the time and ran counter to the "Siberian Land Bridge Only" doctrine. The site was Ch'en Mul, a sinkhole referred to as a "cenoté" or water hole.[337] BYU FARMS reported the following about horse finds in the Yucatan in an article titled "Out of the Dust":

> [In1895,] American paleontologist Henry C. Mercer went to Yucatan hoping to find remains of Ice Age man. He visited 29 caves in the hill area—the Puuc—of the peninsula and tried stratigraphic excavation in 10 of them. But the results were confused, and he came away disillusioned. He did find horse bones in three caves (Actun Sayab, Actun Lara, and Chektalen). In terms of their visible characteristics, those bones should have been classified as from the Pleistocene American horse species, then called Equus occidentalis L. However, *Mercer decided that since the remains were near the surface, they must actually be from the modern horse, Equus equus, that the Spaniards had brought with them to the New World, and so he reported*

them as such. In 1947 Robert T. Hatt repeated Mercer's activities. He found within Actun Lara and one other cave more remains of the American horse (in his day it was called Equus conversidens), along with bones of other extinct animals. Hatt recommended that any future work concentrate on Loltun Cave, where abundant animal and cultural remains could be seen.

It took until 1977 before that recommendation bore fruit. Two Mexican archaeologists carried out a project that included a complete survey of the complex system of subterranean cavities (made by underground water that had dissolved the subsurface limestone). They also did stratigraphic excavation in areas in the Loltun complex not previously visited. The pits they excavated revealed a sequence of 16 layers, which they numbered from the surface downward. Bones of extinct animals (including mammoth) appear in the lowest layers.

Pottery and other cultural materials were found in levels VII and above. But in some of those artifact-bearing strata there were horse bones, even in level II. A radiocarbon date for the beginning of VII turned out to be around 1800 B.C. The pottery fragments above that would place some portions in the range of at least 900 to 400 B.C. and possibly later. The report on this work concludes with the observation that "something went on here that is still difficult to explain." Some archaeologists have suggested that the horse bones were stirred upward from lower to higher levels by the action of tunneling rodents, but they admit that this explanation is not easy to accept. The statement has also been made that paleontologists will not be pleased at the idea that horses survived to such a late date as to be involved with civilized or near-civilized people whose remains are seen in the ceramic-using levels. Surprisingly, the Mexican researchers show no awareness of the horse teeth discovered in 1957 by Carnegie Institution scientists Pollock and Ray. Some uncomfortable scientific facts seem to need rediscovering time and time again.[338]

How Could Horses Have Arrived in Mesoamerica?

In addition to the above-mentioned finds is a Roman terra-cotta head found in a pre-Hispanic burial offering near Mexico City. Due to its discovery during controlled archaeological excavation, and in context without apparent traces of alterations, this find suggests that several centuries before the memorable voyages of Columbus and the Vikings, there had been another, perhaps accidental, crossing of the Atlantic ocean from ancient Mediterranean mariners. It is a genuine Roman artifact. Thermoluminiscence (TL) age test has established its age (Circa the 2nd Century A.D.).[339]

Romeo H. Hristov, Professor of Anthropology at the University of New Mexico, has established the authenticity and the dating of the above head to as early as the 1st century A.D. In any case it is pre-Columbian and demonstrates that those from across the Mediterranean crossed the Atlantic. It has been suggested that they may have been Romans, Vikings, Berbers, and even Phoenicians. All these cultures have a history of bringing horses with them. It was just one more nail in the coffin of the exclusive "Siberian Land Bridge Only" club.

> In 1987, a Roman settlement dated between the first century B.C. and the fourth century A.D. has been discovered in the Lanzarote Island (Canary Islands) and more recent archaeological research has proved that not only Romans but also Phoenicians and Berbers reached at least two of the Canary Islands as early as the sixth or fifth century B.C. The implications of these discoveries in the discussion of possible Pre-Columbian Trans-Atlantic contacts are obvious, and it is not entirely unreasonable to expect in the near future that systematical archaeological studies in the Caribbean, Central America and Brazil may provide more—and more conclusive—data related to small scale Trans-Atlantic voyages before 1492.[340]

It is important to recall a basic claim of the Book of Mormon that the Lehites and the Mulekites fled from the Mediterranean area. The Book of Mormon does not suggest that they brought horses with them. It does claim they found horses when they arrived. It is believed by many that the Lehites made a Pacific crossing while the Mulekites may have fled with Phoenician sailors across the Atlantic. Some maintain a Pacific or Atlantic crossing for the Jaredites. Regardless of which body of water they traversed, they arrived in Mesoamerica via sea going vessels. So also did many non Book of Mormon immigrants cross the great waters and settle throughout North and South America.

Pre-Columbian Traditions of the Horse Among the Lacandon

The Lacandon Maya, located in the jungles near Palenque, Mexico, believed that in a time long ago before the coming of the Spanish, they had *horses, pigs, cattle and chickens.* In the story, the Lacandon and Ladinos [Spanish] are both given *pigs, cattle, and horses*, but the Lacandon do not care for their animals.[341] The gods had entrusted to both the foreigners and the Lacandon these animals. Because of neglect these animals perished among the Lacandon until they were reintroduced by the Spanish. In A.D. 1974, Robert D. Bruce recorded this Lacandon belief in his book, "*El Libro de Chan K'in,*" published in Mexico City. It is footnoted again in Jon McGee's book.[342] The title of the belief is "U Tsimin ti Hach Winik," or "Horses for the [True Men] Lacandon." Professor McGee was steeped in the belief that "The first cattle, horses, chickens, and pigs were all brought to the New World by the Spanish."[343] He was mistaken. Both cattle and chickens were mentioned as imports brought to the New World, "Vinland," by the Vikings. Pre-Columbian chickens have also been discovered in Chile.

Once a theory like the "Siberian Land Bridge Only" becomes an established doctrine, there are few who are willing to risk excommunication from future research grants. However the real problem for science is being open to any finding of facts to the contrary of a revered theory. We saw this lack of openness with Thompson and the deciphering of Mayan, with Mercer and the horse bones of the Yucatan caves, with Dr. Ritzenthaler, with the LA Times DNA gatherers, and now with Professor McGee and the Lacandon. The thought that these animals were simply reintroduced by the Spanish was never considered nor given serious thought. The story is called a "myth" because of the dogmatic assertions of archaeologists and because of the narrow spectrum of scientific options available to Professor McGee if he wanted to remain in the good graces of the politically correct.

The Book of Mormon declared that cattle, swine, horses, fish, and even the honey bee were brought to America as early as 2200 B.C. (see Ether 2:1-3, Ether 9:17-19). As more and more evidence of maritime crossings to settle America are discovered, it is a bit egotistical to think that the Spanish were the only ones who thought of the idea of bringing animals with them in a ship when they immigrated to the New World.[344] Noah and the Ark advocates could make a strong case for carrying animals in ships before the Spaniards. The Norsemen who settled in the L'Anse Aux Meadows near the mouth of the St. Lawrence brought with them both cattle and small Shetland size ponies in A.D. 800-1000. How do we know that the Vikings traveled any farther south than Newfoundland? The answer is "Butternut." The Vikings of L'Anse Aux Meadows had numerous objects of butternut or "Juglandaceae cinerea."[345] The closest butternut trees are found more than seven hundred miles south of L'Anse aux Meadows along the St Lawrence Sea way. The U.S. Forest Service reported the following:

> Butternut is found from southeastern New Brunswick throughout the New England States except for northwest Maine and Cape Cod. The range extends south to include northern New Jersey, western Maryland, Virginia, North Carolina, northwestern South Carolina, northern Georgia, northern Alabama, northern Mississippi, and northeast into Ontario and Quebec.[346]

Most likely, the Vikings sailed down the St. Lawrence Seaway to acquire the needed Butternut wood.

> Butternuts and worked pieces of butternut wood-a tree that was not native to Newfoundland ... This discovery indicates that the people who lived at L'Anse aux Meadows had traveled further south into the Gulf of St Lawrence, and had brought back nuts and wood native to those southern areas and were sampling the region's resources as described in the [Viking] sagas.[347]

Excavations in 1985 of Native American mounds near Aztlan Park, Wisconsin revealed the remains of a small horse five hundred years before the Spanish arrived. After the Spaniards, other later immigrants to the Americas did bring animals with them, and various breeds of dogs, cats and rats as well. Why should one think that ancient people were not smart enough to bring animals with them when they immigrated? Part of the problem is the mindset of the social evolutionist who thinks that the ancient forbearers of man were knuckle-dragging simpletons who were not capable of building a boat, carrying animals with them, and crossing the oceans.

Ancient Greeks traveled to the oracle of Delphi to receive a vision-quest. The legend named, as one of the best, a woman named "Epiphany," and ever since the name epiphany has stood for a great insight, a sudden inspiration, a revelation of knowledge which was life changing. The February 1998 A.A.A.S. meeting was an epiphany. It was announced that primitive man had the ability and intelligence to build a boat sufficient to sail the seas at least 7500 B.C. or 9500 years ago. This is definitely pre-Columbian and before A.D. 1492. In light of this life-changing insight, it will now be necessary to go back and reexamine a ton of archaeological material that was summarily rejected. It may be time to reevaluate the "Bat Creek Stone," the "Heavener Stone," and even pre-Columbian horses.

It is difficult for those who live on the outside of the academic community to appreciate the "strangle hold" of the supporters of the status quo. Challenging a basic premise of the intellectually entrenched, such as the "Siberian Land Bridge Only" doctrine or the issue of pre-Columbian horses in America is tantamount to a declaration of war. Dr. Barry Fell was Professor of invertebrate Zoology at the Harvard Museum of Comparative Zoology. Like Thor Heyerdahl, Dr. Fell was "persona non grata." He was a thorn in the flesh of archaeologists, anthropologists, and epigraphers because of his willingness to examine any evidence which might suggest pre-Columbian contact in the Americas. The most vitriolic epitaphs were hurled at Barry Fell for questioning the status quo. Evidence of pre-Columbian horses in America will continue to be rejected by the hard liners.

Maybe the Lacandon of Mesoamerica really did know about "U Tsimin Ti Hach Winik," horses for the Lacandon. A more productive question would be, "What happened to the pre-Columbian horses?" There are several excellent theories as to what happened to the horses, chickens, and cattle. Sorenson suggested that some animals were misnamed and mislabeled. The Greeks, for example, when they saw large gray animals swimming in the Nile River called them "River Horses," and today we still know them by that name: hippopotamus. The turkey is indigenous to the Americas. When the Spaniards brought European chickens to America, the Native Americans referred to them as "small turkeys."

The Vikings who landed in Newfoundland brought chickens, cattle, and sheep. These animals would have been regional and confined to specific areas.

Also, if various small groups of people settled in remote regions and brought with them horses and other animals, there is no reason to assume that these animals were everywhere.[348]

Obviously, the Vikings and their animals were separated by several hundreds of years from the time of the Book of Mormon. The relevance of pre-Columbian cattle, chickens, sheep and horses in America is that it establishes the viability of other pre-Columbian crossings of the Atlantic and Pacific oceans. It also says the overwhelming majority of former supporters of the "Siberian Land Bridge Only" doctrine were wrong, dead wrong. They were also wrong about no pre-Columbian cattle, horses, chickens, sheep and multiple maritime crossings of the Atlantic and Pacific voyages for the peopling of the Americas. From a historical view the scientific community was far too eager to dismiss the Viking sagas as fairy tails, myths and absurd legends. The same is true of the *Popol Vuh, The History of Mexico* by Ixtlilxóchitl, *The Annals of the Cakchiquel, The Lords of Totonicapán,* and the writings of Guaman Poma about how the pre-Columbians in Peru believed in Christ before the arrival of the Spaniards.[349] These were all dismissed without serious examination. Several Mesoamerican histories specifically claim their forefathers came from across the sea. Not just one obscure document of questionable origin, but many native histories were summarily rejected because they supported a "diffusionist" point of view.

My own belief is that horses were regional and eaten in times of war and extended famine. The Book of Mormon reports on several eras of extended draught and famine, as do Mesoamerican histories:

> And it came to pass that there began to be a dearth upon the land, and the inhabitants began to be destroyed exceedingly fast because of the dearth, for there was no rain upon the face of the earth … and it came to pass that the people did follow the course of the beasts, and did devour the carcasses of them which fell by the way, until they had devoured them all (Ether 9:30-34).

Hundreds of years later, a similar experience occurred with another group of people living on the same land. In the year 18 B.C. it was written

> …the famine did continue and the work of destruction did cease by the sword but became sore by famine. And this work of destruction did also continue … [17 B.C.]. For the earth was smitten that it was dry, and did not yield forth grain in the season of grain; and the whole earth was smitten, even among the Lamanites as well as among the Nephites, so that they were smitten that they did perish by thousands … (Helaman 11:5-6).

Prolonged draught, disease, and domestication may have rendered the animals vulnerable to beasts of prey as well as human consumption. Cannibalism, known to be a part of Mesoamerican history, may have been the means for many to survive the extended famines. Mormon records that in addition to extended draught and famine, wars were the primary destroyer of whatever life was found. Like unto the Civil War and General Sherman's march through Georgia, one Book of Mormon army commander, Shiz, swept the earth before him:

> And there went a fear of Shiz throughout all the land; yea, a cry went forth throughout the land—Who can stand before the army of Shiz? Behold, he sweepeth the earth before him!...And so great and lasting had been the war, and so long had been the scene of bloodshed and carnage, that the whole face of the land was covered with the bodies of the dead. And so swift and speedy was the war that there were none left to bury the dead ... (Ether 14:18-22, 300 B.C.).

Humans were not the only species destroyed by war, pestilence, and famine. The habitat and the population of many animals were also destroyed. Lack of proper habitat would render survival difficult if not impossible. This is especially true for domesticated animals that were dependent upon man. It is evident from the stone carvings and the bones, that the horses mentioned in the Book of Mormon would have been more like the size of the Shetland pony. These horses would have been used for food by humans and easy targets for beast of prey.

Is the Loss of Species a Surprise?

The loss of species is an almost daily occurrence according to most environmentalists. The Tarpan, *Equus caballus gmelini*, was the original European horse. "The very last true Tarpan died in captivity in [the] Munich Zoo in 1887."[350] For whatever reason, famine, disease, etc., the pre-Columbian Mesoamerican horse also disappeared. That does not mean they never existed.

What if scientists were to proclaim, there were no wolves in Yellowstone prior to the introduction of thirty-one Canadians wolves in 1995?[351] Their assumptions would be that only prehistoric wolves lived in Yellowstone and they perished 10,000 years ago. In fact, a sixty-three year old eye witness who had lived in Yellowstone his entire life said he had never seen a wolf in Yellowstone prior to 1995. Does this mean there were no pre-Canadian wolves in Yellowstone? The American wolf was entirely eliminated from Yellowstone National Park by human intervention of hunters, shepherds, and cattle ranchers in 1930. Would any rational person suggest that prior to the reintroduction of Canadian wolves into Yellowstone after an absence of wolves for seventy years, there were no pre-1930 American wolves?

What current evidence could prove the pre-Canadian existence of the American wolf in Yellowstone? Where is the "convincing evidence?" All that exists as evidences of wolves are the journals and stories from old-timers. The journals of the mountain men in the early 1800s reported on the abundance of wolf packs in Yellowstone. However, for the same reasons that scholars have rejected the historical accounts of the *Popol Vuh*, the *History of Mexico* by Ixtlilxóchitl, the *Annals of the Cakchiquel*, the *Title of the Lords of Totonicapán*, and the writings of Guaman Poma, the written and oral traditions of the mountain men must be discounted as myths and legends. The same is true for the wolf stories and wolf dances of the Native Americans. Any bones that pretended to be the American Yellowstone wolves would be rejected as obvious fakes and frauds and unworthy of any serious scientific evaluation according to this line of reasoning. What if everyone in the scientific community believed that until the Canadians brought wolves to Yellowstone, there were no wolves in Yellowstone since the prehistoric era? Assume that all those with doctoral degrees agreed and said that anyone who believed otherwise made as much sense as someone believing in "alchemy, Ouija boards, flying saucers and moon cheese."

The comparison between pre-Canadian wolves in Yellowstone and pre-Columbian horses in America is a valid one. A far more correct statement would be that there were no Canadian wolves in Yellowstone before the Canadians introduced the thirty-one Canadian wolves to the park. There were no Spanish horses in America until the Spanish brought Spanish horses in 1519. The early evidence of pre-Columbian horses in Mesoamerica, such as those discovered in the caves at Uxmal, Mexico, also suggests that the American Pre-Columbian horses were a different species and considerably smaller than the horses brought by the Spanish.

There are two points that need attention. The first is the flexibility and prerogative of science to change theories on a few pieces of evidence and to ride off on a new horse, pardon the pun, proclaiming dogmatically that the new course is the way to absolute truth. This seems inherently arrogant and self-serving. In fairness there are many scientists who acknowledge the limitations of their finds as their best educated guesses.

The second point is there appears to be a double standard for evaluating evidence. *Convincing evidence* is the phrase used to accept a theory as the best current explanation. One standard is applied to Book of Mormon evidence while a more flexible standard is used to support scientific theories such as "The Floating Sweet Potato" theory.

The Book of Mormon as History

A fair and honest evaluation of the Book of Mormon in scientific terms would be the same standard that is used to examine the historicity of the Bible. Many Biblical archaeologists are avowed atheists. Although it is an oxymoron of the highest irony to be a Biblical atheist, it is quite accepted and lauded in the scientific community. Biblical archaeologists use the Bible to find cities and to verify wars, kingdoms, and historical facts. They ignore any claims to divine origin. When the Bible placed Jericho at the north end of the Dead Sea and identified Jericho in a historically correct time and place, it was accepted as evidence of Biblical accuracy. Divine claims were set aside. Whether the walls of Jericho "came tumbling down" after the Israelites marched around them seven times blowing their "shofars" remains an unanswered question for the researcher, but not the believer. There was a Jericho. It did exist at the time and place the Bible designated. The scientific community is not yet at this level of acceptance with the Book of Mormon.

Fear of being labeled as a promoter or as a detractor of the Book of Mormon, or of becoming embroiled in a theological debate is sufficient impetus for most to adopt a "hands off" policy. However, one need not accept the Bible's claim to a universal monotheistic God on the basis of the evidence that Jericho existed. Nor does one have to accept the divine guidance of the Book of Mormon on the basis of maritime crossings of the Atlantic and Pacific oceans by pre-Columbian sailors as claimed by the Book of Mormon when it was published in A.D.1830.

A study of the evidences for why the Book of Mormon is a real history of a real people may spark the very interest needed by some for an honest scientific evaluation. If this is the case, then one cannot help but be impressed with the plethora of evidence. Truman S. Madsen explained,

> The bottom line? That culture to which the Book of Mormon narrative is the most similar is likely the root of the narrative. And enough striking parallels exist between the Book of Mormon and the cultures it claims to represent to rule out coincidence. There are at least 150 cultural patterns in Mesoamerica which anthropologist and archaeologist have found in common with the Book of Mormon since it was published and about which Joseph Smith could not have known. It is hardly a rational explanation to say "he just guessed right."[352]

What is the Current Level of Knowledge About Book of Mormon Geography?

The last twenty-five years has advanced the knowledge of the history and the geography of the Book of Mormon significantly. From the time of its publication in 1830 there was no external evidence to support the claim that the Book of Mormon was real history until 1841. With the publication of the Stephens and Catherwood book *Incidents of Travel in Central America, Chiapas and Yucatan* progress began. In 1901 the Brigham Young Academy sponsored a Zarahemla Expedition. Most Church historians refer to the experience as less than successful. Political upheavals in Mexico and Central America, shortness of supplies, and the lack of general support are the reasons given for its demise.

In the early 1950s the New World Archeological Society was created. Wells Jakeman and Paul Cheesman began a serious study of the Book of Mormon geography and history. The 1960s, 1970s, and the 1980s saw the publication of a few books, the establishment of various archaeological foundations, and numerous articles published in Church related magazines. Brigham Young

University remained the hub for the study of Book of Mormon geography. FARMS, John Welsh, and John E. Clark of the Maxwell Institute became a screening ground to improve scholarship consistent with the scientific community.

Sometime in the 1990s with the wide spread availability of computers, the internet, and access to a knowledge base in all fields of science, the study of the Book of Mormon as a real history acquired "a life of its own." With the growth of the Church and with the ease of travel, the interest in the geography and the history of the Book of Mormon has skyrocketed. There are people in nearly every LDS stake in the United States especially that have traveled to Mesoamerica on a Book of Mormon cruise or land tour.

What is the current level of knowledge about Book of Mormon geography? For Book of Mormon scholars, it is difficult to keep abreast of all the fields of knowledge. Every discipline of science is bursting with significant finds. Linguistics, the study of pottery, and the larger fields of archaeology, anthropology, geography, history, biology, genetics, etc., are narrowing the search for the specific sites of the Book of Mormon.

Although still in its infancy, there is general agreement by most LDS scholars that Mesoamerica is the place where the primary events of the Book of Mormon took place. Eliminating contending claims by the Great Lakes advocates and the South American advocates is one of the major objectives of this book. Concentrating all of the combined energies and resources of researchers in Mesoamerica will assist in future discoveries. In a free thinking society there will always be some who disagree.

The general membership of the Church is interested in but not concerned about the geography or history of the Book of Mormon. Only when the media attacks the Book of Mormon does the general populous of the Church become concerned. The anti-Mormons persist in making outrageous and dogmatic claims which always manage to find their way into the local or national media. In 2006, the Los Angeles Times reported a DNA study that claimed that all of the Native Americans were of Asian origin.[353] The writers of the LA Times were unaware, inept, or willfully negligent of the 1998 Emory study which declared that haplo-group X represented 3% of Native Americans as Caucasians, and not Asians. They confronted various members of the LDS Church with bogus claims. A few members of the Church had their faith shaken and indeed some left the Church. The reporter claimed that this inadequately researched DNA study had disproved the Book of Mormon. Like the "Siberian Land Bridge Only" doctrine, these claims have already fallen by the wayside and taken their place in the graveyard among the other failed attempts to discount the Book of Mormon as a real history of real people. These spreaders of doubt hope to prevent others from going to God and asking for themselves. When confronted with contrary DNA studies, or when the statistical sampling of the study they quote is challenged because they excluded from their sample contrary information, they simply jump to another topic. Many of the doubters carry a bias against all religions and look for any opportunity to put down men and women of any faith. The entire DNA controversy is typical of members being confronted with information from science for which at the time they have no answer. It bears repeating: Don't lose faith in what you know by the Spirit because of what current science advocates. There will always be some questions in the present for which we may not have an answer until a future time.

No amount of evidence will influence the critic, the doubtful, or the entrenched. This is why this work is not intended to convert the skeptical naysayer. They lack the humility and sincerity required by God to receive the promised spiritual witness of the Holy Ghost to the divine origins of the Book of Mormon (Moroni 10:4-5). It is a waste of time and resources to engage the disingenuous or the sign seeker. There are more productive and exciting things to do with one's time than to waste time with a naysayer. One of them is to focus on the question, "Why is there a need in today's world for the Book of Mormon?"

CHAPTER SIXTEEN

Why is There a Need for Another Testament of Jesus Christ?

The Need for the Book of Mormon

The Bible answers the question, "Why is there a need for the Book of Mormon?" In the mouth of two or three witnesses every word may be established (Deuteronomy 17:6, 19:15).[354] The Bible is the first witness. The Book of Mormon is another witness or testament for Jesus as the Resurrected Redeemer of all mankind. In order to qualify as a Biblical witness, one had to see with his physical eyes or hear with his physical ears. Otherwise it was considered "hearsay" and not allowed as evidence. The entire Anglo-American legal system of accepting evidence is based upon this principle. The Book of Mormon is either a true witness or it is a false witness of the Bible's veracity.

The law of witnesses is both an Old Testament doctrine as well as a New Testament doctrine. It was a Law of Moses principle which was perpetuated by Jesus in the New Testament. It is still in effect today and will be when all men and women are required to give an accounting at the Judgment Seat of God. Bearing witness is a serious matter. It required at least two such eye or ear witnesses in order to establish the truth of any matter. Bearing false witness was not only a sin, as outlined in the Ten Commandments, but the person bearing the false witness, if discovered, was to suffer the same fate as the person he accused. "Then shall ye do unto him, as he had thought to have done unto his brother" (Deuteronomy 19:19). When the High Priest could not find any to witness against the Savior, two false witnesses were conjured up (Matthew 26:59-60). Justice would have required that the liars, including the High Priest, be crucified instead of the Savior.

The Apostles, for example at the Council in Jerusalem, when considering the matter of circumcision of the Gentiles, sent two faithful witnesses, Judas (not Iscariot) and Silas, to Antioch to testify of the council's decision (Acts 15:27).

This law is still in effect today. As a preface to the current edition of the Book of Mormon are the testimonies of eleven men who, like Judas and Silas, have born their solemn witnesses to the fact they "have seen ... [With our eyes]" or "we have seen and hefted..." the golden plates from which the Book of Mormon was translated. Three of the witnesses heard the "voice of the Lord." These eleven men were eye and ear witnesses as required by the Law of Moses and the Law of Christ.

Under the Law of Christ, God has given the opportunity for all people to have the truth of eye and ear witnesses to be confirmed by his personal emissary, the Holy Spirit. This is the reason it is important for the serious searcher of truth to go directly to God in sincere prayer to discover the truth or falsity of the witness of the Book of Mormon.

The Crisis in Modern Day Christianity

Many in the leadership of modern Christianity reject the literal resurrection of Jesus Christ. They are neither eye witnesses nor ear witnesses. Additionally, they lack a spiritual witness to the divinity of Jesus. They are skeptics and doubters who substitute the philosophies of men for the eye witness Bible accounts of Peter, Paul, Matthew, Mark, Luke, John, Mary Magdalene, and more than five hundred others who saw with their very own eyes and heard with their ears the Resurrected Christ (1 Corinthians 15:4-10).

What the Book of Mormon doesn't do is to support a liberal position in traditional Christianity which has evolved through the counsels of men over centuries of time. Much of modern Christianity rejects the divinity of Jesus Christ as the literal Son of God. These modern day Pharisees and Sadducees who masquerade as Bible scholars deny the divinity and resurrection of Jesus Christ. When the Chief Priest and the Elders of the Jews discovered that Jesus was not in the tomb, they paid the Roman soldiers much "money" to bear false witness and say, "His disciples came by night, and stole him away while we slept" (Matthew 28:11-15). Of course the leadership of the Jews of that day would be expected to continue to deny that Jesus was the resurrected Messiah.

What is astonishing is that many Christian educators today would deny the resurrection of Jesus. The Bible doctrine of the Fall of Man and the need for Atonement by Jesus Christ is dismissed as unnecessary by the vast majority of scholars and professors at various university schools of divinity. From where do these professors come? According to *Time, Newsweek,* and *U.S. News & World Report,* they come from Harvard, Oxford, Union Theological Seminary, Catholic University of America, and DePaul University. In April of 1996, the now infamous "Jesus Seminar," made the front covers of all three news magazines. The Jesus Seminar is a collection and consortium of Biblical scholars who deny what the Bible teaches about the words of Jesus. Their message was, and is, simple and to the point. They believe Jesus was not divine and did not resurrect. They acknowledge, however, He was a fine teacher and taught wonderful principles.

Robert Funk, a leader in the "Jesus Seminar," said that Jesus was more of a "Jewish Socrates ... than the divine Son of God."[355] Along with Marcus Borg, John Meier, and John Crossan, the "Jesus Seminar" has decided that Jesus really didn't say what is recorded in the New Testament Gospels. These men believe that overzealous disciples fabricated "most" of the sayings of Jesus in order to enhance his image:

> Jesus was a revolutionary peasant who resisted economic and social tyranny in Roman-occupied Palestine. He was a Jewish cynic who wandered from town to town, teaching unconventional wisdom and subverting oppressive social customs.[356]

These renowned scholars have "reinvented Christianity" so that Jesus never resurrected. These men are the professors of religion who are teaching their seminary students, the future ministers and pastors of the body of Christ, not to believe in the resurrected Jesus. Their faithless teachings are working. Less than 30% of graduating ministers believe in the literal resurrection of Jesus Christ. Crossan and others teach that "his body was eaten by dogs at the foot of the cross."[357]

These people have not gone away. The April 17, 2006, edition of *US News & World Report* gave a similar insight. James Tabor, a University of North Carolina at Charlotte professor of religion, wrote a book titled *The Jesus Dynasty.* In it he states his belief that "I don't think that Jesus taught that he was the savior, believe in me and you will be saved."[358] Dr. Tabor goes on to teach that Jesus was not trying to set up a Heavenly Kingdom; rather he was trying to establish an earthly family dynasty with his brother James as his successor.[359] A recent popular book by Dan Brown reflects this same kind of denial of Christ's divine nature. It is *The DaVinci Code.*

The term "historical Jesus" is a dead giveaway for those who want to deny the divinity of Jesus. They are code words for identifying Christ as only a mortal. Over a hundred years ago Albert Schweitzer wrote *The Search for the Historical Jesus.* In 1906 Schweitzer's basic point was that Jesus really did exist but not as the Divine Son of God; rather as a kind, loving, compassionate teacher who rejected social violence and war and embraced a doctrine of love and peace. The "Historical Jesus people," then and now, believe that it makes Jesus more real and more palatable if he is humanized. A Divine Jesus detracts in their minds from his message:

> From the beginning, some seekers of the historical Jesus have been motivated by the desire to discredit the supernatural claims of the Christian faith in order to discredit religion more generally.[360]

Dr. Barbara Thiering of Sydney, Australia wrote a book titled *Redating the Teacher of Righteousness,* and is considered an expert on the Dead Sea Scrolls. In an interview with the Discovery Channel in 1990, she identified herself as a Christian but rejected any notion of Jesus being divine. She characterized Jesus as having a very human paternity and dismissed the miracles of Jesus, his virgin birth, his death on the cross, and his resurrection. "I think I myself side with those scholars and other Christians who would wish to assert that Jesus had a natural father."[361] These spurious and repugnant speculations are not eye or ear witness testimonies as required by the law of witnesses. They are instead the machinations of rationalists. They are probably very good people who accept the teachings of Jesus but who lack the faith to believe in Jesus as the Divine Son of God. The declarations of the Jewish community and of the Traditional Christian scholars are sufficient justification alone for the second witness of the divinity of Jesus Christ and of his resurrection provided by the Book of Mormon.

The Book of Mormon refutes the cunning schemes of pseudo-intellectuals and those who lack the faith, like doubting Thomas. Humility is the first step to spiritual knowledge, and prayer is the second. Those who are puffed up by their own wisdom are blinded by their pride from seeing with their spiritual eyes or hearing with their spiritual ears. The proud will not humble themselves as a child and grow in their spirituality until they are sufficiently prepared to appreciate the experience. The promised witness of the Holy Ghost is only extended to the humble, the prayerful, and the penitent.

Jesus Christ appeared to individuals and groups as a resurrected being in both the Old World and the New World. The mere fact that Jesus appeared as a resurrected being and repeated his teachings nearly word for word to his disciples here in the Americas is sufficient evidence for the need for a second witness (3 Nephi 12-18). These New World disciples were physical eye witnesses and physical ear witnesses to the Resurrected Christ on the North American continent. More than twenty-five hundred saw him and felt the wounds in his hands and feet:

> The multitude went forth, and thrust their hands into his side and did feel the prints of the nails in his hands and in his feet; and this they did do, going forth one by one until they had all gone forth, and did see with their eyes and did feel with their hands, and did know of a surety and did bear record, that it was he, of whom it was written by the prophets, that should come (3 Nephi 11:15)....and they were in number about two thousand and five hundred souls; and they did consist of men, women, and children (3 Nephi 17: 25).

This one appearance of the resurrected Jesus alone may be why the Lord saw fit to have another testament of his literal resurrection as found in the Book of Mormon. The good news is the vast majority of the Christian flock does believe in the Resurrected Christ. This they believe in spite of the fact that many of their pastors do not believe in the Bible's witness of the words of the resurrected Jesus. "Behold my hands and my feet, that it is I myself: handle me, and see; for a spirit hath not flesh and bones, as ye see me have" (Luke 24:39).

Those who would rob Jesus of his divine nature do not understand the Bible's witness to Jesus being both divine and mortal. The dual nature of Jesus allowed him to carry out the dual missions which required a power over death in addition to his mortal nature. This power was given to Jesus by virtue of his unique birth wherein Heavenly Father was able to announce that Jesus was the "only begotten of the Father" (John 1:14). Later, Jesus would declare that the power over death he received came exclusively from his Father:

> Therefore doth my Father love me, because I lay down my life, that I might take it again. No man taketh it from me, but I lay it down of myself. I have power to lay it down, and I have power to take it again. This commandment have I received of my Father (John 10:17-18).

The second mission of Jesus did not require a divine birth. The mortal mission of Jesus as the son of Mary was to be man's great exemplar. In this capacity as the righteous son of Mary, He would invite all of mankind to "Come follow me." Because He was also mortal He could relate to man and teach his flesh and blood kin to love God and to render loving service to their fellowman. As the LDS hymn by Eliza R. Snow declares, "He marked the path and led the way and every point defines to light and life…[362]

Jesus would use his divine power for his divine mission and his mortal power for his mortal mission and never confuse the two. Many in Traditional Christianity are struggling to humanize his divinity. The "Jesus Seminar" people and their adherents are uncomfortable with miracles and Jesus as the Divine Son of God. They are embarrassed by those of us of simple faith. They find it hard to justify intellectually a belief in Jesus as divine. Instead, they find it easier to believe in a mortal Messiah as a great teacher, but certainly not divine. The Book of Mormon and the Bible declare Jesus as the Divine Son of God and the mortal son of Mary (see John 1:14, Mark 9:7; Mosiah 3:8). With his divine powers he carried out the Infinite Atonement and overcame both physical death through the resurrection and spiritual death through his sacrifice in the Garden of Gethsemane and on the Cross. As our mortal exemplar, Jesus taught us how to love the unlovable. What a surprise awaits the Jesus Seminar and the skeptics when they too resurrect. For surely, the Bible and the Book of Mormon teach this:

> But now is Christ risen from the dead, and become the first fruits of them that slept. For since by man came death, by man came also the resurrection of the dead. For as in Adam all die, even so in Christ shall all be made alive (1 Corinthians 15:20-22).

> There is a space between death and the resurrection of the body and … the time which is appointed of God that the dead shall come forth, and be reunited, both soul and body, and be brought to stand before God … (Alma 40: 21).

The world is approaching the great winding up scenes of this dispensation and the eventual return of the Descending God, even Jesus Christ. One can read in the Book of Mormon about His appearance as a resurrected Being in the New World, shortly after His resurrection. Soon this event will be repeated. The Book of Mormon testifies of His promised return and reinforces the Bible's witness to a doubting world. The Bible proclaims the advent of the Second Coming of Jesus Christ:

> For the Lord himself shall descend from heaven with a shout, with the voice of the archangel, and the dead in Christ shall rise first; Then we which are alive and remain shall be caught up together with them in the clouds, to meet the Lord in the air: and so shall we ever be with the Lord. Wherefore comfort one another with these words (1 Thessalonians 4:16-18).

A New Generation of Eye Witnesses and Ear Witnesses to The Resurrected Christ.

There will be a new generation of eyewitnesses and ear witnesses to the resurrected Messiah. Unlike the Book of Mormon Prophet Samuel who foretold the day and the hour of the Savior's First Coming, no man knows the day or the hour of this great event of the Lord's Second Coming. What is known is that latter-day prophets are preparing the people for this great event. President Ezra Taft Benson said the best way to prepare for the second coming and to understand the signs of the times was to read the Book of Mormon and study the social conditions that existed before Christ's coming to the Americas the first time. "The record of the Nephite history just prior to the Saviors visit reveals many parallels to our own day as we anticipate the Saviors second coming."[363]

The truth is that it doesn't matter when He comes. What matters is that disciples of the Lord Jesus Christ are fully engaged in loving their hard-to-love fellow men; that they are being the best examples they can be; that they teach those who are willing to be taught; that they bear testimony to all mankind; and that they endure to the end of their mortal lives temple-recommend worthy.

The Bible and the Book of Mormon: A Personal insight

I love the Bible, and it is under attack from the very people who ought to be defending it. The Bible is God's word and poetry to the soul. As a young man I was motivated by the stories of Daniel in the lion's den, by David's conquest of Goliath, and by God's love for Nineveh as told through the experience of Jonah and the whale. In the New Testament, I fell in love with Jesus. I identified with the weaknesses of the Apostle Peter and was encouraged by his growth and discipleship to the Master. The letters of Paul were more difficult for my young mind to grasp, but I was impressed with the raw courage of Paul who had come to love Jesus more than he loved his own life.

All of these things are under assault by Bible scholars. These men and women are undermining the faith that built a nation by saying that Jesus really didn't say what he said. Is there a need for another testament of Jesus? My own passion for the Old Testament drove me into a study of Biblical Hebrew and to several pilgrimages to Israel, Egypt, Syria, Jordan, and the Sinai. I thrilled, and still do, at the geography where the great events of the Bible were unfolded. I became an efficient researcher in ancient Greek through the use of *Strong's: Exhaustive Concordance of the Bible.* Jerusalem, Bethlehem, the Sea of Galilee, Gethsemane, Golgotha, and the Garden Tomb are places I have been many times. Each visit has been a journey to the sacred. I have led tours with bus loads of fellow pilgrims whose silent prayers along with mine ascended to the God of Heaven in gratitude for the life and mission of Jesus Christ as we walked near where Jesus walked in the Holy Land. When I became familiar with the geography of these sacred sites, it made the Bible stories come alive.

Now those who want to make the Bible a fairytale have a stanch voice against them that will not go away. It is the Book of Mormon. Latter-day Saints are often accused of not accepting the Bible as God's word. Nothing could be further from the truth. The Bible is a primary reference; a standard by which Mormons are to live their lives. It is part of their Standard Works of scriptures. God's word is God's word wherever it may be found. The Book of Mormon does not compete with the Bible; it supports it.

Does the Bible Speak of the Book of Mormon?

Why then does not the Bible speak of the Book of Mormon? It does! There are many references, but only a few will be highlighted. The Book of Mormon is Ezekiel's promised "Stick of Ephraim" (Ezekiel 37:15-17). The Bible is the "Stick of Judah" and "they [The Bible and the Book of Mormon] shall become one in thine hand" (Ezekiel 37: 17). As pointed out earlier, it was the ancient law of Israel that "at the mouth of two witnesses," (Deut 17:6) "every word may be established" (Matt 18:16). The Book of Mormon is another witness, another testament of the resurrected Messiah, the God of all the continents, of all the tribes of Israel and of worlds without number (Hebrews 1:2, 11:3).

Another Bible reference to the Book of Mormon is the coat of many colors worn by Joseph of old whose jealous brothers cast him into a pit from which he was sold into Egypt (Gen 37:3-35). This coat was a type or example of what was going to happen to the descendants of Israel. The rent coat was a symbol of future Israel which would be scattered abroad upon the earth. The Book of Mormon is primarily the history of remnants of Joseph and Judah who were led out of the Holy Land to a place of safety in the New World. These scattered refugees become the main characters in the Book of Mormon. The father of Joseph's New World descendants is Lehi and his sons are Laman, Lemuel, Sam, Nephi, Jacob, and Joseph. Somewhat reminiscent of Esau and Jacob of the Old Testament, these sons divided into two warring factions representing the older verses the younger sons, Laman and Nephi respectively. Those who followed Laman were called Lamanites, and those who followed Nephi were referred to as Nephites. Ninety plus percent of the Book of Mormon is the interaction of these two groups.

The immigration of these descendants of Joseph to America was foretold in the scriptures. The Bible speaks of these wandering descendants of Joseph who would be led to a place referred to as the "Everlasting Hills." Only in the Americas do we find the "Everlasting Hills" which begin in the Aleutians and run the length of two continents to return to the sea as the Andes disappear into the Tierra del Fuego off the southern coast of Chile. Again the Bible foretold this great event in the blessing given to Joseph by his father, Jacob: "Joseph is a fruitful bough…, whose *branches [Children] run over the wall…* unto the utmost bound of the *everlasting hills…*" (Gen 49:22-26). When Moses blessed the tribes of Israel, he said of Joseph he would "push people together to the ends of the earth…" (Deut 33:17). Speaking from Mesopotamia as the cradle of civilization, the Americas represented the "ends of the earth."

The "marvelous work and a wonder" spoken of by Isaiah 29:14 is the Book of Mormon. A person who was *"not learned,"* would be given the "book [of Mormon]" (Isaiah 29:11). Joseph Smith was that person. In a day when people would denigrate the Bible and claim that the "wisdom of their wise men" (Isaiah 29:14) was greater than God's word as seen by the "Jesus Seminar," the Lord would bring forth a "book," even the Book of Mormon, and those who were spiritually *"deaf"* and spiritually *"blind"* (Isaiah 29:18) would receive a second witness of the Bible's message that Jesus was and is the Messiah. "And in that day shall the [spiritually] *deaf* hear the words of the book, and the eyes of the [spiritually] *blind* shall see out of obscurity, and out of darkness" (Isaiah. 29:18).

The Book of Mormon is also the history of a remnant of Judah; even of some Jews who escaped at the time of the Babylonian captivity. Because the main character from the tribe of Judah is named Mulek, his followers are called Mulekites. The Bible predicted this exodus in 2 Kings 19:30-31:

> And the remnant that is escaped of *the house of Judah* shall yet again take root downward, and bear fruit upward. For out of Jerusalem shall go forth a remnant, and they that are escaped out of mount Zion: the zeal of the Lord of hosts shall do this. (See also Isaiah 37:31-32.)

The Bible and the Book of Mormon combat the false doctrines of our day. They teach the reality of Jesus and the two fold mission which Jesus possessed. He was the Promised Messiah and man's great exemplar. He resurrected and sits on the right hand of his Father. He will come again because He loves us and wants each of us to become our highest and best selves. He is a God of Justice and He will require of each person an accounting. He is the universal Messiah; we need not look for another.

There is a God. He has a wonderful plan to bring his children back to Him through the supernal sacrifice and Atonement of Jesus Christ. "It is not all to be comprehended in this world; it will be a great work to learn our salvation and exaltation even beyond the grave..."[364] Joseph taught. What we can accomplish on earth is to learn to love God and our fellow man.

How Does One Obtain A Divine Witness?

The Apostle James addresses this issue. "If any of you lack wisdom, let him ask of God, who giveth unto all men liberally and it shall be given him" (James 1:5). The simplicity of the way is to read the Book of Mormon, ponder its messages, and ask God in humble, honest prayer if the Book of Mormon is His word and a companion witness to the Bible (Moroni 10:4-5).

Pondering means to think about it. After you have read at least the first fifty-two pages, examine your feelings. Do you feel the desire to be a better you? Do you feel uplifted? Do you feel a quiet assurance there is a God? Does Heavenly Father have a plan of salvation for all of his children and are you, as one of his children, a part of that plan? Is the Book of Mormon another witness to God's divine intervention in the lives of his individual children? Finally, by reading the Book of Mormon is not your soul confirmed in the personal knowledge that Jesus is the universal Messiah and in a very intimate way your Lord, Savior, and Redeemer? The Book of Mormon is a true history of the Jaredites, Mulekites, and Nephites. The Book of Mormon is exactly what it claims to be: Another Testament of Jesus Christ.

Recognizing an Answer to My Own Prayer

Not everyone recognizes answers to prayers in the same way. Some have experienced a burning in the bosom. Others have received peace of mind. There are those who have described their minds as being enlightened while others have felt confident in a quiet assurance. One man, who prayed and pondered to see if the Book of Mormon was another witness of Jesus said, "I've had no external manifestation, no voice, no light, no vision, no dream, no burning in the bosom, but I accept the Book of Mormon because it makes sense, and when I read it I want to be a better person." His particular spiritual gift may be logic confirmed by the Spirit. It makes sense. There can be no middle ground. The Book of Mormon is either true or it is a fake. He read it and pondered its message about Jesus Christ and decided to put his spiritual house in order. The fact that the Book of Mormon made sense and inspired him to be a better person was his answer to his prayer.

As a convert to the LDS faith I can speak of my own experience. After I had read fifty-plus pages in the Book of Mormon, I prayed about its validity. Before my prayer was concluded I felt an absolute assurance and a peace of mind which caused my soul to rejoice. Now I recognize that the promise of Isaiah 65:24 was my particular gift. "And it shall come to pass, that before they call, I will answer; and while they are yet speaking, I will answer." I knew the Book of Mormon was a true record, although I had no evidence other than my prayer. I was eleven years old and the only member of my family to act in the faith of that answered prayer. That was more than fifty-five years ago and I have never wavered in my support of that experience. There are many ways to receive spiritual confirmation. Keep your mind and heart open for God to reveal to you the truthfulness of the Book of Mormon in a way and in a manner that you will know for yourself.

There is one very special spiritual gift which comes from the Holy Ghost. It is the ability to believe on the testimony of another and have the Holy Ghost confirm in your heart while another is speaking that their witness is of God (D&C 46:14; 1 Nephi 2:17). Some have thought that this spiritual gift to "believe on the testimony of another" is living on borrowed light. It is not. It is one of the gifts of the Spirit. President Harold B. Lee made reference to living on "borrowed light." It was my opportunity to be interviewed by President Lee and at the conclusion of the interview he asked if I had any questions. I said that I did. I asked if Sam's believing on the testimony of Nephi was living on borrowed light (1 Nephi 2:17). I explained that some people were claiming that President Lee's talk on "Borrowed Light" was being interpreted that way. He emphatically, and without parsing words, said that was not his intention. He was addressing those who had not paid a price to obtain their own testimony. The Spiritual gift of believing on the words of a prophet, the scriptures, or any servant of God is not living on borrowed light. I left his office thrilled at the clarity I had received. My heart was also concerned about those who may have this gift and about those who would diminish their gift by misunderstanding President Lee's statement. On more than one occasion I have heard prophets speak or have read their words in the scriptures. I remember saying to myself, "I don't know, but I feel that what he has said is true." After Paul spoke to the Jewish leaders in Rome, the Book of Acts records, "And some believed the things which were spoken and some believed not" (Acts 28:24).

I have now read the Book of Mormon more than a hundred times from cover to cover. I have pondered its message and meaning by study and prayer. I add my own humble witness that I have received the promised testimony of the Holy Spirit that Joseph Smith was an instrument in the hands of God to translate these records which declares another testament of Jesus as the Promised Messiah, the Son of God, and Universal Savior of mankind. The most significant contribution of the Book of Mormon for me is the second witness and personal knowledge that Jesus is my Savior, God and King, and the Redeemer of my loved ones as well as my own soul.

The Simplicity of the Way

As a student of the scriptures, and as one who loves the great Jehovah and the Bible, the Book of Mormon has given me an even greater appreciation of Jesus Christ. I can do no more than to invite the honest in heart to go to the source of all knowledge, even our Father in Heaven. It is a simple task. It is much like Moses asking the children of Israel who had been bitten by poisonous serpents to look upon a rod with a brazen serpent. They were promised this simple act of faith would heal them. Because of the simple nature of the request and the easiness of the way, many refused this minimal effort and perished (Numbers 21:8-9). If the Book of Mormon is not true, the consequences of rejecting it are nonexistent. If, however, the Book of Mormon is another testament of Jesus Christ and its claims are valid, there are spiritual and eternal consequences of rejecting it. The consequences have more to do with lost blessings and lost opportunities than with the loss of your soul. But maybe the greatest loss on the part of those who fail to avail themselves of a serious examination of the Book of Mormon is the loss of greater knowledge of the Savior, his words and counsel, to a concerned mind.

Joseph Smith was God's prophet, like unto John the Baptist, to restore the Gospel of Jesus Christ anew upon the earth; the Church of Jesus Christ of Latter-day Saints is God's restored work. It is also true that the Book of Mormon is, therefore, what it claims to be: another witness that Jesus is the Promised Messiah.

A Summary Statement

This has been by no means a comprehensive review of all Mesoamerican things related to the Book of Mormon. The scope of my writing has been to point out why Mesoamerica is the land of the primary events of the Book of Mormon. It is because the Prophet Joseph Smith said so, and he is supported by convincing evidence. It was also my hope that students of the Book of Mormon who already have a testimony of the validity of the Book of Mormon will begin to acquire an appreciation for the "Spirit of Place." It is time to take our physical feet to where our spiritual feet have walked in the scriptures. Walking upon the same geographical sites of Lehi's Land of First Inheritance, the Land of Nephi, the Land of Zarahemla, or the Land of Desolation gives us a "Spirit of Place." Our testimonies are strengthened in the reality of the Book of Mormon. The scriptures become more than words on a page. The sights, the sounds, and even the smells in the air contribute to a greater appreciation of the message of real flesh and blood people whose lives are unfolded in the Book of Mormon. The descendants of the Book of Mormon people, and those with whom they have mixed, still live upon the land. Most of all, walking in Mesoamerica is walking once again where Jesus walked. It is where he picked up the little children and blessed them one by one. It is where he prayed and tongue could not tell nor do words describe the power of his prayer unto the Father.

There will be some who will feel the power of the Holy Ghost like Columbus and embark upon a great quest to help identify specific sites in the Land of First Inheritance, the Land of Nephi, and the Land of Desolation. It will not be to convert the skeptic. It will be to strengthen the membership, to proclaim the Gospel, and to honor the dead who died in Christ.

I have been called a scholar; I'm not sure what that means, but I am surely a serious student of the Bible and of the Book of Mormon. I strive to be a disciple of the Lord. It is my personal witness to all within the circle of my influence that Jesus is the Promised Messiah. The Bible and the Book of Mormon bear witness of the resurrected Jesus. I took the challenge to read the Book of Mormon and to ask God in personal, private prayer for a confirming witness born of the Holy Spirit to my soul as to the validity of the Book of Mormon. I received that witness and invite you to do the same in the name of that Jesus who loves us both.

List of Credits for Illustrations, Maps, and Photography

Figures 1. *Reconstruction View of Palenque, Mexico.*
Used by permission of National Geographic.

Figure 2. Map: *Three Geographical Candidates for The Lands of the Book of Mormon.*
Cartography by Joseph A. Lund © 2007.

Figure 3. Map: *Guatemala in Joseph Smith's Day, 1830.*
Cartography by Joseph A. Lund © 2007.

Figure 4. Map: *Lehi's Landing and Subsequent "Journey in the Wilderness."*
Cartography by Joseph A. Lund © 2007.

Figure 5. Map: *Palenque, Quirigua, Copan, and the Isthmus of Tehuantepec.*
Cartography by Joseph A. Lund © 2007.

Figure 6. *Palenque, Mexico Lithograph by Frederick Catherwood.*
Courtesy of Covenant Communications.

Figure 7. Map: *McBride and Hamilton Map #1.* Courtesy of the Church Archives, The Church of Jesus Christ of Latter-day Saints.

Figure 8. Map: *McBride and Hamilton Map #2.* Courtesy of the Church Archives, The Church of Jesus Christ of Latter-day Saints.

Figure 9. Map: *Distance Between the Two Cumorahs.*
Cartography by Joseph A. Lund © 2007.

Figure 10 *Mexica Altar Stone.*
Image preparation by Geoff Shupe.

Figure 11. *Mexican Flag Symbols.*
Image preparation by Geoff Shupe.

Figure 12. *Island Capital of the Aztecs, Tenochtitlán,* circa A.D.1521 by Luis Covarrubias (1919-1987) © Musea Nacional de Antropologia, Mexico City, Mexico/ Sean Srague/ Mexicolore. Used by permission of The Bridgeman Art Library.

Figure 13. Map: *Mormon's Map* by John L. Sorenson. Courtesy of the Neal A. Maxwell Institute for Religious Scholarship, Brigham Young University.

Figure 14. Map: *Proposed Landing Sites of the Jaredites, Mulekites, and the Lehites* by John L. Lund. Cartography by Joseph A. Lund © 2007.

Figure 15. Map: *Current Cities, Current Ruins, and Geographical Approximations for the Book of Mormon Sites* by John L. Lund. Cartography by Joseph A. Lund © 2007.

Figure 16. *Mayan Scribe.* Image design by Geoff Shupe © 2007.

Figure 17. *Egyptian Demotic Glyphs.* Image preparation by Geoff Shupe.

Figure 18. *Anthon Transcript.* The "Caracters" [*sic*] given to Charles Anthon, known as the Anthon Transcript. Used by permission of The Community of Christ Church Archives, Independence, Missouri.

Figure 19. *Proto-Hebrew Script of 600 B.C.* Image preparation by Geoff Shupe.

Figure 20. *Anthon Transcript.* Used by permission of The Community of Christ Church Archives, Independence, Missouri.

Figure 21. *Egyptian Hieratic Script.* Image preparation by Geoff Shupe.

Figure 22. *Anthon Transcript.* Used by permission of The Community of Christ Church Archives, Independence, Missouri.

Figure 23. *Reformed Egyptian; Meroitic Demotic Script.* Image preparation by Geoff Shupe.

Figure 24. *Anthon Transcript.* Used by permission of The Community of Christ Church Archives, Independence, Missouri.

Figure 25. *Thin Gold Plate with Hieroglyphic Writing* extracted from the well at Chichen Itzá by Harvard Archaeologist, Herbert Thompson, in 1904. Courtesy of Peabody Museum, Harvard, University. Image design by Geoff Shupe © 2007.

Figure 26. "*And It Came to Pass,*" Mayan Glyph. © Artist, Cliff Dunston. Used by permission of Joseph L. Allen.

Figure 27. *Stone Box of the Time of Moroni.*
Photograph by Dr. John L. Lund,
Musea Nacional de Antropologia, Mexico City, Mexico.
Image preparation by Geoff Shupe.

Figure 28. *Tree of Life, Stela #5,* Izapa, Mexico.
Image design by Geoff Shupe.

Figure 29. *Stela "F" at Quiriguá.* Lithograph by Frederick Catherwood. Courtesy of Covenant Communications.

Figure 30. *John Lund by Olmec Head.*
Photography by Bonnie Lund.

Figure 31. *Stela "C" at Tres Zapotes, Mexico.*
Image design by Geoff Shupe.

Figure 32. *Large Round Stone, Quiriguá, Guatemala.*
Photo by Dr. John L. Lund. Image preparation by Geoff Shupe.

Figure 33. *Mayan Codex.*
Image preparation by Geoff Shupe.

Figure 34. *Reconstruction View of El Mirador, Guatemala.*
Courtesy of National Geographic.

Figure 35. *Highly Stratified Society.* Photograph by John L. Lund, Musea Nacional de Antropologia, Mexico City, Mexico. Image preparation by Geoff Shupe.

Figure 36. *John Lund on a Sacbé* at Chichen Itzá, Mexico.
Photography by Eric Towner.

Figure 37. *Sacbé*, Chichen Itzá, Mexico.
Photograph ©Jeffrey Jay Foxx/nyc.
Used by permission of Jeffrey Jay Foxx.

Figure 38. *Fattening Pens*, Codex Nuttall.
Used by permission of Dover Publications.

Figure 39. *Chacmool.* Photograph by John L. Lund.
Image preparation by Geoff Shupe.

Figure 40. *Ball Player.* Photograph © Don O. Thorpe.
Used by permission of Don O. Thorpe.

Figure 41. *Kings Fight Kings*, Codex Nuttall.
Used by permission of Dover Publications.

Figure 42. *Taking of Heads*, Codex Nuttall.
Used by permission of Dover Publications.

Figure 43. *Slavery*, Codex Nuttall.
Used by permission of Dover Publications.

Figure 44. *Marriage Alliance*, Codex Nuttall.
Used by permission of Dover Publications.

Figure 45. *Taking of an Arm*,
Diego Rivera, National Palace, Mexico City, Mexico.
Photograph by John L. Lund. Image preparation by Geoff Shupe.

Figure 46. *Quetzalcoatl Teaching Twelve Men*,
Diego Rivera, National Palace, Mexico City, Mexico.
Photograph by John L. Lund.
Image preparation by Geoff Shupe.

Figure 47. *Representation of The Descending God.* Photo by Bonnie Lund,
Musea Nacional de Antropologia, Mexcio City, Mexico.

Figure 48. *Tzolkin Calendar.*
Photograph by John L. Lund.
Image preparation by Geoff Shupe.

Figure 49. *Tropic of Cancer.*
Image design by Geoff Shupe.

Figure 50. *Loincloth.* Photograph © Justin Kerr, K2837b.
Used by permission of Justin Kerr.

Figure 51. *Sacrifice Altar "Q," Copán, Honduras.*
Lithograph by Frederick Catherwood.
Courtesy of Covenant Communications.

Figure 52. *Egyptian Sons of Horus, Maya Sons of Itzamna (Bacab).*
Image design by Geoff Shupe.

Figure 53. *Headless Man Standing by Pre-Columbian Horse.*
Chichen Itza, Mexico. Photograph by John L. Lund.
Image preparation by Geoff Shupe.

ENDNOTES

Introduction

1 Gordon B. Hinckley, "Four Cornerstones of Faith," *Ensign*, February 2004, p. 6.

Chapter One

2 E.A. Matisoo-Smith, et al., "Radiocarbon and DNA evidence for a preColumbian introduction of Polynesian chickens to Chile," *Proceedings of the National Academy of Sciences*, June 19, 2007, vol. 104, no. 25, pp. 10335-10339.
3 Joseph F. Smith, "Joseph Smith Jr., as a Translator," *Improvement Era*, February 1913, p. 380.
4 Mesoamerica: Meso means middle. It is a term used by archaeologists to include Southern Mexico with Central America. It defines the lands of the Maya and in a broader context the geographical region of Southern Mexico to Panama.
5 Joseph Smith—History 1:33-34.
6 Joseph Smith—History 1:54.
7 John L. Sorenson, *Mormon's Map*, (Provo, Utah: FARMS, 2000), p. 78. Emphasis added will be referenced in the footnote and not in the body of the text. Exceptions will be noted in the text.
8 Joseph Fielding Smith, *Doctrines of Salvation*, comp. Bruce R. McConkie, (Salt Lake City, Utah: Deseret Book, 1956), 3:227-241.
9 Gordon B. Hinckley, "Four Cornerstones of Faith," *Ensign*, February 2004, p. 6.
10 B. H. Roberts, *History of the Church,* 2nd ed., Revised, (Salt Lake City: Deseret News, 1949), 1:12, emphasis added.
11 Roberts, *History of the Church,* 4:535-541, emphasis added.
12 Joseph Smith, ed., *Times and Seasons,* July 15, 1842, vol. 3, p. 860, emphasis added.
13 Charles Lowell Walker, *Diary of Charles Lowell Walker,* A. Karl Larson and Katharine Miles Larson, eds., (Logan, Utah: Utah State University Press, 1980), 2:525-526.
14 Brigham Young quoting Oliver Cowdrey, in *Journal of Discourses,* London, 1878, 19:38.
15 Heber C. Kimball, in *Journal of Discourses,* London, 1857, 4:105.
16 Moses 1:8-11, Pearl of Great Price.
17 1 Nephi 8:2-33.
18 1 Nephi 11:1.
19 Genesis 15:1.
20 H. Donl Peterson, "Moroni the Last of the Nephite Prophets," Monte Nyman and Charles Tate, eds., *The Book of Mormon: Forth Nephi Through Moroni, From Zion to Destruction* (Provo, Utah: BYU Religious Studies Center, 1995), pp. 243-247.
21 Kenneth W. Godfrey, "The Zelph Story," *BYU Studies,* (Provo, Utah: Brigham Young University Studies, Spring 1989), 29:31-49.
22 "Zelph," *Book of Mormon Reference Companion,* ed. Dennis L. Largey, (Salt Lake City: Deseret Book, 2007), pp. 801-802.
23 Godfrey, "The Zelph Story," *BYU Studies,* Spring 1989, 29:45.
24 Godfrey, "The Zelph Story," *BYU Studies,* Spring 1989, 29:44-45.
25 John A. Widtsoe, *The Improvement Era,* July 1950, p. 547.
26 Joseph Smith, *The Personal Writings of Joseph Smith,* ed. Dean Jesse, (Salt Lake City, Utah: Deseret Book Co., 1984), p. 324.
27 Peterson, *The Book of Mormon: Forth Nephi Through Moroni,* pp. 243-247.

Chapter Two

28 Roberts, *History of the Church,* 4:535-541.
29 Joseph Fielding Smith, *Teachings of the Prophet Joseph Smith,* 14th ed., (Salt Lake City: Deseret Book Co., 1964), pp. 12-13, hereafter cited *Teachings.*
30 *Teachings,* pp. 166-173.
31 *Teachings,* p. 169.
32 Joseph Smith—History 1:50.
33 Joseph Smith, ed., *Times and Seasons,* March 1, 1842, 3:707, emphasis added.
34 Dan Vogel, compiler, *Early Mormon Documents* (Salt Lake City: Signature Books, 1996), 1:295-296, emphasis added.
35 Hyrum Andrus, *They Knew The Prophet,* (Salt Lake City, Utah: Bookcraft, 1974), p. 116, emphasis added.
36 John Lloyd Stephens, Frederick Catherwood, Illustrator, *Incidents of Travel in Central America, Chiapas and Yucatan,* 1841 (New York: Unabridged Reprint by Dover Press, 1969, two volumes); hereafter cited as Stephens and Catherwood, *Incidents of Travel.*
37 Joseph Smith, ed., *Times and Seasons,* October 1, 1842, 3:927.
38 Joseph Smith, ed., *Times and Seasons,* September 15, 1842, 3:922; also *Teachings,* p. 267, emphasis added.
39 Joseph Smith, ed., *Times and Seasons,* September 15, 1842, 3:922, emphasis added.
40 *Noah Webster: American Dictionary of The English Language,* 1828 edition, vol. II., p. 25, ocean 1.
41 Thomas Suarez, *Early Mapping of the Pacific,* (Edinburgh: Periplus, 2004), p. 211.
42 Joseph Smith, ed., *Times and Seasons,* October 1, 1842, 3:927, emphasis added.
43 Joseph Smith, ed., *Times and Seasons,* October 1, 1842, 3:927.
44 Walker, *Diary of Charles Lloyd Walker,* 2:526.
45 Joseph Smith, ed., *Times and Seasons,* October 1, 1842, 3:927.
46 Book of Mormon, 1840, "Nauvoo edition," p. 281, Alma 22:32.
47 Joseph Smith, ed., *Times and Seasons,* September 15, 1842, 3:914.
48 Joseph Smith, ed., *Times and Seasons,* October 1, 1842, 3:927, emphasis added.
49 Joseph Smith, ed., *Times and Seasons,* July 15, 1842, 3:860.
50 Joseph Smith, ed., *Times and Seasons,* March 15, 1842, 3:710.
51 Joseph Smith, ed., *Times and Seasons,* September 15, 1842, 3:914, emphasis added.
52 W. Cleon Skousen and M. Richard Maxfield, *The Real Benjamin Franklin, Part II,* (Salt Lake City: Freemen Institute, 1982), p. 482.
53 Personal Conversation between Dr. John L. Lund and Alfonso Morales on September 12, 2005, Palenque, Mexico.
54 Joseph Smith, ed., *Times and Seasons,* October 1, 1842, 3:927, emphasis added.
55 Joseph Smith, ed., *Times and Seasons,* October 1, 1842, 3:927, emphasis added.
56 Joseph Smith, ed., *Times and Seasons,* March 15, 1842, 3:710, emphasis added.
57 Joseph Smith, ed., *Times and Seasons,* July 15, 1842, 3:860.
58 Joseph Smith, ed., *Times and Seasons,* October 1, 1842, 3:927.
59 John A. Widtsoe, *The Improvement Era,* July 1950, pp. 547, 596.
60 Peterson, *The Book of Mormon: Forth Nephi Through Moroni,* pp. 243-247.
61 Fayette Lapham, "The Mormons: Interview With The Father of Joseph Smith, The Mormon Prophet, Forty Years Ago. His Account of the Finding of the Sacred Plates," *Historical Magazine,* May, 1870, Vol. VIII, No. 5, p. 307. Although clearly an anti-Mormon source, it reports on an interview with Joseph Smith, Sr. about the contents of the stone box. It is a mix of truth and error and reports the ball (Liahona) as gold and not brass.
62 Joseph Smith—History 1:52.
63 Walker, *Diary of Charles Lloyd Walker,* 2:526.
64 Joseph Heinerman, *Temple Manifestations* (Salt Lake City: Lyon and Associates, 1974), p. 62.
65 Heinerman, *Temple Manifestations,* pp. 60-61.
66 Orson F. Whitney, *Life of Heber C. Kimball,* (Salt Lake City, Utah: Bookcraft, 1967), p. 436.
67 Walker, *Diary of Charles Lloyd Walker,* 2:526.
68 Walker, *Diary of Charles Lloyd Walker, 2*:524-525.
69 Peterson, *The Book of Mormon: Forth Nephi Through Moroni,* pp. 244-247.
70 Peterson, *The Book of Mormon: Forth Nephi Through Moroni,* p. 247.
71 *Teachings,* p.122.
72 Peterson, *The Book of Mormon: Forth Nephi Through Moroni,* p. 247.
73 Walker, *Diary of Charles Lloyd Walker,* 2:525-526.
74 Omni 1:20-21, The Mulekites fled from Jerusalem and the Babylonian invasion around 587 B.C. Coriantumr, the last of the Jaredite kings, stayed with the people of Mulek for nine months.

75 Brigham Young quoting Oliver Cowdrey in *Journal of Discourses*, 19:38; See also Heber C. Kimball in *Journal of Discourses*, 4:105.
76 Walker, *Diary of Charles Lloyd Walker*, 2:525-526.
77 Lapham, *Historical Magazine*, 1870, 7:306.
78 Orson Hyde, "Celebration of the Fourth of July," in *Journal of Discourses*, 6:368.
79 Truman Madsen, "Part 2: The Book of Mormon and the Restoration Begins," *On Sacred Ground: Reflections on Joseph Smith*, 8 DVD series, (Provo, Utah, Novus Visum, 2006), Volume I.
80 "The Testimony of Eight Witnesses," Book of Mormon (Salt Lake City: The Church of Jesus Christ of Latter-day Saints, 1981).
81 Sydney B. Sperry, *Book of Mormon Compendium*, (Salt Lake City, Utah: Bookcraft, 1968), pp. 20-21.

Chapter Three

82 Ted E. Brewerton, "The Book of Mormon: A Sacred Ancient Record," *Ensign*, November 1995, pp. 30-31.
83 Spencer W. Kimball, "Our Paths Have Met Again," *Ensign*, December 1975, p. 5, emphasis added.
84 Read the full text of Alma 42 to understand the context of the laws of justice and mercy.
85 Read the entire 28th chapter of Deuteronomy, all sixty-eight verses, and notice how the first fourteen verses are the blessings that will come to the faithful and obedient. From verses fifteen to sixty-eight are the curses. God gives his covenant people a blessing, a cursing, or destruction when they are "past feeling" or hearing his call to repentance. See Moroni 9:18-20 and 1 Nephi 17:45.
86 The reference to Judah, after 930 B.C., can be a geographical or a literal one. People may call themselves Jews because they lived in Judah. They may or may not be of the tribe of Judah. However, Mulek, who was the son of King Zedekiah, was a literal Jew *and* a geographical one.
87 Demetrio Sodi, *The Great Cultures of Mesoamerica*, (Mexico City, Mexico: Panorama Editorial, S.A., 1988), p. 161.
88 Sodi, *The Great Cultures of Mesoamerica*, p. 161.

Chapter Four

89 Dr. John E. Clark, "Archaeology, Relics, and Book of Mormon Belief," Address given May 25, 2004 in the de Jong Concert Hall at BYU <http://mormanity.blogspot.com/2005/05/mp3-download-prof-john-e-clarks-2004.html>.
90 John A. Widtsoe, "Is The Geography of The Book of Mormon Known?" *Improvement Era*, July 1950, p. 547.
91 "Sidon River," Book of Mormon Index, 1981 Edition, p. 331.
92 Keith C. Heidorn, Ph.D., "Wind-Driven Ocean Currents: Of Shoes and Ships and Rubber Ducks and a Message in a Bottle," *THE WEATHER DOCTOR*, See <www.islandnet.com/~see/weather/elements/shoes.htm>.
93 Romeo Hristov and Santiago Genovés, "The Roman Head from Tecaxic-Calixtlahuaca, Mexico: A Review of the evidence," April 18-22, 2001, <http://www.unm.edu/~rhristov/Romanhead.html>, pp. 4-5.
94 "Sidon River," Book of Mormon Index, 1981 Edition, p. 331.
95 "Ups and Downs," See 1 Nephi 2:5; 1 Nephi 3:4, 9, 10, 15, 16, 22, 23, 29; 1 Nephi 4:1, 2, 3, 4, 33, 34, 35; 1 Nephi 5:1, 5, 6; 1 Nephi 7:2, 3, 4, 5, 15, 22 .
96 "Down to the Land of Zarahemla" from the Land of Nephi, See Omni 1:13; Alma 27:5, 7, 8, 9; Alma 27:26 (the land Jershon, a lowland near Zarahemla); Alma 49:10, 11; Alma 51:12; Alma 53:10, 12; Alma 56:25; Alma 63:15; Helaman 4:5; 3 Nephi 3:3, 4, 8; 3 Nephi 4:1; Mormon 3:7, 8.
97 "Up to the Land of Nephi," from Zarahemla, See Omni 1:27, 28; Mosiah 7:1, 2, 3, 4, 9, 13; Mosiah 9:3; Mosiah 10:18; Mosiah 28:1, 5, 6, 7, 9; Mosiah 29:3; Alma 17:8; Alma 26:9, 23; Alma 47:1; Mormon 3:10, 14, 16; Mormon 4:1, 4.
98 See also Alma 6:7, Alma 8:3, Alma 16:7.
99 Mormon 1:6, 10.
100 Book of Mormon, 1981 ed., Index, p. 331.
101 Joseph Smith, ed., *Times and Seasons*, March 1, 1842, 3:927.
102 Joseph Allen, *Sacred Sites*, (American Fork, UT: Covenant Communications, 2003), p. 34.
103 *Langenscheidt's Pocket Dictionary, Spanish-English*, pp. 122 and 158, "Golfo Dulce."

Chapter Five

104 Matisoo-Smith, et al., "Radiocarbon and DNA evidence for a pre-Columbian introduction of Polynesian chickens to Chile," *Proceedings of the National Academy of Sciences*, pp. 10335-10339.
105 William Robertson, *History of America*, 2nd Edition, (Philadelphia: Simon Probasco Publisher, 1821), p. 3, as quoted from Stephens and Catherwood, *Incidents of Travel*, 1:97, emphasis added.

106 George Bancroft, *History of the United States, from the Discovery of the American Continent*, Eighth Edition (Boston: Charles C. Little and James Brown, 1841), vol. I, pp. 3-4.
107 Stephens and Catherwood, *Incidents of Travel*, 1:104.
108 Michael Coe, *America's First Civilization*, (New York: American Heritage Publishing Co, 1968), pp. 11-12.
109 Maurice Collis, *Cortés and Montezuma*, (London: Faber and Faber, 1972), p. 50.
110 Joseph Smith, ed., *Times and Seasons*, May 1, 1843, 4:185.
111 *The Teachings of Joseph Smith*, eds. Larry E. Dahl and Donald Q. Cannon, (Salt Lake City: Bookcraft, 1997), p. 91, emphasis added (this is a different book than *Teachings of the Prophet Joseph Smith*).
112 John Taylor in *Journal of Discourses*, September 13, 1857, 5:240-241; Also John Taylor, *The Gospel Kingdom*, (Salt Lake City: Bookcraft, 1987), p. 357.
113 John Warren, *Jean Francois Champollion, the Father of Egyptology*, <www.touregypt.net/featurestories/champollion.html>.
114 Franklin S. Spalding, *Joseph Smith, Jr., As a Translator*, (Salt Lake City: Arrow Press, 1912), p. 25.
115 Joseph Smith-History, 1:62.
116 Reginald Smith, "Investigating the Ancient Meroitic Language Using Statistical Natural Language Techniques," <http://stuff.mit.edu/people/rsmith80/SSA%20Meroitic%20Zipf%20Paper.doc>.
117 Joyce Marcus, "Zapotec Writing," *Scientific American*, 1980, 242:50-65, <www.angelfire.com/ca/humanorigins/writing.html>.
118 JR Minkel, "Stone Etchings Represent Earliest New World Writing," *Science News*, September 14, 2006, p. 1.
119 Marion G. Romney in Conference address, *Ensign*, September 1979, p. 4. See also Joseph Allen, *Exploring the Lands of the Book of Mormon*, pp. 141, 260-261.

Chapter Six

120 Robert J. Sharer, *The Ancient Maya*, 5th ed., (Stanford, CA: Stanford University Press, 1994), pp. 604-605.
121 Mark Twain, *Roughing It*, (New York: Signet Classics, 1962), pp. 102-103.
122 Joseph L. Allen, *Exploring the Lands of the Book of Mormon*, (Provo, UT: Brigham Young University Print Services, 1989), pp. 31-43.
123 Laura J. Howard, " The Ancient Maya Site of Lamanai, Belize: A Brief History," 2007, p. 1, <www.lasr.net/travelarticles.php?ID=1165>.
124 David Pendergast and Elizabeth Graham, "What Do We Know about Lamanai?" p. 1, <www.belizecubadigs.com/what-we-know.html>
125 Bruce W. Warren, "'Kish,' A Personal Name," Ancient America Foundation, p. 1, <www.ancientamerica.org>.
126 Stanley B. Kimball, "Kinderhook Plates Brought to Joseph Smith Appear to be a Nineteenth-Century Hoax," *Ensign*, Aug 1981, p. 73.
127 Shelby Saberon, Book of Mormon Lecture, January 24, 2005, Yaxchilán, Mexico.
128 "Haskalah," <www.jewishencyclopedia.com/view. jsp?artid=350 & leller=H>.
129 Joseph Smith along with other church elders took Hebrew lessons from Joshua Seixas in 1836. A certificate attesting to Joseph Smith's knowledge of Hebrew was signed by J. Seixas in March 1836 at Kirtland, Ohio, (LDS archives).
130 Cameron Walker, *National Geographic News*, April 20, 2004, emphasis added.
131 Allen J. Christenson, Translator, *Popol Vuh*, (New York: O Books, 2003), p. 47, emphasis added
132 Donald W. Parry, *The Book of Mormon Text Reformatted, According to Parallelistic Patterns* (Provo, Utah: FARMS, 1992), p. xxxiv.
133 Noel B. Reynolds, "The Authorship of the Book of Mormon," *The Foundation for Ancient Research and Mormon Studies*, (FARMS), BYU Devotional, May 27, 1997, p. 268.
134 "The Testimony of Eight Witnesses," The Book of Mormon, p. iv, emphasis added.
135 Ariel L. Crowley, *Metal Record Plates in Ancient Times*, 1947, pp. 3-13.
136 Christenson, *Popol Vuh*, p. 217, emphasis added.
137 Emphasis added; See also 2 Nephi 4:32; Jacob 2:10; 3 Nephi 9:20, 12:19; Mormon 2:14; Ether 4:15; and Moroni 6:2.
138 "Thin Gold Plates," Santo Domingo Covenant and Monastery, Oaxaca, Mexico, <www.delange.org/MonteAlban5.htm>.
139 "Testimony of the Prophet Joseph Smith," 1981 Edition, Book of Mormon, p. v.
140 "Testimony of the Eight Witnesses," 1981 Edition, Book of Mormon, emphasis added, p. iv.
141 Mark Twain, *Roughing It*, p. 102.
142 Sean Markey, "Priceless Maya Stone Vessel Looted in Guatemala," *National Geographic News*, May 5, 2006, p. 1; see also <http://news.nationalgeographic.com/news/2006/05/0505_060505_maya.html>.
143 Paul R. Cheesman, *These Early Americans*, (Salt Lake City: Deseret Book, 1974), p. 126.

144 Cheesman, *These Early Americans*, p. 128.
145 Robert Sharer, *A Classic Maya Center & Its Sculptures*, (Durham, NC: Carolina Academic Press, 1990), p. 39.
146 Michael D. Coe, *America's First Civilization; Discovering the Olmec*, (New York: American Heritage Publishing, 1968), pp. 6-7.
147 Michael D. Coe, *America's First Civilization; Discovering the Olmec*, p. 51.
148 Stephens and Catherwood, *Incidents of Travel*, 2:122.
149 Joseph Smith, ed., *Times and Seasons*, 3:927.
150 Joseph Smith—History, 1:33.
151 *2006 Church Almanac*, (Salt Lake City: Deseret News, 2005), p. 658; See also <http://www.lds.org/newsroom/showpackage/0,15367,3899-1—44-2-491,00.html>.
152 Diego de Landa, *An Account of the Things of Yucatan*, (Mérida, Mexico: Editorial Dante S.A., reprinted, 2003), p. 3.
153 Roberts, *History of the Church*, 1:71.
154 Jeff Hecht, "Earliest New World Writing Revealed," *Science*, vol. 298, p. 1984.

Chapter Seven

155 Michael D. Coe, *The Maya*, 6th ed., (New York: Thames & Hudson, 1999), p. 152.
156 Charles C. Mann, *1491*, (New York: Vintage Books, 2006), p.104.
157 Mann, *1491*, p. 104.
158 John E. Clark, "Archaeology, Relics, and the Book of Mormon Beliefs," Maxwell Institute BYU, <http://farms.byu.edu/display.php?table=jbms&id=376&mp=T>.
159 Michael D. Coe, *The Maya*, 6th ed., p. 152, emphasis added.
160 Bruce E. Johansen, *"Dating the Iroquois Confederacy,"* pp. 1-2, <http://www.ratical.org/many_worlds/6Nations/DatingIC.html>.
161 "Original Inhabitants and the Iroquois," <http://www.co.seneca.ny.us/history/Chapter%20One%20—%20Geography-1.doc >.
162 Sharer, *The Ancient Maya*, p. 57.
163 Linda Schele and Peter Matthews, *The Code of Kings*, (New York: Simon & Schuster, 1999 ed.), pp. 13-61.
164 Schele and Mathews, *The Code of Kings*, p. 18.
165 Jacob 3:5-7.
166 Edward Herbert Thompson, *People of the Serpent*, (Boston: Houghton Mifflin Co, 1932, reprinted New York: Capricorn Books, 1965), pp. 75-79.
167 Thompson, *People of the Serpent*, pp. 75-79, emphasis added.
168 Stephens and Catherwood, *Incidents of Travel*, 1:17.
169 "Machu Pichu," <http://www.mnsu.edu/emuseum/prehistory/latinamerica/south/sites/machu_picchu.htm>.
170 Michael D. Coe, *Mexico From Olmecs to the Aztecs*, 4th ed., (New York: Thames and Hudson, 1994), p. 80.
171 Coe, *Mexico From Olmecs to the Aztecs*, p. 81.

Chapter Eight

172 Gilberto Crespo y Martinez, *Mexico Industria Minera*, (Mexico City, Mexico: Oficina de Formento, 1903), p.27.
173 Collis, *Cortés and Montezuma*, p.74. Cempoalan, where Cortés met the Totonacs, is near Cerro de Oro and the Hill Vigia in the state of Vera Cruz, Mexico.
174 Sharer, *The Ancient Maya*, p. 455.
175 Sharer, *The Ancient Maya*, p. 463, emphasis added.
176 Sharer, *The Ancient Maya*, p. 546.
177 Sharer, *The Ancient Maya*, p. 730.
178 Linda Schele and Peter Mathews, *The Code of Kings*, p. 359, emphasis added.
179 Sharer, *The Ancient Maya*, pp. 454-455, 730.
180 Joseph Smith—History 1:56-57.
181 Reed Carter, "A Unique Place in Connecticut," Norwalk, Connecticut, June 2002, <http://www.silverminetavern.com/press_releases.htm>.
182 Ether 15:2, 14.
183 "Turkey Vultures" <http://www.mbr-pwrc.usgs.gov/id/framlst/i3250id.html> [go to BBS Map] There is a void of any vultures in the "Lower Great Lakes Plains" because of the lack of an updraft. See <www.mbr-pwrc.usgs.gov/id/framlst/i3250id.html>.

Chapter Nine

184 Diego de Landa, *An Account of the Things of Yucatan*, pp. 8-31.
185 Diego de Landa, *An Account of the Things of Yucatan*, p. 14.
186 Christenson, *Popol Vuh*, p. 21.
187 Sharer, *The Ancient Maya*, p. 530.
188 Michael D. Coe, *The Maya*, 6th ed., p. 190, emphasis added. For the full text go to <http://www.myweb.cableone.net/subru/Chilam.html> The Spaniards were believed to be the representatives of "Elder Brother." The Maya referred to them as Elder Brothers.
189 *Teachings*, pp. 356-357.
190 See "Remarkable Fulfillment of Indian Prophecy," *The Evening and the Morning Star*, (Independence, Missouri: September 1832), vol. I, no. 4, p. 8.
191 R. Jon McGee, *Life, Ritual, and Religion among the Lacandon Maya*, (Belmont, California: Wadsworth Publishing Company, 1990), p. 97.
192 Lacandon Maya <http://www.geocities.com/RainForest/3134/lacgods.html>.
193 Christenson, *Popol Vuh*, p. 60. See also fn #14.
194 McGee, *Life, Ritual, and Religion among the Lacandon Maya*, p. 18.
195 McGee, *Life, Ritual, and Religion among the Lacandon Maya*, p. 65.
196 McGee, *Life, Ritual, and Religion among the Lacandon Maya*, p. 30.
197 *Teachings*, pp. 347, 361, 372.
198 This review of the Lacandonian religious beliefs is adapted from the book by R. Jon McGee entitled *Life, Ritual and Religion among the Lacandon Maya*, pp. 60-70, and my own personal knowledge of the Maya.
199 Christenson, *Popol Vuh*, p. 77 (footnote 88), and p. 89 (footnote 143).
200 Joseph Smith, ed., *Times and Seasons*, 3:914.
201 Cannibalism, <http://www.chemistrydaily.com/chemistry/Cannibalism,> p. 3.
202 Sharer. *The Ancient Maya*, p. 487. See also McGee, *Life, Ritual, and Religion among the Lacandon Maya*, p.6.
203 Jacob Wassermann, *Columbus, Don Quixote of the Seas* (Boston: Little, Brown &Co., 1930), pp. 19-20.
204 Christenson, *Popol Vuh*, p. 34.
205 Christenson, *Popol Vuh*, p. 34.
206 Rock Crystals of Tomb #7, Monte Alban, Oaxaca, Mexico. <www.planetware.com/oaxaca/monte-alban-tomb-7-mex-oax-mart7>.
207 Sodi, *The Great Cultures of Mesoamerica*, p. 124.
208 See also Leviticus 8:8, Joseph Smith—History 1:35.
209 Merrill Unger, *Unger's Bible Dictionary*, (Chicago: Moody Press, 1985), pp. 1128-1129.
210 Chacmool has a number of spelling variants because it is phonetic, i.e., Chac Mol, Chak Mul, Chaac Mool, etc. Michael Coe and Robert Sharer prefer Chacmool.
211 Michael D. Coe, *America's First Civilization: Discovering the Olmec*, p. 131.

Chapter Ten

212 Guy Gugliotta, "The Maya Glory and Ruin," *National Geographic*, August 2007, p. 106.
213 Michael D. Coe, *The Maya*, 6th ed., p. 191.
214 Collis, *Cortés and Montezuma*, p. 52.
215 Sharer, *The Ancient Maya*, pp.738-739, p. 740.
216 Sharer, *The Ancient Maya*, p. 740.
217 Sharer, *The Ancient Maya*, emphasis added.
218 Collis, *Cortés and Montezuma*, p. 29.
219 Sharer, *The Ancient Maya*, p. 734, emphasis added.
220 Michael D. Coe, *The Maya*, 6th ed., p. 191, emphasis added.
221 Linda Schele and Mary Ellen Miller, *The Blood of Kings*, (New York: George Braziller, Inc., 1986), pp. 214-215, emphasis added.
222 Schele and Miller, *The Blood of Kings*, p. 219, emphasis added.
223 Schele and Miller, *The Blood of Kings*, p. 209.
224 Collis, *Cortés and Montezuma*, pp. 62-63.
225 LDS Bible, p. 110, Footnote 13a.
226 Sharer, *The Ancient Maya*, p. 92.
227 Sharer, *The Ancient Maya*, p. 105.
228 Sharer, *The Ancient Maya*, p. 503, emphasis added.
229 Michael D. Coe, *The Maya*, 6th ed., p. 26, emphasis added.
230 Collis, *Cortés and Montezuma*, pp. 43-46.
231 Collis, *Cortés and Montezuma*, pp. 81-83.

232 Collis, *Cortés and Montezuma*, pp. 102-104.
233 Sharer, *The Ancient Maya*, pp. 732-733.
234 This is a reconstruction of a Pre-Columbian Yucatec marriage: McGee, *Life Ritual and Religion;* Sharer, *The Ancient May;* and personal interviews with two Yucatec Maya (Ah Kinin) Holy Men.
235 Christenson, *Popol Vuh*, pp. 97-98.
236 Collis, *Cortés and Montezuma*, p.143.
237 The "SB" combination in ancient Egyptian is often used to refer to Sobek, the crocodile god of the underworld, meaning these waters in the Book of Mormon could have been appropriately called something like "Submerged Crocodile." The oldest known name for the city-state of Laman Ayaim, (called Lamanai by contracting the two words) is Submerged Crocodile. It can be found today on the New River in Belize. It dates to the time of Ammon, but is located too far north to be the same location.
238 Gugliotta, "The Maya Glory and Ruin," *National Geographic*, August 2007, pp. 108-109.
239 Gugliotta, "The Maya Glory and Ruin," *National Geographic*, August 2007, pp. 97-98.

Chapter Eleven

240 Collis, *Cortés and Montezuma*, pp. 123-124.
241 Collis, *Cortés and Montezuma*, p. 54.
242 L. Taylor Hansen, *He Walked the Americas*, (Amherst, WI: Legend Press, 1997)
243 Personal interview with the author on October 14, 2006. Elder Jeff Granlich was sent to open up missionary work in Adjunta, Puerto Rico in November of 1980 for the LDS Church, native history.
244 Collis, *Cortés and Montezuma*, p.110.
245 Collis, *Cortés and Montezuma*, pp.55-56.
246 Randolph Widmer, *The World of the Maya*, Royal Olympic Cruise, Pamphlet, March 1524, 2003, p 13, emphasis added.
247 Collis, *Cortés and Montezuma*, pp. 189-190.
248 Christenson, *Popol Vuh*, p. 70.
249 Dennis Tadlock, *Popol Vuh*, (New York: Touchstone, 1996), pp. 16, 21.
250 Dionisio José Chonay and Delia Goetz, translators, *Title of the Lords Totonicapán*, (Norman, OK: University of Oklahoma, 1953), p. 170.
251 Chonay and Goetz, *Title of the Lords of Totonicapán*, p. 194.
252 Chonay and Goetz, *Title of the Lords of Totonicapán*, p. 194.
253 Fernando de Alva Ixtlilxóchitl, *Obras Históricas* (Mexico City, Mexico, in Spanish, reprinted 1952).
254 Ixtlilxóchitl, *Obras Históricas*, 1:11-12, emphasis added.

Chapter Twelve

255 Christenson, *Popol Vuh*, "The Defeat of the Lords of Xibalba," pp. 185-186.
256 Collis, *Cortés and Montezuma*, p. 53.
257 Wallace Budge, *Book of the Dead*, (New York: Gramercy Books, copyright 1895, reprinted 1960) p. 53, footnote number 3.
258 Collis, *Cortés and Montezuma*, p. 43, emphasis added.
259 Keepers of the Law of Moses: See also Jarom 1:11, 2 Nephi 25:24-30, Mosiah 2:3-4, Alma 25:15-16, Alma 30:3, 3 Nephi 1:24-25, 3 Nephi 5:29, 3 Nephi 12:18, 4 Nephi 1:12.
260 Book of Mormon, 1981 Edition, Index, p. 331.
261 "Climate," <www.weatherbase.com/weather/vacation>.
262 "Climate," <www.weatherbase.com/weather/vacation>.
263 Stephens and Catherwood, *Incidents of Travel*, 1:40.
264 "Under the Weather," <htlp://www.cdc.gov/ncidod/> emphasis added.
265 Center for Disease Control, <http://www.pancanal.com/eng/history/history/end.html.> <www.cdc.gov/malaria/history/panama_canal.htm.>.
266 Herbal Gram. 1995; 35:55 American Botanical Council, p. 56, <www.conservatoryofflowers.org/education/plants.htm>.
267 Herbal Gram, p. 56, <www.conservatoryofflowers.org/education/plants.htm>.
268 Herbal Gram, p. 56,<www.conservatoryofflowers.org/education/plants.htm>.
269 Stephens and Catherwood, *Incidents of Travel*, 1:161.
270 Stephens and Catherwood, *Incidents of Travel*, 1:369-370.
271 Stephens and Catherwood, *Incidents of Travel*, 1:vi.

Chapter Thirteen

272 This story and others I shall relate in this book are true. I have changed some elements to protect the identities of the people but not the principle being taught.

273 Robert R. Bennett, "Barley and Wheat in the Book of Mormon," Maxwell Institute Papers, BYU, pp. 1-2; <http://www.maxwellinstitute.byu.edu/display.php?table=transcripts&id=126%20-%2016k%20-> quoting Daniel B. Adams, "Last Ditch Archaeology," *Science*, December 1983, p. 32.

274 Richard Norton Smith, *Patriarch George Washington and the New American Nation,* (New York: Houghton Mifflin Company, 1993), pp. 351-355.

275 Davistown Museum, Liberty, Maine, June 2007, <www.davistownmuseum.org/bibPreColumb.htm>.

276 Michael D. Lemonick, "Mysteries of the Mayans," <www.indians.org/welker/maya.html>.

277 Michael D. Coe, *Mexico From the Olmecs to the Aztecs*, 4th Ed., pp. 89-90.

Chapter Fourteen

278 *Encyclopedia Smithsonian,* "Siberian Land Bridge," <www.si.edu/Encyclopedia_SI/nmnh/origin.htm>.

279 Mann, *1491*, pp. 4, 17-18.

280 Matt Zimmerman, "The Kennewick Man Controversy," *Professional Ethics Report,* Summer 1998, volume XI, number 3, p. 1.

281 Michael D. Coe, *The Maya*, 6th ed., p. 41.

282 I do not agree that the dating system currently used by the scientific community is correct in dating the age of man. Evolutionists now claim that primitive man was able to make transoceanic voyages 30,000 to 50,000 years ago. This is not the time or place to introduce into the discussion a new dating system juxtaposed with theirs. I use the evolutionist community's dating system as a convenience only.

283 Coe, *The Maya*, 6th ed., p. 41, emphasis added.

284 Alan Mairson, Expeditions: "Kon-Tiki: The Sequel," *National Geographic*, August 2007, p.21.

285 *New Zealand Encyclopedia,* 1984 Edition, Bateman, *p. 306.*

286 Cowley, *Matthew Cowley Speaks*, (Salt Lake City: Deseret Book Co., 1954), p. 114.

287 *New Zealand Encyclopedia,* 1984 Edition, Bateman, *p. 306.*

288 The Mystery of the Sweet Potato, "The Accidental Drift Theory," 11 June 2004. <www.bbc.co.uk/dna/h2g2/A1984421>.

289 McGee, *Life, Ritual, and Religion among the Lacandon Maya*, p. 22; See also, "Statement Regarding the Book of Mormon," Office of Anthropology, National Museum of Natural History, Smithsonian Institute, Washington DC, 1996. The Statement can be quickly accessed by going to the Jeff Lindsay site, <www.jefflindsay.com/LDSFAQ/smithsonian.html>.

290 E.A. Matisoo-Smith, et al, "Radiocarbon and DNA evidence for a pre-Columbian introduction of Polynesian chickens to Chile," *Proceedings of the National Academy of Sciences*, June 19, 2007, vol. 104, no. 25, pp 10335-10339.

291 Adrian Recinos and Delia Geotz, translators, ***The Annals of the Cakchiquels*; Dionisio José Chonay and Delia Goetz, translators, *Title of the Lords Totonicapán*,** (Norman, Ok: University of Oklahoma Press, 1953), pp. 43-45, 49.

292 Peter N. Spotts, "First Americans May Have Crossed Atlantic 50,000 Years Ago," *Christian Science Monitor,* Nov 18, 2004, p. 3.

293 Encyclopedia Smithsonian: Paleoamerican Origins, <www.si.edu/Encyclopedia_SInmnh/origin.htm>.

294 Michael D. Brown, et al., "mtDNA Haplogroup X: An Ancient Link between Europe/Western Asia and North America?" University of Chicago, Nov 25, 1998, <http://www.journals.uchicago.edu/AJHG/journal/issues/v63n6/980554/980554.test.html>.

295 Brown, et al., "mtDNA Haplogroup X: An Ancient Link between Europe Western Asia and North America?" <http://www.journals.uchicago.edu/AJHG/journal/issues/v63n6/980554/980554.text.html, emphasis added.>

296 Brown, DNA, p. 2., emphasis added. <http://www.greaterthings.com/Book_of_Mormon/DNA/Terry_Silva.htm >.

297 Brown, DNA p. 5, <http://www.greaterthings.com/Book_of_Mormon/DNA/Terry_Silva.htm >.

298 DNA, Sidia M. Callegari-Jacques, et al., "GM Haplotype Distribution in Amerindians: Relationship with Geography and Language," *American Journal of Physical Anthropology*, ABR-91540, April 1993, 90:4, p. 427.

299 Carrie A. Moore quoting Gordon B. Hinckley, Deseret Morning News, March 1, 2006.

300 Wallace Budge, *The Book of the Dead*, (New York: Gramercy Books, 1895, reprinted 1960), pp. 192, 240-241.

301 Budge, *The Book of the Dead*, pp. 130-131.

302 Budge, *The Book of the Dead*, p. 192.

303 Diego de Landa, *Yucatan Before and After the Conquest*, A.D. 1566, translated by William Gates, (Mérida Yucatán, Mexico; reprint Mineola, New York: Dover Publications, 1978), pp. 88-89.
304 Diego de Landa, *Yucatan Before and After the Conquest*, pp. 88-89.
305 Chilam Balam, The Four World-Quarters, Appendix A <www.sacredtexts.com/nam/maya/cbc/cbc30.htm>.
306 Stephens and Catherwood, *Incidents of Travel*, 1:103.
307 Sharer, *The Ancient Maya*, p. 6.
308 Sharer, *The Ancient Maya*, p. 6.
309 J. Marcus, "Zapotec Writing," *Scientific American*, 1980, 242:5065.
310 *Teachings*, p. 267; See also Suarez, *Early Mapping of the Pacific*, p. 211.
311 "Statement Regarding the Book of Mormon," Office of Anthropology, National Museum of Natural History, Smithsonian Institute, Washington DC, 1996 Statement as quoted by Jeff Lindsay, "The 1996 Smithsonian Statement Regarding the Book of Mormon," <www.jefflindsay.com/LDSFAQ/smithsonian.html>.
312 Mann, *1491*, p. 4.
313 Davistown Museum, Liberty, Maine, June 2007, <www.davistownmuseum.org/bibPreColumb.htm>.
314 E.J.Vajda, "The Siberian Origins of Native Americans," <www.pandora.cii.wwu.edu/vajda/ea210/SiberianOriginsNA.htm>.
315 "Paleoamerican Origins," *Encyclopedia Smithsonian*, <www.si.edu/Encyclopedia_SInmnh/origin.htm>.
316 David Lore, "Bering Strait May Not Have Been Only Route to Americas," *Columbus Dispatch*, March 17, 1998; <http://www.science-frontiers.com/sf119/sf119p10.htm>.
317 J. Houston McCulloch, "Pre-Columbian Horses?" <http://www.trends.net/~yuku/tran/9h8.htm>, pp. 1-2; See also *Wisconsin Archaeologist*, vol. 45, #2, June 1964, pp. 118-120.
318 Davistown Museum, Liberty, Maine, June 2007, <www.davistownmuseum.org/bibPreColumb.htm>.
319 William Shakespeare, *Julius Caesar*, Act III Scene II.

Chapter Fifteen

320 "Statement Regarding the Book of Mormon," Office of Anthropology, National Museum of Natural History, Smithsonian Institute, Washington DC, 1996 Statement as quoted by Jeff Lindsay, "The 1996 Smithsonian Statement Regarding the Book of Mormon," <www.jefflindsay.com/LDSFAQ/smithsonian.html>.
321 McGee, *Life, Ritual, and Religion among the Lacandon Maya*, p. 22.
322 Davistown Museum, Liberty, Maine, June 2007, <www.davistownmuseum.org/bibPreColumb.htm>.
323 "The Icelandic Horse," <http://www.gaitedhorse.com/icelandi.htm>.
324 Roger Daniels, *Coming To America: A History of Immigration and Ethnicity in American Life*, (New York: Harper Collins, 2002), p. 14.
325 "Vinland: Historical Accounts," <www.libraryoflibrary.com/E_n_c_p_p_Vinland_map.html>.
326 Hakon Hjelmqvist, Cayennepeppar från Lund medeltid, *Svensk Botanisk Tidskrift*, 1995, Vol. 89:193-195.
327 "Cayenne: A History of the Healing Chili," Herbal Legacy, p. 1, <www.herballegacy.com/history_m.htm>.
328 Vinland Archeology, <www.mnh.si.edu/viking/voyage/subset/vinland/archeo.html>.
329 "The Heavener Runestone," www.heavener.k12.ok.us/community/runestone/rune.
330 "Cayenne: A History of the Healing Chili," Herbal Legacy, p. 1, <www.herballegacy.com/history_m.htm>.
331 Stanley B. Kimball, "Kinderhook Plates Brought to Joseph Smith Appear to be a Nineteenth-Century Hoax," *Ensign*, Aug 1981, p. 73.
332 Henry C. Mercer, *The Hill-Caves of the Yucatan*, (Philadelphia: J. B. Lippincott Company, 1896), p. 172.
333 J. Houston McCulloch, "Pre-Columbian Horses?" <http://www.trends.net/~yuku/tran/9h8.htm> p 1. See also *Wisconsin Archaeologist*, vol. 45, #2, June 1964, pp. 118-120.
334 McCulloch, "Pre-Columbian Horses?" <http://www.trends.net/~yuku/tran/9h8.htm> p 1.
335 McCulloch, "Pre-Columbian Horses?" <http://www.trends.net/~yuku/tran/9h8.htm> p 1.
336 "No Horses in Wisconsin," <www.archaeology.about.com/od/frauds/a/spencer_lake_2.htm>.
337 Clayton Ray, "Pre-Columbian Horses from Yucatan," *Journal of Mammalogy*, 1957, 38:278.
338 "Out of the Dust." FARMS, 2001, <http://farms.byu.edu/display.php?table=jbms&id=246>.
339 Romeo H. Hristov and Santiago Genovés, "The Roman Head from Tecaxic-Calixtlahuaca, Mexico: A Review of the evidence," April 18-22, 2001, <www.unm.edu/-rhristov> p. 1.
340 Hristov, "The Roman Head from Tecaxic-Calixtlahuaca, Mexico: A Review of the evidence." p. 1.
341 McGee, *Life, Ritual, and Religion among the Lacandon Maya*, p. 22, emphasis added.
342 McGee, *Life, Ritual, and Religion among the Lacandon Maya*, pp. 20-21, 132-133.
343 McGee, *Life, Ritual, and Religion among the Lacandon Maya*, p. 22.
344 "The Heavener Runestone," <http://www.heavener.k12.ok.us/community/runestone/rune.htm>.
345 Vinland Archeology, <www.mnh.si.edu/viking/voyage/subset/vinland/archeo.html>.

346 George Rink, "Butternut Tree," U.S. Forest Service, 2007, p. 1, <http://wildwnc.org/trees/Juglans_cinerea.html>.
347 Vinland Archeology, <www.mnh.si.edu/viking/voyage/subset/vinland/archeo.html>.
348 Viking Historical Accounts, <www.libraryoflibrary.com/E_n_c_p_p_Vinland_map.html>.
349 Guaman Poma, *Nueva corónica y buen gobierno;* Stephen Kaplan, *Indigenous Responses to Western Christianity,*(New York: New York University Press, 1995), pp.56-58.
350 Tarpan, <www.home.conceptsfa.nl/~pmaas/rea/tarpan.htm>.
351 Douglas W. Smith, Rolf O. Peterson, and Douglas B. Houston, "Yellowstone after Wolves," *Bioscience*, April 2003, 53:4, p. 330.
352 Truman G. Madsen, "B.H. Roberts After Fifty Years Still Witnessing for the Book of Mormon," *Ensign*, December 1983, p. 17.
353 William Lobdell, "Bedrock of a Faith is Jolted," *L.A.Times*, February 16, 2006.

Chapter Sixteen

354 See also Matthew 18:16, 2 Corinthians 13:1.
355 *U.S. News and World Report,* April 8, 1996, p. 48.
356 *U.S. News and World Report,* April 8, 1996, p. 52.
357 *Time,* April 8, 1996, p. 55.
358 *U.S. News and World Report,* April 17, 2006, p. 53.
359 *U.S. News and World Report,* April 17, 2006, pp. 50, 52.
360 *U.S. News and World Report,* April 17, 2006, p. 50.
361 Dr. Thomas Holland, "Lesson Nine: The Dead Sea Scrolls," pp.16, 18, <www.purewords.org/kjb1611/html/lesson09.htm>.
362 "How Great the Wisdom and the Love," *Hymns,* (Salt Lake City: LDS Church, 1985), no. 195.
363 Ezra Taft Benson, Conference Report, April 1987, p. 3.
364 *Teachings,* p. 348.